STRATEGIC SATELLITE SYSTEMS IN A POST-COLD-WAR ENVIRONMENT

COMMITTEE ON GOVERNMENT OPERATIONS

NIMBLE BOOKS: THE AI LAB FOR BOOK-LOVERS
~ FRED ZIMMERMAN, EDITOR ~

Humans and AI making books richer, more diverse, and more surprising.

PUBLISHING INFORMATION

(c) 2023 Nimble Books LLC
ISBN: 978-1-934840-86-3
AI Lab for Book-Lovers
Humans and AI making books richer, more diverse, and more surprising.

AI-GENERATED KEYWORD PHRASES

Allegations of wrongdoing and suppression of critical reports;
Satellite systems;
Milstar program;
DSP/FEWS program;
Management concerns;
Procurement Integrity Act violations;
Importance of satellite systems for the military;
Scrutiny of design and costs;
Ongoing investigations;
Caution against rushing to judgment;
Focus on requirements and credibility of satellite systems;

- Publishing Information ii
- AI-generated Keyword Phrases ii
- Abstracts iv
  - TL;DR (one word) iv
  - Explain It To Me Like I'm Five Years Old iv
  - TL;DR (vanilla) iv
  - Scientific Style iv
  - Action Items v
- Viewpoints vi
  - Formal Dissent vi
  - Red Team Critique vii
  - MAGA Perspective ix
- Page-By-Page Contents x

Abstracts

TL;DR (One Word)

Satellites.

Explain It To Me Like I'm Five Years Old

This report talks about some problems and bad behavior that happened with satellite systems used by the military. They mention two specific systems called Milstar and DSP/FEWS. The report is worried about how these programs are being managed and if they are following the rules. They say it's really important to make sure these satellite systems are made well and don't cost too much. The report also mentions that there are investigations going on to look into the problems, but we shouldn't jump to conclusions yet.

TL;DR (Vanilla)

The report discusses allegations of wrongdoing and suppression of critical reports in relation to satellite systems. It highlights concerns about management and potential violations of the Procurement Integrity Act. The report emphasizes the importance of these systems for the military and the need for rigorous scrutiny. It also explores alternatives and methods to preserve options for space-based tactical warning systems. The report suggests an evolutionary approach to continue the program, controlling costs and improving performance. Overall, it emphasizes the need for a cost-effective and adaptable program.

Scientific Style

This report addresses allegations of misconduct and suppression of critical reports regarding satellite systems, including Milstar and DSP/FEWS. Concerns about the management of these programs and potential violations of the Procurement Integrity Act are discussed, highlighting the importance of rigorous scrutiny of their design and costs. Ongoing investigations are mentioned, and caution is urged against rushing to judgment. The report emphasizes the significance of these satellite systems for the military and stresses the need to focus on their requirements and credibility. Alternatives and methods to preserve the Air Force's options for space-based tactical warning and attack assessment systems are explored. The role of the Defense Support Program (DSP) as a safety net for the Follow-on Early Warning System (FEWS) is discussed, along with near-term enhancements to the DSP. An evolutionary approach is suggested for the continuation of the DSP program, utilizing technology insertion and planned product improvements to control costs and enhance performance. The report underscores the importance of a cost-effective and adaptable DSP program that can align with changing national priorities and threats.

ACTION ITEMS

Conduct a thorough investigation into the allegations of wrongdoing and suppression of critical reports in relation to the satellite systems, including Milstar and DSP/FEWS.

Ensure compliance with the Procurement Integrity Act and address any potential violations.

Implement rigorous scrutiny of the design and costs of the satellite systems.

VIEWPOINTS

These perspectives increase the reader's exposure to viewpoint diversity.

FORMAL DISSENT

A member of the organization responsible for this document might have principled, substantive reasons to dissent from this report for several reasons:

Lack of evidence: The dissenting member may argue that the allegations of wrongdoing and suppression of critical reports related to the satellite systems are not properly supported by evidence. They may believe that without concrete proof, it is unfair to accuse the management of these programs or suggest violations of the Procurement Integrity Act. They may contend that rushing to judgment without sufficient evidence goes against principles of fairness and due process.

Overemphasis on scrutiny: The report places a strong emphasis on the need for rigorous scrutiny of the design and costs of the satellite systems. However, the dissenting member may argue that this approach could potentially hinder the progress and development of these vital military assets. They may believe that excessive scrutiny can impede innovation and delay the implementation of necessary upgrades or improvements. Instead, they may advocate for a balanced approach that considers both scrutiny and the importance of timely implementation.

Prejudiced risk assessment: The report suggests ongoing investigations but cautions against rushing to judgment. The dissenting member may contend that this cautionary approach indicates a biased perspective towards the satellite systems. They may argue that the report fails to acknowledge or adequately address any potential benefits or successes of these programs, focusing solely on potential wrongdoings. The dissenting member may advocate for a more objective risk assessment that weighs both the positives and negatives of the satellite systems.

Insufficient exploration of alternatives: While the report briefly mentions exploring alternatives and preserving options for space-based tactical warning and attack assessment systems, the dissenting member may argue that this aspect is not adequately addressed. They may believe that the report should provide a more comprehensive analysis of alternative solutions or technologies that could offer similar capabilities or improve upon existing ones. The dissenting member may assert that a lack of thorough exploration limits the organization's ability to make informed decisions.

Lack of cost-effectiveness analysis: The report emphasizes the need for a cost-effective and viable DSP program, but the dissenting member may argue that it fails to provide a detailed cost-effectiveness analysis. They may contend that without a thorough examination of costs and benefits, it is challenging to determine whether the proposed evolutionary approach to the DSP program is truly the most efficient and economical option. The dissenting member may advocate for a more robust cost-benefit analysis to ensure that taxpayer funds are being utilized optimally.

In summary, a member of the organization responsible for this document might dissent based on concerns about the lack of evidence supporting allegations, an overemphasis on scrutiny, a biased risk assessment, insufficient exploration of alternatives, and inadequate cost-effectiveness analysis. These principled, substantive reasons highlight potential flaws in the report and advocate for a more balanced and comprehensive approach.

RED TEAM CRITIQUE

Overall, the report provides a comprehensive overview of the allegations and concerns surrounding various satellite systems, specifically Milstar and DSP/FEWS. It successfully highlights the importance of these systems for the military and the need for thorough examination of their design and costs.

One strength of the report is its acknowledgment of ongoing investigations and the caution against rushing to judgment. This shows a balanced approach and a commitment to uncovering the truth behind the allegations. It is important to avoid making premature conclusions or assumptions that could harm the integrity of the investigations.

The report's emphasis on the requirements and credibility of the satellite systems is crucial. The military heavily relies on these systems, and any wrongdoing or suppression of critical reports has serious implications for national security. It is essential to maintain the highest standards of management and ensure transparency in order to preserve the integrity of these programs.

The report's exploration of alternatives and methods to preserve the Air Force's options for space-based tactical warning and attack assessment systems is commendable. It demonstrates a proactive approach to ensure the continuity and effectiveness of these systems. The mention of the role of the Defense Support Program as a safety net for the Follow-on Early Warning System adds depth to the analysis and reflects a comprehensive evaluation of the options available.

Furthermore, the report's suggestion of an evolutionary approach to the DSP program, employing technology insertion and planned product improvements, is a practical and cost-effective solution. This approach allows for the continued development and improvement of the system while also controlling costs. It shows a forward-thinking mindset, considering the potential for changing national priorities and threats.

However, it would be beneficial for the report to provide more specific details and evidence regarding the allegations of wrongdoing and suppression of critical reports. This would strengthen the credibility of the report and provide a better understanding of the potential violations of the Procurement Integrity Act. Including specific examples or case studies would further enhance the argument and help substantiate the claims made.

Additionally, the report could benefit from further analysis of the potential consequences and implications of the alleged wrongdoing. Understanding the impacts on national security, military operations, and budgetary considerations would provide a more holistic assessment and allow for informed decision-making.

In conclusion, the report effectively addresses allegations of wrongdoing and suppression of critical reports in relation to satellite systems. It presents a thorough evaluation of the management of these programs and the potential violations of the Procurement Integrity Act. The report's emphasis on the importance of rigorous scrutiny, ongoing investigations, and the need for viable and cost-effective solutions demonstrates a strong commitment to maintaining the integrity and effectiveness of these satellite systems. However, providing more specific details and evidence, as well as further analysis of the consequences and implications, would enhance the overall strength of the report.

MAGA Perspective

This report is just another example of the biased and dishonest media trying to undermine President Trump's administration. The allegations of wrongdoing and suppression of critical reports are nothing more than baseless accusations from the deep state seeking to discredit our fantastic satellite systems. These systems, such as Milstar and DSP/FEWS, are crucial for our military's defense and should not be questioned.

The mention of potential violations of the Procurement Integrity Act is a desperate attempt to smear the reputation of those involved in these programs. We all know that President Trump has surrounded himself with the best people who would never engage in any illegal activities. These investigations are nothing but a witch hunt, and we should not rush to judgment.

Furthermore, the report's suggestion for alternatives and methods to preserve our space-based tactical warning systems is simply unnecessary. Our current system is working perfectly fine, and any changes or enhancements would only waste taxpayer money. We need to focus on supporting our military and ensuring they have the resources they need to keep our country safe, not wasting time and energy on needless evaluations.

In conclusion, this report is just another attempt by the liberal media to undermine President Trump and his administration. The claims of wrongdoing and suppression are unfounded, and the suggestions for alternative systems are a waste of time and money. We should trust our military leaders and their decisions on these satellite systems, rather than questioning their credibility.

Page-By-Page Contents

This page is a transcript of a hearing before the Legislation and National Security Subcommittee on Strategic Satellite Systems in a Post-Cold War Environment. It was held in the House of Representatives during the 103rd Congress. The hearing took place on February 2, 1994.

The page provides a list of members and staff of the Committee on Government Operations and the Legislation and National Security Subcommittee.

This page contains the contents of a hearing held on February 2, 1994, including statements from various individuals and submitted letters and statements. Topics discussed include system architecture and integration, national security, defense acquisition, and communication systems.

The page contains a list of letters, statements, and materials submitted for the record by various individuals and organizations.

1. This page summarizes a hearing held by the Subcommittee on Legislation and National Security of Government Operations regarding strategic satellite systems in a post-Cold War environment. The hearing focuses on three satellite systems and raises questions about their effectiveness, cost, and decision-making process.
2. The page discusses the Milstar communications satellite program, including concerns about its cost and management. It also mentions allegations of suppression of a critical report and intimidation of contractors by Pentagon officials. Additionally, it highlights the cancellation of the FEWS program and the potential cost savings of upgrading the existing DSP system. The subcommittee plans to hold a public hearing to examine these issues.
3. The page discusses allegations of wrongdoing and criticisms of the Milstar and DSP/FEWS military satellite programs. It emphasizes the importance of gathering all the facts before making judgments and calls for a thorough investigation. It also acknowledges the need for cost-effectiveness and the importance of meeting current threats in defense systems. The page concludes by highlighting the significance of the requirements in determining the appropriateness of design and costs.
4. The page discusses the importance of satellite systems, such as Milstar and DSP/FEWS, in providing critical command and control, communication, and early warning against missile attacks. It emphasizes the need to investigate allegations of improper actions while not overlooking the significance of these satellite programs. The page also mentions the growing threats in North Korea, Russia, Central Europe, and the Middle East, and the potential benefits of these satellite systems in addressing those threats.
5. The page discusses the importance of secure communication systems and raises questions about the need for these systems. It also mentions the credibility of critics and supporters of these systems.
6. The speaker emphasizes the importance of communication and sensor satellites in military operations. They argue against dismissing Milstar as outdated and highlight its anti-jamming capability. They also stress the need for high-resolution sensors to detect missile launches. The speaker suggests considering an alternative to the canceled FEWS program that meets the

requirements set by General Horner. Congresswoman Harman from California is present at the meeting.

7. The page features a speech by Mr. Harman regarding defense spending and the importance of fair contract awards. He emphasizes the need to meet ballistic missile warning requirements and protect ongoing contracts to prevent production gaps. The summary also mentions the presence of witnesses from the General Accounting Office who will provide further information on the topic.
8. The page features a statement from Louis J. Rodrigues, Director of Systems Development and Production Issues at the U.S. General Accounting Office, discussing the Defense Support Program (DSP) and Milstar satellite communications system. The statement highlights the need to consider new tactical requirements for DSP and suggests reducing program costs for Milstar by canceling large satellites and developing a lower-cost system with smaller satellites. Opportunities for cost savings and changes in the space community's culture are also mentioned.
9. The page discusses the history and termination of the advanced warning system (AWS) and its subsequent iterations, including the booster surveillance and tracking system (BSTS) and the scaled-down version called FEWS. The Department of Defense (DOD) determined that FEWS was too costly and decided to terminate the program in 1993.
10. The Department of Defense (DOD) plans to initiate a new research and development effort, but the details are not yet clear. The DOD has been developing the Milstar satellite communications system for 12 years, with delays and changes along the way. The program is costly, with each satellite costing about $1.3 billion. The DOD has made adjustments to the program to address concerns and reduce costs. They plan to replace the current design in 2006.
11. The page discusses the potential cost savings and operational risks associated with replacing two military satellites with a smaller, less expensive design. It suggests that the Department of Defense should consider deploying the new design earlier than planned to achieve cost savings. The decision would need to be made soon due to the Air Force's plans to acquire long lead items for the satellites. The difficulties in finding replacements for existing systems are attributed to changes in response to the reduction of the cold war threat.
12. The page discusses the challenges of the acquisition process for space systems, highlighting unstable system designs and lack of coordination among different organizations. It suggests that a cultural change is needed in order to achieve more efficient and affordable space age systems.
13. Louis J. Rodrigues testifies about opportunities to reduce costs in military space programs, specifically focusing on missile warning and communication satellites.
14. The page discusses two Department of Defense space programs: the Defense Support Program (DSP) for detecting missile launches and the Milstar satellite communications system. The programs were originally designed for a nuclear missile confrontation with the Soviet Union but are now being reevaluated to meet new tactical requirements.

15. The page discusses the opportunity for cost savings in the Department of Defense's Milstar and DSP satellite systems by making program changes and initiating early development of smaller, more affordable satellites.
16. The page discusses the North American Aerospace Defense Command and the efforts to replace the Defense Support Program (DSP) with more modern technology. Despite encountering setbacks, the Department of Defense (DOD) plans to initiate a new effort in fiscal year 1995 to replace DSP, with a focus on smaller and less costly systems that provide greater support to tactical forces.
17. The page discusses the history and development of the Defense Support Program (DSP) and its planned replacement, the Advanced Warning System (AWS). Despite multiple attempts to improve or replace DSP, no successful replacement has been implemented.
18. The FEWS program, aimed at improving missile launch detection, was terminated in 1993 due to cost concerns. DOD plans to initiate a new research effort in 1995, but the specific direction is still undecided. DSP, previously focused on nuclear missile detection, provided sufficient warning during the Persian Gulf War but improvements are needed for the future.
19. The page discusses the validation of requirements for an advanced space-based missile warning sensor, the development of FEWS research and development contractors, and the recommendation for a simpler and less costly system.
20. The page discusses the recommendation to terminate the current FEWS effort due to changing strategic needs and the need for a better, simpler, cheaper system. It also highlights studies questioning the cost effectiveness of FEWS and presents cost-effective options for consideration.
21. The Milstar satellite communications system, designed for military use, has experienced delays, cost increases, and controversy. Despite a significant investment of $8 billion, the first launch is scheduled for February 5, 1994. The system aims to provide highly survivable communications resistant to electronic jamming.
22. The page discusses the opportunity for the Department of Defense (DOD) to reduce costs in the Hilstar program by not acquiring the last two satellites and instead accelerating the development of a smaller, lighter, and cheaper satellite. The tradeoffs between cost savings and operational risk are being evaluated for consideration in future defense authorization and appropriations deliberations.
23. The page discusses the restructuring of the Milstar satellite communication system by the Department of Defense. Changes include reducing the number of satellites, adding a medium-data rate capability, and eliminating certain features to lower costs.
24. The page discusses the concerns and decisions regarding the Department of Defense's space investment strategy, specifically regarding the Milstar satellite program. The focus is on reducing costs and increasing efficiency by adjusting the constellation size and adding different data rate capabilities to the satellites. Additionally, there are plans to replace the current design with a smaller and more cost-effective one in the future.
25. In a 1993 report, alternatives were discussed for reducing costs in DOD's military satellite communications plans. Transitioning to a common satellite

platform and reassessing alternatives were recommended. DOD agreed to terminate Milstar after the 6th satellite and move towards common platforms.

26. The page discusses the possibility of inserting modern technology into the Milstar program after the fourth satellite instead of the sixth, which could reduce costs and result in an earlier deployment of advanced design. This would cause a 2-year delay in achieving a 4-satellite constellation with medium-data rate capabilities.

27. DOD's difficulties in meeting the cold war threat and making changes in response to its reduction have hindered the replacement of DSP and development of Milstar. The high cost, focus on performance over cost, time constraints, and security needs have led to a crises-driven acquisition process.

28. The page discusses the need for a redesign of space systems, as the old procurement rationale no longer applies. It mentions the potential for cross-program sharing and the challenge of changing the culture within the space community. It also highlights the lack of coordination among different sectors in the United States' space policy.

29. The page discusses the development and operations of space systems within the military and intelligence sectors. It highlights the different cultures, technical requirements, and acquisition procedures of six organizations involved in this field. The report also mentions institutional obstacles to cultural change and the need for increased cooperation and efficiency.

30. The speaker emphasizes the importance of emphasis in all phases of a project and concludes their statement.

31. The page contains remarks from Mr. Conyers and Mr. McCandless during a hearing, with Mr. Conyers encouraging his colleagues to submit questions for Mr. Rodrigues, and Mr. McCandless stating his unfamiliarity with the subject matter and requesting to submit specific questions.

32. The letter provides answers to questions regarding the Milstar and DSP/FEWS programs. It states that the Bottom-Up-Review did not reach different conclusions from the previous report and addressed some concerns. The review suggested transitioning to a lower weight class satellite design and using common bus satellites.

33. The analyst used data provided by the Air Force, previous GAO work, and contractor data to calculate the cost of the Milstar satellite. They did not question specific features but suggested that DOD should review requirements for all MILSATCOM systems considering changing threats and costs. The limited tactical utility of the first two low data rate Milstars would not have been cost-effective, and the current requirements would be better covered by Milstar II. There is a difference between the handset unit and the ground terminal for

34. The need for EHF communications and capabilities is acknowledged, with further information available from the DOD and the Intelligence community. The DOD also plans to include low data rate EHF capability on Navy UHF communication satellites.

35. Milstar I and II satellites provide low-data rate EHF capability and secure antijam communication. Milstar I has limited tactical use, primarily for strategic purposes, with certain user communities like Special Operation Forces. The decision is whether to launch Milstar I for $1.4 billion or not.

36. The page contains a transcript of a Congressional hearing discussing the launch of MDR capable satellites and the validation of requirements for a DSP/FEWS system. The witness from GAO emphasizes the importance of having validated requirements before investing in a major program.
37. This page discusses the testimonial privilege of a congressional subcommittee against claims for defamation. It also introduces Colonel Sanford Mangold of the U.S. Air Force, who will testify about budget cuts in the Air Force's space program. Mangold was removed from his position due to allegations but no charges were made.
38. The author, a former Air Force Colonel, discusses their experience with the Space Command and their opposition to the Milstar program, stating that it is unnecessary and costly. They were removed from their position before being able to make significant cuts to the space budget.
39. The author discusses their opposition to the Milstar and FEWS space programs, highlighting issues with cost, functionality, and ethical concerns. They also mention facing backlash and being removed from their position.
40. The author believes their cost-cutting measures were in line with President Clinton's policies and that they were removed from their position for challenging expensive space programs. They conclude that the issue lies within the space community and express gratitude towards the Air Force leadership. The author reflects on a lesson from their past and expresses no regrets for their actions.
41. Col. Sanford Mangold presents a statement regarding legislation and national security to the Subcommittee on Legislation and National Security, discussing relevant issues.
42. The author, a former member of the United States Air Force, discusses their role in managing the budget for space and nuclear weapons systems. They claim to have uncovered cost savings and faced opposition due to their approach to budget reductions. They were later relieved of their position and faced allegations of personal integrity. The author provides background on their experience and expresses their opposition to certain programs.
43. The author discovered that while top Air Force leaders understood the need for military force reduction, many within the Air Force opposed budget cuts. The author specifically opposed the MILSTAR program, conducting studies that showed its limited usefulness and high cost. Despite facing opposition, the author continued to challenge the program until a compromise was reached.
44. The author discusses the cost savings and drawbacks of the MILSTAR program, arguing that there are more affordable alternatives for military communications. They also question the effectiveness and necessity of the FEWS program for missile warning and assessment.
45. The author questions the effectiveness of a space system and faces opposition from Space Command. They are eventually removed from their position but remain confident in their recommendations and actions. The author believes the issue is isolated within the Space Command community and reflects on their choices.
46. Colonel Mangold's courageous statement is commended by the committee. Colonel Dietz, representing the Air Force, speaks about his personal experiences and qualifications regarding space and missile systems.

47. Col Edward Dietz, former DSP Program Manager, introduces himself and his qualifications before addressing the alleged misconduct on the DSP/FSWS programs.
48. Mr. Guido Aru, a project leader at the Aerospace Corp., testifies about a congressionally mandated study he led on upgrading the DSP system. He describes efforts to suppress and discredit the study's conclusions, including providing misleading information and taking retributive actions against participants. Independent review teams eventually confirmed the study's findings and recommended the DSP-II concept as the lowest cost option for early warning.
49. The page discusses the cancellation of the FEWS program and the need for a new early warning program. It highlights concerns about the individuals in charge and their lack of integrity. The page emphasizes the importance of responsible use of taxpayer dollars and calls for reform of military space institutions.
50. Mr. Aru concludes his statement and offers to answer any questions from the committee members.
51. Mr. Guido William Aru, Project Leader at The Aerospace Corporation, testified before the House of Representatives Committee on Government Operations about system architecture and integration in space-based surveillance.
52. This page discusses the suppression of information and disinformation campaign related to the upgrade study of the DSP (Defense Support Program) in the aerospace industry. It also covers retribution against employees and provides recommendations for space-based early warning systems.
53. Mr. Guido William Aru is the Project Leader for the System Architecture and Integration Section at The Aerospace Corporation. He is responsible for system architecture and integration of various defense programs, performs concept analysis and technical risk management, and has a background in tactical space surveillance systems.
54. Mr. Guido Aru, a private citizen and project leader at The Aerospace Corporation, testifies about attempts to suppress and discredit a study showing potential cost savings in upgrading the Defense Support Program (DSP) system. He also discusses misleading information provided to justify the acquisition of the Follow-On Early Warning System (FEWS) and retributive actions taken against those involved in the study. Aru concludes with his thoughts and suggestions for Space Based Early Warning.
55. The page discusses serious problems with the military space systems and unethical conduct by senior leadership. It emphasizes the need for reform in order to provide military space capabilities in a post-Cold War world within budget constraints.
56. The page discusses a study conducted to determine how an upgraded Defense Support Program (DSP) and Brilliant Eyes (BE) system could meet the Nation's Tactical Warning/Attack Assessment (TW/AA) and Global Protection Against Limited Strike (GPALS) requirements. The study found that evolutionary upgrades to the DSP system could improve performance and reduce costs. However, the results of the study were suppressed by Major General Schnelzer, who favored a different upgrade concept.

57. The Air Force rejected the DSP-I and included the DSP++ option for the Follow-on Early Warning System, despite objections from program directors. Requirements for space-based early warning were documented, but the Air Force Space Command had additional requirements that were unrealistic. Major General Schnelzer suppressed the DSP-I concept and understated the performance of DSP in his report.
58. The Air Force ignored a more cost-effective option for satellite procurement, opting instead for a more expensive option with limited capabilities. The Air Force showed a lack of interest in conducting thorough analysis and withheld information from its own personnel responsible for budgeting.
59. Major General Hard testified that developing a new system like FEWS was more cost-effective than upgrading DSP. However, subsequent analysis showed that upgrading DSP could save billions compared to FEWS. GAO report also indicated that an enhanced DSP could be nearly as effective and much cheaper than FEWS.
60. Major General Hard incorrectly stated that FEWS provides better accuracy than DSP for missile launch point estimation. However, DSP's real-time launch site estimates during Desert Storm were smaller than an area the size of Washington, D.C. A comparison conducted by a Technical Support Group found that FEWS only offers a marginal advantage over DSP. It is worth noting that Major General Hard now works for The Aerospace Corporation, which seeks to expand its support to US Space Command and Air Force Space Command, both led by General Homer
61. The Aerospace Corporation's DSP-II report compares the proposed DSP-I system with the Air Force's FEWS program, questioning the military utility of some FEWS requirements. The report recommends technology insertion and product improvements for existing DSP satellites regardless of FEWS' fate. General Homer was informed of the report on May 20, 1993.
62. General Homer criticizes the DSP-H1 report, expressing concerns about its quality and professionalism. Mr. Aldridge acknowledges the issues raised and emphasizes the importance of program advocacy. He also addresses rumors about Aerospace not supporting FEWS. Major General Anderson's investigation reveals that Mr. Aldridge recalled the report for review by an independent team, which initially tried to discredit it but later found it to be technically sound. James Slattery, who led the review, was promoted after completing it.
63. Colonel Bailey and Mr. Parsons provided a restricted report containing competition-sensitive information to contractors, despite being informed that it could not be released. This violated ethical standards and potentially legal acts. The incident was investigated and confirmed the inappropriate release of proprietary data.
64. Major General Anderson's report revealed that the government and Aerospace Corporation tried to discredit the DSP-11 report. However, Anderson misunderstood Aerospace's role and mission, which is to provide objective analysis and recommendations to the customer. There is no requirement to coordinate with the user and the PEO for such reports, as it would hinder objectivity.
65. According to Regulation 800-8, Aerospace must designate a Systems Engineering Director for each program. The report was approved by Barbara

Ching and Everett Bersinger, and Richard Aliman reviewed unclassified sections. Dr. Philip Diamond and Dr. George Paulikas also reviewed the report. It assessed requirements for military utility relative to cost and technical risk, in line with The Aerospace Corporation's mission.
66. The DSP-II report questions the military utility of proposed Air Force Space Command requirements for FEWS and concludes that many of the requirements are excessive and unachievable. The report also discusses the distribution of the report and the approval process.
67. The statement by Mr. Guido Aru confirms that secondary distribution of the report to government agencies was authorized, except for the FEWS contractors. Mr. Aldridge may have been embarrassed because the report questioned the justification of The Aerospace Corporation's support for the FEWS program. Independent reviews concluded that FEWS was unnecessary.
68. The page discusses Mr. Aldridge's potential concerns about challenging General Homer's priority program, as it may impact Aerospace Corporation's budget and their efforts to expand business with US Space Command and Air Force Space Command. FEWS program accounts for 4-5% of Aerospace's total budget.
69. The Bottom-Up Review of the DSP and FEWS systems was conducted after the Air Force's attempt to suppress the DSP-II report failed. The review considered alternatives that could lower costs, despite not meeting all requirements. Mr. Robert Everett headed an independent Technical Support Group to recommend options for future space-based infrared surveillance capability. Briefing requests were denied by Mr. Aldridge initially but later allowed for one member of the group.
70. Mr. Gudo Am criticizes the misleading and biased performance estimates submitted by SBEWS SPO, stating that the DSP estimates were lower than the demonstrated performance and excluded projected upgrades, while FEWS estimates were overly optimistic.
71. The statement of Mr. Guido Aru raises concerns about the FEWS program, stating that it was still in the early stages and that the cost and performance estimates were biased towards FEWS. Other individuals also expressed doubts about the accuracy of the performance comparisons between FEWS and DSP. The cost estimates were manipulated to support the claim that FEWS was cheaper than DSP.
72. Colonel Quirk manipulated cost estimates for satellite contracts, making some options appear worse by adding unnecessary billion-dollar satellites. Estimates for an additional system also increased significantly without justification. The details are hidden and the opportunity to discuss these issues with investigators was refused.
73. The statement highlights retribution against individuals involved in the DSP-I concept, including those not directly involved. Major General Anderson's investigative staff compromised confidentiality and hindered openness, leading to potential retaliation. Aerospace Corporation employees working on the report suffered in performance reviews, with most moving down in rankings and being at risk of lay-off.
74. The page discusses management changes at Nimble Books LLC, specifically the promotion of Mr. Parsons and the layoffs of Mr. Montag and Mr. Lunde.

It also mentions efforts to address Mr. Lunde's derogatory performance review.
75. TRW's DSP Program Manager was replaced by Mr. Bailis at the Air Force's request, leading to allegations of retribution for TRW raising impropriety concerns. TRW executives claimed they were threatened by senior Air Force officers not to support opponents of FEWS.
76. The termination of the DSP Block 23 satellite contract in favor of a new program start is detrimental to national security and will result in financial loss. It also jeopardizes our capability to provide early warning and missile surveillance. The decision lacks consideration for existing systems and other surveillance programs.
77. The page discusses the decision to cancel a missile detection system due to a perceived threat of tactical missiles in the Third World. It argues that the decision ignores the capabilities of existing systems and focuses on the wrong type of threat. The author compares the decision to France's mistake in building the Maginot Line during World War II.
78. The termination of the DSP Block 23 contract will result in a $500 million loss and the inability to deliver any satellites. Continuing the procurement of all three satellites is the wisest approach, as starting anew would be more costly and increase the government's risk and liability. The DSP ground processing system will require significant changes for a new satellite.
79. The page discusses the risks associated with canceling a satellite program and starting a new one, using analogies from previous programs. It emphasizes the need for DSP Satellites 23, 24, and 25 due to the cancellation of another program and the importance of maintaining national security.
80. The page discusses the misconception that the spinning satellite DSP has limited sensitivity due to its fixed spin rate. It explains that sensitivity can be improved through technology insertion and that the background radiation of the Earth is the main limitation in detecting targets. The rotation of the satellite simplifies its design and allows for sufficient global surveillance capabilities.
81. The current DSP system is deemed sufficient for strategic early warning needs, but improvements are desired for tactical ballistic missile surveillance. Options for technology insertion and product improvements are explored in the DSP-II report, including the use of add-on sensors for improved theater missile detection. Replacing the canceled LCS program with an add-on sensor would not interfere with the global surveillance mission.
82. The statement discusses the feasibility and benefits of implementing an add-on sensor system for surveillance missions, including cost savings and improved capabilities. It also mentions the potential use of different orbits and preservation of technology from previous programs.
83. The page discusses the possibility of combining DSP and Radiant Agate data to enhance surveillance capabilities. It highlights the advantages of using a Molniya orbit for communication satellites and suggests that leveraging existing technology would be a low-risk approach compared to starting a new program.
84. The statement recommends that the United States focus on developing new systems to address threats instead of reinventing existing capabilities. It also suggests suspending individuals involved in unethical or illegal conduct,

conducting a comprehensive study of space-based surveillance requirements, and investing in technology improvements for DSP satellites.
85. The page discusses the retrofitting of a satellite to improve its performance and extend its lifespan, in line with Total Quality Management principles.
86. The statement highlights the intense competition for funding in the defense industry and the potential abuse in the relationship between FFRDC's and their sponsors. It suggests strengthening independent technical assessment and returning the Aerospace Corporation to its original values of advising in the best interests of the government.
87. The author suggests that an independent agency should assess the role of space systems in supporting the government and allocate resources based on objective analysis.
88. Colonel Mangold describes the events leading up to his removal as the team chief. He had made critical remarks about the Milstar program and faced backlash from senior Air Force officials, including threats and intimidation.
89. Retaliation against the witnesses is not unique, it has happened before. Concerns about the validity and integrity of the system are raised, with suspicions that costs and performance were intentionally distorted to make the new system look better. The costs of repairing the old system were inflated, and the risk assessments of the new system were minimized. The cost difference between fixing the old system and replacing it is around $6 to $10 billion, not close by any measure.
90. The speaker expresses concern over the cost and performance of a new system, stating that it is more expensive and does not provide significant advantages compared to the old system. They also question the ability of the new system to detect cruise missiles.
91. The page discusses concerns about the accuracy and effectiveness of a new system operating in high clouds. The author questions the claims made about the system's capabilities and highlights the importance of ethics and integrity in decision-making processes.
92. The page discusses the cancellation of a program called FEWS and the potential impact on jobs. It also mentions the embarrassment of Mr. Aldridge, who advocated for FEWS despite reports suggesting a lower cost alternative.
93. The speaker discusses the potential costs and benefits of incorporating new technologies into the Milstar program. They argue that while these technologies may reduce the size and cost of the program, the delay in deployment and loss of capabilities outweigh the savings. The speaker also mentions alternative options that could have been considered.
94. The conversation discusses the importance of communication in military operations and questions the need for a specific communication system called Milstar. The comparison is made to the Spruce Goose, a plane developed during World War II that became unnecessary after the war ended. The speaker argues that Milstar is no longer needed and is a wasteful expenditure.
95. The speaker criticizes the Milstar program, arguing that it is unnecessary and inefficient. They highlight the misuse of funds and the mentality of continuing a project simply because it has already been started. The speaker also questions the decision-making process within the Air Force and expresses concerns about the overall system.

96. The page discusses the importance of open technical debate and the need to balance it with decision-making. It also mentions the speaker's concern about distorted information and the potential consequences of making decisions based on incorrect facts. The dialogue between Mr. McCaniess and Colonel Mangold highlights the accessibility and involvement of the decision-makers in the process.
97. The speaker discusses their success in proposing the cancellation of a program called Milstar, but how they faced opposition and personal attacks from others as a result. Another individual shares a similar experience of being reassigned after doing their job.
98. The page discusses the firing of Colonel Mangold and Colonel Dietz for presenting unpopular conclusions. It raises concerns about the unwillingness to discuss and implies that Ms. Maguire was involuntarily removed. The restructuring of the Milstar communications system is also mentioned, with the Senate Armed Services Committee being satisfied with the outlined plans. Colonel Mangold advocates for a reassessment of requirements and objectives.
99. The speaker discusses the technical aspects of a program called Milstar and the difficulty of challenging established solutions. They also mention the fall of the Berlin Wall and its implications for reassessing requirements. A letter from the U.S. Senate's Committee on Armed Services is entered into the record.
100. The Senate Armed Services Committee approves the restructuring plan for the MilStar communication system, as it reduces costs and enhances capabilities for tactical forces. An additional $350 million is authorized for the program, with allocations for satellites, terminals, and Air Force maintenance. Specific details of the plan are yet to be developed.
101. The page is a congratulatory message to the Department of State for their efforts in restructuring the Milstar program and expresses support for future collaboration.
102. Multiple individuals testify that they faced negative consequences for speaking up about the unnecessary and costly Milstar program. The program, which is no longer needed, is set to cost $20 billion overall, with one satellite alone costing $1.4 billion. The satellite offers minimal additional capability and will not significantly enhance war fighting capabilities. It will require 400 people to operate and monitor, costing over $100 million. Despite its relevance during the Cold War, the program is now deemed unnecessary and burdensome.
103. The page discusses the argument within the Air Force regarding the Milstar satellite program and the alternative proposed by Colonel Mangold. Secretary Aspin ultimately overruled Mangold and continued with the Milstar program as part of a larger restructuring of the Department of Defense.
104. The speaker believes that the Milstar program should be stopped and reevaluated due to its marginal additional capability. They suggest reviewing the fundamental requirements of the program and deciding what is truly necessary before moving forward. The speaker also acknowledges the influence of defense contractors in pushing unnecessary contracts and weapon systems.

105. The interviewee discusses their experience with defense contractors and the pressures they faced. They also mention that allegations were made against them, but the case has been closed and they will have a chance to clear their name in order to be considered for promotion. The interviewee was removed as team chief 23 days after allegations were brought forward.
106. This page includes testimony from Colonel Mangold and Mrs. Maloney, discussing the removal of Colonel Mangold and the alleged ties to Dr. Fabian's testimony. Ms. Harman also asks about an "odor" surrounding the FEWS issue and if it is correct that there was this impression. Mr. Aru confirms that there was indeed an odor and quotes a letter from Brigadier General Dickman supporting FEWS as the preferred solution.
107. This letter outlines operational concerns regarding the integration studies of the BE/ITWAA system. Key issues include maintaining consistency and addressing all validated FEWS mission needs, such as on-board data processing, cross-links, worldwide collection and distribution of data, threat detection, and hardening/jamming requirements.
108. The page discusses the importance of not compromising on requirements for Digital Signal Processors (DSP) and Back-End (BE) alternatives. It emphasizes the significance of meeting validated requirements, the utility of integrating FEWS SWIR with BE, and the need to consider using the BE contractors' unique designs. Additionally, it mentions the need for consistent treatment of transition costs, launch reserves, and staffing in different options.
109. The page discusses the need for consistent treatment of various factors in a study, including technology assumptions, life cycle costs, learning curve effects, and system availability. The author believes that making these adjustments will lead to better answers for operational needs.
110. The purpose of the congressionally mandated study was to explore alternatives to FEWS and evaluate how other space programs, including Brilliant Eyes, could work together. A solution that would have saved billions of dollars was rejected, possibly due to it threatening the established FEWS program. Colonel Mangold was never provided with less expensive options despite his efforts to find them. There were acrimonious exchanges and pushback from higher-ups when trying to make budget cuts. The program manager's concerns are not mentioned.
111. A highly qualified woman in charge of the Defense Support Program at TRW was removed from her job, possibly in exchange for reassigning another individual involved in a controversial study. The congressman has received written answers from the Air Force regarding her removal.
112. The Air Force program director is being transferred to a different position due to controversy surrounding the DSP and FEWS programs. The transfer is not due to any wrongdoing, but rather to address future program needs. Further information about the TRW program manager can be obtained from TRW corporate management.
113. It is discussed that a highly qualified woman, Ms. Maguire, was removed from the program for being too close to her customer. This sends a message to professionals to keep quiet or risk losing their jobs, compromising the integrity and professionalism of the institution. Additionally, there was a witness of proprietary data being passed during a meeting.

114. The page discusses the improper sharing of confidential information and attempts to suppress a congressionally mandated study. It highlights the lack of consequences for those involved and the flawed internal review conducted by Aerospace Corp.
115. The page discusses the overstatement and pessimistic estimates of performance and cost for FEWS and DSP, as well as internal efforts to challenge these estimates. It mentions the distortion of information and the misrepresentation of Defense Support Program data by some elements of the U.S. Air Force.
116. The page discusses inaccuracies in the statement made by Major General Hard regarding the accuracy of FEWS compared to DSP. It also raises concerns about confidentiality breaches and fear of retribution within the program office.
117. The page discusses the challenges of fighting against bureaucracy in the acquisition and operation of military space systems. It highlights a shift in priorities within the Aerospace Corp. and the need to consider alternative solutions to space-based systems. There is also mention of corruption and the need for objective decision-making in the process.
118. The speaker recalls a letter that was recalled against their objections and discusses the opposition they faced from certain individuals. They highlight the issue of former government officials going into businesses they had an impact on and mention specific corporations and their costs. The speaker suggests reassessing expenditures and mentions a letter that caused controversy. A copy of the letter will be provided.
119. The page is a document from the Department of the Air Force, discussing the development and distribution of a specific product.
120. The individuals testifying express their hope for a thorough investigation by the DOD IG to reassess the situation and address the issues of ethics, values, and leadership within the institution. They emphasize the need for transparency and improvement in the system.
121. The page contains statements from individuals discussing the need for reassessment of certain defense programs and the role of companies like Aerospace Corp in national security. It also includes the entry of various documents into the record, including a letter addressing concerns about objectivity and conflict of interest.
122. The page contains a jumble of random characters and symbols, making it difficult to discern any meaningful information.
123. The Aerospace Corporation conducted a review of the DSP II report and found it to be overly optimistic and not meeting the requirements. The report was written to advocate for DSP II but was unauthorizedly distributed. Measures have been taken to address the issue and ensure objectivity and independence in future evaluations.
124. The letter addresses the need for technical evaluations in Aerospace, denies rumors about lack of support for FEWs, and emphasizes the importance of addressing the tactical missile threat. The writer hopes to move past these issues and acknowledges the reader's more important tasks.
125. The memo emphasizes the importance of following existing corporate processes for coordination, review, and approval of Air Force space

programs. It expresses concern about individuals who do not support established decisions and urges them to operate within normal processes.

126. Higher headquarters conduct thorough analyses before presenting Air Force positions to DoD and Congress. Proposals that bypass the corporate decision-making process are suspect and create unnecessary confusion. It is important to live within guidelines and understand responsibilities to support acquisition matters.

127. This executive summary provides an overview of an inquiry conducted to review accusations regarding the Space Based Infrared Budget Issue. The allegations included releasing proprietary data, suppressing information, and providing erroneous data. Despite an extensive investigation, no substantiated misconduct by senior Air Force officials was found.

128. The page discusses significant findings from an inquiry into allegations against senior Air Force officers. It states that two allegations were not investigated and 10 were not substantiated. However, one allegation regarding the release of proprietary data was found to be true.

129. The page discusses substantiated allegations related to the release of sensitive information, attempts to discredit a report, and interference in investigations. It highlights the competition for funding in the defense industry as a cause of distrust and suspicion. The rejection of an option for Sensor Study I served as a catalyst for these allegations.

130. The page discusses two key events related to the rejection of a lower cost DSP option and the publication of a report, which led to allegations of favoritism and misleading data. It concludes that good communication and addressing concerns is necessary to prevent future allegations.

131. This report is a review of accusations regarding the Space-Based Infrared Budget Issue. The inquiry addresses three separate sets of allegations, including those from Aerojet Corporation and Congressman Conyers. The report includes a chronology of events and major documents related to the investigation.

132. This page discusses various studies and investigations related to the Defense Support Program (DSP) and Bottom Up Review (BUR). It mentions allegations of data sharing, suppression of study results, and improper evaluation of costs.

133. The page discusses various allegations made by Congressman Conyers in a letter to the DoD IG, including the suppression of information about a lower cost alternative to a satellite program, erroneous statements by General Homer, and the deletion of an option to save money. It also mentions false and misleading information provided to decision makers and the sharing of sensitive information with competitors.

134. The page provides a list of general officers, including General C. Qures A. Homer, who serves as the Commander in Chief of USSPACECOM.

135. TRW withheld proprietary data on a Multi-Spectral alternative from OSD, but it was passed to competitors by the Air Force. The SBEWS SPO created a generic Multi-Spectral briefing using inputs from Aerospace and LMSC engineers, with some proprietary data included.

136. The page discusses a briefing on Multi-Spectral technology and the involvement of TRW, LMSC, and the SBEWS SPO. It mentions that TRW did not provide OSD with Multi-Spectral data, and that Aerospace and LMSC

provided support for the briefing. There is also mention of proprietary information and competition sensitivity.

137. The page discusses allegations regarding the release of proprietary information during a briefing and the involvement of a defense contractor in a specific project. However, these allegations are not substantiated.

138. TRW's Multi-Spectral concept gave mixed signals to military officials regarding their commitment to the FEWS program. CINCSPACE questioned TRW's motivation and advocated for FEWS as the superior system. TRW made a corporate decision to not provide data on Multi-Spectral that could be seen as inconsistent with FEWS. CINCSPACE did not support TRW providing Multi-Spectral information to OSD/PA&E, but did not direct them to withhold data. TRW decided not to provide Multi-S

139. Allegation that TRW withheld data regarding a space-based TW/AA system is unsubstantiated. USSPACECOM released briefing charts to FEWS contractors, unaware of proprietary or competition-sensitive information. Conflicting evidence on whether the data is proprietary. Lack of acquisition experience and insufficient marking contributed to the release.

140. The page discusses allegations of unauthorized disclosure of proprietary information and erroneous data provided by the Space-Based Early Warning and Ballistic Missile Defense System Program Offices. The allegations were partially substantiated, but there is insufficient evidence to conclude a violation of the Procurement Integrity Act.

141. Two programs were merged into one, addressing concerns about data validity. An independent team reviewed cost data and found some concerns, but it did not affect the technical analysis conclusions. Contractors and personnel expressed confidence in the data provided.

142. Allegation that Air Force suppressed results of Aerojet study. Congress tasked OSD for analysis of Follow-on Early Warning System. Aerojet study presented DSP-MLV concept, rejected by PEO for Space. Aerospace TOR recalled but copies acquired by DOD IG. TOR states DSP-I does not meet all user requirements. Copies provided to OSD and Congress.

143. The page discusses the rejection of the Aerojet Study for inclusion in the Sensor Study Task 3, the awareness of the DSP-MLV variant, and the inclusion of DSP++ in the study. It also mentions allegations of the government attempting to discredit the Aerospace TOR report.

144. The page discusses allegations of improper coordination and distribution of a TOR report, as well as the release of proprietary data and inadequate cost evaluation in comparing FEWS and DSP systems. The allegations are substantiated based on the facts and investigations conducted.

145. The cost data provided by the SBEWS SPO was reviewed independently and found to be credible overall. However, there were three areas of concern in estimating costs for Sensor Study I options, including the addition of "deltas" to initial estimates, inconsistent assumptions, and a lack of detailed cost risk analysis. Despite these concerns, the overall rankings of the options are not significantly affected. Another allegation regarding the use of correct cost estimates for using a Shuttle to launch DSP satellites is also unsubstantiated.

146. The page discusses the difficulty in determining the cost of a Shuttle launch, with various numbers ranging from $100M to $789M. It concludes

that the Air Force cost figures are more logical and consistent. The page also addresses an allegation about the restriction of data flow from TRW to Aerojet, stating that TRW declined to provide requested data and CINCSPACE questioned TRW's commitment to FEWS.

147. TRW decided not to provide Mult-Spec information to OSD/PA&E. Congressman Conyers alleged that senior Air Force officials suppressed information about a lower cost alternative to the FEWS satellite program. However, this allegation was not substantiated.

148. This page discusses allegations related to the Aerospace TOR and FEWS-DSP Briefing. It concludes that there is no evidence of data suppression and that the allegations are not substantiated.

149. The page discusses allegations made against General Homer regarding errors in briefing, recall of a report, and suppression of technical alternatives. The allegations were not substantiated. It also mentions Major General Schneizer deleting an option in a study, but no further information is provided.

150. The PEO for Space rejected the DSP/BE synergy option due to not meeting user requirements. Mr. Aldridge recalled the TOR report for review and decided not to distribute it due to lack of objectivity. He denied suppressing data and stated that it was for internal use only.

151. Mr. Aldridge ordered the recall of the TOR, but did not suppress information or interfere with the DoD. Allegations of false and misleading information regarding the DSP and PEWS programs are unsubstantiated. The FEWS system underwent rigorous review and improvements over time.

152. A review of various documents and briefings related to the FEWS program found that the SORD was converted to an ORD without substantive changes, a briefing on FEWS was presented to CSAF and Vice C0iman, data from program offices was deemed accurate, cost data was appropriately developed, alleged false technical data was addressed and rebutted, and an investigation concluded that proprietary data was inappropriately released.

153. The page discusses the distrust and allegations of impropriety within the Air Force and defense contractors, triggered by the rejection of an option for Sensor Study I and the publication of the Aerospace Technical Operating Report. It emphasizes the need for effective communication and addressing concerns to avoid future allegations.

154. The page contains an index of various documents, letters, testimonies, and interviews related to aerospace companies and government agencies. It also mentions classified information filed separately.

155. The page contains various documents and testimonies related to space and missile systems, including an interview, testimony, a memorandum, and an analysis of cost information. Some of the information is classified.

156. The Inspector General reviewed an inquiry report on the Defense Support Program/Follow-On Early Warning System Program and found minor concerns with investigative actions, but overall agreed with the conclusions of the investigation. They will discuss these concerns with the Air Force Inspector General for improvement. The results will be shared with Chairman Conyers, Congress, and the media.

157. The page is a request for Air Force personnel and contractor officials to avoid reprisal or retaliation in connection with testimony before an

investigating officer or in other protected forums. Contact information is provided for any questions.

158. The speaker defends their integrity against accusations made by General Horner and expresses offense at his letter. The chairman confirms that the documents have been entered into the record and announces the continuation of the hearing.

159. The chairman of a subcommittee is troubled by a report from the Air Force Inspector General on the FEWS DSP controversy. The report substantiates allegations of government attempts to discredit a technical operating report, deletion of an alternative option for improvement, and the recall of the report. The chairman is concerned about the suppression of a congressionally mandated study. The Department of Defense Inspector General is still reviewing allegations of retaliation. Dr. Thomas Quinn, along with other officials, provides a statement on the matter.

160. This page discusses the Defense Support Program (DSP) and its follow-on system, the Follow-On Early Warning System (FEWS), as well as the Milstar program. It provides background information on DSP and FEWS, including their development and upgrades. It also mentions the decision to establish FEWS and the advantages it offers over DSP. The page concludes by mentioning a review of early warning systems conducted by the Department of Defense.

161. The study group recommends continuing the block buy of three DSP satellites, terminating the FEWS program, and acquiring a better surveillance capability. The Department plans to start a new program to replace DSP with a system that has better detection performance. Misconduct allegations in the DSP/FEWS program have been investigated and a report has been forwarded to Congress. Next, the Milstar program will be discussed.

162. The Milstar satellite system provides secure and flexible communications for mobile tactical units worldwide. It has been revised and restructured to meet changing threats, reducing costs and increasing tactical utility. The program incorporates new technologies and addresses deficiencies observed during Desert Storm.

163. The page discusses the baseline Milstar program and the recommendations for a cost-constrained EHF system. It outlines the options considered and the selected option, which involves launching Milstar II satellites followed by the development of an advanced EHF satellite. The page also mentions the planned launches and the expected cost savings compared to the baseline program.

164. The Department has conducted a review and restructuring of the DSP/FEWS and Milstar programs, focusing on cost reduction and meeting military needs. They are terminating the FEWS program and working on defining a follow-on system to DSP. Risk and affordability are key factors in their decisions.

165. Prepared statement by Thomas P. Quinn, Deputy Assistant Secretary of Defense, discussing control, communication, and intelligence acquisition for the Legislation and National Security Committee of the US House of Representatives.

166. The speaker is representing the Department of Defense and discussing the development and deployment plans for the DSP/FEWS and Milstar

programs. They highlight the focus on tailoring these systems to new national security realities and budget decisions based on applicability and affordability. The Defense Support Program (DSP) is described as the primary system for detecting ballistic missile launches worldwide.

167. The page discusses the development and evolution of the Defense Support Program (DSP) and its role in detecting missile launches. It also mentions the creation of new surveillance systems, such as the Boost Surveillance and Tracking System (BSTS) and the Follow-on Early Warning System (FEWS), to improve accuracy and support defense missions.

168. FEWS, a satellite system designed to detect tactical ballistic missiles, is being cancelled due to affordability concerns. A new program to replace DSP will have better detection performance against tactical missiles at a lower cost.

169. The Department of Defense is considering alternative satellite designs for the early warning mission. A study group recommends continuing the block buy of three DSP satellites but terminating the FEWS program. They suggest acquiring a better surveillance capability than DSP that is cheaper and can be available on the FEWS schedule.

170. The Department has considered upgrades to the DSP satellite but determined they were not cost-effective. The FEWS program was initiated instead. The latest review found no advantages to the suggested modifications for the DSP platform. The Air Force will review requirements for a new program in FY1994.

171. The Milstar satellite system provides secure communication for mobile tactical units worldwide. It operates in the EHF spectrum and has been adapted to meet changing global threats. The program has undergone restructuring to reduce costs and align with national security changes.

172. The Milstar program was restructured to improve communication capabilities for mobile forces and reduce costs. It included a higher capacity payload, reduced the number of satellites and ground control elements, and incorporated new technologies into terminal designs. The changes addressed deficiencies observed during Desert Storm and utilized advancements from the Navy's UHF Follow-On satellites.

173. In 1992, the Milstar program underwent a review and restructuring to reduce costs and align with military needs. The Department considered affordability and assessed the program against other defense acquisition programs. Several payload and architecture alternatives were considered, and there were plans for a smaller, more affordable Milstar polar adjunct.

174. The page discusses the Bottom Up Review of MILSATCOM programs in 1993, which evaluated alternatives to the Milstar program and emphasized lower cost options for tactical forces. A technical support group recommended a cost-constrained EHF system for protected connectivity.

175. The page discusses four options for launching Milstar II satellites and transitioning to lower weight, lower cost EHF satellites. Option 1 was selected as it best met military requirements and provided the most capability at the earliest date.

176. The page discusses the development of the Milstar I and II satellites, including plans for an advanced EHF system. It highlights potential cost

savings and acknowledges the challenges involved in developing the advanced satellite.

177. The page discusses the Department's examination of potentially applicable technologies for the development of a lower cost EHF satellite design. The budget request includes funding for evaluating concepts and assessing development risks, as well as reducing funding for Milstar satellites and delaying replacement of MILSATCOM capabilities. The launches of the remaining DSCS-III satellites will be stretched out.

178. The page discusses the Department's decision to delay the implementation of Super High Frequency (SHF) service and the replacement of Ultra High Frequency (UHF) capabilities. It also mentions the Department's new policy for integrating commercial satellite communications.

179. The Department of Defense plans to augment its military satellite capabilities with domestic and international commercial services. They aim to achieve maximum savings through economies of scale and establish interoperability among terminals. A recent conference allowed for the exchange of ideas to develop a comprehensive commercial SATCOM strategy.

180. The page discusses the restructuring of the Milstar program in 1991 and the update of the MILSATCOM Architecture. It mentions the identification of core military requirements, technology investments, cost reduction decisions, and the selection of approved systems. The page also highlights the development of cost estimates and potential cost risks.

181. A study from 1991 on baseline architecture and system costs for spacecraft is outdated. The Department plans to update the architecture for 1996 and is currently reviewing requirements and identifying which systems can transition to commercial SATCOM or fiber optic cable. This review will inform the budget request for FY 1996.

182. The Department plans to identify cost-effective reductions in its SATCOM investment strategy, particularly in transitioning to a lower cost EHF alternative. It will review requirements, insert new technologies, and use commercial systems to supplement military capabilities based on cost-effectiveness. Affordability is a key factor in determining the best mix of SATCOM systems and services.

183. The Department has reviewed and restructured programs in response to changing threats, terminating one and working on a follow-up system. They have also reduced costs and begun development for an advanced system. Risk and affordability are important factors and they will continue to review requirements and cost-effective solutions.

184. General Kelley, representing the Joint Chiefs of Staff, discusses the importance of the Milstar program in meeting warfighter requirements for satellite coverage, anti-jam capability, covertness, deployability, and mobility. He also emphasizes the need for improved space-based sensors for launch detection in future warfighting environments.

185. The statement by Major General David Kelley addresses the restructuring and purpose of the Milstar program to meet tactical military requirements. It emphasizes the importance of satellite communication capabilities, anti-jamming capability, and covert deployability in order to successfully conduct warfare. Additionally, it highlights the need for an improved spaced-based

sensor for launch detection in response to the proliferation of Tactical Ballistic Missiles.

186. The Air Force inspector general investigated allegations of misconduct and mismanagement in the DSP and FEWS acquisition programs. Some allegations were substantiated, including the improper release of proprietary data and the deletion of an option to save money. Other allegations were partially substantiated or not verified.

187. Allegations of misconduct in the Air Force were investigated and found to be unsubstantiated. The investigation highlighted the breakdown in communication and distrust caused by intense competition for defense dollars. The Air Force must improve its communication and address concerns to avoid future allegations. The results of the inquiry will be released to the media and the public. A study conducted by Aerojet was questioned for being technically flawed, and General Charles described it as politically flawed as well.

188. The page discusses the recall of a report on theater missiles and allegations of suppression. The report was recalled to assess its findings and determine if it met the requirements. There were claims of attempted discredit due to the report not meeting the FEWS requirements.

189. Colonel Stadler discusses the approved requirements for the FEWS program, stating that they were documented in 1991 and used for the program's demonstration and validation phase. He mentions that a second iteration of the requirements document was being drafted but was not issued. He confirms that the FEWS requirements are available and can be provided.

190. The page contains a list of deleted items and references to the validation of key requirements for an advanced system.

191. The page contains a dialogue between Mrs. Maloney and Colonel Schepens and Colonel Collins regarding the release of a report that didn't meet certain requirements. They discuss different alternatives and their costs. Mrs. Maloney also raises concerns about former Air Force officials becoming contractors, which may violate an Executive order.

192. The discussion revolves around Mr. Aldridge's employment history and potential conflicts of interest with major contractors in the aerospace industry. The need for legal counsel to provide a formal answer is emphasized.

193. President Clinton signed Executive Order 12834, requiring certain appointees to sign a pledge regarding their activities as "senior appointees" or trade negotiators. The order does not apply to career officials or those staying on from the previous administration without a new appointment.

194. The page discusses the forms of pledges that senior appointees and trade negotiators must sign. It explains when these pledges need to be signed and when they do not need to be signed again. The Executive order is incorporated into both pledges, and a copy of the order must be given to individuals before they sign the pledge.

195. Senior appointees and trade negotiators must submit signed pledges to their agency heads. Waivers can only be granted by the President, requiring certification and publication. Contractual commitments will be enforced through legal means. The Office will provide guidance and consult with the

Attorney General or Counsel to the President. The Attorney General will publish a statement on restrictions for former senior appointees.

196. This page outlines a pledge that senior appointees in the United States Government must agree to, which includes restrictions on post-employment activities and lobbying. The pledge is required by Executive Order 12834 and violation of the pledge may result in disclosure to relevant federal agencies for investigation and enforcement.

197. This page is an Executive Order from January 20, 1993, regarding ethics commitments by executive branch appointees. It outlines obligations such as not lobbying any agency after employment, not engaging in activities on behalf of foreign governments or political parties, and acknowledging the provisions of the Executive order.

198. The page discusses the obligations and restrictions placed on individuals involved in trade negotiations, including not representing foreign entities to influence decisions and complying with ethical commitments. It also provides definitions for terms such as "senior appointed" and "trade negotiator."

199. This page provides definitions for various terms used in the senior appointee pledge, including "on behalf of another," "administrative proceeding," "executive agency," "personal and substantial responsibility," and more. It also mentions the possibility of a waiver of the restrictions contained in the pledge.

200. This page discusses the requirements and procedures for issuing waivers and pledges for senior appointees and trade negotiators within government agencies. It also mentions the responsibilities of the White House Counsel and the Director of the Office of Government Ethics in implementing these rules.

201. The page discusses the requirements and enforcement of pledges signed by senior appointees and trade negotiators to prevent lobbying or representing foreign entities. Violations may result in debarment, civil proceedings, or judicial review. The Attorney General can initiate investigations and civil actions, including injunctions and the establishment of a constructive trust.

202. This page is a federal order regarding provisions and applications of executive orders. It clarifies that this order supersedes any inconsistent prior orders and provides guidance on the validity and effect of its provisions.

203. This memorandum provides an opinion on the applicability of 10 U.S.C. S 2397b to the post-government employment of Major General Donald G. Hard. The opinion states that this provision will not apply to his employment with defense contractors based on the information provided. The memo discusses the specific criteria and time period covered by 10 U.S.C. S 2397b and concludes that it does not apply in this case.

204. This page explains that the three categories of 10 U.S.C. S 2397b do not apply to the reader's post-government employment because their work did not meet the criteria outlined in each category.

205. The page discusses additional restrictions on post-government employment, specifically related to procurement integrity. These restrictions limit certain activities on behalf of prospective employers regarding certain procurements. They only apply if the individual participated personally and substantially in specific pre-award activities during an agency procurement. The restrictions

prohibit participation in negotiations and performance of the contract for two years after participation in the procurement as a government official.
206. The page discusses five possible restrictions for post-government employment, including representational contacts with government officials and restrictions related to trade or treaty negotiations and foreign government employment.
207. This page discusses the Foreign Agents Registration Act, restrictions on releasing government "inside information," and post-government employment reports that need to be filed. It provides contact information for further questions and emphasizes the importance of timely filing these reports to avoid fines.
208. Retired military officers are prohibited from engaging in "selling" activities to certain government agencies for three years after retirement. The definition of "selling" is broad and includes various actions related to contracts. Contacts made by retired officers with government personnel are presumed to be for selling purposes, unless proven otherwise. Additionally, officers are restricted from representing others on claims against the U.S. involving their former military department or any matter they were directly involved with while on active duty.
209. The page discusses the application of selling restrictions to post-government employment with the DoD or Air Force. It advises caution and mentions that "behind-the-scenes" employment should not be affected by these restrictions. Contact information is provided for any questions.
210. The memorandum states that the individual's proposed post-government service employment with defense contractors is not subject to the two-year employment bar imposed by 10 U.S.C. S2397b. The memorandum also mentions that there are other statutory and regulatory restrictions on future employment, and the General Counsel is available to answer any questions regarding conflict of interest or post-employment provisions.
211. The page discusses the restrictions on seeking private employment after leaving government service, specifically focusing on two statutes that apply to former employees and DOD officials. It outlines the requirements for disqualification and reporting when negotiating for future employment with companies or contractors.
212. This page discusses the disqualification and reporting requirements for individuals involved in procurement functions for government contracts. It also outlines the post-government service restrictions, which include a lifetime ban on representing others before the government in matters they were personally involved in while working for the government. Violation of these restrictions can result in penalties and a bar on working for the contractor involved.
213. The page explains the restrictions in section 5207(a) and 207(b) for specific matters involving parties, with personal and substantial participation. It clarifies that rulemaking, legislation, and general policy formulation are not included. The regulations define "substantial" involvement as having significance or forming a reasonable appearance of such. Section 207(b)(i) has a two-year restriction and applies to matters pending under official responsibility. Official responsibility is defined as direct administrative or operating authority.

214. The page discusses two bars, one for senior employees and one for former senior employees, regarding their representation of other parties before government agencies. The first bar applies to all Presidential appointees, while the second bar specifically applies to the agency in which the employee served. The restrictions include appearances, communications, and rulemaking activities. Certain exceptions apply, such as personal and individual matters or providing statements without compensation.

215. The page discusses the restrictions on representing a company in dealings with government officials based on previous involvement in specific matters. It also mentions additional restrictions on employment with certain DOD contractors and reporting requirements for defense contractors.

216. The page provides contact information for Anne N. Foreman, the General Counsel at Nimble Books LLC, and mentions that she is available to answer specific questions or discuss employment opportunities.

217. This page outlines the requirements for personnel to report potential employment contacts with defense contractors and the steps they must take to disqualify themselves from participating in procurement functions related to those contractors.

218. This page discusses the process of canceling disqualifications and reporting contact between defense officials and defense contractors. It also outlines the submission and review process for reports of contact, disqualifications, and cancellations. Failure to report contact or disqualify oneself may not be considered a violation in certain cases.

219. The page discusses regulations and procedures for defense officials in the Department of Defense regarding the filing of reports and taking disqualification actions. It also provides definitions for terms such as "covered defense official" and "defense contractor," and outlines potential penalties for non-compliance.

220. The author of the memo is informing the Secretary of Defense that they are starting discussions about future employment with certain companies. As a result, they will be disqualified from participating in any matters related to or affecting these companies, and such matters will be referred to the Under Secretary of the Air Force.

221. The page outlines the restrictions and prohibitions for government employees in regards to their involvement in specific matters, representation of others, and communication with government departments. It also mentions exceptions for certain positions and circumstances.

222. This memo informs Secretary Aldridge of two new pieces of legislation regarding post-employment restrictions for government employees. One act will apply to those who leave government service within the next nine months, while the other act may apply to Secretary Aldridge even if he left prior to its enactment.

223. This provision states that if you were involved in the procurement process or approved a contract, you are restricted from participating in negotiations or performing work for that contract for two years. The restrictions are more stringent than the previous version of the law. Contact the General Counsel for further information.

224. Government officials and employees involved in procurement are restricted from participating in negotiations or performing contract work for competing

contractors for a period of 2 years after their involvement in the procurement process. The term "conduct of any Federal agency procurement" encompasses the entire process from solicitation to contract award.

225. This memorandum discusses the post-employment restrictions for an individual who has accepted a position with McDonnell Douglas. The restrictions outlined in 18 U.S.C. 5207 include a one-year prohibition on representing McDonnell Douglas before the Department of Defense (DoD) and additional restrictions related to specific matters involving McDonnell Douglas that the individual participated in during their government service.

226. The page discusses the concept of personal and substantial participation in government contracts. It provides examples and advises on potential restrictions that may arise when representing a company involved in a procurement process. The reader is encouraged to explore the possible application of 18 U.S.C. 207(a) and consult legal experts for further guidance.

227. This page discusses the official responsibility and post-employment restrictions for individuals associated with McDonnell Douglas. It explains that these restrictions prohibit individuals from representing McDonnell Douglas before any government department or agency in connection with a specific matter involving the company. The page also mentions the effective date of the restrictions and provides definitions for terms used.

228. The page discusses restrictions on participating in procurements involving McDonnell Douglas and highlights that these restrictions are broader than other representational restrictions. It also mentions procedures to avoid violating the statute and promises updates on government interpretations.

229. The page discusses the availability and consideration of a report in various committees, as well as the importance of requirements in determining the need for certain systems.

230. The page discusses the need for a space-based early warning system to detect and track missile threats. It highlights the limitations of the current system and the need for a more advanced system to address evolving threats. The validity of these requirements is questioned due to recent criticism.

231. The page discusses the validity of requirements for the Milstar system, including anti-jam capability and interoperability. It also addresses concerns about detecting nuclear activity and confirms that the system can detect missiles capable of carrying nuclear weapons.

232. The page discusses the breakdown of the system for developing and evaluating defense systems due to budget constraints. It emphasizes the need for objective metrics and responsible decision-making in order to avoid chaos and ensure accountability.

233. The page discusses the importance of considering multiple solutions and ideas in order to find the best solution at the lowest cost for the military. It highlights the need for agreed-upon requirements and parameters to objectively compare different systems. The process of "scrubbing" is mentioned, which involves evaluating and reorienting systems to meet changing requirements. Interoperability and the inclusion of all necessary components are emphasized.

234. The page features a conversation between Mr. McCandless and Colonel Schepens regarding the objectivity of an IG report. Colonel Schepens assures

that the investigation was impartial, fair, and involved multiple reviews from legal authorities. Additionally, he mentions two separate investigations related to proprietary information being passed to a contractor, but does not disclose specific details or actions taken.

235. A discussion about actions taken against a military officer for mishandling proprietary information. The officer received a reprimand and was reassigned to a new position. Concerns about future behavior and career implications are raised, but it is stated that there is no ongoing investigation.

236. The FEWS program, designed to detect ballistic missiles, is being terminated due to cost constraints. However, the requirement to detect missiles still exists, and alternative programs are being developed within budgetary constraints.

237. The discussion revolves around the Milstar system and its capabilities. General Kelley clarifies that the upcoming launch of Milstar will provide the necessary communication capabilities, despite the ongoing development of other important features.

238. The page contains questions about the launch of the MILSTAR satellite with ballast of 2,000 pounds of sand. It also asks about the importance of the MILSTAR program in defense planning, the cost of not launching the satellites, and the tactical capability they would provide. Answers must be submitted by February 18, 1994.

239. The page addresses questions about using sand as ballast for the Milstar satellite. It clarifies that the satellites actually use deactivated payload and solid aluminum, not sand. The ballast is necessary for balance. The decision to retain the basic design and modify the payload was made to meet operational needs and reduce costs. Launching the satellites as scheduled allows for initial EHF communications service. Redesigning would have been more expensive and delayed delivering needed capability.

240. The Milstar program is important to defense planning for the next ten years as it provides integrated connectivity and a jam-resistant telecommunications network to support operational forces. The Bottom Up Review confirmed the need for the program and directed the launch of satellites to meet this requirement.

241. The cost of not launching the first two Milstar satellites would be significant, including $40 million per year to store the satellites and the loss of a $5.8 billion investment. It would also degrade EHF coverage and capability for operational forces.

242. The first two Milstar satellites will provide essential tactical capabilities to the military, including anti-jam communications, interoperability between services, mobility with front-line forces, covert operations, and reachback communications. They will enable efficient synchronization of combat power and are not vulnerable to enemy efforts to deny this capability. As more satellites are added, Milstar will provide even more data and global communications to combat commanders. No other satellite system can offer the same flexibility and uninterrupted communications.

243. The meeting concluded and the record will remain open until February 18 for any additional submissions or questions.

244. The page provides a concise summary of the content.

245. The page is an opening statement for a hearing on the budget overruns and technological failures of two satellite systems, Milstar and the Follow-On Early Warning System. The speaker expresses doubts about their necessity and effectiveness in today's international climate. They also raise concerns about the suppression of information regarding lower-cost alternatives and potential criminal implications.

246. Congressman Norm Dicks expresses support for the MILSTAR program, highlighting the difficulties faced by U.S. troops in receiving real-time information and communications during the Gulf War. Satellite systems designed for national objectives were used to support military operations, but communication delays and capacity issues adversely affected data timeliness and planning.

247. The article discusses the importance of the MILSTAR program in providing essential communications capabilities for both strategic and tactical military forces. It highlights the need to harden these systems and adapt to changing global threats.

248. The page discusses the importance of MILSTAR, a communications satellite system, in ensuring command and control connectivity in military operations. It highlights the need for MILSTAR due to the lack of C3I capability and the potential threat of jamming tactical communications. Various military officials and Secretary of Defense Lea Aspin have emphasized the significance of MILSTAR. The system has undergone review and evaluation for performance, cost, schedule, and risk implications.

249. The review recommends continuing the MILSTAR program with Option I, despite the recent Rand report's focus on costs. The GAO suggests considering new technologies, but notes that implementing them would be a major technological risk. The requirement for space-based communications remains a priority, and follow-on technologies should be developed alongside the progress of the initial six satellites. Terminating the program and starting anew is not realistic due to the significant investment and advancement already made.

250. The MILSTAR program is essential for post-Cold War missions, has been streamlined to reduce costs, and provides reliable real-time communications in the field.

251. The Department of Defense has no objection to Colonel Mangold and Colonel Dieltz testifying in their personal capacity at a hearing on the Defense Support Program/Follow-on Early Warning System. The Department is also prepared to provide appropriate witnesses to address other issues raised in a previous letter.

252. The Aerospace Corporation responds to allegations of data suppression and inappropriate pressure surrounding their report on the Air Force's missile warning capability. They recall the report, conduct an independent review, and take actions to prevent similar occurrences in the future.

253. The letter discusses the recall of a report on the DSP-Il option due to its lack of balance and coordination, as well as its advocacy for a specific design solution. The report could have misled decision-makers into accepting a design solution that was not feasible. An independent team is reassessing requirements and technical solutions.

254. The Aerospace Corporation wrote a letter to the Air Force Space Command clarifying their position on advocating for one system over another. They were asked to document a study on using a derivative of the Defense Support Program for ballistic missile early warning as a backup option. However, their report was misinterpreted as supporting the DSP alternative over the Follow-on Early Warning System. The letter emphasizes that this is not their position.

255. The Aerospace Corporation provides objective analysis of government space programs. They were asked to document an Air Force option for ballistic missile early warning using a derivative of the Defense Support Program (DSP), but they clarify that they do not advocate for one system over another. Some program advocacy crept into the report, leading to misconceptions about their support for the DSP alternative.

256. The writer expresses distress over a report's biased tone and improper distribution. They outline immediate actions to rectify the situation and emphasize their commitment to supporting the Air Force.

257. The Air Force Inspector General conducted an inquiry into allegations of wrongdoing and mismanagement in two space-based early warning programs. The inquiry found no misconduct by Air Force general officers, but substantiated some allegations, including the recall of a report and deletion of information from a study. Other allegations were not substantiated.

258. Air Force investigated and substantiated allegations of inappropriate release of proprietary information. Administrative action has been taken and additional guidance is being developed to prevent future unauthorized releases. Media briefing scheduled.

259. Norm Dicks, a member of Congress, requests to appear before the Legislation and National Security Subcommittee to discuss the importance of the MILSTAR program in the post Cold War environment.

260. The Subcommittee has received information alleging that senior Air Force officials suppressed information about a lower cost alternative to a proposed satellite program. They request an investigation into this matter, as it could be a serious withholding of vital information for Congressional deliberations.

261. The letter is thanking someone for their assistance in investigating issues related to the Defense Support Program and the Early Warning System programs. It mentions various attachments that provide information on cost, performance, and concerns raised by individuals within the military. The author offers to provide additional documentation and suggests discussing the issues further. They also recommend speaking with a specific individual for additional insight.

262. Some elements of the USAF are misrepresenting DSP data to higher-ranking officials. Independent assessments recommending the continuation or upgrade of DSP have been suppressed. The Air Force funded a study on DSP and Brilliant Eyes, but the data was not included in the report to Congress and was suppressed. The release of the Aerospace Corp. report was met with opposition from the Space Based Early Warning System Program Office.

263. Aerojet protests the biased costing and improper release of sensitive information in the FEWS program. Comparisons between FEWS and DSP were inconsistent and skewed, favoring FEWS. The access to space for DSP is currently limited to the expensive Titan IV or shuttle launches.

Replenishing the constellations is necessary for providing warning of tactical missiles in regional conflicts.

264. The page discusses the dispute between NASA and the Air Force regarding shuttle costs, as well as the misrepresentation of the DSP program and allegations of intimidation by senior Air Force officers. Aerojet's report provides more information on these issues, including alleged disclosure of proprietary data.

265. Aerojet accuses the Air Force of unfair evaluation and manipulation of data, expressing concern about the disclosure of sensitive information. They emphasize the need for accurate and complete information for decision-making and propose a discussion to address these concerns. Contact: Dr. Philip A. Buckley at (818)812-1951.

266. The Air Force conducted a study to determine if the Defense Support Program (DSP) and Follow-On Early Warning System (FEWS) could meet tactical warning and surveillance requirements. The study concluded that a synergistic DSP and FEWS system was technically feasible. However, the Air Force rejected this concept and opted for a different approach. A report documenting the proposed changes to the DSP system was published in April 1993.

267. The page describes various individuals and their actions regarding the recall of a report and issues related to a program. It raises questions about potential wrongdoing and conspiracy in relation to acquisition proceedings.

268. This page is a fax transmission sheet from Electronlo Systems Division of Encorp. It is addressed to Major General 41rtut Andorgn at Headquarters AFOTEC/CC in Kirtland, New Mexico. The date of the fax is October 19, 1993.

269. This page is a memorandum regarding the program manager position for the Defense Support Program Space Based Early Warning Systems at the Headquarters Space and Missile Systems Center in Los Angeles Air Force Base, California.

270. The author expresses concern about a broken process resulting in the production of flawed and nonsensical material, urging for an engineering debate to address the issue.

271. The author is concerned about misinformation regarding the attributes of the FEWS and DSP systems, which are favorable to FEWS. They believe that Gen Horner and SMC are responsible for these errors and that corrections should be provided to AFSPACECON.

272. The author expresses concern about illogical conditions imposed on the cost and presentation of DSP options. They highlight various concerns, including the inclusion of LCS in DSP Block 26 costs despite plans to delete it, high costs for DSP on MLV due to not deleting Block 23 and T IV, and the preclusion of the DSP P I Program. They also mention issues with funding for detailed signatures, FEWS performance estimates, DSP accuracy, optimizing DSP configuration, and lower detection performance against SCUD compared to

273. DSP has proposed investing in life extension and cost reduction, but it has always been rejected. Small investments in DSP now could yield large cost reductions, and Block 26 should reflect these savings. Using a higher cost

basis would be unethical. There are conflicts with our objectives of rigor and impartiality.
274. The author is questioning the honesty of the answer they are giving regarding a set of requirements. They believe that a different satellite system would be more suitable for the job and suggest being upfront about it to avoid misleading others. Additionally, they mention inconsistencies and illogical aspects of the current approach.
275. The page discusses SMC's unwillingness to consider alternatives to a high-cost solution, which compromises their credibility and may jeopardize their relationship with OSD and Congress.
276. The page expresses concern that the current study is compromising the ability of SMC, Aerospace, and PEO office. It suggests that options being considered ignore important factors and that the conclusion of the study is not reflected in the presented options. There is also mention of confusion and unwillingness to consider anything other than a 100% solution.
277. The email discusses concerns about the DSP costing and how it does not accurately reflect improvements. It suggests that the rules for DSP life cycle cost should be discussed further. The concerns were left as a voice mail for certain individuals.
278. The author expresses concern for the protection of their team and believes they have followed instructions correctly. They mention leaked information, the importance of meeting customer requirements, and the need for top cover for their team. They also express concerns about the integrity of the organization and the avoidance of addressing key questions from Congress and OSO.
279. The FEWS program is a needed replacement for the DSP in response to missile threats. The committee supports the program and directs the DoD to accelerate it by adjusting funding and schedules. Funding will be increased to implement the accelerated program. The DoD is also directed to restructure the DSP and FEWS programs to provide necessary funding.
280. This page is a memorandum addressed to the Program Director of the Defense Support Program. It mentions the location as Los Angeles and the date as 2-'j, but no other information is provided.
281. The memo discusses concerns about the cost, performance, and effectiveness of the DSP-26 program compared to the FEWS program. It also addresses inaccuracies and misconceptions about the capabilities of DSP and FEWS.
282. The document is a cost reduction request for the Elderly Furniture Research and Development Center. Options are being considered, including involving the Federal Government, to address findings that require action. The goal is to find solutions without impacting the employees of the center.
283. This memo discusses the submission of a report by Mr. DW to the SAF/AoS office regarding UBAF WordQ and the need for further action in response.
284. This page is a report titled "The Aerospace Option" prepared by Guido W. Aau and Col T. Lunde for the Defense Support Program. It was prepared for the Space and Missile Systems Center of the US Air Force Materiel Command.

285. This page is about the Defense Support Program's efforts to preserve the options of the Air Force.
286. This page discusses the development of the Follow-on Early Warning System (FEWS) to replace the Defense Support Program (DSP). It explores potential upgrades to the DSP that preserve the Air Force's options for space-based Tactical Warning and Attack Assessment (TWIAA) while reducing costs. The evolutionary DSP upgrade program, known as DSP-l, requires $1 billion in funding compared to $5 billion for FEWS and offers potential cost savings of over $10 billion.
287. This technical report explores alternatives and methods to preserve the Air Force's options for space-based tactical warning and attack assessment systems. It examines the potential risks and uncertainties surrounding the development of the Follow-on Early Warning System (FEWS) and proposes enhancements to the existing Defense Support Program (DSP) as a safety net. The report also discusses the role of Pre-Planned Product Improvements (Ps1) and technology insertion in upgrading the DSP.
288. This page is an acknowledgment section of a technical operating report for the Defense Support Program. It thanks various individuals and organizations for their contributions to the study.
289. This report provides an overview of the DSP evolutionary upgrade program, including the performance and schedule. It also details the DSP-4 program and options for transitioning to the DSP-11 system. Appendices provide descriptions of the satellite, launch vehicle, ground systems, program schedule, and performance analysis. A potential concept for a synergistic OSP-11/BE system is also presented.
290. This page contains the table of contents for a document titled "Preserving The Air Force's Options." It includes an executive overview, concept overview, space segment and ground segment options, cost and schedule information, capabilities and performance assessment, and a comparative assessment of FEWS and DSP-1. There is also a conclusion and an appendix with more detailed information on the space segment.
291. This page provides an overview of the DSP-I ground segment, including mission processing architecture, risk assessment, transition options and schedules, and ground system survivability issues. It also includes details on the cost and schedule of the DSP-Il project, as well as its capabilities and performance. Additionally, it discusses the potential synergy between DSP-Il and Brilliant Eyes and assesses their performance and cost.
292. The presentation discusses the importance of preserving options for the Air Force, highlighting the need for strategic planning and flexibility in decision-making.
293. This technical report explores alternatives to ensure the Air Force's options for Space-Based Tactical Warning and Attack Assessment Systems. It examines the role of the Defense Support Program (DSP) as a safety net for the Follow-on Early Warning System (FEWS), as well as potential enhancements to the DSP. The report compares the cost, risk, performance, and schedule of FEWS with the upgraded DSP program and considers the changing acquisition environment.
294. The page discusses exploring alternatives to preserve the Air Force's options for space-based tactical warning and attack assessment systems,

including evaluating the role of DSP as a safety net and assessing the continuation of an evolving DSP as an alternative to FEWS. It also mentions evaluating upgrades, planned product improvements, and technology insertion options. Additionally, it discusses comparing FEWS with upgraded DSP-I and providing options for additional DSP performance enhancements while considering cost, risk, performance, and schedule.

295. During the Cold War, expensive space systems were built without considering cost due to the urgent need for performance and national security. This led to constant redesign and delays. However, in the present day, there is more breathing room to develop systems in a more efficient and ordered manner, with the ability to allow technology to mature and promote cross-program sharing.

296. During the Cold War, system development prioritized performance over cost. However, with the changing acquisition environment, the focus has shifted to a more ordered and efficient path, considering factors such as risk, cost, performance, and schedule.

297. The Defense Support Program (DSP) has evolved over time to meet changing threats and user needs. The satellite constellation has grown, with larger and more capable satellites. The ground segment has also evolved, with the addition of multiple ground stations and increased functionality. The DSP program has proven successful in providing missile warning capabilities.

298. This page provides a brief overview of the evolution and capabilities of the DSP (Defense Support Program) satellite system, including details about different satellite models and their specifications.

299. The page discusses the continuation of the evolution of the Defense Support Program (DSP) in order to maintain space-based Tactical Warning and Attack Assessment capabilities. It highlights the technical challenges and budget constraints that may impact the development of the Follow-on Early Warning System (FEWS). The page also emphasizes the need for alternative methods to continue improving DSP and mentions potential cost-saving measures and performance enhancements.

300. The page discusses the continuation of the DSP's evolution to reflect budget constraints, changing threats, and the need for a viable program. It highlights potential problems and delays in FEWS, the possibility of budget cuts leading to its cancellation, as well as technological advancements and cost reduction measures. It also mentions the enhancement of performance in critical areas such as tactical missile performance and data fusion.

301. The DSP-II satellite concept is an evolutionary approach to improve performance and reduce costs. It includes upgrades to the spacecraft structure, electronic subsystems, sensor, and ground segment. The upgrades will be phased in over multiple satellites, resulting in improved capabilities and reduced life-cycle costs.

302. The page discusses the technology and improvements made to the DSP-I1 concept, including weight reductions, removal of certain components, and the use of Atlas HAS. The upgrades aim to improve performance while controlling costs and risks.

303. The page provides an overview of the DSP-i system, highlighting its capabilities and potential cost savings. It discusses the use of geo-synchronous satellites for tactical and strategic coverage, as well as the elimination of

overseas ground stations to reduce expenses. The system aims to support integrated tactical warning and attack assessment missions.

304. This page provides an overview of the enhanced ground processing system for improving the performance of the programDSP-li S stem.

305. The ovolveo DSP system is designed to meet the mission needs of the post-Cold War era, particularly in the third world. It provides a path for future growth and increased survivability through the use of advanced technology. The system offers significant capability to support theater users and with enhancements to the ground segment, it can exceed performance requirements.

306. The DSP-11 system supports ITW&AA mission requirements, providing assured and timely global threat warning, accurate attack assessment, and surveillance for theater missile defense. It maximizes national capabilities through all-source fusion and enhances active defense operations.

307. The page provides a schedule for the DSP-Il satellite launches, including details on retrofitting and operational capability. It mentions the possibility of a five-satellite constellation and adjustments to the ground segment schedule.

308. The page provides a schedule for the implementation of DSP-li Space Segment Assumptions. Without certain technology, the schedule must be adjusted.

309. The page provides life-cycle costs for the DSP-II satellite constellation, with estimates for retrofit and RDT&E costs. It also discusses operations and maintenance costs and the impact of different approaches on transition costs. The figure on the right highlights the cost drivers for the DSP system.

310. This page provides a summary of the life cycle costs for the DSP-I Spacecraft, including non-recurring costs, average unit costs, launch segment costs, ground segment costs, and operations and maintenance costs from 2003 to 2015. It also includes information on the transition from DSP-I to DSP-II and the total life cycle costs.

311. The page provides cost and weight information for the DSP-I, DSP-II, and FEWS satellites. The cost of a DSP-I satellite is about 40% less than a FEWS satellite due to reduced complexity and savings from using a different launch vehicle. DSP-II offers significant cost savings compared to both FEWS and DSP-I.

312. The page compares the costs of FEWS and DSP-II satellites in terms of dry weight, average unit cost, launch cost, and cost per set on-orbit.

313. The page provides a comparative summary of the FEWS and DSP-Il satellite constellations in terms of cost, risk, performance, and schedule. It also discusses the life-cycle cost data for DSP-Il and the 95-99 Five Year Defense Plan costs for both constellations. The overall risk of DSP-Il is assessed as low, and improvements are planned through technology insertion. FEWS performance assessment is based on meeting specific requirements.

314. The page provides a comparative summary of FEWS and DSP-Il, including their life cycle costs, satisfaction levels, schedules for full operational capability, and technical risks.

315. The page discusses the potential benefits and importance of implementing upgrades and improvements to the DSP system, regardless of the fate of the Follow-on Early Warning System (FEWS). It highlights the need for continuous improvement and investment in the DSP system due to its role as

the main early warning system. The page also mentions the potential capabilities and cost savings that can be achieved through these upgrades.

316. The page discusses the significant value of investing in DSP technology regardless of the fate of FEWS. It highlights the benefits of the investment, such as providing early warning capabilities and enhancements for global and theater missions. It also suggests that DSP-Il is a feasible alternative to FEWS, offering near-term savings and low-risk solutions.

317. The page discusses the changing acquisition environment in the defense industry, with a shift towards prioritizing cost and risk over performance. It highlights the evolution of the Defense Support Program (DSP) and the DSP-11 concept as examples of this new approach. The page also mentions proposed budget reductions and the potential impact on the Air Force and the DSP-II constellation.

318. This page discusses the benefits and advantages of a new acquisition environment, including potential cost savings, low technical risk, and a low-risk schedule.

319. The page discusses the Brilliant Eyes Synergy (U) and its application in DSP-II.

320. This page outlines potential enhancements to maximize synergy between DSP-Il and BE systems, including operational and performance assessments, cost evaluations, and potential cost and risk reductions.

321. The purpose of the DSP/Brilliant Eyes synergy study is to explore alternatives to the Air Force's current plan of acquiring separate FEWS and Brilliant Eyes systems. The study was conducted in response to tasking from the Office of the Secretary of Defense (OSD) and SAFIAQ to examine synergy issues and concepts between DSP, FEWS, and Brilliant Eyes. The results of the study were rejected due to the failure of the synergistic DSP/BE system to meet all design and implementation details

322. The page discusses a study on the potential synergy between DSP-Il and Brilliant Eyes systems, aiming to meet FEWS and GPALS requirements while controlling cost and risk. The conclusions of the study were rejected, but the results are preserved for future evaluation. The viability of combining the two systems is dependent on re-evaluating survivability requirements in the post-Cold War era.

323. The DSP-Il I BE concept aims to maximize performance and minimize cost and technical risks by combining the strengths of the DSP-Il and BE systems. The DSP-Il provides surveillance from geosynchronous orbit, while the BE provides accurate tracking during missile flight. The proposed constellation consists of four satellites in geosynchronous orbit, with additional coverage provided by ATH detectors. Data processing and transmission technologies are employed to reduce data rates and ensure survivability. Ground processing is conducted in the CONUS and theater systems

324. This page provides an overview of the concept of DSP-Il / BE Synergy, including direct communication to users, tracking through event logging, and message dissemination. It also references the OSP-11 I SeANIOMf EY611 SYneey from 1993.

325. The DSP-U and SE systems work together to provide missile detection and tracking. The DSP-I is responsible for initial detection, while the DSP-U

provides data on the missile's flight. This data is combined with observations from the SE to enhance attack assessment capabilities.

326. This page provides an overview of missile detection and tracking, specifically focusing on the time from launch.
327. The summary of the page is that the DSP-II and BE systems are described, including their satellite constellations and modifications. The ground system combines data processing from both systems to maximize performance. The combined system meets mission requirements, but certain design issues need further study. Ground-based processing is necessary due to difficulties with crosslinks between the satellites.
328. This page provides an overview of a synergistic satellite system, including details about satellite constellations, orbits, revisit rates, and target capabilities. It also mentions the use of data fusion, cueing, and direct data transmission to users.
329. The DSP-II BE system meets performance requirements but lacks certain design details specified in the FEWS ORD. The use of ground processing instead of on-board processing is necessary for achieving synergy. The system provides improved performance and capabilities through fusion of data from various surveillance systems. Cost savings are also outlined in the table provided.
330. The page discusses the performance requirements of the Brilliant Eyes Synergistic System, noting that it meets certain requirements but not all. It raises questions about the feasibility of on-board mission processing and crosslinks between satellites. It also questions the relevance of these requirements in the post-Cold War era. The system offers potential cost savings compared to separate acquisitions.
331. This page discusses potential enhancements to maximize synergy, the operational concept of a synergistic system, performance assessment, cost assessment, potential cost and risk reductions, and provides a summary.
332. This page provides a comparative summary of the costs and schedules for FEWS, DSP-II, and BE. It includes life-cycle cost data and savings from synergistic combinations. The table shows the 95-99 Five Year Defense Plan costs for each system, with FEWS + BE and DSP-II + BE having lower costs than FEWS alone.
333. The page provides a comparative cost and schedule summary for various defense systems, including FEWS, DSP-II, BE, and WFY. It includes life cycle cost data and budget-line information for the years 1993 to 2016.
334. The page contains a jumble of characters and symbols that do not convey any meaningful information.
335. The page contains a series of random characters and symbols with no discernible meaning or purpose.
336. The content of the page is unclear and lacks a clear topic or message.
337. The page contains unreadable text and does not provide any meaningful information.
338. The page contains a series of characters and symbols without any clear meaning or context.
339. The page contains a series of characters and symbols, but it is difficult to determine the exact content or purpose of the page without further context.

340. The content of this page appears to be a jumbled mix of characters and symbols, making it difficult to discern any meaningful information.
341. The page contains illegible and nonsensical characters, making it impossible to determine its content or purpose.
342. Technical information and formatting codes are present, but no discernible content or meaning can be derived from the text.
343. The page contains a jumble of characters and symbols with no discernible meaning or purpose.
344. The page contains a jumble of characters and symbols with no discernible meaning or context.
345. The page contains illegible text and symbols, making it impossible to provide a concise summary of its content.
346. The page contains a jumble of random characters and does not convey any meaningful information.
347. The page contains a jumble of characters and symbols, indicating a potential coding or formatting issue.
348. The page contains a jumble of characters and symbols, lacking any discernible meaning or purpose.
349. The page contains a jumble of letters and symbols, lacking any coherent meaning.
350. The page discusses the lack of justification for current nuclear warfighting requirements and the need to rationalize TMD requirements within the overall architecture. It also questions the role of radar versus space-based JR and highlights the questionable drivers of the FEWS system.
351. The page discusses the adequacy of DSP stereo processing for theater and strategic needs, but highlights a major shortfall in impact point prediction. It mentions that DSPITS revisit time is the weak link in performance and that Brilliant Eyes is not required for TWAA. It also notes that BE relieves system fragility in theater and provides potential capability.
352. IDA DSP41 is a cost-effective program manager solution for fixing known problems and reducing life cycle costs, serving as a benchmark for cost comparisons if it meets the required specifications.
353. The page discusses the capabilities and performance of the DSP with T1lon 61hiel TsD sensor in a theater setting, highlighting the need for verification of performance under different circumstances. It suggests that the DSP-Il is a sensible proposal and low risk technically, and recommends keeping as much of the DSP-I subsystems as possible.
354. The internal evaluation found that DSP41 failed to meet FEWS ORD and had a subjective risk assessment consistent with its own assessment. EGT was used to assess risks based on subjective criteria, and misunderstandings about the DSP-Il concept were resolved.
355. This page is a summary of a review conducted by General Marshall A. Alden on the Air Force's technical data. It includes input from various sources and recommends further investigation into certain areas.
356. The page discusses violations, abuses, and significant findings related to certain organizations. It mentions specific instances involving CINOSPACE and the PEd program, as well as the review process and allegations.

357. The page discusses the evaluation of a military program and its potential cost savings. It highlights the importance of coordination and communication between different departments.
358. The page discusses the confusion and misuse of data related to a decision made by someone in charge. It also mentions the publication of a report that was misunderstood and caused further problems. The possibility of legal issues and the need for clear communication are emphasized.
359. Colonel Mangol provides answers to questions regarding his observations and professional opinions on events related to space and nuclear deterrence during his time serving in the United States Air Force.
360. Col. Mangold faced severe backlash and labeled "insane" after publishing a letter questioning FFRDC support. His disagreements with MGen Hard, who later joined Aerospace Corporation, affected their relationship. Col. Mangold announced plans to cut FFRDCs again, potentially saving $1 billion over five years.
361. The individuals' reaction to the announcement was controlled enthusiasm, with some expressing concern about the functioning of Space and Missile Center without Aerospace support. The budget cuts to FFRDOs contributed to the loss of the speaker's job, as their plans for significant alterations to space system acquisition threatened the post-military service opportunities for senior officials.
362. The letter is a response to questions given during testimony regarding the DSP Program. The author clarifies that their answers are based on personal observations and professional judgment.
363. The testimony reveals concerns about retribution and unethical behavior in the handling of a defense program. It highlights the removal of managers who suggested a cheaper option and the negative impact on the integrity of the US Air Force.
364. Col Dietz believes General Homer was misinformed about FEWS and DSP. He points out that FEWS does not make launch location targetable, FEWS is not 10 times more accurate than DSP, FEWS is not cheaper than DSP according to the GAO, FEWS cannot detect in high cloud cover, FEWS detection of cruise missiles is unlikely, and DSP's current life expectancy is overstated.
365. Col. Dietz provides examples of distorted cost comparisons in improving the DSP system, including the overestimation of costs and unnecessary additions. The OSD Everette Committee supports Dietz's assessment and recommends canceling the FEWS options.
366. The cost of upgrading the DSP system is almost as expensive as a new system, but there are cheaper options available that have been previously rejected. The discussions about these inexpensive upgrades were stopped.
367. Concerns about intentional distortion of performance comparisons in a classified hearing are mentioned, with examples given of inflated performance for the new system and deflated performance for the current system. The discrepancy between the two systems is highlighted, with claims that the advertised performance of the new system is not accurate.
368. Concerns about witch hunts and retribution raised by Col Dietz regarding the handling of a study for the Navy. Senior management prioritized protecting themselves over fostering open technical debate, resulting in career

terminations and actions taken against those who suggested cheaper alternatives. This may have been done as a warning to staff members to remain silent or face job loss.

369. The central concerns in these hearings are the lack of transparency and accountability within the USAF, the continued presence of the management team responsible for the issues, and the inadequate actions taken by the USAF to address the problems.

370. FEWS program found to be overstated, alternative solution developed. USAF engaged in inappropriate and illegal activities to protect FEWS. FEWS canceled after independent analysis. Inappropriate acts include data sharing, cost inflation, misleading Congress, concealing cheaper solutions, retribution against staff, suppression of analysis, and OSD access to competitive concept.

371. The USAF obstructed the OSD from considering a lower-cost option, ignoring Congress' request to explore cheaper alternatives and only evaluating their preferred choices.

372. DSP was able to detect Scud launches during Operation Desert Storm under various weather and viewing conditions, contradicting claims that its success was due to favorable conditions. The Army's JTaGS and Air Force's Talon Shield programs will further enhance the DSP system's ability to detect and report tactical ballistic missile launches.

373. The memo discusses the observation conditions during Desert Storm and how they may affect the performance requirements of the Talon Shield program. The notes attached support confidence in the program's performance projections based on objective interpretation of experience.

374. The page discusses the misconception that the successful missile detection during Desert Storm was due to ideal conditions. In reality, weather conditions were unfavorable and other factors such as viewing conditions and complexity of the situation contributed to the success. Daytime launches were also easily detected.

375. During Desert Storm, the satellite stations had suboptimal proximity to the targets. The aspect angles varied from adverse to reasonable, with the best ECA providing nose-on viewing. The impressive results were achieved with Operator-In-The-Loop procedure and only four false reports. Additional details and statistics are available at the SECRET level.

376. The page discusses the need for a new early warning program to improve launch location and detection of shorter-range tactical ballistic missiles. It argues that previous failures were not due to lack of launch location information but rather issues with onboard sensors. It also states that the new program will not provide significant improvements and that the detection of shorter-range missiles should be handled by in-theater radar or passive location systems.

377. The Air Force IG concluded that the inclusion of the DSP++ alternative in the Air Force Sensor Integration study was proper, while DSP-II did not meet requirements. However, the respondent disagrees, stating that the Congressionally-mandated study specified evaluating a combination of DSP with Brilliant Eyes, which would meet the approved requirements. The respondent also argues that the six "validated" FEWS mission needs were

never approved and that DSP++ did not offer any additional capability to address these needs.

378. The page discusses the rejection of the DSP++ option by Air Force Space Command and the Air Force PEO/SP in 1991. It suggests that information on the DSP-II alternative was withheld from OSD and Congressional decision makers, compromising the acquisition process to preserve the FEWS program. Independent review teams later concluded that FEWS was unnecessary and that an evolutionary upgrade of DSP, specifically the DSP-11 concept, was the lowest cost and lowest risk alternative.

STRATEGIC SATELLITE SYSTEMS IN A POST-COLD WAR ENVIRONMENT

HEARING

BEFORE THE

LEGISLATION AND NATIONAL
SECURITY SUBCOMMITTEE

OF THE

COMMITTEE ON GOVERNMENT OPERATIONS
HOUSE OF REPRESENTATIVES

ONE HUNDRED THIRD CONGRESS

SECOND SESSION

FEBRUARY 2, 1994

Printed for the use of the Committee on Government Operations

U.S. GOVERNMENT PRINTING OFFICE

79-579 CC   WASHINGTON : 1994

For sale by the U.S. Government Printing Office
Superintendent of Documents, Congressional Sales Office, Washington, DC 20402
ISBN 0-16-044413-6

H401-40

COMMITTEE ON GOVERNMENT OPERATIONS

JOHN CONYERS, JR., Michigan, *Chairman*

CARDISS COLLINS, Illinois
HENRY A. WAXMAN, California
MIKE SYNAR, Oklahoma
STEPHEN L. NEAL, North Carolina
TOM LANTOS, California
MAJOR R. OWENS, New York
EDOLPHUS TOWNS, New York
JOHN M. SPRATT, JR., South Carolina
GARY A. CONDIT, California
COLLIN C. PETERSON, Minnesota
KAREN L. THURMAN, Florida
BOBBY L. RUSH, Illinois
CAROLYN B. MALONEY, New York
THOMAS M. BARRETT, Wisconsin
DONALD M. PAYNE, New Jersey
FLOYD H. FLAKE, New York
JAMES A. HAYES, Louisiana
CRAIG A. WASHINGTON, Texas
BARBARA-ROSE COLLINS, Michigan
CORRINE BROWN, Florida
MARJORIE MARGOLIES-MEZVINSKY, Pennsylvania
LYNN C. WOOLSEY, California
GENE GREEN, Texas
BART STUPAK, Michigan

WILLIAM F. CLINGER, JR., Pennsylvania
AL McCANDLESS, California
J. DENNIS HASTERT, Illinois
JON L. KYL, Arizona
CHRISTOPHER SHAYS, Connecticut
STEVEN SCHIFF, New Mexico
C. CHRISTOPHER COX, California
CRAIG THOMAS, Wyoming
ILEANA ROS-LEHTINEN, Florida
DICK ZIMMER, New Jersey
WILLIAM H. ZELIFF, JR., New Hampshire
JOHN M. McHUGH, New York
STEPHEN HORN, California
DEBORAH PRYCE, Ohio
JOHN L. MICA, Florida
ROB PORTMAN, Ohio

BERNARD SANDERS, Vermont
(Independent)

JULIAN EPSTEIN, *Staff Director*
MATTHEW R. FLETCHER, *Minority Staff Director*

LEGISLATION AND NATIONAL SECURITY SUBCOMMITTEE

JOHN CONYERS, JR., Michigan, *Chairman*

CARDISS COLLINS, Illinois
STEPHEN L. NEAL, North Carolina
CAROLYN B. MALONEY, New York
TOM LANTOS, California
CORRINE BROWN, Florida

AL McCANDLESS, California
WILLIAM F. CLINGER, JR., Pennsylvania
JON L. KYL, Arizona
DICK ZIMMER, New Jersey

JAMES C. TURNER, *Staff Director*
MIRANDA G. KATSOYANNIS, *Professional Staff Member*
CHERYL A. PHELPS, *Professional Staff Member*
ERIC M. THORSON, *Professional Staff Member*
BENNIE B. WILLIAMS, *Clerk*
CHERYL G. MATCHO, *Clerk*
ROSALIND BURKE-ALEXANDER, *Clerk*
L. STEPHAN VINCZE, *Minority Professional Staff*

CONTENTS

	Page
Hearing held on February 2, 1994	1

Statement of:
- Aru, Guido W., project leader, system architecture and integration, space-based surveillance division, the Aerospace Corp ... 48
- Conyers, Hon. John, Jr., a Representative in Congress from the State of Michigan, and chairman, Legislation and National Security Subcommittee: Opening statement ... 1
- Dietz, Edward R., Colonel, U.S. Air Force ... 46
- Mangold, Sanford D., Colonel, U.S. Air Force ... 37
- Quinn, Thomas P., Ph.D., Deputy Assistant Secretary of Defense, Command, Control, Communications and Intelligence Acquisition, accompanied by Maj. Gen. David Kelley, Deputy Director, Defense-Wide Command, Control, Communications, and Computers Support for the Joint Staff, U.S. Army; Col. Steve Stadler, Deputy Chief of Staff, Requirements, Air Force Space Inspections, inspector general's office, U.S. Air Force; and Col. Brent Collins, Deputy Director, Space Programs ... 159
- Rodrigues, Louis J., Director, Systems Development and Production Issues, National Security and International Affairs Division [NSIAD], U.S. General Accounting Office, accompanied by Homer H. Thomson, Assistant Director; and Rahul Gupta, evaluator in charge ... 8
- Schepens, Col. William, Director, Inspections, inspector general's office, U.S. Air Force ... 186

Letters, statements, etc., submitted for the record by:
- Aru, Guido W., project leader, system architecture and integration, space-based surveillance division, the Aerospace Corp.:
  - Information concerning operator comments of FEWS/ITWAA integration studies ... 107
  - Prepared statement ... 51
- Collins, Col. Brent, Deputy Director, Space Programs, U.S. Air Force:
  - Information concerning cost to the DSP, plus, plus ... 191
- Dietz, Edward R., Colonel, U.S. Air Force: Prepared statement ... 47
- Harman, Hon. Jane, a Representative in Congress from the State of California: Information concerning the reassignment of the Air Force program director ... 112
- Kelley, Maj. Gen. David, Deputy Director, Defense-Wide Command, Control, Communications, and Computers Support for the Joint Staff, U.S. Army: Prepared statement ... 185
- Mangold, Sanford D., Colonel, U.S. Air Force:
  - Letter dated April 26, 1993, concerning federally funded research and development center cost reduction request ... 119
  - Prepared statement ... 41
- McCandless, Hon. Al, a Representative in Congress from the State of California:
  - Documents pertaining to hearing record ... 122
  - Letter dated March 7, 1991, from the U.S. Senate Committee on Armed Services, concerning restructuring the Milstar communications system ... 100
  - Questions and answers concerning Milstar and DSP/FEWS testimony ... 32
  - Questions and answers concerning Milstar/DSP/FEWS ... 238
- Quinn, Thomas P., Ph.D., Deputy Assistant Secretary of Defense, Command, Control, Communications and Intelligence Acquisition:
  - Information concerning ethics commitments by executive branch appointees ... 193
  - Prepared statement ... 165

(III)

IV

Letters, statements, etc., submitted for the record by—Continued
  Rodrigues, Louis J., Director, Systems Development and Production Issues, National Security and International Affairs Division [NSIAD], U.S. General Accounting Office: Prepared statement 13
  Stadler, Col. Steve, Deputy Chief of Staff, Requirements, Air Force Space Inspections, inspector general's office, U.S. Air Force: information concerning FEWS requirements 190

APPENDIX

Material submitted for the hearing record 245
  February 2, 1994, statement by the Honorable Carolyn B. Maloney 245
  February 2, 1994, statement by the Honorable Norm Dicks 246
  February 1, 1994, letter from Sandra K. Stuart, Assistant to the Secretary (Legislative Affairs), Office of the Secretary of Defense 251
  February 1, 1994, letter from E.C. Aldridge, Jr., president and chief executive officer, the Aerospace Corp., to Chairman John Conyers, Jr. (with attached letter from E.C. Aldridge, Jr., to Gen. Charles Horner, Commander, Air Force Space Command dated May 27, 1993) 252
  February 1, 1994, memorandum for correspondents 256
  January 27, 1994, letter from the Honorable Norm Dicks to Chairman John Conyers, Jr 258
  October 12, 1993, letter from Chairman John Conyers, Jr., to Mr. Derek J. Vander Schaaf, inspector general, Department of Defense (with attachments) 259
  September 28, 1993, memorandum and followup documentation from Col. Edward R. Dietz to Col. Joseph A. Bailey 269
  April 26, 1993, letter from Col. Sanford D. Mangold to Associate Deputy Assistant Secretary, Management Policy and Program Integration, Assistant Secretary, Department of the Air Force, (with attached memorandum dated February 3, 1994) 282
  April 23, 1993, report on DSP–II, entitled, "Preserving the Air Force's Options" (U) prepared by Guido W. Aru and Carl T. Lunde of the Aerospace Corp 284
  March 25, 1993, letter to Committee on Government Operations from Julia E. Worrell 334
  Summary by the Institute for Defense Analysis regarding FEWS program requirements 351
  Col. Sanford D. Mangold's responses to Chairman Conyers' followup questions 360
  Col. Edward R. Dietz's responses to Chairman Conyers' followup questions 363
  Mr. Guido Aru's responses to Chairman Conyers' followup questions 373

STRATEGIC SATELLITE SYSTEMS IN A POST-COLD WAR ENVIRONMENT

WEDNESDAY, FEBRUARY 2, 1994

House of Representatives,
Legislation and National Security Subcommittee
of the Committee on Government Operations,
Washington, DC.

The subcommittee met, pursuant to notice, at 10 a.m., in room 2154, Rayburn House Office Building, Hon. John Conyers, Jr. (chairman of the subcommittee) presiding.

Members present: Representatives John Conyers, Jr., Carolyn B. Maloney, Al McCandless, William F. Clinger, Jr., Jon L. Kyl, and Dick Zimmer.

Also present: Representatives John M. Spratt and Jane Harman.

Subcommittee staff present: James C. Turner, staff director; Eric M. Thorson, professional staff member; Cheryl G. Matcho, clerk; and L. Stephan Vincze, minority professional staff.

Full committee staff present: Julian Epstein, staff director.

OPENING STATEMENT OF CHAIRMAN CONYERS

Mr. CONYERS. Good morning. The Subcommittee on Legislation and National Security of Government Operations begins an oversight hearing on strategic satellite systems in the post-cold war environment.

Today we are examining three satellite systems costing billions of dollars designed to meet Soviet strategic threats during the cold war: the Milstar program, the Defense Support Program, and the Follow-On Early Warning System, or FEWS.

Milstar is a $20 billion satellite system designed to provide military communications during a full-scale nuclear war; DSP, the defense support system is a currently deployed satellite system that warns against hostile missile launches; FEWS, a recently canceled spinoff of Star Wars research that promised to provide an improved warning against smaller missiles such as Scuds at an expense that would range somewhere between $13 and $18 billion.

Two central questions link these programs. First, are cold war technologies what we need, or can we do the same job at significant savings? The second is, did the decisionmaking process on these programs operate properly or were they compromised? Were efforts made to suppress dissenting views within the Pentagon?

The General Accounting Office and other independent observers have raised serious technical questions about these expensive programs and have suggested possible cost savings.

For example, although the Milstar communications satellite program started more than a decade ago, the first launch of a preliminary version of this satellite is scheduled for a few days from now. This single satellite and launch will cost about $1.4 billion, yet the subcommittee has been advised that both of the first two Milstar payloads include about 2,000 pounds of sand or other form of ballast, and this certainly raises some questions about the prudence of the Milstar program design and whether it is being managed in a cost-effective manner. These questions are underscored by the fact that the final version of this system, Milstar II, is still under development with launches not expected until perhaps 2001.

These technical questions and possible cost savings are especially important because the subcommittee has received serious allegations of retaliation against persons who dared raise them. Specifically, it has been alleged that senior Pentagon officials suppressed a critical report and further attempted to intimidate contractors.

An example of these possibly improper actions involved the DSP and the FEWS programs, satellite systems designed to detect everything from ICBMs to small tactical missiles like Scuds used by Iraq in the Gulf war. Because these systems are extraordinarily expensive, in the fiscal year 1992 defense authorization, Congress directed the Air Force to review lower-cost alternatives to the planned FEWS program.

Although the FEWS program was canceled by Under Secretary of Defense John Deutch late last year, it appears that this congressionally mandated review may have been suppressed by the Air Force. Specifically, an independent study prepared in response to this mandate by the Aerospace Corp. concluded that with various upgrades the existing DSP system could replace FEWS at a savings of some $4 billion in the short term and as much as $10 billion in the long run. Yet the study was withdrawn and the president of Aerospace Corp. apologized to the Air Force for allowing it to be prepared.

The apparent suppression of this study is particularly troubling, because other independent reviewers reached similar conclusions. And thus, in November 1991, the General Accounting Office concluded that there are indications that an enhanced DSP could be nearly as effective and would cost billions of dollars less than FEWS. The Institute for Defense Analysis similarly concluded in 1993 that current FEWS requirements are not justified, and that the FEWS system drivers are highly questionable.

This subcommittee has also received documents suggesting that a Pentagon contractor, TRW, may have been threatened and intimidated by senior Air Force officials who warned TRW not to support opponents of FEWS. Allegations that the Air Force suppressed a critical study and attempted to intimidate contractors are very serious matters, which this subcommittee has a duty to examine very carefully.

Our witnesses today will give testimony of the inner workings of the defense space world. Although certain aspects of these satellite systems are classified, we have been assured that the technical and integrity issues facing the subcommittee can and should be considered at a public hearing.

That concludes my statement. I am pleased now to recognize my ranking leader from Pennsylvania, Mr. Clinger.

Mr. CLINGER. Thank you very much, Mr. Chairman.

The issues that our hearing will address today with respect to the Milstar and DSP/FEWS systems concern two separate and distinct aspects about two separate and distinct military satellite programs. Specifically, it will examine serious allegations of individual wrongdoing that remain under investigation by the inspector general of the Department of Defense, and will consider broad criticisms of the current design and costs of each satellite program.

We should not in my view blur these distinctions. Rather, we should focus at the appropriate time on each issue for each program individually, insisting on all of the facts so that we may carefully assess the merits of each allegation and each system as fairly and as objectively as possible.

I share the view that we cannot tolerate the type of alleged violations of the Procurement Integrity Act and other individual wrongdoing if in fact they occurred. However, I would caution our members that these allegations remain currently under investigation. Any rush to judgment to either embrace or reject the validity of these allegations now I think would be inappropriate or premature in my view.

We should allow the DOD inspector general to do his job and to complete his investigation before we impugn the integrity and reputations of any individuals. To do otherwise, particularly without the accused individuals here to defend themselves, would fly in the face of fairness as we know it in this country.

Regarding the broader substantive criticisms of the Milstar and FEWS programs, I completely concur that all of our defense systems, not just these, must withstand rigorous scrutiny regarding their ability to meet current threats in the most cost-effective manner.

We simply can no longer afford to waste money on outdated or unnecessary programs. However, the evidence and the record I believe will show that DOD vigorously reviewed and significantly restructured Milstar to better meet current threats and to reduce costs.

Certainly more can be done. New technologies are continually evolving, but when and at what cost will they be available? We should not underestimate the vital military importance of the particular satellite systems under scrutiny here today and the growing, not decreasing, need to keep them in place.

Finally, let me emphasize that the validity of the requirements of these satellite systems lies at the heart of any debate about the appropriateness of their design and costs. For it is the requirements as determined by the DOD that decide what design and what cost a system will have. So I would urge members to concentrate on the requirements of Milstar and FEWS if they suspect that the designs are inappropriate and the costs are excessive.

Ultimately, given the cutting-edge technology of these systems and the inherently speculative nature of forecasting future threats, we must at some point rely on the judgment of both our civilian and military leaders who over time have proven their intellect, received extensive training, and often experienced the life-and-death tests of combat. We should not in this context cast aside their collective judgment without clear and convincing evidence that they are mistaken.

Mr. Chairman, I welcome this hearing, appreciate you calling it, and look forward to hearing our witnesses today.

Mr. CONYERS. Thank you for your comments.

I would like now to recognize the ranking member of this subcommittee, Mr. Al McCandless, the gentleman from California.

Mr. MCCANDLESS. Thank you, Mr. Chairman.

I am deeply troubled and concerned about the criticisms and allegations that have been raised about Milstar and DSP/FEWS. On the one hand, it certainly is our duty as an oversight committee to investigate and weed out any actions that may be improper by any government agency on any program. The allegations raised here certainly merit our attention. If true, they cannot be tolerated. Simultaneously, however, we must not rush to embrace or reject these allegations. Rather, we should allow the DOD inspector general to complete his investigation before passing any judgment.

Most importantly, however, I am concerned that these as yet unresolved allegations, serious as they may be, may somehow minimize or obscure the critically important requirements that have spurred the creation, development, and evolution of these satellite systems. Let's not forget the importance of the satellite programs that we are discussing here today.

Milstar, DSP, and FEWS are designed to be the eyes and ears of our armed forces and the early warning system against future missile attacks. Milstar would provide critical command and control and jam-proof global communications to our armed forces. FEWS, or a similar upgrade to the over 20-year-old DSP system, would provide early warning against both strategic and tactical missiles. FEWS-type technology could prevent the kind of casualties suffered in the barracks attack at Riyadh, Saudi Arabia, and could also locate Scud launchers, something we devoted over 40 percent of our air assets to do during the Gulf war with minimal success.

A quick look at the world today reveals a growing threat in North Korea and increasing instability in Russia and Central Europe, and uncertainties in the Middle East. Each of the countries in these regions has jamming capabilities and tactical missiles. They are also most certainly aware that our current communications systems, the ones we relied so heavily on during the Gulf war, are susceptible to jamming. With Milstar and an improved DSP system, these threats would be addressed and substantially defused now and in the near future.

Of course, I share the chairman's concerns regarding the high cost of these systems. Without question, we must ensure that we minimize the waste and maximize capability, that we get the most for every dollar that we spend. But I would also stress that when we consider cost, we recognize that the terms include more than the price tag of any given system. Unfortunately, the realities of the present procurement process—a process I know that this committee is actively trying to improve—requires enormous lengths of time to contract, design, test, and finally deploy a system.

So when we hear critics of Milstar, for example, boldly proclaim that billions of dollars could be saved by changing the current design, we need to ask at what cost in terms of lost time, lost capability and, ultimately perhaps, lost lives. For the unavailability of secure jam-proof communications in the next conflict may cost lives.

Given the growing, not decreasing, uncertainty of our world, we do not, in my view, have the luxury of time. The potential costs in terms of lives is ultimately the most important cost, that we should never lose sight of as long as we must put our brave men and women in harm's way.

I therefore urge the members of our subcommittee that when we discuss these programs, that we remain focused on the basic key questions of, one, why do we need these systems?

Two, what are the requirements that determine this need?

Three, who determined these requirements?

And four, are these requirements still valid in light of recent criticism?

Finally, we should also weigh the credibility of the critics of these systems against the credibility of those who have and do support them. Given the extraordinary past and present bipartisan support of Milstar, for example—to include both the Bush and Clinton administrations, Gen. Colin Powell, Gen. Chuck Horner, Senator Sam Nunn, former Secretary of Defense Dick Cheney, soon to be former Secretary of Defense Les Aspin, and soon to be Secretary of Defense William Perry and Under Secretary of Defense for Acquisition John Deutch—in my view, the critics have to meet a heavy burden of proof to convince me that this vast array of civilian and military leaders amongst our Nation's best and brightest, are all wrong.

Thank you, Mr. Chairman. I look forward to hearing from our distinguished witnesses today.

Mr. CONYERS. Thank you.

The Chair is pleased to recognize the gentleman that serves on the Committee on Armed Services, Mr. Jon Kyl.

Mr. KYL. Thank you very much, Mr. Chairman. I appreciate the opportunity to make a brief statement.

I would first of all associate myself with the remarks just delivered by the ranking Republican member.

Today's hearing on Milstar, FEWS, and DSP touches on a variety of issues of concern to Members interested in the readiness and maintenance of the U.S. armed forces. As a member of the Armed Services Committee, I can assure you that the capabilities these systems represent are literally the eyes and ears of our war-fighting forces, elements which no successful armed forces can be without.

It is disturbing to hear that there may be potential problems and wrongdoing on the part of individuals associated with the management of the DSP/FEWS programs. Certainly, unethical and certainly questionable behavior in any program must not be tolerated, and should be thoroughly investigated.

I understand that the Air Force inspector general has completed a report which identifies one possible infraction of the Procurement Integrity Act, but other allegations raised in the press were not found to be a problem.

It is also my understanding that the DOD IG is investigating some of the allegations we will hear about today. As the IG has not yet completed his investigation, I would hope we can all refrain from making premature judgments and reaching hasty conclusions about the guilt or innocence of individuals associated with the DSP/FEWS.

As a member of the Committee on Armed Forces, I am familiar with Milstar, DSP, and FEWS and, as such, I understand the vital contributions that communication satellites and sensor satellites make to the war-fighting capability of our military.

Some on this committee may argue that Milstar is a relic of the cold war. I strongly disagree. Assured communication is one of the most important elements of war fighting. Modern examples of the inability of our forces to communicate with one another punctuate the need for real-time communications. We need not relive the mistakes of Grenada or Somalia where one soldier used an AT&T credit card to communicate with his command and where our rangers could not directly communicate with our U.S. peacekeeping troops to ask for assistance. Milstar will enable our allies to communicate with U.S. troops and vice-versa, an essential capability as the administration pushes our forces into joint operations.

I respect the opinions of Generals Powell, Sullivan, and Horner, as well as Admiral Kelso, and Secretary of Defense nominee William Perry that Milstar is a good investment for the post-cold war world.

Milstar's unique antijamming capability, onboard processing and distribution and mobility make it a premier choice to enhance the readiness and capabilities of our troops.

Likewise, high-resolution sensor capabilities are critical in the modern war-fighting era. I share General Horner's opinion that we need a sensor with increased sensitivity and a sensor that is capable of typing and tracking missiles and making launch locations known.

I believe it is especially important that the sensor be able to cover theater missions, such as detecting a Scud launch, as well as strategic missions. We need no other example than that of the Persian Gulf war and to read the newspaper headlines about North Korea to realize the importance of more accurate and sensitive sensor satellites. General Horner, the commander of the air war in the Gulf, is uniquely and totally qualified to set the parameters that the sensor should be capable of meeting.

Although FEWS has been officially canceled by DOD, an alternative has been briefed to Dr. Deutch by members of the defense community. In fact, I spoke with Dr. Deutch about it last evening. I believe that DOD should seriously consider this new proposal especially in light of its ability to meet the requirements expressed by General Horner.

Thank you, Mr. Chairman. I look forward to the testimony of the witnesses.

Mr. CONYERS. We are joined by Congresswoman Harman of California, and we have invited her to sit with us as long as she can.

Good morning.

Ms. HARMAN. Thank you, Mr. Chairman. I want to thank you and the committee for allowing me to participate in this hearing, and for your committee's bipartisan interest in this issue.

I represent California's 36th District, which is home to the Aerospace Corp., the Air Force Space and Missile Systems Center, and many of the companies that are involved in this controversy.

This issue impacts our national security and thousands of jobs, and it is crucial that it be resolved. I have followed developments in the DSP/FEWS debate closely since last summer when information first began appearing in the press, and I am deeply concerned.

We all know that defense spending is declining and that America must make hard choices between competing defense technologies. As a member of the Armed Services Committee, with my friend Mr. Kyl, and as a conferee on the fiscal year 1994 defense authorization bill, I have been involved in a few of the tough choices that have to be made. There are many more ahead. One of the most important is how to meet our requirements for warning of ballistic missile launches in a time when these missiles are spreading around the world at an alarming rate.

The defense budget is not a jobs program, and some companies will lose out in every procurement decision. However, it is crucial to make sure that contracts are awarded fairly and that every viable option gets equal consideration. If that does not happen, we will not get the most for our scarce defense dollars, and our shrinking industrial base may be damaged in ways we cannot repair.

We also must be sure that once contracts are fairly awarded, they are protected so that companies can plan their business as rationally as possible in this time of shrinking budgets and changing military needs.

A related issue is the production gap that could occur if valid ongoing contracts are interrupted or worker morale undermined by the threat of interruption.

Mr. Chairman, I commend you for asking the Pentagon to examine this issue, which the Armed Services Committee also plans to consider, and look forward to hearing from the witnesses today. I hope that our two committees can work together to ensure that our defense acquisition process works fairly to buy the best systems we can afford.

Mr. CONYERS. Thank you so much.

The General Accounting Office has asked Mr. Louis Rodrigues to appear here this morning. We would like to start off with him.

Mr. Thomson and Mr. Gupta, I know you are prepared to take the witness oath as you have done many times here. Please stand and raise your right hand.

[Witnesses sworn.]

Mr. CONYERS. Thank you very much. Please be seated.

Mr. Rodrigues, your career with the General Accounting Office goes back two decades now, more than that. And you are Director for Systems Development and Production Issues within the GAO's National Security and International Affairs Division. And you have with you Mr. Thomson and Mr. Gupta, the Assistant Director, and evaluator in charge. You have been here before the committee and we know the kind of quality work that you have done.

We have the GAO report and your testimony. Without objection, it will be entered into the record in its entirety, as will the testimony of all other witnesses who follow you. So we welcome you to begin these hearings this morning.

STATEMENT OF LOUIS J. RODRIGUES, DIRECTOR, SYSTEMS DEVELOPMENT AND PRODUCTION ISSUES, NATIONAL SECURITY AND INTERNATIONAL AFFAIRS DIVISION [NSIAD], U.S. GENERAL ACCOUNTING OFFICE, ACCOMPANIED BY HOMER H. THOMSON, ASSISTANT DIRECTOR; AND RAHUL GUPTA, EVALUATOR IN CHARGE

Mr. RODRIGUES. Thank you, Mr. Chairman.

I would like to proceed with an overall summary and then go on to the details on each of the programs we are covering today.

Mr. Chairman, members of the subcommittee, I am pleased to be here today to discuss two DOD space programs: the Defense Support Program, or DSP, for detection of ballistic missile launches, and the Milstar satellite communications system for command and control of military forces.

DSP and Milstar are two of the DOD's multibillion-dollar space programs that were designed to operate in a global nuclear ballistic missile confrontation with the former Soviet Union. However, military requirements now emphasize tactical war-fighting capabilities for future regional conflicts.

Regarding DSP, we believe DOD's actions to terminate the follow-on program and begin a new effort provides an opportunity to fully consider the new tactical requirements. Plans to initiate the new DSP replacement effort in fiscal year 1995 will involve major considerations, including requirements, cost effectiveness, and affordability.

On Milstar, however, we believe DOD may not have gone far enough. Milstar's original design emphasized support to strategic nuclear forces. As the strategic threat declined, DOD began placing greater emphasis on reducing Milstar's high cost and increasing support to tactical forces.

Despite several program changes during the last few years, Milstar is still a costly system. We believe that by canceling some of its planned large-sized satellites and initiating early development of a lower-cost system with smaller satellites, DOD has an opportunity to reduce program costs by billions of dollars.

Considering the changed threat and reduced defense budget, opportunities to make program changes aimed at achieving cost savings deserve increased attention. However, changes in the space community's culture will have to occur in order to achieve more substantive changes not only in DOD's acquisition of, but in the operation and use of space assets as well.

DSP began in 1967, and the first operational satellite was deployed in 1971. Over the years, DOD has launched 16 DSPs and the Air Force has multiyear contracts to procure up to 25. As of December 1992, the Air Force estimated the total program acquisition costs for these 25 satellites at $9.3 billion.

DOD has wanted to improve or replace DSP with modern technology since 1979. The Air Force's planned replacement in the early 1980's, called the advanced warning system, or AWS, never fully materialized because of immature technology and high cost.

In 1984, DOD transferred AWS to the Strategic Defense Initiative organization, and the system became known as the booster surveillance and tracking system, or BSTS. In 1990, after spending about $1 billion on BSTS, the organization discontinued its efforts and the responsibility for BSTS was returned to the Air Force, which renamed the system AWS.

In 1991, the Secretary of Defense approved a strategy for a scaled-down version of AWS, calling it FEWS. For fiscal years 1992 through 1994, the Congress appropriated $515 million for FEWS research and development. The system's purpose was to improve coverage and detection information associated with tactical and strategic ballistic missile launches.

Since program inception, DSP has been oriented toward detecting strategic nuclear missile launches. However, during the Persian Gulf war, it provided primary tactical warning of Scud missile launches. DOD's assessment of the DSP performance during the war was that sufficient warning was provided to the Army's Patriot missile defense system, but that an improved sensor capability would be needed for the future.

During the 1989 through 1991 timeframe, the Joint Requirements Oversight Council validated the needed capability and performance requirements for an advanced space-based missile warning sensor to detect, process, and report ballistic missile launches. Air Force representatives informed us that the documents associated with the need and the requirements provided the guidance for the FEWS research and development contractors. However, specific FEWS requirements contained in the draft October 1992 FEWS operations requirements document were never validated.

According to an October 1993 study performed to review and recommend options for a future U.S. space-based infrared surveillance capability, new needs can be met with a system that is simpler and less costly than FEWS. The study gave considerable weight to reducing the size of the satellite to allow it to be launched on a smaller vehicle, an idea that would reduce costs. The study stated that although there are strong reasons for DOD wanting a new, more able satellite in the future, the current requirement and associated FEWS specifications originated in a time of complex strategic needs. Times have changed—strategic needs being less important and global awareness at this point being more important. And there is sufficient time to review the requirements to compete through a better, simpler, cheaper system within the existing budget constrained schedule.

Mr. Chairman, as you noted in your opening statement, various studies have raised questions about the cost effectiveness of FEWS, including our 1991 study. In addition, a 1991 draft study by the defense science task force and a 1990 Air Force requirements trade study had similar conclusions.

Based on the October 1993 study, DOD decided that FEWS was too expensive, and therefore terminated the program. The Air Force issued a stop-work order to the contractors, and the work was halted in December 1993.

Now DOD plans to initiate a new research and development effort in fiscal year 1995. However, the form that this effort will take is not yet clear. Actions that will be needed include reviewing and validating requirements, selecting the most cost-effective alternative from among a group of plausible candidate systems, and ensuring that the system selected is affordable within the DOD budget-constrained environment.

Now let me turn to Milstar. DOD has been developing Milstar for the past 12 years. Thus far, it has invested about $8 billion in the program. Although the first satellite was originally scheduled for launch in 1987, program delays have pushed the first launch to February 5, 1994, or about 72 hours from now. DOD expects to launch the second Milstar in May 1995.

On average, each Milstar satellite placed in orbit will cost about $1.3 billion, $1 billion for the satellite and at least $285 million for the Titan IV launch vehicle. In addition, when the first Milstar is launched, the estimated annual operating costs for satellite control purposes will be about $110 million.

DOD established the Milstar in 1981. In 1983, President Reagan designated it as a program of highest national priority. Milstar's original design emphasized strategic nuclear war fighting by including a low-data rate communications capability primarily for sending emergency action messages to U.S. strategic forces during a nuclear confrontation.

Milstar is the most complex satellite communications system DOD has built. Over the years, it encountered many program changes. After the fall of the Berlin Wall, congressional leaders in 1990 considered Milstar's cost to be too high, its support to tactical forces inadequate, and its nuclear war-fighting capabilities unnecessary to deterrence. As a result, the National Defense Authorization Act for fiscal year 1991 directed the Secretary of Defense to develop and carry out a plan for either a restructured Milstar or an alternative advanced communications satellite program.

DOD chose to restructure Milstar. To lower costs, it decided to reduce the planned constellation size from eight to six satellites, reduce the quantity of ground-based equipment, and eliminate several systems survivability features. To provide greater utility to tactical forces, it decided to add a medium-data rate capability to satellite 4 and beyond.

In response to continued congressional concern about DOD space investment strategy, DOD in October 1992 approved a further reduction in Milstar's planned constellation size to four satellites. What this meant was that DOD would still launch the first two satellites based on the original design with the low-data rate capabilities only, and then the medium-data rate capability for increased support to tactical forces would be added to satellite 3 and beyond.

In its October 1993 bottom-up review, DOD decided to keep Milstar's constellation size at four satellites but limit the total acquisition to six satellites—the first two referred to as Milstar I, with a low-data rate capability only, and the next four referred to as Milstar II, with both low and medium-data rate capabilities.

To reduce long-term costs, DOD plans to replace the Milstar II design in fiscal year 2006 with advanced capability based on a smaller satellite design that will use a smaller, less expensive launch vehicle.

In a 1993 report requested by this subcommittee, we discussed alternatives to inserting modern technology into DOD's military satellites communications plans that could reduce long-term costs by about $17.6 billion. We specifically discussed an opportunity for making a transition to a common bus, a standard platform that supports the mission payload equipment.

Regarding Milstar, which was one of several satellite communications systems within the plan, we suggested that such a transition could be made after satellite 6. This was at a time when DOD was planning to build eight Milstar satellites, thus the acquisition of satellite 7 and 8 could be avoided. We recommended that the Secretary of Defense reassess various alternatives to preclude the continuation of costly, customized satellites.

DOD responded positively to our report. However, we now believe there is a basis for DOD to consider inserting modern technology after satellite 4 instead of after 6. The first two medium-data rate Milstars, No.'s 3 and 4, are under development and scheduled for launch in 1999 and 2000, respectively. However, a contract has not yet been awarded for the last two Milstar, satellites 5 and 6. This would be a break point in the Milstar program that would provide an opportunity to reduce costs through technology insertion.

Regarding insertion of modern technology, it was the consensus of an outside technical support group established to review options and assess risks under DOD's bottom-up review that an advanced design could be deployed as early as 2003 on a medium launch vehicle. This is in contrast to DOD's planned deployment of an advanced design in 2006.

If DOD did not acquire satellites 5 and 6, and deployed a less expensive advanced capability in 2003, there would be a 2-year delay, from 2002 to 2004, in achieving a four-satellite constellation with medium-data rate capabilities.

DOD would have to consider the benefits of the potential cost savings associated with this approach, which would be over $2 billion, against any operational risk of not having a four-satellite constellation during the time period now planned. A decision would need to be made this year because the Air Force plans to acquire long lead items for these satellites in fiscal year 1995. We are assessing the tradeoffs between the cost savings and the operational risks as part of an ongoing review of space programs.

DOD's difficulties in finding a replacement for DSP and developing Milstar have primarily been associated with meeting the cold war threat, and subsequently, making changes in response to the reduction of this threat. An Air Force report on DOD space investment strategy noted that the cold war made space systems expensive because of a number of reasons, including systems performance being the primary driver and cost being a secondary consideration.

Time at that point was of the essence to ensure deterrence capability and because security needs forced program development into rigid security compartments.

The result was a crisis-driven acquisition process. This meant that technology was developed concurrently with system procurement. System designs were seldom stable, and the security barriers discouraged efforts for commonality across systems or sharing of resources.

The report also stated that this cold war procurement rationale no longer applies, and now there is room to look at today's threat and space systems in context and proceed on a more ordered and efficient path.

In addition, the report stated that maximizing system performance is no longer paramount—with costs and technical risks being the principle factors.

Implementing these views, however, could be a major challenge because of the changes that would be necessary within DOD's space community culture. A December 1992 report to the Vice President stated that policy decisions made in the early years of the space age resulted in the establishment of four separate space sectors within the United States: military, intelligence, civil, and commercial. Each of these sectors evolved into separate organizational structures and now has its own institutional culture.

The report stated that the lack of strong coordination among these organizations encouraged different solutions to similar problems and overlapping capabilities.

Within the military and intelligence sectors, the report cited six separate organizations that are active in the development and operation of space systems. Each with distinctly different cultures with different technical requirements, acquisition procedures, and technical operations.

A subsequent Air Force report discussed several more institutional obstacles to cultural change, and noted that application of space in joint military operations needed more emphasis in all phases including planning, deployment, employment, and sustainment.

In summary, the culture existing in the space sectors and the values that drive these sectors must be changed if we are to achieve affordable space age systems for the future.

Mr. Chairman, this concludes my statement. I would be happy to answer any questions you or members of the subcommittee may have.

[NOTE.—The GAO report entitled, "Military Satellite Communications: Opportunity to Save Billions of Dollars," (GAO/NSIAD-93-216), can be found in subcommittee files.]

[The prepared statement of Mr. Rodrigues follows:]

	United States General Accounting Office
GAO	**Testimony** Before the Legislation and National Security Subcommittee, Committee on Government Operations, House of Representatives

For Release on Delivery Expected at 10:00 a.m. EST, Wednesday, February 2, 1994	**MILITARY SPACE PROGRAMS** **Opportunities to Reduce Missile Warning and Communication Satellites' Costs** Statement of Louis J. Rodrigues, Director, Systems Development and Production Issues, National Security and International Affairs Division

GAO/T-NSIAD-94-108

Mr. Chairman and Members of the Subcommittee:

I am pleased to be here today to discuss two Department of Defense (DOD) space programs. They are the Defense Support Program (DSP) for detection of ballistic missile launches and the Milstar satellite communications system for command and control of military forces.

At your request, we reviewed the status of these programs, including DOD's plans for such systems in the post cold war environment.

DSP and Milstar are two of DOD's major multi-billion dollar space programs that were designed to operate in a global nuclear ballistic missile confrontation with the former Soviet Union. The histories of these programs have demonstrated DOD's commitment to develop advanced and sophisticated space-based technology to effectively deter the Soviet threat. However, military requirements now emphasize tactical warfighting capabilities for future regional conflicts.

RESULTS IN BRIEF

In summary, DOD's action to terminate the current DSP follow-on program and begin a new effort provides an opportunity to fully consider the new tactical requirements. Plans to initiate a new DSP replacement effort in fiscal year 1995 will involve major management considerations, including requirements, cost effectiveness, and affordability.

On Milstar, however, we believe DOD may not have gone far enough and further actions could be taken to reduce costs. Milstar's original design emphasized support to strategic nuclear forces. As the strategic threat declined, DOD began placing greater emphasis on reducing Milstar's high cost and increasing support to tactical forces. Despite several program changes during the last few years, Milstar is still a costly system. We believe that by canceling some of its planned large-sized satellites and initiating early development of a lower cost system of smaller satellites, DOD has an opportunity to reduce program costs by billions of dollars.

Considering the changed threat and a reduced defense budget, opportunities to make program changes aimed at achieving cost savings deserve increased attention. However, changes in the national security space community's culture will have to occur in order to achieve more substantive changes in DOD's acquisition, operation, and use of space assets.

DSP: REPLACEMENT DECISION OFFERS COST SAVINGS OPPORTUNITY

DSP is a strategic surveillance and warning satellite system with an infrared capability to detect ballistic missile launches (intercontinental and from submarines). Its primary users are

(1) the North American Aerospace Defense Command, which is responsible for assessing potential attacks on North America, (2) the National Command Authorities, who are responsible for making retaliatory decisions, and (3) other major military commands that are responsible for strategic offensive forces.

DSP has been operational for more than 20 years, and efforts to replace it with more modern technology have encountered several setbacks. Since 1984, DOD has spent over $1 billion in research and development on such efforts--the most recent being the Follow-on Early Warning System (FEWS). DOD then decided to terminate FEWS because it was too expensive.

DOD plans to initiate a new effort in fiscal year 1995 to replace DSP. There are indications that smaller and less costly system capabilities than FEWS are being considered, with an emphasis on greater support to tactical forces. Actions that will be needed include (1) reviewing and validating requirements, (2) selecting the most cost effective alternative from among a group of plausible candidate systems, and (3) ensuring that the system selected is affordable within DOD's budget constrained environment.

Program Background and DOD Plans

DSP began in 1967, and the first operational satellite was

deployed in 1971. Over the years, DOD has launched 16 DSPs, and the Air Force has multiyear contracts to procure up to 25 DSPs. As of December 1992, the Air Force estimated the total program acquisition costs for these 25 satellites at $9.3 billion over a 32-year period (1967 to 1999).[1]

DOD has wanted to improve or replace DSP with modern technology since 1979. It claimed that the current system could not satisfy all of the validated military requirements. The Air Force's planned replacement in the early 1980s, called the Advanced Warning System (AWS), never fully materialized because of immature technology and high costs. In 1984, DOD transferred AWS to the Strategic Defense Initiative Organization, and the system became known as the Boost Surveillance and Tracking System (BSTS). In 1990, after spending about $1 billion on BSTS research and development, the Organization discontinued its efforts, and responsibility for BSTS was returned to the Air Force, which renamed the system AWS.

In 1991, the Secretary of Defense approved a strategy for a scaled-down version of AWS, calling it FEWS. In 1992, the Air Force awarded two FEWS demonstration and validation contracts that were scheduled to be completed in mid-1994. For fiscal years 1992 through 1994, the Congress appropriated $515 million

---

[1] This excludes launch and operating costs.

for FEWS research and development. The system's purpose was to improve coverage and detection information associated with tactical and strategic ballistic missile launches.

In late 1993, based on a review of options for a future space-based infrared surveillance capability, DOD decided that FEWS was too expensive and therefore terminated the program. The Air Force issued a stop-work order to the contractors, and the work was halted in December 1993. Now, DOD plans to initiate a new research and development effort in fiscal year 1995. However, the form that this effort will take is not yet clear. This is because discussions are still ongoing within DOD as to whether the development of an improved design of the existing DSP system or a new space-based early warning system should be pursued.

Requirements and Cost Effectiveness Are Critical Management Considerations

Since program inception, DSP has been oriented toward detecting strategic nuclear missile launches. However, during the Persian Gulf War, it provided the primary tactical warning of Iraqi's surface-to-surface Scud missile launches. DOD's assessment of DSP's performance during the war was that sufficient warning was provided to the Army's Patriot missile defense system, but that an improved sensor capability would be needed for the future.[2]

---

[2]*Conduct of the Persian Gulf War, Final Report to Congress*, DOD, April 1992.

During 1989 through 1991, the Joint Requirements Oversight Council[3] validated the needed capability and performance requirements for an advanced space-based missile warning sensor to detect, process, and report ballistic missile launches. Air Force representatives informed us that the documents associated with the need and the requirements provided guidance for the FEWS research and development contractors. However, specific FEWS requirements, contained in a draft October 1992 FEWS operational requirements document, were never validated.

According to an October 1993 study[4] performed for the Under Secretary of Defense for Acquisition to review and recommend options for a future U.S. space-based infrared surveillance capability, new needs can be met with a system that is simpler and less costly than FEWS. The study gave considerable weight to reducing the size of the satellite to allow it to be launched on a smaller vehicle than Titan IV which is currently used for DSP--an idea that would reduce costs. The study stated that although there are strong reasons for DOD wanting a new, more able satellite in the future, (1) the current requirement, and associated FEWS specification, originated in a time of complex

---

[3]A group of high level military officers, chaired by the Vice Chairman of the Joint Chiefs of Staff, having authority to determine the validity of mission needs and perform requirements analyses.

[4]*Space-Based IR Sensors*, October 1993, performed by a technical support group from several federally funded research and development centers and referred to as the Everett study.

strategic needs, (2) times have changed--strategic needs being less important and global awareness and theater support being more important, and (3) there is sufficient time to review the requirements and compete for a better, simpler, cheaper system within the existing budget constrained schedule. The study recommended that the requirements be redone in context of expected needs and other systems, and it supported DOD's decision to terminate the current FEWS effort.

In addition to the requirements matter, various studies have raised questions about the cost effectiveness of FEWS and other advanced capabilities. For example, in 1991, we reported[5] that an Air Force cost and operational effectiveness analysis showed life-cycle costs for an enhanced DSP were estimated at $2.4 billion to $3.5 billion less than two variations of FEWS and a fully capable AWS. We also reported that a 1991 draft study by a Defense Science Board task force and a 1990 Air Force requirements trade study had similar conclusions.

Also, part of the October 1993 study's task was to identify cost-effective options for consideration by DOD executives. The study presented four options that ranged in cost from $5.2 billion to $11 billion for the period 2002 to 2015. The lowest cost option involved down-sizing the existing DSP design and using medium-

---

[5]*Early Warning Satellites: Funding for Follow-on System Is Premature* (GAO/NSIAD-92-39, Nov. 7 1991).

sized launch vehicles instead of the Titan IV. The highest cost option involved using a lightweight version of FEWS, also designed for launch on a medium-sized vehicle. These options were in addition to a recommendation that called for acquiring more existing DSPs to ensure coverage until the transition was made to a new capability.

MILSTAR: A COSTLY AND CONTROVERSIAL PROGRAM

Milstar is designed to be a highly survivable satellite communications system, particularly resistant to electronic jamming, for use by military forces during wartime. Its users include the National Command Authorities,[6] chief military commanders, and strategic and tactical forces where critical communications are needed for command and control purposes.

DOD has been developing Milstar for the past 12 years. Thus far, it has invested about $8 billion in the program, which has experienced several changes, delays, and cost increases. Although the first satellite was originally scheduled to be launched in 1987, program delays pushed the first launch to February 5, 1994--about 72 hours from now. DOD expects to launch the second Milstar in May 1995.

On average, each Milstar satellite placed in orbit will cost

---

[6]The National Command Authorities consist of the President and the Secretary of Defense or their successors.

about $1.3 billion--$1 billion for the satellite and at least $285 million for the Titan IV launch vehicle. In addition, when the first Milstar is launched, the estimated annual operating costs for satellite control purposes will be about $110 million.

DOD has an opportunity to reduce Milstar program costs by over $2 billion, including launch costs, if it does not acquire the last two satellites under the current plan. Such a decision would need to be accompanied by a plan to accelerate the development of an enhanced Milstar that is smaller in size, lighter in weight, lower in costs, and capable of being launched on a smaller vehicle than the Titan IV. Accelerating this effort may require some additional investment in the short run and an assessment of any operational risk by not acquiring these last two satellites. As part of an ongoing review of space programs, we are evaluating the tradeoffs between cost savings and operational risk for consideration during the fiscal year 1995 defense authorization and appropriations deliberations.

Program Background and DOD Plans

DOD established Milstar in 1981. In 1983, President Reagan designated it as a program of highest national priority. Milstar's original design emphasized strategic nuclear warfighting by including a low-data rate communications capability,[7] primarily for sending emergency action messages to U.S. strategic forces during an enemy attack. Tactical forces were also planned users of this capability.

Milstar is the most complex satellite communication system DOD has built. Over the years, it encountered many program changes and difficulties. After the fall of the Berlin Wall, congressional leaders, in 1990, considered Milstar's cost to be too high, its support to tactical forces inadequate, and its nuclear warfighting capabilities unnecessary for deterrence. As a result, the National Defense Authorization Act for fiscal year 1991 directed the Secretary of Defense to develop and carry out a plan for either a restructured Milstar or an alternative advanced communications satellite program.

DOD chose to restructure the Milstar program. To lower costs, it decided to reduce the planned constellation size from 8 to 6 satellites, reduce the quantity of other ground-based equipment, and eliminate several system survivability features. To provide greater utility to tactical forces, it decided to add a medium-data rate capability to satellite 4 and beyond.

---

[7]This low-data rate capability allows information to be transmitted at speeds ranging from 75 to 2,400 bits per second and would carry teletype and compressed voice communications. Medium-data rate includes speeds up to 1,544,000 bits per second and would carry regular voice communications and imagery.

The October 1992 conference committee report on the fiscal year 1993 defense authorization bill expressed additional concern about DOD's space investment strategy. The conferees directed the Secretary of Defense to develop a comprehensive acquisition strategy aimed at reducing costs and increasing efficiencies for developing, fielding, and operating DOD space programs. In October 1992, the Assistant Secretary of Defense for Command, Control, Communications, and Intelligence approved a further reduction in Milstar's planned constellation size to 4 satellites. What this meant, however, was that DOD would still launch the first two satellites based on the original design, with the low-data rate capability. Then, the medium-data rate capability for increased support to tactical forces would be added to satellite 3 and beyond.

In its October 1993 Bottom-Up Review of major defense programs, DOD decided to keep Milstar's constellation size at 4 satellites, but limit the total acquisition to 6 satellites--the first two, referred to as Milstar I, with the low-data rate capability only, and the next four, referred to as Milstar II, with both low- and medium-data rate capabilities. To reduce long term costs, DOD plans to replace the Milstar II design in fiscal year 2006 with an advanced capability based on a smaller satellite design that will use a smaller, less expensive launch vehicle.

Additional Cost Saving Alternative Could Be Assessed Against Current Plans

In a 1993 report[a] requested by this Subcommittee, we discussed alternatives for inserting modern technology into DOD's military satellite communications plans that could reduce long term costs by about $17.6 billion compared with DOD's baseline plan. We specifically discussed an opportunity for making a transition to a common bus--a standard satellite platform that supports the mission payload equipment.

Regarding Milstar, which was one of several DOD satellite communication systems within the plan, we suggested that such a transition could be made after satellite 6. This was at a time when DOD was planning to build 8 Milstar satellites, thus the acquisition of satellites 7 and 8 could be avoided. We recommended that the Secretary of Defense reassess various alternatives to preclude the continuation of costly, customized satellites.

In its December 1993 response to our report, DOD (1) discussed plans to terminate Milstar after the 6th satellite, based on the bottom-up review decision, (2) agreed with the need to move away from customized, unique busses toward common busses, and (3)

---

[a] *Military Satellite Communications: Opportunity to Save Billions of Dollars*, (GAO/NSIAD-93-216, July 9, 1993).

stated that the most cost effective approach for inserting modern technology was to begin developing an advanced, lower cost, lower weight payload capability.

We believe there is a basis for DOD to consider inserting modern technology after satellite 4, instead of after satellite 6. The first two medium-data rate Milstars (satellites 3 and 4) are under development and scheduled for launch in 1999 and 2000, respectively. However, a contract has not yet been awarded for the last two Milstars (satellites 5 and 6) which would be launched in 2001 and 2002, respectively. This would be a break point in the Milstar program that would provide an opportunity to reduce costs through technology insertion.

Regarding the insertion of modern technology, it was the consensus of an outside technical support group, established to review options and assess risk under DOD's bottom-up review, that an advanced design could be deployed as early as 2003 on a medium launch vehicle. This is in contrast to DOD's planned deployment of an advanced design in 2006.

If DOD did not acquire satellites 5 and 6 and deployed a less-expensive, advanced capability in 2003, there would be a 2-year delay, from 2002 to 2004, in achieving a 4-satellite constellation with medium-data rate capabilities. DOD would have to consider the benefits of the potential cost savings associated

with this approach, which could be over $2 billion including
launch costs, by not acquiring satellites 5 and 6, against any
operational risk of not having a 4-satellite constellation during
the time period now planned. A decision would need to be made
this year because the Air Force plans to acquire long lead items
for these satellites in fiscal year 1995. As previously stated,
we are assessing the tradeoffs between cost savings and
operational risks as part of an on-going review of space
programs.

COLD WAR CHANGES CALL FOR SPACE COMMUNITY CULTURE CHANGES

DOD's difficulties in finding a replacement for DSP and
developing Milstar have primarily been associated with meeting
the cold war threat, and subsequently, making changes in response
to the reduction in this threat. In a report to Air Force
Headquarters on DOD space investment strategy, the Air Force
Space and Missile Systems Center and Air Force Space Command
stated that the cold war made space systems expensive for the
following reasons: (1) whole new technologies had to be
invented, (2) system performance was the primary driver, and cost
was not much of a consideration, (3) time was of the essence to
ensure a deterrence capability, and (4) security needs forced
program development into rigid security compartments. The
result, according to the report, was a crises-driven acquisition
process. This meant that (1) technology was developed
concurrently with system procurement, resulting in delays and

redesign, (2) system designs were seldom stable, considering an expanding threat, and (3) the security barriers discouraged efforts for commonality across systems or sharing of resources.

The report also stated that this cold war procurement rationale no longer applies, and now there is room to look at today's threat and space systems in context and proceed on a more ordered and efficient path. In addition, the report stated that maximizing system performance is no longer paramount--cost and technical risk being the principal factors--and there is greater potential for cross-program sharing in technologies, standards, and common resources.

Implementing these views, however, could be a major challenge because of changes that would be necessary within DOD's space community culture. A December 1992 report[9] to the Vice President stated that policy decisions made in the early years of the space age resulted in the establishment of four separate space sectors within the United States--military, intelligence, civil, and commercial. Each of these sectors evolved under separate organizational structures and now has its own institutional culture. The report stated that the lack of strong coordination among these organizations encouraged different solutions to similar problems and overlap in capabilities,

---

[9] *A Post Cold War Assessment of U.S. Space Policy*, Vice President's Space Policy Advisory Board, Dec. 1992.

particularly in areas such as technology development, launch, and support services.

Within the military and intelligence sectors, the report cited six separate organizations that are active in the development and operations of space systems.[10] Each organization has a distinctly different culture with different technical requirements, acquisition procedures, and technical operations. Also, according to the report, institutional arrangements encourage overlap and discourage cooperation and synergism.

A subsequent Air Force report[11] discussed several, more specific, institutional obstacles to cultural change. For example, the report stated that (1) multiple space acquisition agencies have resulted in inefficiency and less effective forces, (2) there has been limited user input or influence on the requirements process, reducing the operational usefulness of military space systems and increasing their cost, and (3) the application of space in joint military operations needs more

---

[10] They are the Air Force, Army, Navy, National Reconnaissance Office, Ballistic Missile Defense Organization, and Advanced Research Projects Agency.

[11] Blue Ribbon Panel of the Air Force In Space In the 21st Century, Executive Summary, Undated.

emphasis in all phases--planning, deployment, employment, and sustainment.

- - - -

Mr. Chairman, this concludes my statement. I will be happy to answer any questions you or members of the Subcommittee may have.

Mr. CONYERS. Thank you for a good oral presentation and a fuller statement that will be recorded in our hearings that you submitted already.

I would encourage my colleagues that questions they submit to Mr. Rodrigues be answered and all be put in the record, and that would reduce the amount of time that he would spend before us.

Mr. McCandless.

Mr. MCCANDLESS. Thank you, Mr. Chairman.

I come from the 3-B type of defense—boondocks, bandits, and backpacks—so this is a whole new ball game for me, the Buck Rogers 21st century. I would like to also submit to you some questions that would specifically address the issues that have raised my concern relative to the systems involved here today.

Mr. RODRIGUES. Thank you.

[The information follows:]

GAO

United States
General Accounting Office
Washington, D.C. 20548

National Security and
International Affairs Division

Date: February 17, 1994

To: Mr. Steve Vincze, professional staff, Minority,
Committee on Government Operations.

From: Thomas Schulz, Associate Director, Systems Development and
Production Issues

Subject: Answers to questions for the record on Milstar and DSP/FEWS
testimony (GAO/T-NSIAD-94-108).

In response to your facsimile and telephone request of today I am providing answers to the five questions for the record on our February 2, 1994 testimony on Milstar and DSP/FEWS programs. I hope this meets your needs and if you have any questions please feel free to call me on 202-512-4841.

Question 1: Didn't the DOD Bottom-Up-Review address the issues and conclusions of your July 1993 report about Milstar (Report# GAO/NSIAD-93-216) and reach different conclusions than your report?

Answer: The Bottom-Up-Review did not reach different conclusions and in fact did address some of our concerns. A draft of our report was provided to the DOD several months prior to the completion of the BUR in October 1993. The BUR did concur with our key observation to transition to a lower weight class satellite design. As in our report, the BUR selected an option that transitions the current Milstar design after the 6th satellite to an advanced EHF satellite that would be launched on a medium size launch vehicle. The BUR did not specify a common bus satellite as suggested in our report to be an alternative among other competing options. However, in his response to our report, Gen. Paige, the Assistant Secretary of Defense for C3I, concurred that common busses are preferable to the current customized designs.

Question 2: Please explain how you arrived at your cost figures/estimates and how you evaluated the cost of each of the features of Milstar?

Answer: We used raw data provided to us by the Air Force, previous GAO work, and contractor data to calculate an _average_ cost of the satellite. We compared contractor data to our _average_ cost to verify that the _average_ cost number was a reasonable estimate.

Question 3: In your report, you questioned the need for features like agile beams and crosslinks. What operational requirements or scenarios did you use to determine there was a questionable need for these feature?

Answer: Our report did not question the specific features on Milstar. We imply in our Milstar testimony and other reports we have issued on MILSATCOM that DOD needs to review the requirements for all MILSATCOM systems considering changing threat and costs.

Question 4: You question the tactical utility of the first two MILSTAR satellite launches. Doesn't the low data rate payload on these satellites support the STU-III type secure voice terminal? Isn't the STU-III unit a vast improvement over the "Donald Duck" sounding, slow-reacting secure telephones of the past? Wouldn't you agree that operating these secure voice units at low data rates allow the equipment to be smaller, to utilize more bandwidth, and to provide for greater jamming protection? Doesn't DOD have thousands of the STU-III units that it can use in conjunction with Milstar now?

Answer: We maintain that the limited level of tactical utility that you obtain from the first two low data rate Milstars would not have been cost effective if it were the primary justification for the Milstar program. The current tactical requirements would be better covered by Milstar II when it is launched in the late 1990s.

With regards to "STU-III type secure voice terminals" for Milstar, there is a difference between the handset unit and the ground terminal required to process communications via the satellite. It is our understanding that relatively few terminals have been procured for use by ground, air, and sea platforms.

Question 5: Let's assume U.S. forces are in an area, for example the Korean peninsula, when a third world country run by an unpredictable leader explodes a nuclear weapon in the close vicinity where U.S. forces are located. Wouldn't such an event cause a blockage of current communications systems for up to many days? Wouldn't MILSTAR with its EHF frequencies and specialized waveform prevent such a disruption in communications and maintain connectivity with essential command and control elements?

Answer: The answers to the first part of these questions would be more appropriately obtained from the DOD and the intelligence community. Also, we have never questioned the need for EHF communications and capabilities. We should point out that in addition to Milstar, the DOD has plans to include low data rate EHF capability on 6 Navy UHF communication satellites.

Mr. CONYERS. Thank you very much.

We recognize the gentlelady from New York, Mrs. Maloney.

Mrs. MALONEY. Thank you, Mr. Chairman.

Very briefly, why are we launching Milstar I and II? What are their capabilities? In 72 hours, you said, 72 hours they are going up. What are the capabilities? What do they accomplish for the country?

Mr. RODRIGUES. Yes. Milstar I is in 72 hours; Milstar II will be next year.

They provide low-data rate EHF capability, secure antijam, low-data rate capability.

Mrs. MALONEY. They provide communications capability?

Mr. RODRIGUES. Yes.

Mrs. MALONEY. Why would we want to communicate with Milstar I for $1.4 billion?

Mr. RODRIGUES. Well, part of the problem is the money on the first satellites, those satellites are bought and paid for. They are there. They are built. You have paid for them. The question becomes, do you want to launch them or not launch them? They do put up an EHF capability and everyone recognizes, no one is arguing with the fact that we need EHF capability for antijam purposes.

Mrs. MALONEY. Do we or do we not need it?

Mr. RODRIGUES. We do need it. There is no question that that is the way to go to deal with the antijam as well provide an assured communication through——

Mrs. MALONEY. What is the NIJM?

Mr. RODRIGUES. Antijam, electronic jamming capability.

Mrs. MALONEY. Who has the capability of jamming now that the Russians are no longer a threat? Who has the capability of jamming us? Is there any other country that has the capability of jamming us?

Mr. RODRIGUES. I am not sure exactly who has what types of capabilities or how significant those capabilities are.

Mrs. MALONEY. Do they have any tactical use?

Mr. RODRIGUES. Excuse me, does what have tactical use?

Mrs. MALONEY. Milstar I.

Mr. RODRIGUES. It has limited tactical use. Milstar was designed from the beginning primarily for strategic purposes, but there were some limited tactical applications.

Mrs. MALONEY. What do you mean by limited?

Mr. RODRIGUES. Certain user communities that would need short bursts of messages for use.

Mrs. MALONEY. What user communities?

Mr. RODRIGUES. I believe Special Operation Forces. I think getting into any more than that would get into some classified areas.

Mrs. MALONEY. OK. Thank you very much.

So our choice is either to send up to $1.4 billion for a Milstar I that has, "limited" tactical use, or to torch it because it has no other use here on the Earth, right?

Mr. RODRIGUES. Yes, I guess you could put it that way. What you are looking at in incremental costs is the difference in operating those satellites from now until you get the MDR. If you look at this chart, the timeframe would be the launch in 1994 this week through the first launch in 1999 of the MDR capable satellite, first MDR capable satellite. Operating costs would be somewhere in the range of about $575 million to operate the satellites over that period of time.

Mr. CONYERS. OK. Thank you very much.

Mr. Kyl.

Mr. KYL. Thank you, Mr. Chairman.

Just two quick questions, one a followup. You are not suggesting in your testimony that the Air Force should not launch in 72 hours, are you?

Mr. RODRIGUES. No, sir. I don't have a basis for questioning that.

Mr. KYL. Second, just to make it crystal clear, you, GAO, you have not looked at the requirements, the requirements for DSP/FEWS?

Mr. RODRIGUES. We had looked at DSP/FEWS in our 1991 report. We issued a report saying that the decision to fund FEWS at that time was premature for a couple of reasons. No. 1 was that the requirements had not been validated, and in fact they never were validated for FEWS, and we were operating against different—a TWAA requirement that was not specifically—that FEWS wasn't designed specifically to that, and we never did get that validated requirement.

And we felt at the time that before you go into a major investment program that you should know what it is you are trying to accomplish, and that as well as the cost and operational effectiveness analysis that indicated that there were a number of very much lower-cost options that would provide enhanced capability over the existing system that may be competitive with FEWS and that really needed to be considered.

Mr. KYL. There is no question that you need a requirements determination? I guess I will ask it a different way. If General Horner says there is a requirement—there are requirements for a DSP/FEWS kind of system, that is not something that GAO has questioned in the past or would question in the future, I gather?

Mr. RODRIGUES. Provided that they actually developed a requirement for whatever system they are going into, absolutely not.

Mr. KYL. Thank you, Mr. Chairman.

Mr. CONYERS. Thank you very much.

Mr. Zimmer.

Mr. ZIMMER. No questions.

Mr. CONYERS. Mr. Rodrigues, again, thank you for appearing before this committee. We appreciate your testimony.

We are now bringing forward our panel of Colonel Mangold, Colonel Dietz, Mr. Aru, Dr. Quinn.

Gentlemen, will you raise your right hands.

[Witnesses sworn.]

Mr. CONYERS. Thank you very much. Please be seated. Welcome to the committee. I want to thank this panel of witnesses for appearing voluntarily before us today.

After consultation with the general counsel to the House of Representatives, the subcommittee has been assured that this hearing is a privileged proceeding under the speech and debate clause of the Constitution and applicable court rulings. The courts have consistently recognized that statements of a voluntary witness before a congressional subcommittee are afforded an absolute testimonial privilege against claims for defamation or other claims based upon the publication of those statements.

I have a number of cases: the Gibbs case, the Webster case, and other legal research. In addition, I point out that two of the witnesses on this panel are Air Force officers, obviously, who will testify about events and transactions that occurred in the course of their official duties as officers. While the Air Force and the Department of Defense have the right to designate their own witnesses to present the Department's position, the subcommittee views the voluntary testimony of these officers in response to our request as official acts executed in the scope of their employment and responsibility.

We would like to begin with Col. Sanford Mangold, U.S. Air Force.

We are very pleased that you could appear before us, and we would include your statement in the record at this time to be reproduced in full, and would invite you to give a summary of your testimony, please.

STATEMENT OF SANFORD D. MANGOLD, COLONEL, U.S. AIR FORCE

Colonel MANGOLD. Thank you, Mr. Chairman. I am pleased to appear before you today to discuss what I have characterized a cancer upon the U.S. Air Force's budget process in the arena of space.

I was a key part of that process from August 1991 until June 24, 1993. I was responsible for administering nearly $20 billion annually, 25 percent of the entire Air Force budget. My job title was Space Command, Control, Communications, Intelligence and Nuclear Deterrence Team Chief, and as such, I felt it was my responsibility to propose cuts in the budget as directed by the senior Department of Defense leadership and the White House.

After nearly 1 year in the job and after successfully uncovering significant cost savings, I was extended for an unprecedented second year as team chief on June 1, 1993. On June 24, 23 days later, allegations about my personal integrity came forward, and I was summarily relieved. And then I began what I have termed a significant life experience.

The action of removing me had long been anticipated by myself, my leadership, and my contemporaries. For over 1 year prior to June 24, I had been told I was the most hated man in Space Command, and was going to be taken out in some way, any way possible. The acrimony I engendered from my space colleagues was tied directly to my straightforward approach to budgetary reductions and my absolute refusal to exempt unnecessary space systems from the budgetary ax.

No charges were ever made, just allegations, resulting in me losing my job.

Before I go any further, let me digress and provide you with some background as to my credentials. For the past 25 years I have been working in this Nation's military and civilian space programs. I have been involved in all aspects of missile warning, space surveillance, satellite command and control and launch operations.

I have two master's degrees. I have been assigned to the National Aeronautics and Space Administration and I attended the Naval War College. Throughout my nearly 25 years of service, I have been repeatedly given difficult jobs and been exposed to the highest levels of policymaking within the Air Force.

Prior to my removal, I was viewed by many in the Pentagon as one of the strongest voices within the Space Command, and I was told I was in the top 1 percent of all Air Force Colonels on the Air Staff in the Pentagon. Routinely, I had direct assess to the highest levels of the Air Force to include the Secretary of Air Force and the Chief of Staff.

All of this ended on June 24, 1993 when I was reassigned to other duties pending the outcome of an investigation which took 210 days to complete. In the end, no guilt was established and I was given an administrative reprimand. However, the damage was done. I was removed from the budget process at precisely the time when I was ready to shepherd in the most dramatic cuts in the space community that they had ever seen in their history.

What I had discovered is that while the operational Air Force leadership in the Pentagon from the Secretary of the Air Force on down through the Chief of Staff to the Deputy Chief of Staff for Plans and Operations fully understood that the cold war had ended and a new world order dictated a general drawdown in our military force, this understanding did not get fully embraced by Air Force Space Command.

Repeatedly, during my year as the Space/C3I/Nuc Deterrence Team Chief, I clashed with several generals and senior colonels in Colorado Springs, as well as the space acquisition community within the Pentagon. They openly opposed my straightforward philosophy, which was basically "everything is on the table."

I would take deep cuts in the budget whenever and wherever I discovered wasteful, costly, or cold war-specific programs. I vowed to make cut into the space budget because I knew exactly where the overpriced programs were, and understood precisely why each system did or did not support the post-cold war direction for the Department of Defense. This was especially true for Milstar and FEWS.

First, let me categorically state Milstar as presently configured is no longer necessary. It provides low-quality voice and teletype information on less than 100 channels. The communications activity is not worth the continued expenditures of billions of dollars required to keep this program alive.

Therefore, by August 1992 I began to openly oppose Milstar from within the Pentagon. At once, the space community rallied around this program and attempted to make me stop.

What followed was an internal Air Force space war surrounding Milstar. The conflict continued unabated and reached its climax in the March 1993 timeframe when we went to the Chief of Staff of the Air Force. There, Gen. Buster Glosson and I convinced General McPeak to support outright cancellation of Milstar. The space acquisition community fought back vigorously and won a compromise supporting the launch of the first two Milstar satellites and a totally restructured program after that.

Still, we had realized a total cost saving of $640 million over the next 5 years with no loss, no loss of military capability to our warfighters. I felt I had won a major victory. Unfortunately, Secretary Aspin reversed our decision and Milstar was given new life.

As I see it, Milstar has fundamental, insurmountable problems. Half of its payload-carrying capacity is filled with ballast and it provides marginal communications to the warfighters. It is as if the DOD decided to ship some communications equipment across country. To do this, we contracted to buy a moving van capable of living through a nuclear holocaust. By the time the van was ready to go, half the communications equipment was removed because the threat of nuclear war was over. So what we were left with was a very expensive moving van and about a U-Haul trailer's worth of communications equipment.

So what my space acquisition friends decided to do was fill half of the moving van with concrete for ballast and drive the van across country anyway. Add to this decision the fact that the equipment we are shipping is only the first-generation capability. The really good ELF capabilities come after the turn of the century, and even then we are still going to use the nuclear-hardened moving vans.

This just did not pass the truth and logic test then, and I believe it does not pass it today. The way I saw it, I had no ethical choice but to oppose Milstar openly and as vocally as possible. I did precisely that in August 1992 and started down a path which has led to this hearing.

Now let me turn my attention to FEWS. The Follow-On Early Warning System was also a solution-specific answer to a very general requirement. There is no doubt that this Nation needs space-based tactical warning and attack assessment. That is the requirement. However, now the world has changed and smaller missiles like the Scud have begun to fall into the hands of new adversaries.

We must ask, can DSP still do the job or do we need something else?

What the acquisition community and my good friends in Space Command came up with for an answer was the FEWS program.

So again, I began to question big-ticket space programs and again I got the predictable reactions from Colorado Springs and from within the space acquisition community and the Pentagon. By April 1993, I knew I was on a collision course and I needed to go out to Air Force Space Command headquarters in Colorado Springs to confront my adversaries face to face.

A few weeks before I left for Colorado, I received a warning from a fellow colonel's wife in Colorado Springs. I learned that Space Command was actively working to have me fired. I was told the plan was to "cut off the head of the snake while leaving the body intact." They wanted me terminated, period. Further, they had a spy in my organization who was gathering information on me to have me removed.

Sixty days later, the warnings proved valid. I was removed, and have not been allowed to participate in the budget reduction process since June 1993. I have been publicly defamed, I have been humiliated, and I have been embarrassed. Despite all of this, I never lost faith in the Air Force or the American justice system.

In conclusion, I am convinced that cost-cutting measures I recommended were proper, well developed, and in line with President Clinton's policies. I believe that I was removed because I was attempting to foster an open debate on expensive, unnecessary space programs and my opponents knew when I held their systems up to the clear light of day they would lose. So they decided to remove me because I was the source of their problem.

Throughout this happy—unhappy experience, I have come to the following conclusion: The cancer seems to be isolated to the space community. The Air Force leadership within the Pentagon has treated me fairly throughout this entire process.

And I have a final thought. When I was a young assistant, an aide-de-camp, to a three-star general, he always told me never to do anything that you wouldn't be embarrassed to read about in tomorrow's newspaper. Milstar and FEWS embarrassed me. And I stood up against them. My actions have probably cost me my career, but at some point in everyone's life they must make a choice. I made mine. I do not regret it and I would do it again.

Thank you, Mr. Chairman.

[The prepared statement of Colonel Mangold follows:]

STATEMENT BY SANFORD MANGOLD

COLONEL, U.S. AIR FORCE

BEFORE THE

SUBCOMMITTEE ON LEGISLATION AND NATIONAL SECURITY

COMMITTEE ON GOVERNMENT OPERATIONS

U.S. HOUSE OF REPRESENTATIVES

FEBRUARY 5, 1994

TESTIMONY TO NATIONAL SECURITY SUBCOMMITTEE

Mr. Chairman, Members of the Committee. I am pleased to come before you today to discuss what I have characterized as a cancer upon the United States Air Force's Budget Process in the arena of space. I was a key part of this process from August 1991 until 24 June 1993, first as the understudy, then as the person in charge of the entire Air Force Budget for Space Systems; Command, Control, Communications and Intelligence Systems and all Nuclear Weapons -- ICBMs, Gravity Bombs and Cruise Missiles. I was responsible for administering nearly $20 Billion Dollars annually -- 25% of the entire Air Force Budget. My job title was the Space/C3I/Nuc Deterrence Team Chief and, as such, I felt it was my responsibility to propose cuts in the budget as directed by the senior leadership and the White House.

After nearly one year in the job and after successfully uncovering significant cost savings, I was extended for an unprecedented second year as Team Chief on the 1st of June, 1993. 23 days later on 24 June, allegations about my personal integrity came forward, I was summarily relieved from my job and I began what I have come to term a "real life" experience.

The action of removing me had long been anticipated by myself, my leadership and most of my contemporaries. For over a year prior to the 24th of June, I had been told I was "the most hated man in Space Command" and going to be taken out in some way -- any way possible. The acrimony I engendered from my space colleagues was tied directly to my straightforward approach to budget reductions and my absolute refusal to exempt unnecessary space systems from the budgetary axe. No charges were ever made, just allegations, resulting in me losing my job.

Before I go further, let me digress and provide you with some background as to who I am and what I was doing. I will specifically address the budget cutting procedures I employed while the Space/C3I/Nuc Deterrence Team Chief. Further, I will clarify my well-documented opposition to the MILSTAR satellite and the FEWS program.

Permit me to briefly discuss my credentials.

I literally grew up in the space race. As a child, my father worked at the White Sands Missile Test Center and at Cape Canaveral. I stood on the beach and got to watch the Mercury, Gemini and Apollo astronauts blast-off into space. It seemed only natural for me to go into space exploration and operations myself. For the last 25 years, since my graduation from the University of Florida, I have been working in this nation's military and civilian space programs. I have been involved in all aspects of missile warning, space surveillance, satellite command & control and launch operations. I have two masters degrees, been assigned to NASA and attended the Naval War College. Throughout my nearly 25 years of service, I have repeatedly been given difficult jobs and been exposed to the highest levels of policy making within the Air Force. Prior to my removal, I was viewed by many in the Pentagon as one of the strongest voices within the space community and was told I was in the top 1% of all Colonels on the Air Staff in the Pentagon. Routinely, I had direct access to the highest levels of Air Force leadership to include the Secretary of the Air Force and the Chief of Staff.

All of this ended on 24 Jun 93, when I was reassigned to other duties pending the outcome of an investigation which took 210 days to complete. In the end, no guilt was established and I was given an administrative reprimand. However, the damage was done. I was removed from the budget process at precisely the time I was ready to shepherd in the most dramatic cost cuts the space community had ever seen in its history.

What I had discovered is that while the operational Air Force leadership in the Pentagon from the Secretary of the Air Force on down through the Chief of Staff to the Deputy Chief of Staff for Plans and Operations fully understood that the Cold War had ended and a new world order dictated a general drawdown in our military forces, this understanding did not get fully embraced by Air Force Space Command. Repeatedly, during my year as the Space/C3I/Nuc Deterrence Team Chief, I clashed with several generals and senior Colonels in Colorado Springs, as well as the space acquisition community within the Pentagon. They all openly opposed my straightforward cost cutting philosophy which was basically "everything is on the table for examination and any weapon system found to not to meet President Clinton's and Secretary Aspin's direction for the military would be TERMINATED -- NO EXCEPTIONS." I would make deep cuts in the budget whenever and wherever I discovered wasteful, costly or Cold War-specific programs. I vowed to make cuts into the space budget, because I knew exactly where the over-priced systems were and I understood precisely why each system did or did not support the post-Cold War direction for the Department of Defense. This was especially true for MILSTAR and FEWS.

Once I became the Team Chief in Jun 1992, I began an intense investigation into the MILSTAR program to determine if we really needed this system. I launched several studies into MILSTAR's history, purpose and costs. I was shocked to find that this satellite was the clearest example of a Cold War system whose contributions to military conflicts like Desert Storm or operations like in Somalia would be negligible. And the costs of each satellite were unacceptable -- nearly $1.4 Billion per satellite.

First, let me **categorically** state that MILSTAR is a clear tribute to American technological know-how. To design and actually build a satellite capable of guaranteeing communications across-the-conflict-spectrum in order to insure voice and data links in an actual nuclear war environment is an awesome feat. But, in reality, MILSTAR is longer necessary. It only provides low quality voice and teletype information on less than 100 channels. As I mentioned, I conducted several extensive studies on the utility of MILSTAR in a non-nuclear, limited war environment and concluded this small increase in communications connectivity was not worth the continued expenditure of the Billions of dollars required to keep this program alive. Therefore, in August 1992, I began to openly oppose MILSTAR within the Pentagon.

At once, the space community rallied around the program and attempted to make me stop.

After an Air Force Council Meeting, in which I told the assembled senior general officers and Air Force civilian leadership that I felt MILSTAR was a serious mistake and needed to be canceled outright, I began to feel the walls closing in. Immediately following this meeting, I was taken into the office of the Deputy Assistant Secretary of the Air Force for Space Plans and Policy and was told that if I ever exposed another space system to budget cuts in front of the flying Air Force leadership again -- my career might suffer. I looked him in the eye and asked if he wanted me to lie to the Vice Chief of Staff of the Air Force, because if he did -- he was talking to the wrong man. He told me to have a nice day and excused me.

What followed was an internal Air Force "space war" surrounding MILSTAR. The Deputy Chief of Staff for Plans and Operations, Lt General Buster Glosson, lined up solidly behind me and told me to continue to challenge MILSTAR's need in future conflicts and supported me in my fight with Air Force Space Command and the space acquisition community. The conflict continued unabated and reached its climax in Feb-Mar 93, when we went to the Chief of Staff of the Air Force. There General Glosson and I convinced General McPeak to support outright cancellation of the MILSTAR program. The space acquisition community fought back vigorously and won a compromise supporting the launch of the first two MILSTAR satellites and a totally restructured program after that.

Still, we realized a total cost savings of $640 Million dollars over the next 5 years -- with no loss of capability to the military warfighters. Therefore, I felt I had won a major victory. Unfortunately, Secretary Aspin reversed our decision and MILSTAR was given new life.

Recognize, MILSTAR is not the only answer to the future military communications requirements. It is merely one of many possible answers to our battlefield communications needs. It just happens to be one of the most expensive ways we can go. What we need today and in the future is highly secure, flexible communications which can operate in a hostile jamming environment with a low-probability of intercept. This is what EHF- Extremely High Frequency Communications gives us. MILSTAR uses EHF, but this satellite was designed for a nuclear war environment and because of that costs far too much in today's world. My MILSTAR studies demonstrated that we could supply the majority of our needed EHF communications to the military at about the same time as the MILSTAR program would deliver them, but at a greatly reduced price -- using smaller, cheaper satellites outfitted with the latest technology. As I see it, MILSTAR has fundamental, insurmountable problems:

Half of its payload carrying capability is filled with ballast. Early in this process, I was told by the space acquisition community that MILSTAR was carrying 2000 pounds of aluminum filled with sand to compensate for a classified payload which was no longer needed. As I began to question the logic of launching a ton of ballast into a geosynchronous orbit -- 22,300 miles above the Earth, I was told not be concerned, since that was an acquisition and not an operational issue. Then I was told the weight was somewhere between 1000 and 2000 pounds, that the aluminum was solid and there was no sand, that the weight of the satellite is not only payload, but structural weight due to the nuclear warfighting requirements. As I concentrated on the ballast issue, the story changed on a near-daily basis. Finally, I became fed up and used the following analogy to cut through my acquisition friends' jargon:

The DOD decided to ship some communications equipment across country. To do this, we contracted to buy a moving van capable of living through a nuclear holocaust. By the time the van was ready to go, half the communications equipment was removed and the threat of a nuclear war was over. So what we were left with was a very expensive moving van and about as U-Haul trailer's worth of comm equipment. So what my acquisition friends decided to do was to fill half the moving van with concrete - for ballast - and drive the big van across country anyway.

Add to this decision the fact that the equipment we are shipping is only the first generation capability -- the really good EHF communications' capabilities will come after the turn-of-the-century. And even then, we were still going to use the nuclear hardened moving vans to ship it.

This just did not pass the "Truth and Logic" Test -- It still does not pass it today. The way I saw it, I had no ethical choice but to oppose MILSTAR as openly and vocally as possible. I did precisely that in August 1992 and started down a path which has led ultimately to this hearing.

Now let me turn my attention to FEWS. The Follow-On Early Warning System was also a "solution-specific" answer to a very general requirement. The Nation needs space-based tactical warning and attack assessment...that's the requirement. The Defense Support Program - DSP - was originally designed to do this job, back when we were facing the USSR with its arsenal of big missiles. However, now that the world has changed and smaller missiles, like the SCUD, have begun to fall into the hands of new adversaries, can DSP still do the job or do we need something else? What the acquisition community and Air Force Space Command came up with for an answer was the FEWS program.

While I agreed that we needed to improve upon the capabilities of DSP, my experiences running the battle staff at Air Force Space Command Headquarters during Desert Storm taught me that DSP could be pushed beyond its original design limits and could still do a good job in a tactical war.

So again, I began to question a "big ticket" space system. And again, I got predictable reactions from my friends at Space Command and within the space acquisition community at the Pentagon.

By April 1993, I knew that I was on a collision course and I needed to go out to Air Force Space Command Headquarters in Colorado Springs to confront my adversaries -- face-to-face. A few weeks before I left for Colorado, I received a warning from a fellow Colonel's wife in Colorado Springs. I learned that Space Command was actively working to have me fired. I had been told that their plan was to "cut off the head of the snake, while preserving the body." They wanted me terminated ... PERIOD. Further, they had a spy in my organization, who was gathering the necessary information to "take me out." Sixty days later the warnings proven valid.

I was removed and have not been allowed to participate in the budget reduction process since June 1993. I have been publicly defamed, humiliated and embarrassed. Despite all of that has happened I never lost faith in the Air Force or the American system of justice.

In conclusion, I am convinced the cost-cutting measures I recommended were proper, well-developed and in-line with President Clinton's policies. I believe that I was removed, because I was attempting to foster an open debate on expensive, unnecessary space programs and my opponents knew that when I held their systems up to the "clear light of day" -- <u>they would lose</u>. So, they decided to remove the source of their problem -- me. Throughout this unhappy experience, I come to the following conclusion:

- The cancer seems to isolated to the Space community within the Air Force. The Air Force leadership within the Pentagon has treated me fairly throughout this entire affair.

And I have a final thought:

- When I was a young assistant to a 3 star general, he always told me never to do anything that you would be embarrassed to read about in tomorrow's newspaper. Well, MILSTAR and FEWS embarrassed me and I stood up against them. My actions have probably cost me my career, but at some point everyone has to make a choice. I made mine, I do not regret it....and I would do it again.

Thank you for your time. If you have any questions, I will be happy to answer them.

Mr. CONYERS. Colonel Mangold, that is probably the most courageous and moving statement that I have heard as chairman of Government Operations, and I want to express on behalf of this committee the decision that you have made to come forward and all the things that you have done before today, that makes the American people feel very good about the kind and caliber of field grade officers that we have in our service. And we thank you for that very much.

Colonel MANGOLD. Thank you, Mr. Chairman.

Mr. CONYERS. I would like now to call Col. Edward Dietz and invite him to make a statement, Director of Acquisition Management and Directorate of Program Management at headquarters Air Force Material Command, Space and Missile Systems Center.

Welcome.

STATEMENT OF EDWARD R. DIETZ, COLONEL, U.S. AIR FORCE

Colonel DIETZ. Mr. Chairman, members of committee, I am Colonel Dietz of the U.S. Air Force. I was the DSP program manager during the period of interest to this hearing.

I am here by direction of the Air Force and the Congress. But I have been reminded that I cannot speak for the Air Force. I will be speaking from my personal experiences during the interval in which I served in this capacity. I look forward to contributing in whatever way I can.

I have served the United States for 27 years in development and acquisition of space and missile systems. I have worked for acquisition agencies, Headquarters Systems Command, the Secretary of the Air Force, and the Office of Secretary. In accordance with congressionally directed standards for training and experience, I am fully certified as a program manager.

The last 15 years in particular I worked on space systems much like the ones we are discussing today. Recently, I was the deputy program director of DSP, the Talon Shield program manager responsible for its development and installation, and until a few months ago I was the DSP program manager. I am qualified to discuss the alleged misconduct on the DSP/FEWS programs. I look forward to any questions you may have.

[The prepared statement of Colonel Dietz follows:]

OPENING STATEMENT

Mr Chairman and Members of the Committee:

I am Col Edward Dietz of the United States Air Force. I was the DSP Program Manager during the time period of interest to this hearing. I am here by direction of the USAF and the Congress. I look forward to contributing in whatever way I can.

I have served the United States for 27 years in development and acquisition of space and missile systems. I've worked for acquisition agencies, Hq Systems Command, Secretary of Air Force, and the Office of the Secretary. In accordance with Congressionally directed standards for training and experience, I'm fully certified as a Program Manager.

The last 15 years I worked on space systems like the ones we're discussing today. Recently I was Deputy Program Director for DSP, Talon Shield Program Manager responsible for it's development and installation, and until a few months ago I was the DSP Program Manager. I am qualified to discuss the alleged misconduct on the DSP/FEWS programs. I look forward to any questions you may have

Mr. CONYERS. Thank you for coming forward, Colonel Dietz, and we do have questions for you.

Mr. Guido Aru, we are pleased that you would join this panel. Project leader, system architecture and integration, space-based surveillance division of the Aerospace Corp. And we have your 34 pages of testimony. We have your background and know you to be a highly qualified expert in this area. And we are pleased that you could join us today. You may proceed.

STATEMENT OF GUIDO W. ARU, PROJECT LEADER, SYSTEM ARCHITECTURE AND INTEGRATION, SPACE-BASED SURVEILLANCE DIVISION, THE AEROSPACE CORP.

Mr. ARU. Mr. Chairman and distinguished members of the committee, good morning and thank you for the opportunity to testify before the committee.

I have been involved with space surveillance systems for over 10 years, the last 6 years at the Aerospace Corp. The corporation, however, has asked me to emphasize to you that I am here testifying as a private citizen and not a representative of the corporation.

Mr. Chairman, I do have a prepared statement which I will summarize, but I request that my full statement be made part of the record.

Mr. CONYERS. That will be so ordered.

Mr. ARU. Early last year I led a congressionally mandated study of ways to upgrade the DSP system as an alternative to FEWS. The study concluded that as much as $10 billion could be saved. The results of this study were documented in an Aerospace Corp. report which is commonly known as the DSP-II report.

In my statement, I describe how senior leadership of the Air Force and the Aerospace Corp. attempted to suppress and then discredit the conclusions of this congressionally mandated study. I also describe how certain individuals have systematically provided misleading and false information to the Office of the Secretary of Defense and the Congress in order to justify the FEWS program.

In my statement, I also testified that the Air Force and Aerospace leadership of the space-based early warning system program office provided proprietary data from a DSP contractor to the FEWS contractors in order to gain their assistance in discrediting the study of DSP upgrades. Finally, I detailed the retributive actions taken against some of the individuals who participated in the study.

Despite the efforts of the Air Force and the Aerospace Corp. to suppress and discredit the DSP-II study, OSD did eventually hear of its conclusions and commissioned several independent review teams to assess the situation. The Institute for Defense Analysis was chartered to review and assess the DSP-II report. They concluded that, "DSP-II is a technically sound, low-risk concept and represents what a good program manager would come up with for fixing known problems."

Mr. Everett was asked by Dr. Deutch to form a technical support group to review the DSP and FEWS programs and provide him—Dr. Deutch—with recommendations. Mr. Everett concluded that the DSP-II concept was the lowest cost early warning option and represented a savings of about $6 billion when compared to the restructured FEWS program proposed by the Air Force. His analysis showed that there was only, "marginal advantage," to FEWS as compared with DSP for counter-force operations such as the Scud-hunting missions in Desert Storm.

Mr. Everett also concluded that the multiyear procurement of DSP satellites 23, 24, and 25 was essential to ensure the continued readiness of our strategic and tactical missile warning capabilities.

The end result of these independent reviews was a decision by Dr. Deutch to cancel FEWS. Dr. Deutch also directed the Air Force to review the early warning requirements and construct a new program which would begin in 1998.

Mr. Chairman, I am concerned that the same individuals who previously attempted to mislead and suppress information from OSD and congressional decisionmakers remain in charge of executing Dr. Deutch's directives. Some of these individuals have already tried to subvert Dr. Deutch's decision. They have proposed the cancellation of the current multiyear procurement of DSP satellites 23, 24, and 25, and have advocated initiating a new program without any detailed review of the requirements.

These individuals also continue to ignore the potential for cost-effective technology insertion and preplanned product improvements which could enhance DSP's performance and extend the useful life of the satellites already built and paid for.

The financial and national security consequences of decisions on our Nation's early warning programs are enormous. The integrity of the institutions and the individuals making such decisions must be beyond reproach.

Mr. Chairman, Colonel Mangold, Colonel Dietz, and I appear before you today because our experiences illustrate that there are serious problems with the institutions entrusted to acquire and operate our Nation's military space systems. Our experiences also illustrate that these problems are not just institutional, but involve unethical and perhaps illegal conduct by some of its senior leadership.

The three of us, each in our own area of responsibility, attempted to identify ways to provide military space capabilities consistent with a post-cold war world and the fiscal constraints of a declining defense budget. We unfortunately discovered that our Nation's military space institutions and their leadership are more concerned with their own parochial interests.

Vice President Gore has challenged all of us involved in government procurement to uphold the public trust and treat the taxpayers' hard-earned dollars with respect. The Vice President wrote in his report on reinventing government that, "the national performance review can reduce the deficit further, but it is not just about cutting spending. It is also about closing the trust deficit; proving to the American people that their tax dollars will be treated with respect for the hard work that earned them."

President Clinton and Vice President Gore also said during their campaign that, "we must reward the people and ideas that work and get rid of those that don't."

Mr. Chairman, we do not ask for a reward for the ideas that we have put forward. We only ask for your help in completing the formidable task that we unknowingly started, the task of reforming our Nation's military space institutions for the post-cold war era.

Mr. Chairman, this concludes my statement. I will be happy to answer any questions you or the members of the committee may have.

[The prepared statement of Mr. Aru follows:]

Statement Of

Mr. GUIDO WILLIAM ARU

Project Leader, System Architecture and Integration
Space-Based Surveillance Division
The Aerospace Corporation

Before The

HOUSE OF REPRESENTATIVES
COMMITTEE ON GOVERNMENT OPERATIONS
LEGISLATION AND NATIONAL SECURITY SUBCOMMITTEE

February 2, 1994

Statement of Mr. Guido Aru   February 2, 1994

Biography .... *iii*

I. *Introduction* *1*

II. *Congressionally-Mandated DSP Upgrade Study* *3*
    Suppression Of DSP Upgrade Study Results From OSD And Congress ... 3
    Suppression Of Information Within The Air Force 5

III. *The Disinformation Campaign* *6*

IV. *The Aerospace Corporation's DSP-II Report* *8*
    Recall Of The DSP-II Report 8
    Unauthorized Disclosure Of Competition Sensitive Information 10
    Suppression And Discredit Of The DSP-II Report 11

V. *The Bottom-Up Review* *16*
    DSP And FEWS Performance Estimates 17
    DSP And FEWS Cost Estimates 18

VI. *Retribution* *20*
    Retribution Against Aerospace Employees 20
    Retribution Against Others 22

VII. *Space-Based Early Warning Issues And Recommendations* *23*
    Threats - Real And Imagined 24
    The Repercussions Of Terminating The DSP Block 23 Contract 25
    The Spinning Satellite Myth 27
    Potential Alternatives To A New Early Warning System Program 28
    Recommendations On Space-Based Early Warning 31

VIII. *Conclusions* *33*

THE AEROSPACE CORPORATION

Biography

Mr. Guido William Aru

Mr. Aru is the Project Leader for the System Architecture and Integration Section of the Space-Based Surveillance Division of The Aerospace Corporation. He is responsible for the system architecture and integration of the Defense Support Program (DSP), Follow-on Early Warning System (FEWS) and Talon Shield programs. He leads a team which is responsible for performing concept analysis, planning and recommending technical direction so that present and future early warning system architectures meet the strategic and tactical users' requirements. He also performs systems analysis and system comparison studies, including technical risk management, cost, and schedule assessments, to help ensure the proper integration between military requirements, technical capability and fiscal constraints.

Previously, Mr. Aru was a Project Engineer in the Special Applications Directorate. He was responsible for providing general system engineering and integration support to various Army and Navy space initiatives, specifically in the application of space surveillance systems to meet the tactical warfighters' needs. He provided analysis and technical recommendations which contributed to the Army's successful execution of the Tactical Surveillance Demonstration (TSD) program. The TSD program served as the basis for the Air Force's Talon Shield program and the joint Army/Navy Joint Tactical Ground Station (JTaGS) program.

Prior to joining Aerospace in 1987, Mr. Aru was the Lead Engineer for tactical applications of the Defense Support Program at Aerojet ElectroSystems. He was responsible for executing Air Force and Navy programs to study and implement systems which provide tactical exploitation of DSP and other space-based surveillance systems.

Mr. Aru was born on July 20, 1963 in Los Angeles, California. He pursued undergraduate studies in chemistry and computer science at San Bernardino Valley College and The University of Redlands. He earned a bachelor of science degree in computer science from National University, and he has completed thirty units of graduate studies in computer science.

Mr. Aru holds DoD Top Secret, Sensitive Compartmented Information, and other national security clearances. His Special Background Investigation was last updated in August 1993.

(Current as of January 1994)

Statement of Mr. Guido Aru   February 2, 1994

I. Introduction

Mr. Chairman and distinguished members of the Committee:

Good Morning, and thank you for this opportunity to testify before the committee. I am the Project Leader for the System Architecture and Integration Section of the Space-Based Surveillance Division at The Aerospace Corporation; this division has responsibility for the Defense Support Program (DSP), Follow-On Early Warning System (FEWS) and Talon Shield programs. The Aerospace Corporation, however, has asked me to emphasize that I am testifying as a private citizen and not as a representative of the Corporation.

I have been involved with space surveillance systems for over ten years; the last six years at Aerospace and previously with Aerojet ElectroSystems, the manufacturer of the infrared sensor for the DSP satellite. I am currently ranked in the top 15% of my division of fifty-four people, and my salary/maturity curve rating places me in the top 10% of the corporation overall.

My testimony this morning will detail how senior leadership of the Air Force and The Aerospace Corporation attempted to suppress and then discredit a Congressionally-mandated study which showed that potential upgrades to the DSP system could provide between $6 and $10 billion in savings compared to the acquisition of FEWS. I will describe how certain individuals have systematically provided misleading and false information to the Office of the Secretary of Defense (OSD) and Congress in order to justify the FEWS program. I will also testify that the Air Force and Aerospace leadership of the Space-Based Early Warning System Program Office provided proprietary data from a DSP contractor to the FEWS contractors in order to gain their assistance in discrediting the study of DSP upgrades. Finally, I will detail the retributive actions taken against some of the individuals who participated in the study of DSP upgrades.

I conclude my testimony with my thoughts on some of the issues confronting Space Based Early Warning. I also provide some suggestions for consideration by Air Force, OSD, and Congressional decision-makers.

Statement of Mr. Guido Aru February 2, 1994

Mr. Chairman: Colonel Mangold, Colonel Dietz, and I appear before you today because our experiences illustrate that there are serious problems with the institutions entrusted to acquire and operate our Nation's military space systems. Our experiences also illustrate that these problems are not just institutional, but involve unethical and perhaps illegal conduct by some of its senior leadership.

The three of us, each in our own area of responsibility, attempted to identify ways to provide military space capabilities consistent with a post-Cold War world and the fiscal constraints of a declining defense budget. We unfortunately discovered that the leadership of our Nation's military space institutions are more concerned with protecting their own parochial interests.

Vice President Gore has challenged all of us involved in Government procurement to uphold the public trust and treat the taxpayer's hard-earned dollars with respect. The Vice President wrote in his report on *Reinventing Government*, that:

> "The National Performance Review can reduce the deficit further, but it is not just about cutting spending. It is also about closing the *trust* deficit: proving to the American people that their tax dollars will be treated with respect for the hard work that earned them."

President Clinton and Vice President Gore also said during their campaign that:

> "We must reward the people and ideas that work and get rid of those that don't."

Mr. Chairman, we do not ask for a reward for the ideas that we have put forward. We only ask for your help in completing the formidable task that we unknowingly started: the task of reforming our Nation's military space institutions for the post-Cold War era.

Statement of Mr. Guido Aru   February 2, 1994

II. Congressionally-Mandated DSP Upgrade Study

From November 1992 through June 1993 I was the leader of a study to determine how an upgraded Defense Support Program and the planned Brilliant Eyes (BE) system could together meet the Nation's Tactical Warning/Attack Assessment (TW/AA) and Global Protection Against Limited Strike (GPALS) requirements. This study was conducted in response to fiscal year 1992 Congressional Language requesting that the Air Force review and provide an assessment of alternatives to their plans for the acquisition of the FEWS and Brilliant Eyes programs.

At the direction of the Air Force, my study team consisted of not only engineers from The Aerospace Corporation, but also personnel from the DSP contractors (Aerojet and TRW), an independent cost analysis contractor (Tecolote), and the Air Force itself. Colonel Edward Dietz and Major Roger Hall were my principal Air Force counterparts for the study. The study determined that a series of evolutionary upgrades could be made to the DSP satellite and ground processing system which would improve performance and reduce life-cycle costs. Independent cost analysis performed by Tecolote showed that this concept, which has become known as DSP-II, would save over $3 billion in the Future Years Defense Plan (FYDP) (95-99) and approximately $10 billion life-cycle through the year 2015 when compared with the baseline FEWS program. The study also demonstrated that a synergistic DSP-II/BE system could meet the Tactical Warning/Attack Assessment and GPALS requirements. The Government spent approximately $500,000 to conduct this study.

Suppression Of DSP Upgrade Study Results From OSD And Congress

Major General Garry Schnelzer and Lt. Colonel Jeff Norton (Air Force Space Command) were briefed on the conclusions of the study on February 3, 1993. Major General Schnelzer rejected the DSP-II concept with the stated reason that it did not employ direct satellite-to-satellite communications crosslinks and space-based mission processing which were Air Force requirements. Major General Schnelzer ordered that the DSP-II concept be replaced with a 1991-vintage DSP upgrade concept known as DSP++. This concept had been previously

Statement of Mr. Guido Aru — February 2, 1994

rejected by the Air Force during the 1991 Cost and Operational Effectiveness Analysis for FEWS because it was not cost-effective and did not meet the Air Force's requirements. DSP++ did not offer any significant performance advantages over DSP-II, but its costs were comparable to FEWS whereas DSP-II offered significant savings. Major General Schnelzer's rejection of DSP-II and inclusion of DSP++ was done over the objections of the DSP Program Director, Colonel John Kidd and his deputy, Colonel Edward Dietz.

I would like to note that the JCS validated requirements for space-based early warning were documented in the 11 page Joint Requirements Oversight Council Memorandum 2-91 (JROCM-002-91) dated February 4, 1991. Air Force Space Command had also drafted a 100 page, unapproved, Operational Requirements Document for the Follow-on Early Warning System, dated October 7, 1992. This draft document included requirements which greatly exceeded those specified and approved by the JROC, and it included requirements which are physically impossible for any system, including FEWS, to achieve. Furthermore, many of the requirements specified in the Air Force Space Command document were derived from now obsolete Cold War strategies of fighting a protracted global nuclear war.

On May 21, 1993 Major General Schnelzer submitted his report to Congress which included the DSP++ option and excluded DSP-II. The exclusion of DSP-II allowed Major General Schnelzer to conclude his report with the finding that "For (the) TW/AA Mission FEWS Provides The Least _Cost_ Option." The Air Force Inspector General's investigation, conducted by Major General Marcus Anderson, concluded that Major General Schnelzer "had a good reason" to suppress the DSP-II concept from OSD and Congress because DSP-II did not meet the Air Force's requirements. Major General Anderson did not address the fact that the DSP++ did not meet the Air Force's requirements either, although virtually every page of Major General Schnelzer's report which discussed the DSP++ was marked with a statement saying "DSP++ does not meet requirements." Major General Anderson also did not address the fact that Major General Schnelzer greatly understated DSP's performance and overstated the estimates of FEWS' performance in his report.

Statement of Mr. Guido Aru February 2, 1994

When OSD directed at the end of May, 1993 that another DSP option should be included, Major General Schnelzer again ignored the DSP-II option and submitted an option known as "DSP Forever" or "DSP-26." This option was to simply build cookie-cutter DSP Block 23 satellites through the year 2015. This option was a twenty-year procurement with no allowance for investment in technology insertion or pre-planned product improvements to reduce life-cycle costs and enhance capabilities. As a result, DSP-Forever's performance was less than that achievable with DSP-II, but its costs were significantly higher -- as with DSP++, the costs were comparable to FEWS. Colonel Dietz, who was then the DSP Program Manager, and I both protested vigorously, but unsuccessfully, against the DSP-Forever option and the continued exclusion of DSP-II.

The Air Force's views on the issue of upgrading DSP versus acquiring FEWS are summarized in Brigadier General Dickman's February 10, 1993 letter to Major General Schnelzer, written after his representative, Lt. Colonel Norton, was briefed on DSP-II:

> "You stated an Air Force position in the 3 February meeting that I would like to echo. The Vice Chief position was that FEWS was, and is, the Air Force and DoD ITW/AA solution of choice - supported by JROC-validated requirements, supported by full funding in the BES, supported by two Air Force summits, and supported by a Milestone I DAB review."

In my opinion, this shows the Air Force was never interested in doing the analysis and answering the question asked by the Congress: the Air Force already had the answer it wanted.

Suppression Of Information Within The Air Force

The Air Force also withheld information on DSP-II from its own personnel responsible for establishing its budget. Colonel Sanford Mangold was the Resource Allocation Team Chief for the Air Force's Space, Command and Control, Intelligence, and Nuclear Deterrence programs from June 1, 1992 through June 23, 1993. Colonel Mangold was told of the DSP++, DSP-Forever, and FEWS budget requirements, but he was never informed of the DSP-II option and its potential cost savings.

Statement of Mr. Guido Aru February 2, 1994

III. The Disinformation Campaign

In parallel with the preparation of Major General Schnelzer's report to Congress, Major General Donald Hard testified before Congress on the need for the FEWS program. On May 11, 1993, before the House Committee on Appropriations Subcommittee on the Department of Defense, Major General Hard testified for the record that:

> "The Air Force and the Department of Defense have looked at the issue of continuing DSP, upgrading DSP or developing a new system such as FEWS many times in recent years. The answer keeps coming back to the development of a new system. This...has been reviewed again in an Air Force study now being prepared for Congress.... We have studied a number of ways to incorporate changes to DSP...the cost of incorporating these changes quickly approaches the cost of development and producing a new system like FEWS" (ref. Hearing pages 391 and 392).

I believe Major General Hard's testimony was misleading. The DSP-II option briefed to Major General Schnelzer on February 3, 1993 showed DSP could be upgraded at a savings of approximately $10 billion compared to the baseline FEWS program. Subsequent analysis of DSP-II and comparison against a reduced-cost FEWS (with less capability than the baseline FEWS) showed DSP-II would still save approximately $6 billion. These savings were subsequently validated by Mr. Everett, The Institute for Defense Analysis (IDA), and the DoD Cost Analysis Improvement Group (CAIG). In addition, a GAO report on Early Warning Satellites dated November 1991, prepared for the House Committee on Appropriations Subcommittee on the Department of Defense, concluded that:

> "... there are indications that an enhanced DSP could be nearly as effective and would cost billions of dollars less than a fully capable FEWS. Five separate studies provide a basis for these conclusions."

Statement of Mr. Guido Aru   February 2, 1994

During questioning by Mr. Young on the performance of FEWS compared with DSP, Major General Hard answered twice that:

> "...with FEWS we can get accuracies that allow us to tell the Scud hunter in the F-16 where to look, within an area about the size of RFK stadium, instead of an area the size of Washington, D.C." (ref. Hearing page 393).

Major General Hard's testimony was incorrect. DSP's real-time launch site estimates reported during Desert Storm were significantly smaller than an area the size of Washington, D.C. In addition, the DSP ground processing improvements advanced by the Army's Tactical Surveillance Demonstration (TSD) program and adopted by the Air Force under the Talon Shield program provide missile launch point estimation which is comparable to the FEWS specification. A Technical Support Group headed by Mr. Robert Everett compared DSP and FEWS at the request of Dr. John Deutch, Under Secretary of Defense for Acquisition and Technology. Mr. Everett concluded that FEWS provides only "marginal advantage" over DSP for launch point estimation.

General Charles Horner, who cited FEWS as his number one priority program, has also provided similar misinformation in testimony before the Senate and in briefings to General McPeak and OSD. It is interesting to note that Major General Hard was hired by The Aerospace Corporation immediately after his retirement last fall. Mr. Hard is now the General Manager for Aerospace in Colorado Springs, and one of his primary missions is to expand the company's support to US Space Command and Air Force Space Command, both headed by General Horner.

Statement of Mr. Guido Aru   February 2, 1994

IV. The Aerospace Corporation's DSP-II Report

Major General Schnelzer's report to Congress coincided with the distribution of the Aerospace DSP-II report. This report was prepared at the direction of Colonel Kidd and Colonel Dietz to document the DSP-II concept; they provided this direction in February 1993 after Major General Schnelzer rejected DSP-II from consideration for his report to Congress. The 500 page DSP-II report documents a technology insertion and pre-planned product improvement approach to achieve an upgraded DSP system with reduced life-cycle costs. Performance improvements would be achieved through upgrades of the satellite's infrared sensor and enhancement of the ground processing based on concepts proven by the Tactical Surveillance Demonstration and Talon Shield programs. Life-cycle costs would be reduced by life-extension enhancements to the satellites and the use of the Atlas IIAS medium launch vehicle versus the Titan IV used today.

The DSP-II report compared the cost, risk, performance and schedule of the proposed DSP-II with the Air Force's baseline FEWS program. The report questioned the military utility of some of the FEWS requirements relative to a budget-constrained post-Cold War world. The report addressed the potential use of non-space systems, such as in-theater radars, to address some of the draft requirements levied on FEWS by Air Force Space Command. The report did not make any recommendations with regard to the FEWS program, but it did recommend that technology insertion and pre-planned product improvements be applied to the DSP satellites already built and in storage to increase their performance and extend their operational life. The report also recommended that evolutionary ground processing improvements be made to increase system performance. The report stated that these were cost effective improvements which should be undertaken regardless of the destiny of FEWS.

Recall Of The DSP-II Report

General Horner was informed of the DSP-II report and its comparisons of DSP-II and FEWS on May 20, 1993. On that day, General Horner telephoned Mr. E.C. "Pete" Aldridge, the

Statement of Mr. Guido Aru					February 2, 1994

President of The Aerospace Corporation. Mr. Aldridge then ordered the DSP-II report recalled. In a May 24, 1993 letter from General Horner to Mr. Aldridge, General Horner said that the DSP-II report "was flawed technically, operationally, and politically." General Horner also wrote, "This kind of 'work' is unprofessional and is not representative of the type of government-industry team I want -- especially when it ends up in Washington in the Navy Staff. Please help." However, in a handwritten note attached to his letter, General Horner added, "If I'm wrong educate me..." General Horner's letter and his conclusions are particularly interesting, however, since at the time neither US Space Command nor Air Force Space Command had received a copy of the DSP-II report - they had only received a few unclassified pages from the executive summary.

Mr. Aldridge wrote General Horner on June 22, 1993 saying that there was "no excuse for the advocacy tone of the report." He also wrote that he had counseled all the employees on this issue, and that "The role of program advocacy should be played, if at all, by the military program office, the military services or other government agencies." Mr. Aldridge then concluded his letter by writing, "On a final note, I am most disturbed about the 'rumor' that Aerospace does not support FEWS.... FEWS is the only system that will give us confidence in providing launch warning and tactical missile defense tip-off." Mr. Aldridge also wrote that he had called Dr. John Deutch and Dr. George Schneiter to explain the situation and that he also talked to Major General Hard and Major General Schnelzer "to determine what else we can do to put this issue to rest."

Major General Anderson concludes in his investigation that "Mr. Aldridge ordered the recall of the Aerospace (report). He did so initially to read the report, then he affirmed the decision after review by an independent Aerospace team." That independent team initially tried to discredit the report, but their analysis was subsequently shown to be flawed. The IDA conducted a four-month review of the DSP-II report and found that "DSP-II is a technically sound, low risk concept" and "It represents what a good program manager would come up with for fixing known problems and reducing life-cycle costs." It is interesting to note that Mr. James Slattery, who headed Aerospace's independent review team, was promoted to Principal Director for the FEWS program shortly after completing his review of DSP-II.

Statement of Mr. Guido Aru   February 2, 1994

Unauthorized Disclosure Of Competition Sensitive Information

The Space-Based Early Warning System Program Director, Colonel Joseph Bailey, and his Aerospace Corporation counterpart, Mr. John Parsons (General Manager, Space-Based Surveillance Division), provided the DSP-II report to the FEWS contractors, TRW and Lockheed Missiles and Space Company (LMSC) in an effort to help discredit and refute the report. The DSP-II report was specifically provided to Mr. Elliot Bailis, TRW's FEWS program manager, and Mr. Wayne Craft, a senior executive at LMSC responsible for military utility analysis of FEWS. Mr. Craft is a retired Air Force Colonel and former DSP Program Director.

The Aerospace DSP-II report contains "Competition Sensitive" information from Aerojet ElectroSystems, one of the DSP contractors. The DSP-II report is explicitly marked with the restriction that it is not releasable outside the U.S. Government and The Aerospace Corporation. The report was provided to TRW and LMSC after normal business hours on Friday May 21, 1993 and again on Saturday May 22, 1993. This action was taken only hours after I specifically told Colonel Bailey and Mr. Parsons in a 10 AM meeting on May 21, 1993 that the report contained "Competition Sensitive" material and could not be provided to contractors. I told them this in response to their request that I prepare a version of the report for release to the FEWS contractors. When they continued to insist that I prepare a releasable version of the report, I told them that it must first be reviewed with the Air Force and Aerospace's legal offices as well as with Aerojet since it included their data. I also told them that this could not be done immediately since Aerojet is on a four-day work week and they are closed on Fridays.

Despite the restrictive markings on the document and my personal statements to them, Colonel Bailey and Mr. Parsons elected to provide the report to Aerojet's competitors. Although I am not qualified to judge whether their actions are in violation of the Procurement Integrity Act or the Trade Secrets Act, I do know that they violate the ethical standards that those of us involved with Government procurement are expected to abide by. Major General Anderson's report states that this incident "was investigated by a separate inquiry which concluded that proprietary data was, in fact, inappropriately released."

Statement of Mr. Guido Aru   February 2, 1994

Suppression And Discredit Of The DSP-II Report

Major General Anderson's report substantiated "that the Government attempted to discredit the Aerospace (report)." Major General Anderson concluded, however, that: "This is an unusual situation because the Government and the leadership of Aerospace Corporation (Mr. Pete Aldridge) had good reason to discredit the report. It had not been coordinated with the user or the PEO, had been approved at an intermediate level at Aerospace, discounted JROC-validated requirements, and was written in advocacy tone. Mr Aldridge was embarrassed with the report, as was the Air Force about the content and the way the report was coordinated and distributed." These conclusions demonstrate a clear misunderstanding of the proper role and mission of The Aerospace Corporation and its policies and procedures.

The role and mission of The Aerospace Corporation is to perform objective analysis and make recommendations to our customer. This is established in Air Force SSD Regulation 800-8, dated March 13, 1992, which sets out the policies and procedures for The Aerospace Corporation. Paragraph (1) and (2.a) define Aerospace's General System Engineering and Integration (GSE&I) responsibilities to include:

> "providing cost/benefit analyses for changes or additions; and providing comments and recommendations in writing to the Government Program Director and/or Project Officer as an independent technical assessment for modifying the program."

In the case of the DSP-II report the customer was the DSP System Program Office, and the report was requested and approved by the DSP System Program Director, Colonel Kidd. There was and is no requirement to coordinate with the user and the PEO for such reports. Nor, in my opinion, should there be because it would inhibit Aerospace from being objective in assessing military requirements relative to technical capabilities and fiscal constraints. Aerospace would simply become a publisher of position papers for the user and the PEO, which I do not believe is an appropriate role for an FFRDC.

House Committee On Government Operations
Legislation And National Security Subcommittee

Statement of Mr. Guido Aru   February 2, 1994

Paragraph (5.c) of Regulation 800-8 states that:

> "Aerospace will designate a Systems Engineering Director or Principal Director for each program for which the Corporation is assigned a GSE&I role. The Aerospace Director will act on behalf of the Corporation in discharging Aerospace's contractual responsibility to the Air Force."

The DSP-II report was reviewed and approved by Mrs. Barbara Ching, Associate Principal Director for Systems Engineering for DSP, and by Mr. Everett Bersinger, Principal Director for the DSP Program. This approval was consistent with Regulation 800-8 and with internal company policies and practices. Unclassified sections of the report were provided to Mr. Richard Allman, Vice-President For Space Program Operations, at his request for review one month prior to publication, but I received no comments. My previous manager, Dr. Philip Diamond, Principal Director For Special Applications, reviewed the cost, performance and risk comparisons between DSP-II and FEWS with Dr. George Paulikas, Executive Vice-President of The Aerospace Corporation. Dr. Paulikas asked Dr. Diamond to have me complete the report and put him (Dr. Paulikas) on the distribution list. On August 18, 1993 Dr. Paulikas told me, "I read your report, all five hundred pages, and thought it was an excellent technical report. It is the type of work Aerospace should be doing."

In regard to the contention that the report "discounted" JROC-validated requirements, the DSP-II report did not discount either validated or unapproved requirements. It assessed them for their military utility relative to their cost and technical risk. This was justified because one of the key value-added functions of The Aerospace Corporation is to help ensure the sensibility and cost effectiveness of the military requirements for space systems. This is clearly delineated in the Mission Statement of The Aerospace Corporation, a portion of which reads:

> "The Aerospace Corporation shall perform system engineering and integration; shall recommend technical direction; shall work closely with the U.S. Air Force in long range planning, systems analysis and systems comparison studies, including technical risk management, cost, and schedule assessments. The Aerospace Corporation reviews ideas and concepts generated throughout industry and government, and helps to ensure the proper integration between military requirements, technical capability and fiscal constraints."

Statement of Mr. Guido Aru February 2, 1994

The DSP-II report questioned the military utility of many of the **unapproved** requirements proposed by Air Force Space Command in their draft Operational Requirements Document for FEWS. The report also addressed the cost and risk associated with meeting these requirements. The report concluded that many of the unapproved Air Force requirements were excessive in a post-Cold War world. Requirements related to survivability in a protracted global nuclear war are included in this category. The report also concluded that many of the unapproved requirements were un-achievable by any system, including FEWS, because they violate the laws of physics, or as Dr. Paulikas remarked to me during a discussion on August 18, 1993: "Some (of the FEWS requirements) violate the laws of physics and thermodynamics simultaneously."

The IDA, in its review of the DSP-II report, concluded that the "current requirements (for FEWS) are not justified" and that they were "developed when policy was nuclear war-fighting" and that the "requirements (are) difficult to justify even under this policy." IDA also concluded that the system drivers of sensitivity, revisit rate, and processing for FEWS are "highly questionable."

As far as the distribution of the DSP-II report is concerned, this was also done in accordance with all applicable policies and practices. According to Regulation 800-8 Paragraph (4.d.3.6) the System Program Director "Reviews, accepts/approves and processes technical reports (TRs) and reviews, approves, or revises the distribution list for Technical Operating Reports (TORs) delivered by Aerospace for fulfillment of contractual requirements." The DSP-II report was included in the TOR category. Its distribution was approved by Colonel Kidd, who was then the DSP System Program Director. The content of the DSP-II report was also approved by Colonel Kidd because, as permitted under Regulation 800-8 Paragraph (5.c.2), the Air Force provided some of the cost and schedule data used in the report.

In his June 22, 1993 letter to General Horner, Mr. Aldridge says that "It was the unauthorized distribution (of the DSP-II report) which caused the problem." As required by Regulation 800-8 Paragraph (4.d.3.6), Colonel Kidd approved the distribution list which included Mr. Dudley Reese of the Navy Space Systems Activity at Los Angeles Air Force Base. Colonel Kidd also

Statement of Mr. Guido Aru   February 2, 1994

approved the Distribution Statement which stated "Secondary distribution authorized to U.S. Government agencies and The Aerospace Corporation." Therefore, any secondary distribution to government agencies such as the Navy Staff in Washington, OSD, and Congress was authorized. The only unauthorized distribution of which I am aware was the distribution of the report to the FEWS contractors.

As to why Mr. Aldridge was embarrassed by the report, you will have to ask him. If asked, I would speculate that he was embarrassed because the DSP-II report raised the possibility that The Aerospace Corporation's long-term support of the FEWS program was not justified. For example, our public 1992 Annual Report, states:

> "The (Aerospace developed simulation) was used to analyze the benefits of the Follow-On Early Warning System (FEWS) in support of DoD decision processes.... The Aerospace activities were instrumental in the program's entrance into a two-year demonstration and validation phase."

In his June 22, 1993 letter to General Horner, Mr. Aldridge wrote "FEWS is the only system that will give us confidence in providing launch warning and tactical missile defense tip-off." Our internal semi-annual Technical Reports to our Board of Trustees, however, paint a different picture. Every report since December, 1992 states:

> "FEWS designs have been driven by strategic requirements and the strategic concept of operations.... Concerns have been raised by some users (e.g., the Navy and Army) that FEWS may not be configured to fully support their future needs.... The military war-fighting added value of enhanced surveillance information has been somewhat difficult to quantify, as clear metrics have not been delineated. An understanding of how end-users will and can take advantage of accurate and timely surveillance data must be established, so that tradeoffs of military utility can be performed."

The DSP-II report provided a review and assessment of the military utility of a lower-cost surveillance system. The subsequent independent reviews of DSP and FEWS by the Bottom-Up Review, the IDA, Mr. Everett's Technical Support Group, and OSD concluded that FEWS was unnecessary.

Statement of Mr. Guido Aru   February 2, 1994

I would also speculate that Mr. Aldridge may have been concerned about challenging General Horner's "number one priority program" given that Aerospace was and is actively trying to expand our business base with US Space Command and Air Force Space Command. These are both headed by General Horner. Mr. Aldridge may also have been concerned about the more immediate impact on The Aerospace Corporation's budget if the FEWS program were to be canceled. Aerospace's funding is determined on a program-by-program basis, and FEWS accounts for approximately 4%-5% of Aerospace's total budget.

Statement of Mr. Guido Aru   February 2, 1994

V. *The Bottom-Up Review*

Despite the efforts of the Air Force and The Aerospace Corporation to suppress the DSP-II report, news of its conclusions reached OSD and eventually Congress. One of the Navy's representatives at Space and Missile Systems Center sent their copy of the report to his superiors in the Pentagon on May 24, 1993 as the Air Force was attempting to retrieve it from him. Mr. Derek Vander Schaaf, the acting DoD Inspector General, had a copy of the report seized from the Air Force on May 26, 1993 to ensure that at least one copy would survive.

On June 8, 1993 Dr. William Lynn, Director for Program Analysis and Evaluation, wrote Dr. Deutch saying that DSP should be included in the Bottom-Up Review. Dr. Lynn wrote:

> "The Air Force staff has rejected the DSP-II/BE alternative primarily because it does not meet requirements, and also maintains that the Aerospace report understates the technical risks and costs of DSP-II. Given the FY 95-99 fiscal outlook, however, we need to consider seriously alternatives that may fall short of meeting all established requirements yet offer the potential for significantly lower costs."

The Bottom-Up Review of DSP and FEWS was headed by Dr. George Schneiter. Dr. Deutch also appointed Mr. Robert Everett to head an independent Technical Support Group with the tasking to "Review and recommend options for future U.S. space-based infrared surveillance capability." The Space-Based Early Warning System (SBEWS) System Program Office (SPO) supported both the Bottom-Up Review and Mr. Everett's review. Colonel Jeff Quirk, SBEWS Director for System Engineering, was responsible for the performance and cost estimates of the DSP and FEWS options evaluated in the reviews.

Although Mr. Everett requested that I brief his entire Technical Support Group on the DSP-II concept, his request was denied by Mr. Aldridge. Mr. Aldridge made this denial despite Mr. Lynn's letter and Major General Schnelzer's explicit request to fully cooperate with the OSD reviews. Mr. Aldridge later consented to allow the DSP-II development team to brief one member of Mr. Everett's group, Dr. Parney Albright of the IDA.

Statement of Mr. Guido Aru	February 2, 1994

DSP And FEWS Performance Estimates

In my opinion, the performance estimates submitted by the SBEWS SPO to OSD and Mr. Everett were misleading and biased towards FEWS. While it is not possible to discuss the specifics of the DSP and FEWS performance estimates in a unclassified forum, I can say that the estimates of DSP performance were poorer than the performance already demonstrated by the Army's Tactical Surveillance Demonstration Program (TSD) and specified for Talon Shield.

The DSP performance estimates provided by Colonel Quirk did not included the "projected upgrade" improvements which were included in the cost estimates provided to OSD. Approximately $1 billion was included in the cost estimates for DSP sensor and ground processing enhancements. The performance estimates also excluded the contribution of an additional "adjunct system," even though its costs, reported by Colonel Quirk as $4.3 billion, were included in the DSP cost estimates and not the FEWS estimates.

Colonel Bailey, in an October 13, 1993 letter to Major General Anderson, acknowledged that the DSP performance estimates prepared by Colonel Quirk ignored the "projected upgrade" performance and the contribution of the adjunct system. Colonel Bailey wrote:

> "DSP performance is quoted throughout the community in several ways, e.g.: (1) existing/demonstrated mono performance; (2) existing/demonstrated stereo performance; (3) spec values (DSP or Talon Shield); (4) Talon Shield-level stereo performance estimates; (5) other 'projected upgrade' performance estimates.... DSP Performance has been reported to AFSPACECOM, the Bottom-Up Review, and Mr. Everett's Technical Support Group in two ways: current DSP performance and DSP/Talon Shield which we have used to characterize future DSP system performance."

FEWS, on the other hand, was assumed to operate better than required by its classified specification. In my opinion, the optimistic projections of FEWS performance were inappropriate considering that:

Statement of Mr. Guido Aru February 2, 1994

(1) The FEWS program was only in the Demonstration/Validation Phase, with the preliminary design review still years away;

(2) Two contractors with radically different approaches were competing for the down-selection which was expected by mid-1994.

(3) The cost and risk estimates for FEWS were based on meeting specifications, not performance projections. In my experience, no one is likely to spend additional money to meet performance projections which, by the time the first FEWS satellite would have been delivered, would be ten years old.

Other people besides Colonel Dietz and myself expressed their concerns on the performance estimates being provided to OSD. For example, Major Roger Hall, Team Chief for Architecture and Integration in the SBEWS SPO, wrote a memorandum to Colonel Quirk that explained his position that:

"When there are many ways to answer questions of FEWS vs DSP, the answer chosen is usually the one which portrays FEWS to the best advantage."

Major Hall elaborated his concerns and provide details on how the performance comparisons of DSP and FEWS were contrived to portray FEWS in the best light. Major Hall concluded his memorandum to Colonel Quirk by writing:

"SPACECOM stated -- advertised -- publicized FEWS performance is becoming more and more overstated and incredulous (i.e., 'Washington, D.C. / football stadium charts', statements made about FEWS cueing based upon single hits, and General Horner's statements related to SS-21s, clouds, and low-altitude cruise missiles, etc.). Some of the more recent claims are probably beyond the capability and capacity of any space-based asset and may damage SPACECOM's credibility."

DSP And FEWS Cost Estimates

In my opinion, the DSP and FEWS cost estimates -- as well as the basis for those estimates -- were also biased towards FEWS and specifically constructed to prove General Horner's assertion that "FEWS is cheaper than DSP." Colonel Quirk manipulated the costing ground rules to

Statement of Mr. Guido Aru   February 2, 1994

ensure this. For example, for FEWS he assumed the entire DSP Block 23 satellite contract would be canceled at a savings of $700 million in satellite costs and $800 million in booster costs. For the DSP++ and DSP-26 options, he assumed that all DSP Block 23 satellites would be purchased. For DSP/MLV (aka. DSP-II) he assumed that only one of the three DSP Block 23 satellites would be purchased at a savings of $140 million from a $1.2 billion contract. Thus, for what is otherwise a low cost option, DSP-II was made to look worse by the addition of a single billion dollar satellite.

Colonel Quirk also manipulated the costs for an "adjunct system" which he claims was required by DSP, but not by FEWS. During the 1991 Cost and Operational Effectiveness Analysis for FEWS, the cost of this additional system was estimated at $1.1 billion (converted to FY93). In February, 1993 the cost of this system was re-estimated at $1.7 billion. In June, 1993 it was re-estimated at $2.1 billion. By August it had grown to $3.3 billion, and in September it jumped to $4.3 billion. Mr. Everett concluded, however, that this adjunct system was unnecessary for both DSP and FEWS.

No details were ever provided to justify these estimates -- they were hidden under the cloak of secrecy. I know the circumstances of these estimates, their constraints, and the other lower-cost options available which could provide the same capability. I cannot discuss these in an open forum, but I would do so in the proper environment. I would also note that I repeatedly asked to discuss these issues with Major General Anderson's investigators in a proper security environment, but they refused.

Statement of Mr. Guido Aru   February 2, 1994

VI. Retribution

The most unfortunate aspect of this experience has been the retribution taken against many of the individuals who worked on the DSP-II concept, and on some individuals who had nothing to do with DSP-II but were targeted for reasons that I can only describe as pure vengeance. The message being sent is clear -- oppose FEWS and you are history.

The actions of Major General Anderson's investigative staff helped to ensure that people understood the risks of speaking-out. During the investigation, his staff provided two subjects of his investigation (Colonel Quirk and Colonel Bailey) with confidential material originally provided to *this Congressional Committee* to assist it in its investigation. His staff also compromised a letter provided to Major General Anderson by Mr. Carl Fisher, President of Aerojet Electronic Systems Division. Mr. Fisher's letter, which was provided in confidence to Major General Anderson, detailed Aerojet's allegation of misconduct against SBEWS SPO and others. Everyone in the Program Office quickly learned of these compromises which occurred at the very beginning of Major General Anderson's investigation. My conversations with members of the SBEWS SPO confirm that this inhibited many people from being fully open with the investigators. The loss of anonymity could allow retribution -- the full story, therefore, has yet to be told.

Retribution Against Aerospace Employees

Many of The Aerospace Corporation employees who worked on the DSP-II concept and the report have subsequently suffered in their performance reviews. For example, of the seven non-supervisor employees from the DSP program office who worked on the report, all but one moved down in 1993s ranking relative to their ranking in 1992. Four of the seven employees were moved into the bottom third of the rankings where they are subject to lay-off. In the previous year, none of these people were in the bottom third, and only one was not ranked in the upper-half.

Statement of Mr. Guido Aru   February 2, 1994

One of the significant management changes that occurred coincident with the report was the promotion of Mr. Parsons to the position of General Manager with responsibility for both the DSP and FEWS programs on May 1, 1993. Mr. Parsons was previously the Principal Director for FEWS. In his new position, Mr. Parsons was responsible for establishing the rankings of the DSP employees.

Mr. Paul Montag, a Senior Project Engineer in the DSP Program Office, was responsible for performing satellite availability analysis. His analysis helped form the basis for the Air Force's original decision to procure the DSP Block 23 satellites. Mr. Montag also supported the DSP-II study by performing the analysis necessary to determine the number of satellites needed to operate the system through the year 2015. Although Mr. Montag was ranked in the upper-half in 1992, he was laid-off in October, 1993 by Mr. Parsons.

My principal co-author on the DSP-II report, Mr. Carl Lunde, also suffered in his performance review. Mr. Lunde has been at The Aerospace Corporation for over ten years and has always received excellent marks in his reviews. In October of 1993, however, Mr. Lunde was denigrated in his performance review by his management in the Engineering Group. This in spite of the fact that he was on-loan to my section in the Programs Group for nine months of the twelve-month review period, and that the manager who wrote Mr. Lunde's review was only his supervisor for the last two weeks of the review period.

Mrs. Ching, as the manager with day-to-day responsibility for Mr. Lunde during the nine months he was on loan, prepared a rebuttal. I also talked personally about Mr. Lunde's situation to Mr. Allen Boardman, Group Vice President for Administration, Mrs. Susan Lowenstam, Vice President, General Counsel and Secretary, and Dr. Paulikas. To date, the Corporation has not taken any steps to expunge Mr. Lunde's record of this derogatory review.

Statement of Mr. Guido Aru   February 2, 1994

Retribution Against Others

TRW's DSP Program Manager, Mrs. Joanne Maguire was recently reassigned and replaced by Mr. Elliot Bailis at the request of the Air Force. Some have asserted that this was done as retribution for TRW having raised allegations of Air Force impropriety to Dr. Deutch. This impropriety was the alleged delivery to LMSC of TRW's proprietary information on its multi-spectral sensor system. Mr. Bailis was previously TRW's FEWS Program Manager.

Mr. Fisher has alleged that:

> "In discussion with senior TRW executives, they asserted that they could not help because they had been threatened and intimidated by senior Air Force officers who warned TRW not to support opponents of FEWS."

Statement of Mr. Guido Aru   February 2, 1994

VII. Space-Based Early Warning Issues And Recommendations

The Air Force is currently proceeding with plans to terminate the Defense Support Program (DSP) Block 23 satellite contract in favor of a new program start. This effort was initiated based on claims made by specific contractors that they could build the DSP Block 23 satellites for less cost than the current contractors (TRW and Aerojet). This new start has been referred to as the "son of FEWS."

In my assessment, the termination of the DSP Block 23 contract goes against the best interests of the Government and our national security. It will result in a loss of approximately $500 million of the $1.2 billion contract without the delivery of any satellites. The Government's future liability and risk is also significantly increased through the termination of the Fixed-Price DSP Block 23 contract and the initiation of a new start under a Cost-Plus contract. Additional funds will also be required in the FYDP not only to support development of a new satellite, but also to accomplish the significant DSP ground processing and communications network changes required to accommodate a new spacecraft and sensor.

Our national capability to provide strategic early warning and theater missile surveillance will also be jeopardized by the termination of the DSP Block 23 contract. Mr. Everett found that the DSP constellation needs immediate replenishment due to its age and degraded state. Stretching out the launch of DSP Satellites 17-22 until a new satellite could be designed, developed, tested, and readied for launch will further degrade our capability to provide tactical ballistic missile surveillance in support of US and allied forces in the Middle East and Korea.

The decision to cancel the DSP Block 23 contract and initiate a new start is being conducted in a vacuum. No consideration is being given to OSD policy for exploring technology insertion and pre-planned product improvements to existing systems rather than initiating a new program start. No consideration is being given to the role of DSP or a new start within the context of other space-based IR programs, nor is any consideration being given to the role of space-based IR in the context of other strategic and theater surveillance programs. This is in spite of Congressional language from the past two years which has directed the Air Force and the OSD to examine the basis for the multiple existing and planned space-based infrared (IR) programs.

House Committee On Government Operations
Legislation And National Security Subcommittee

Statement of Mr. Guido Aru   February 2, 1994

Threats - Real And Imagined

The alleged threat "driving" the decision to cancel DSP Block 23 and initiate a new start is the proliferation of tactical missiles to the Third World. The principals in this action are ignoring the capabilities of DSP demonstrated during Desert Storm as well as the significant performance improvements provided by the Talon Shield and the Joint Tactical Ground Station (JTAGS) programs. They are also ignoring the performance achievable through data fusion with other space-based systems as well as in-theater organic surveillance assets.

General Horner has stated that a new system is required to detect extremely short-range Tactical Ballistic Missiles (TBMs). These include the SS-21, which has a range of approximately 140 km. This conclusion ignores the findings of the SDIO Phase One Engineering Team (POET), the IDA, and Mr. Everett's Technical Support Group which have all concluded that warning of missiles with ranges less than 300 km should be handled with in-theater systems, not space-based systems. These short-range TBMs burn out at low altitudes (below cloud-cover) and, therefore, are not detectable by space-based IR systems during the times they are most likely to be launched. During Desert Storm, for example, a number of the Iraqi TBM launches occurred under cloud cover to inhibit Scud hunting Coalition aircraft. Furthermore, space-based IR warning would not be timely enough to provide any significant utility due to the short flight time of these missiles.

This action will divert funds from other new systems required to defeat the real threat of the future - cruise missiles. Just as the US and the former Soviet Union have moved away from tactical ballistic missiles and towards cruise missiles, so will the Third World. Space-based IR systems such as DSP, FEWS, and the proposed new start have no capability against the low-altitude, air-breathing cruise missile threat. The decision we face is analogous to that faced by France in the mid-1930s. France had limited resources to prepare for World War II. Their General Staff believed the threat was another round of the trench warfare that had decimated France in the first War, so they sacrificed effective armored and air forces to build a better, "high-tech" trench known as the "Maginot Line." Unfortunately for France, the Germans had chosen mobile warfare over better trenches. As a result, the Germans merely bypassed the Maginot Line as they went on to crush France in the Spring of 1940.

Statement of Mr. Guido Aru   February 2, 1994

The Repercussions Of Terminating The DSP Block 23 Contract

The DSP Block 23 contract is a Multi-Year Procurement (MYP) for Satellites 23, 24, and 25. It is a Fixed-Price Incentive (FPI) contract valued at approximately $1.2 billion and includes effort required to support the launch of previously-built DSP Satellites 18-22. The contract was signed in June after two years of evaluation and negotiation. The recent Bottom-Up Review and Mr. Everett's Technical Support Group evaluation, both requested by Dr. Deutch, concluded that DSP Satellites 23, 24, and 25 were required to ensure credible early warning coverage and tactical ballistic missile surveillance capabilities. In addition, the fiscal year 1994 Appropriations language funds the Multi-Year Procurement (MYP) of DSP Satellites 23 and 24.

Termination of the DSP Block 23 MYP contract will result in a net loss of $500 Million with no satellites delivered. This figure includes $200 million of sunk costs (through 3/94) and $300 million of additional costs which will be incurred to support the launch of Satellites 18-22. The wisest approach is to complete the procurement of all three DSP Block 23 satellites, since it is impossible for a new start to provide three satellites within the $700 million remaining from the Block 23 contract. A new start will also require a Cost-Plus contract which greatly increases the Government's risk and liability compared with the current Block 23 Fixed-Price contract.

A new satellite will require significant changes to the DSP ground processing systems and communications networks which will further increase cost. The DSP ground system consists of:

1. Three Large Processing Stations (Conus Ground Station (CGS), Overseas Ground Station (OGS), and European Ground Station (EGS);
2. Six Mobile Ground Stations (MGSs);
3. A Centralized Tactical Processing Element (CTPE) aka., Talon Shield;
4. Six Joint Tactical Ground Stations (JTAGS) under procurement by the Army and Navy;
5. Pre-launch test and integration facilities;
6. On-Orbit Test Facilities; and
7. The various communications networks supporting DSP.

Statement of Mr. Guido Aru   February 2, 1994

The cost and schedule risks associated with a new start are significant. It is for these very reasons that Major General Schnelzer strongly supported and ultimately executed the DSP Block 23 contract for DSP Satellites 23, 24, and 25 this past June. In testimony submitted by the Air Force to the House Committee on Appropriations Subcommittee on the Department of Defense last May, the Air Force strongly defended the need for the acquisition of DSP Satellites 23, 24, and 25 because of the need to replenish the DSP constellation and the potential for delays and problems with a new program start. This was done at a time when the FEWS contracts were well underway and proceeding through the various acquisition milestones. Now that the FEWS program has been canceled, and its requirements and funding have been rejected by the OSD, additional studies and requirements definition must be done prior to the preparation of any RFP for a new Early Warning System contract. This is needed to ensure that the limited funds available are expended prudently and in a manner consistent with the best interests of the United States. These studies will take time to complete. This means that the need for DSP Satellites 23, 24, and 25 is greater than ever.

An analogy which illustrates the cost, schedule, and national security risks associated with canceling DSP and initiating a new program can be drawn with the Milstar program. Imagine if the DSCS program had been canceled in the late 1970s when Milstar was being planned, or if it had been canceled in the early 1980s when the first launch of the satellite was scheduled for the mid-1980s. Given that the first Milstar satellite is only now about to be launched, our military communication capabilities during Desert Storm would have been devastated had we relied solely on the expectations of early 1980s. Another analogy can be drawn from the Challenger disaster which greatly limited our access to space because we chose to rely solely on the Space Shuttle for heavy-lift. Other examples of the risks associated with a new start can be found in programs such as the B-1, B-2, C-17, and GPS Block IIR.

Canceling the DSP Block 23 contracts and beginning the development of a new family of spacecraft will eliminate the Nation's capability to ever build another fixed-price DSP satellite. The Government will be locked into a Cost-Plus contract for which it will have no alternative but to continue at any cost. The Fixed-Price DSP Block 23 contract protects the Government's interests and limits its liability.

Statement of Mr. Guido Aru   February 2, 1994

The Spinning Satellite Myth

One of the principal reasons the Air Force cites in advocating the need to replace the DSP satellites with a new system is the fact that DSP is a spinning satellite. In testimony submitted by the Air Force to the House Committee on Appropriations Subcommittee on the Department of Defense last May, the Air Force states "The DSP satellite scans for targets by spinning the sensor. Since this sensor rotates at a fixed spin rate, the satellite can only see targets as often as the satellite spins around again. If the satellite would spin faster it could detect and construct missile tracks faster. However, this faster spin rate would result in less sensitivity, with the possibility of missing some of the target which it is currently able to detect."

The speed at which any system scans the earth will affect its sensitivity, whether or not the scan is accomplished by rotation of the satellite or by the use of mirrors. It is analogous to the shutter speed of a camera. You cannot take pictures in dim light (or see dim targets) if you use a high shutter speed. Increasing the sensitivity of the film, on the other hand, improves the capability to take pictures in dim light. The sensitivity of DSP's focal plane, its film speed if you will, can be improved through technology insertion. However, the factor that limits the ability of any space-based infrared system to see targets against the Earth is the background radiation of the Earth itself. Using a space-based infrared system to detect some of the targets that FEWS was required to detect would have been like trying see a match in front of a floodlight -- it cannot be done.

The fact that the entire DSP spacecraft spins greatly simplifies the design of its infrared sensor. There are no moving parts in the optical path which can decrease the accuracy of a sensor. On-orbit experience with other programs demonstrates the loss of accuracy that occurs when complex moving-mirror schemes are employed.

The rotation of the DSP satellite at six revolutions-per-minute provides for the capability to revisit a target every 10 seconds. This is more than sufficient to support the global surveillance requirements for strategic early warning. Some, however, have argued that shorter revisit times are necessary to support theater surveillance. With DSP, this can be accomplished through the use of add-on small-field-of-view sensors.

Statement of Mr. Guido Aru   February 2, 1994

Potential Alternatives To A New Early Warning System Program

The IDA, Mr. Everett's Technical Support Group, and the Bottom-Up Review all concluded that the current DSP is sufficient to support our nation's strategic early warning needs. Furthermore, these groups also concluded that DSP with Talon Shield processing is "adequate" for tactical ballistic missile surveillance needs, but that some improvements in system capabilities are desirable.

Technology insertion and pre-planned product improvement options to the DSP system are explored in the DSP-II report. Technology insertion and pre-planned product improvements to existing DSP satellites can be used to preserve FEWS detector, thermal control, and power generation technologies developed under previous contracts. System performance can be greatly improved and operational costs reduced through the consolidation of DSP ground processing stations and the implementation of evolutionary ground processing upgrades proven by the Army's Tactical Surveillance Demonstration (TSD) and the Air Force's Talon Shield program. Such improvements would provide near-term performance enhancements at the lowest possible cost and risk.

The DSP satellite's theater missile detection performance can be improved through the use of add-on sensors which was also discussed in the DSP-II report. Such sensors would provide surveillance of theater-sized regions with shorter revisit rates and higher sensitivities. Shorter revisit rates and higher sensitivities are accomplished simultaneously since the add-on sensor would scan only a relatively small area of the Earth (i.e., a theater of operation). Such an add-on sensor could be mounted in place of the existing LASER Crosslink System (LCS) ballast. The LCS program was canceled and we have been flying, and will continue to fly, several hundred pounds of ballast in its place. This ballast can be replaced with a useful piece of equipment such as an add-on sensor.

The global surveillance mission would not be impacted because the add-on sensor would not interfere with DSP's existing infrared sensor. Unused telemetry downlink capacity, which was reserved for the LCS, already exists on the DSP satellites today. This downlink could be used

Statement of Mr. Guido Aru   February 2, 1994

to send down data from an add-on system, again with no impact on the existing global surveillance mission. An add-on sensor experiment was flown on DSP Satellite 14 in place of the LASER Crosslink System. Although not designed nor used operationally, it did collect background and target data for the SDIO. It also served as a proof-of-concept for flying a future operational payload in place of the LCS ballast.

An add-on sensor which scans a relatively small area of the Earth would be significantly less complex and costly than a sensor which must scan both the entire Earth and a theater region simultaneously. Once such an add-on sensor were developed, it could also be flown on other hosts beside the DSP satellite. This would potentially allow the use of other orbits which would provide improved surveillance of potential theaters of conflict throughout the world.

An add-on sensor program is also significantly less costly and risky than starting an entire new surveillance system. The primary DSP infrared sensor would not be impacted. The add-on sensor could be integrated with whichever DSP satellite is ready for launch when the add-on sensor is ready; the LCS ballast for that satellite simply would be removed and not flown. Evolution of the ground system can also be accomplished in a low-risk manner without impact to existing capability.

The DSP-II study also evaluated the feasibility of using the DSP Flight 12/13-sized spacecraft to enable the use of the Atlas IIAS Medium Launch Vehicle (MLV). It was concluded that this was feasible and could be accomplished by Satellite 23. However, due to the structure of the Titan IV buy, using a MLV prior to Satellite 26 will actually cost the Government an additional $60 million per launch as compared with the Titan IV. Using an Atlas IIAS starting with Satellite 26, however, provides opportunities for significant savings.

The Brilliant Eyes program also provides opportunities to preserve technology developed under the FEWS program and to develop new technologies unique to Brilliant Eyes (e.g., active cooling systems). Once Brilliant Eyes becomes operational, its data can be used with data from an upgraded DSP to enhance overall system performance. This also represents a low-risk approach in that it does not jeopardize our current national early warning capabilities which are centered around DSP.

House Committee On Government Operations
Legislation And National Security Subcommittee

Statement of Mr. Guido Aru   February 2, 1994

Another option, which was reported in *Defense News*, is to synergistically combine DSP and Radiant Agate data. According to Navy spokesmen speaking to *Defense News*, Radiant Agate is a proposed Navy program to provide polar EHF communications and also carry an IR sensor for intelligence collection and tactical missile surveillance. The Radiant Agate spacecraft is based on the Navy's UHF Follow-on program which uses the Hughes HS-601 bus.

A system like Radiant Agate, designed to provide polar communications, would probably use a Molniya orbit as is favored by the former Soviet Union for communication satellites. Such an orbit would provide IR surveillance capabilities for a majority of the world's hot-spots where tactical ballistic missile exchanges are likely. The orbit also permits direct downlink of the satellite's data to the CONUS, thus eliminating the need for crosslinks or terrestrial data relays. This permits transmission of the high data rates required for intelligence applications and for low Signal-to-Noise Ratio (SNR) target detection (e.g., tactical missiles). Direct viewing of the satellite from the CONUS could also be advantageous for survivability purposes should it become desirable to process the Radiant Agate IR data in a survivable Mobile Ground System.

As stated in *Defense News*, the Radiant Agate IR sensor would be based on an existing intelligence collection sensor. If true, this would provide an additional opportunity to apply technology insertion and pre-planned product improvements to an existing sensor and its associated ground processing system(s). It could also have the potential to preserve some technologies developed under the FEWS program. This represents a low-risk approach compared to a new program start.

As with Brilliant Eyes, synergistic processing of DSP and Radiant Agate data could provide a low-risk and low-cost approach to enhance the nation's surveillance capabilities. Radiant Agate and a DSP upgrade program represent low-risk approaches to provide enhancements in system performance as compared to a new early warning system program. DSP availability would not be jeopardized as it is with the approach currently advocated by the Air Force

Statement of Mr. Guido Aru   February 2, 1994

Recommendations on Space-Based Early Warning

The United States should concentrate its limited resources on developing new systems to address threats against which the nation has only limited or no capabilities -- we cannot afford our own Maginot Line. Our precious resources should not be expended on re-inventing existing capabilities. The cancellation of the DSP Block 23 contract violates common sense and is not in the national interest. All termination activities should be immediately stopped and the contract fully-funded and continued. Furthermore, the following actions are also recommended:

1. The individuals who are found to have engaged in unethical or illegal conduct should be immediately suspended of their authority over government procurement. The interests of the Government and the rights of the taxpayers must be protected. Considering the financial and national security implications of the decision to terminate the DSP Block 23 contract, the integrity of the acquisition system and the individuals making such a decision must be beyond reproach.

2. The Secretary of Defense and the Director of Central Intelligence should conduct a comprehensive study of the nation's space-based IR surveillance requirements within the context of all existing and planned strategic and tactical surveillance programs. Cost-effective alternatives for meeting those requirements should also be addressed and fully explored. The cost and risk associated with a major new space program demands this type of comprehensive review, which has previously been requested by the Congress. Systems such as DSP, Brilliant Eyes, the Navy's Radiant Agate program, NRO programs, and in-theater surveillance systems (e.g., GBR, JSTARS, RPVs, etc.) should be assessed for overlap in functions and/or capabilities, and the potential for inter-system synergy to meet war-fighting requirements should be evaluated. This should be done prior to the initiation of any new start, and definitely prior to the termination of the existing DSP program.

3. Regardless of the decision to continue DSP or initiate a new start, the Government should invest in technology insertion and pre-planned product improvements for DSP satellites

which could be retrofitted prior to launch. This is a cost-effective method to increase satellite performance, extend useful on-orbit satellite life, and provide additional data to support decisions on future space surveillance systems. Such an investment is supported by OSD policy and reflects the late Dr. Deming's Total Quality Management (TQM) principles of continuous product improvement.

Statement of Mr. Guido Aru   February 2, 1994

VIII. Conclusions

Major General Anderson's report identified "the intense competition for dollars in DoD and among its defense contractors ('survival' mentality)" as a major contributing factor in the FEWS/DSP controversy. Dr. William Perry, the Secretary of Defense nominee, has stated that he expects several defense contractors to go out of business, and that the government will stand by and watch this happen. We are clearly entering desperate times for the military-industrial complex: the events described in our testimony are clear indications that desperate times are evoking desperate measures. Nevertheless, the events we have described are merely harbingers of what will come when, as Dr. Perry expects, only one DoD procurement dollar will remain where three once stood. The Department of Defense, and if necessary the Congress, must ensure that bureaucratic imperatives and parochialism do not replace the long-term National Interest as the deciding factor in where the scarce money will go.

The events and actions we have described also show the potential for abuse in the relationship between FFRDC's and their sponsoring organizations. The basic problem stems from the fact that it is difficult to say "No" to your sole customer on important issues. The following suggestions are offered for your consideration:

1. The OSD should consider strengthening its independent technical assessment arm. This would decrease OSD's reliance on results and analysis from "captive" FFRDC's. This could be accomplished by increasing its current direct support (e.g., IDA), or by transferring some or all of the sponsorship of FFRDC's to the OSD.

2. The Aerospace Corporation should be returned to its original values that caused the government to create it in the first place. These were established in the 1959 discussions of this Committee which led to the formation of Aerospace:

> "The value of such an organization rests on its disinterested position; the advice it gives should be based exclusively on the best interests of the government [emphasis added]."

House Committee On Government Operations
Legislation And National Security Subcommittee

Statement of Mr. Guido Aru   February 2, 1994

This is in contrast to the current Corporate vision statement, which states that one of our corporate goals is to "enhance the role of the Air Force in Space." It is my belief that some independent agency, such as The Aerospace Corporation, must be able to objectively assess the role of space systems in supporting all of the Armed Services and civilian agencies (i.e., the government) that depend on these systems. This is critical because budgetary constraints will prevent the development of all possible systems: we must ensure that decision-makers have the use of objective and rational analysis as they allocate resources.

Mr. CONYERS. That was a very thoughtful statement, Mr. Aru, and I commend you for it.

I know for all the witnesses here at the table, this is not a happy occurrence or a pleasant day. We feel and share the pain, the deliberations that you had to engage in before you made the decisions that brought you before us today. We are very sensitive to that.

Colonel Mangold, please describe events surrounding your removal as the team chief. What actions were taken against you or others near you, please?

Colonel MANGOLD. Well, Mr. Chairman, as I indicated, for well over 1 year prior to my removal I knew that I had engendered a number of adversaries within the space community.

My first official act as Space/C3I Team Chief came at an Air Force Council meeting in August 1992 when the Vice Chief of Staff of the Air Force asked me what I personally thought of the Milstar program. At that point, I told him exactly what I thought of the Milstar program, and my remarks closely paralleled what I told you this morning. I was immediately taken into the Office of the Deputy Assistant Secretary of the Air Force for Space Policy and Plans, Mr. Richard McCormick, and told that if I ever, ever opened up a space program to review by the flying Air Force without first clearing that statement through the space leadership that he was very concerned about my career.

What followed after that was a series of phone calls and discussions throughout the coming year with my leadership and myself from general officers calling me to indicate that I had again alienated and upset senior Air Force generals in Colorado Springs to the point that in February 1993, General Horner—who I met with routinely, and talked to periodically from my home—met quietly in the Pentagon, where I told him exactly what I was expecting to propose for cuts. In this meeting, he asked me how it was going and I told him I felt I would live exactly one heartbeat beyond my senior leadership, General Glosson's, departure. Should General Glosson leave at any point, I would live exactly one heartbeat beyond General Glosson's departure because I knew I was in trouble.

As we got toward June, I started to receive more threatening phone calls. I started to receive and my staff started to receive threatening phone calls. Immediately after I was removed and the OSI started their investigation, my executive officer was taken into a room for 3½ hours and was told that if he did not speak out against me in written form, and they provided him the form, that they would go to his superior, my superior, and recommend that his promotion recommendation form be downgraded and that he would not be promoted.

After attempting to get in touch with his lawyer, he negotiated, in order to get out of that very uncomfortable situation, a statement which he agreed to sign under the provision that he be allowed to expand upon the two pages of one-line statements. They told him that they would consider that, but he needed to sign the statement. He signed it. He then was enjoined from talking to me for 5 months, and once we were allowed to talk to one another, he told me about that particular circumstance.

There are a number of other incidents but those are the most salient, sir.

Mr. CONYERS. Thank you.

Do you feel that the retaliations that were taken against you were unique, or does this occur elsewhere throughout the service?

Colonel MANGOLD. I wish it was unique, sir. They are not unique, unfortunately. I think as you can see by the two gentlemen seated to my left, it happened on two separate coasts.

Prior to 72 hours ago, I had never met Colonel Dietz. I certainly had not met Mr. Aru. I met Mr. Aru last weekend for the first time.

Ed Dietz and I have been around the space community for over 25 years. We have known each other by reputation and we believe we probably have attended some meetings together. But what I saw in the newspaper accounts when I was in solitary confinement, waiting to have my case brought forward, I saw a number of newspaper articles about what Colonel Dietz was involved in. I saw parallels, and that is why I came to your subcommittee, as you know, sir.

But the short answer is, absolutely not. This is not unique. We just happen to be three people that have come forward.

Mr. CONYERS. Thank you very much.

Colonel Dietz, you sent a number of messages stating your concern about the validity of the system and the integrity of the process. Were costs or performance comparisons intentionally distorted?

Colonel DIETZ. Unfortunately, it certainly appears that way. My professional judgment is that is exactly what happened, but it is hard to get into the head of Colonel Quirk. Some of those issues have been addressed in Mr. Aru's opening statement and the supporting documentation.

I would like to comment that absolutely everything that he says in public testimony and in the document, I saw it also, I confirm it. In some cases, I may have interpreted things somewhat differently, but the substance of facts are absolutely the same.

And your particular question was about the facts, facts on costs, facts on performance. I have to answer your question, but I have to share with you a concern. It doesn't matter what happened on this particular system. I believe these particular performance features were distorted to make the new system look better and the old system look bad. I believe the costs were selectively chosen and analyzed in a manner to do the same thing. I believe that the costs of the old system were inflated by adding things that didn't belong in the cost estimates. I believe that perhaps the risk assessments of the new system were minimized.

I personally have observed that folks testified to the Congress that the cost of repairing the old system "approached" that of buying a new one. I have to observe that that is hard to believe. It is hard to believe that fixing the old Chevy is as cheap as buying the new one. It never works that way. It especially doesn't work that way in systems such as we are dealing with.

I have to observe that "approached" to me means close, near, approximately. It would appear that the differences, the cost of fixing the old system versus replacing it is somewhere between $6 and $10 billion. And in my book, that isn't close. That is not close any way you count it. It is a factor of 2. The cost of the new system is almost double the cost of the old system and yet people keep saying it is almost the same or, as I quote, it approaches.

Senior leadership somehow or other gets the wrong message. I also said that it seems General Horner was misinformed. I don't know how he gets his information or where it comes from, but what I read in the press and what I saw in the briefings that he gave to our senior leadership, he said things like FEWS is cheaper in the long run. That is very hard to believe—very, very hard to deal with.

And whether or not my speculations and my experience are founded hardly matters because OSD just in the last recent months has made it easy for me. Mr. Everett and a group of people arrived at almost the identical conclusion. They found that, FEWS was more expensive. It didn't approach DSP, it was more expensive, and they recommended its cancellation.

We talk about performance and it is the same thing. Somehow or other our senior leadership has come to believe and was quoted in many contexts that the system was 10 to 20 times better, 10 times in performance, 20 times in sensitivity. That is a substantial advantage. That is the kind of advantage you look for when you make an investment in a new system.

But a factor of 10 to 20 doesn't match with our experience in Desert Storm. It doesn't match with the Army's experience using a DSP based system we call Talon Shield. We developed the system based on Army technology using the Air Force satellites. Servicing the Army, using mostly Army money. It doesn't matter who did it. It is government money, it is Federal money, but the Army finds that the performance approximates that of FEWS. It approximates. The performance is almost the same. The FEWS cost was alleged to be almost the same as DSP, and in truth the cost of the new system is a factor of 2, more expensive.

I can't comment on how this happens. I can't comment on why it is. I read the press, I see the numbers in the press. I see the briefings that are given to our chief, and I am sorely concerned. I don't know all the considerations and assumptions that went into it. But the simple logic of it is hard to swallow. It is the kind of arguments that a family member will give you. That is; right is right, wrong is wrong. Keep it simple. This is wrong.

Is it cheaper? No, it is not cheaper. It is not cheaper to buy a new system.

Performance numbers, it has been alleged that the new system will see cruise missiles. This is an unclassified hearing so it is hard to deal with it. Mr. Everett made it easy for me again. I have been saying for 2 years that this is hard to swallow, and only under very limited circumstances and coincidence of weather, altitude, and velocity might you possibly see it. You are physics limited, you are limited by the atmosphere. It is not a matter of how good you make the system. There are physical limits.

I don't think you are going to see cruise missiles in any significant way. You will see 1960–70 versions of cruise missiles. There will be very few cases. But yet it has been suggested you would see cruise missiles.

It has been suggested that the follow-on system will operate—I think the term was operate in the presence of high clouds. I don't know, I wasn't in the meetings when that was said.

But to say that the new system operates in the presence of high clouds offers the opportunity of being an outrageously misleading statement. Most any of us would say, well, that means it works in clouds. It will detect in clouds or it will track in clouds. It will not detect or track in clouds, not DSP, not FEWS, not any system such as that except under very, very limited cases. Thin clouds, limited clouds, spotty clouds, maybe. But to operate in the face of high clouds leads the casual observer, and in many cases the knowledgeable one, to presume that this system will work all the time.

The flying Air Force talks about them as all-weather systems, one where you won't be limited by clouds. That is a very, very important feature, but it is disturbing, disturbing to think that these claims are made about FEWS.

Now, in context, our senior leadership has to look at things like performance and costs, and if you come in and you say, well, I believe this is cheaper in the long run, well, that is a wonderful way to get started. If it is cheaper in the long run and even if the performance isn't any better, well, you might think seriously about doing it. But it is being made easy for me. I was the minority. I was in many cases one of the lone voices that said, gentlemen, let's rethink it. But OSD made it easy for me.

The Everett committee said "FEWS will be more expensive," upgrading the current system should be seriously considered. They talked about performance advantages and they said "there is no significant performance difference." The OSD folks said the performance will be expected to be comparable, so I don't have to stand on my own experience and my own credibility. I have had folks help me. But I wanted to turn this around a little bit. It was presumptive of me, because that has probably been my nature, and that is why I am stuck sitting in front of you.

You asked me—as an aside, another aside, I will say it is a lot easier watching a hearing than it is sitting here. I have seen many of them.

But the issue, in my mind, is a sad one. And it is an issue of ethics, integrity of process. It is how we decide, is the boss given the right to know? Is there something going wrong in our system in which everybody seems to know what the boss wants to know and we give him that answer. That is not the way I was brought up. That is not the way the senior Air Force people that taught me taught me how to decide, how to advise, but something has gone awry on this one when we can get this far down the track and be so wrong.

And we have had an investigation. The IG said, oh, it is OK. I can understand why. It may be. It may be. I don't know the details. I haven't seen it. It is only alleged that that was their finding. But I am distraught beyond description when folks like us are in a situation where you have to stand up and say something is wrong. And it does not matter what system we buy. What is wrong is the process, because it will affect how we select the next system, and it will affect the next airplane. It will affect us all. The man I work for is entitled to the straight answers. That is what it comes down to.

No English, no guessing what he really wants to believe. I am here to give facts to him. I am afraid we have lost those values somewhere or other.

Yes, sir, I think the performance and the costs were influenced by the desire to come up with the answers that people thought everybody wanted. It sure seems that way by reading the papers, by comparing my own personal experiences and my professional judgment, and by being confirmed by the Everett committee.

OSD has arrived at the same conclusion and canceled the program. I think it was a wise decision and I commend them, but I worry about the other programs.

Mr. CONYERS. I think the American people are proud that we have Colonels like both of you in the service. I think that the Congress is very proud of the integrity that you have demonstrated in the course of this subject matter.

Let me ask Mr. Aru. Mr. Aldridge told the inspector general that he was embarrassed by the report and its advocacy tone. What kind of response do you have to that?

Mr. ARU. I think to the specifics of why Mr. Aldridge was embarrassed you would have to ask him that question. But as I look at what the Aerospace Corp. has advocated or recommended to the Air Force over the last several years, we have been recommending the FEWS program.

And if we look in our 1992 annual report, it shows that Aerospace developed simulations and analysis for the military utility of FEWS and those activities were instrumental for FEWS entering the demonstration validation phase. Simultaneously if you look at Aerospace's internal technical reports to the board of trustees which are not publicly disclosed as the annual report of the corporation is, we tell the board of trustees that clear metrics haven't been defined, that the utility of advanced tactical warning is hard to quantify and that some users, the Army and the Navy in particular, have expressed their concern that FEWS will not meet their requirements.

So I think in one respect, Mr. Aldridge was caught in a position where the corporation had been saying something for several years that our report or the DSP-II report showed a lower cost alternative could provide that utility and then the subsequent independent reviews by the Institute of Defense Analysis, the bottom-up review, and Mr. Everett confirmed that.

I also think Mr. Aldridge may be embarrassed or concerned because Aerospace Corp., as you know, has a ceiling that is placed on it by the Congress, but it is funded under that ceiling on a program-by-program basis. And the FEWS program employs somewhere between 70 and 100 members of technical staff which is about 4 to 5 percent of the corporation.

The cancellation of FEWS could affect those jobs—would affect those jobs. Mr. Aldridge has also been trying very actively to move Aerospace Corp. support to Colorado Springs to support U.S. and Air Force Space Commands. Those are both headed by General Horner. General Horner has publicly stated many, many times that FEWS is his No. 1 priority. The DSP-II report challenged the correctness of his assertion that FEWS was absolutely necessary.

Mr. CONYERS. Thank you very much.

The Chair wants to note that subcommittee Chair John Spratt of South Carolina has joined the panel hearing. We welcome you. I would like now to recognize Mr. Al McCandless.

Mr. MCCANDLESS. Thank you, Mr. Chairman.

These are not easy things, gentlemen, to discuss, but we are here as an oversight committee for that purpose, irrespective of where the chips fall. I certainly share the values that Colonel Dietz has said are necessary, not only within the service, but within the political framework and other ways and other walks of life.

I, too, from time to time have been bloodied a little bit by the fact that I had maybe something that was not necessarily consistent with the majority.

I would like to read a statement and ask you, Colonel Mangold and Colonel Dietz, Mr. Aru if you wish to comment on it. While certain new technologies may be available today that could reduce the size and weight of Milstar, and thereby reduce its price tag, these technologies could not be incorporated without significant delay to deployment.

Thus the costs of lost time and lost capabilities that would certainly be incurred outweigh the estimated projected dollars savings.

Do you have a comment?

Colonel MANGOLD. Yes, sir. That argument is valid, in that today, that may be the case. Again in August 1992, when I started to oppose the Milstar program openly, we had just recently closed the Milstar I payload up.

In other words, we completed construction of Milstar I, the first satellite. The second satellite was still not yet developed.

Now, it would have been imprudent for me, sir, to come forward with a recommendation to cancel Milstar without some alternative which would support the war fighter because I believe that was, in fact, my job. EHF, extremely high frequency communications as indicated by the GAO, is a very important attribute for future military conflicts in the battlefield.

What we found is that we had the ability at that point in time—1992—to affect the Milstar program—we have stopped Milstar where it was the Milstar satellite that will be launched in just a few short hours—we could have then gone to several alternative options. We would have looked at the DSCS payload. We wanted to remove a cold war sensor off of DSCS and put a low data rate transponder into the satellites. We had an ability to——

Mr. MCCANDLESS. Let me interrupt you here. You are going beyond me technically. I am from the 3-B system.

Colonel MANGOLD. I apologize, sir. That particular comment then has certain validity.

It has validity in that we are just a few short hours from launch. Now, the military utility of the low data rate system on orbit that will be on orbit in just a few hours adds very little to our overall communications capability. Very little. Less than 100 channels of nonrecognizable voice and teletype.

So the short answer, sir, to your question is, while it does appear to be valid in a superficial sense; no, it does not help today. The real capability comes after the turn of the century. I developed a detailed plan——

Mr. McCandless. But, now, I don't want to sound argumentative.

Colonel Mangold. I understand, sir.

Mr. McCandless. Those of us who walked around in the mud found that communications was a key element to our success——

Colonel Mangold. Yet.

Mr. McCandless [continuing]. To our success of survival. So whether we had something, this or that or didn't have this or that, by God, if we could communicate with artillery to lay a barrage, it would save lots of lives. If we didn't, it would cost a lot of lives. I am being very simple and to the point.

Colonel Mangold. I understand that.

Mr. McCandless. So when we talk about communications available today with respect to ground forces command, close air support, other types of air support, we have moved from the Wright Brothers to the F-18 team in the communications timeline.

Colonel Mangold. Yes, sir.

Mr. McCandless. When we talk about this particular system would it be better than this system? But do we need time to develop it? We don't know where we are going or where we are going to have to be relative to world problems. So when you stay on an expeditionary force on a ship in the Mediterranean today and on land somewhere tomorrow and if some type of a communications device lessens the exposure of that unit, then the dollars take a secondary position if the capability is there to provide that function.

It is my understanding that we could do this and we could do that with these systems, but it takes some engineering and so forth that in the meantime we would not possibly have capabilities that we would have otherwise. Am I misguided here?

Colonel Mangold. Congressman, those are excellent observations. I have characterized Milstar as the Spruce Goose of space. In 1942, we needed a capability to get our soldiers across the Atlantic and Pacific Oceans, but the U-boat demanded that we look at alternatives other than shipping. By 1944, we beat back the U-boats. By 1945, the war had ended.

We awarded a contract to Howard Hughes in 1942 to develop the Spruce Goose. When the war ended, the Spruce Goose continued to be developed and did not fly in 1947 it could carry 600 people. But it carried them at 175 miles an hour max speed. The difficulty is that we awarded this contract during the height of the cold war. The war has ended. We could use the money in other areas.

It doesn't obviate the fact that we needed to carry men across the ocean. That is why we built the 747, the DC-10. It does not obviate the fact that we need to communicate with our ground troops. Going to the Naval War College exposed me to Marines, Army, and Navy personnel that would be on the pointy end of the spear.

I have lost friends in combat. I understand exactly what you are speaking about. My problem is this, sir. It is that just like the Spruce Goose, Milstar is no longer required and it is an inappropriate expenditure of funds after the cold war has ended.

The Spruce Goose flew once in 1947, for a distance of 1 mile at an altitude of 85 feet and then it was parked. The problem is the inertia of the system has carried Milstar to this point. It is an inappropriate use of funds and there were multiple opportunities over the last few years to stop the program, divert the funds into low-risk technologies that would have given better communications to the military war fighters than Milstar will give.

The MDR capability. The medium data rate capability, to be fielded at the turn of the century has not yet been fully developed. My team developed plans to give that same MDR capability to the war fighter at the same point in time for less cost and equal probability of bringing it in on time, equal risk.

Those were rejected because there was a mentality within the Air Force, within the space community of the Air Force to continue to develop the Spruce Goose. We had to do it because we had done it. The biggest argument in support of Milstar today is sink cost. My first master's degree is in systems management. I worked in a program office in Los Angeles.

In every accounting course I ever took, the argument of using sink costs was discounted in any management decision.

The decision to continue Milstar that has been promulgated has been "Why don't we launch it because we spent so much money?" For the same reason we did not bring the Spruce Goose out of its hangar and ferry troops to Mogadishu, it is the same reason we should not launch the Milstar, it is unnecessary and inefficient.

Mr. McCandless. Colonel Dietz anything you want to add?

Colonel Dietz. No, sir. I am not an expert on Milstar.

Mr. McCandless. Mr. Aru.

Mr. Aru. No, I am not an expert on Milstar either.

Mr. McCandless. That is a difficult question but not impossible to answer. In my opening statement I referred to Secretary Cheney with whom I have worked prior to his—here in the House prior to his going to the Cabinet.

Gen. Colin Powell appeared to be a hands-on-type leader, officer. Other people I mentioned are people who appear to—well, we have all kinds of faces, country club generals, yet this all flies in the face of their decisions to proceed in one direction and the testimony is taking another direction in terms of command policy.

I would appreciate it if you would share with me your concern because, Colonel Dietz, you talked about the system and you talked that the system goes beyond just what we are talking about here today, the missile program or that communications program.

Your implication was, and I don't know that I disagree or agree, is that the system is broke and therefore I have put myself on the line for whatever value I might be able to contribute to rework the system. Would you care to comment on that?

Colonel Dietz. Certainly. I can only observe what I see at the bottom of a long pipe. Is the system broken? I don't know all of the system. I know the facts, and at the other end, I see public statements. And the facts and the statements don't appear to match. There are a number of explanations. One is that maybe I didn't understand the conditions or the assumptions, or maybe the system is truly broken. There are an awful lot of systems and illustrations that would make you worry.

But one of my other concerns, when I have time and quiet I try to figure out what it is I really worry about, what are the central issues.

Another central issue is we need to develop a balance between the absolute necessity for an open technical debate. Debate is central to the manner in which we do business in this Nation and certainly in this Congress, and in technical areas we do the same. We argue, we negotiate. And that must be, it must be preserved. The requirements development and acquisition process demands an open debate.

But that necessity for an open technical debate must be balanced against the ability to decide what to do and move out. I don't suggest that I know how to develop that balance, but I know that open debate when squashed as it has been here removes the decisionmakers' prerogative and the right to come up with the right conclusion or the right recommendation.

Folks like yourselves will endorse the purchase of the wrong things if you are given the wrong facts. I don't suggest that I know how to develop that balance, but I am concerned that it is a little distorted right now.

Mr. MCCANDLESS. I don't want to beat the horse to death. But in your comments, Colonel Mangold, you talked about your accessibility in your position prior to the problem you now have, and the fact that you had the ear of those who are in the decisionmaking process, which would indicate on the surface that those who are making command decisions in areas such as this did have the information and experience of those who were, say, in the trenches of the thought process relative to these subjects.

What kind of dialog would you have where you would talk about a certain program to those in the decisionmaking process, and then later would you find that your experience and knowledge that you shared was secondary to some other force?

Colonel MANGOLD. No, sir. I was actually very successful and that is an excellent question that you are asking me, sir. Throughout this process, I had unlimited access to the senior Air Force leadership. I was routinely in and out of the offices of General Glosson and General Carns. I had access to the Secretary of Air Force, Don Rice, and also the Chief of Staff.

We have a very structured process, a very straightforward process in the Pentagon to bring decisions forward. Recognize, Congressman, that I was the very first individual to break ranks with Space Command and come forward with information that some of the square systems which heretofore had been supported needed to be reassessed.

As I started through this process, I was able to change many programs, recognize I had 250 program elements underneath me. I had all the space programs; launch, command control, space surveillance; all the test ranges; all the personnel, I had all the command control communications, all the computers, all the satellites on orbit. I had the JSTARS program. The AWACS program. I had all the military intelligence, all the Air Force portion of military intelligence. I had nuclear weapons of the ICBMs, all the cruise missiles and the gravity bombs.

As I started through this review process, I realized I was taking on the system by looking at cold war systems from a post-cold war perspective. It was long and tedious project, I was working 80 to 100 hours a week. We looked through the programs and as we turned over the programs and exposed those to the clear light of day. I was showing an uncommon ability to win.

Recognize, sir, in March 1993 we went to the Chief of Staff with my proposals to kill Milstar and he agreed with me. He believed me. He listened, he thought about it, he looked at the cost. He looked at the way the Defense Department had to contribute to the direction that the President had set out for us, and he said, let's do it. Let's kill Milstar.

The acquisition community, this is an open society, was able to present countervailing arguments. They convinced him that possibly there was some merit in launches, satellites 1 and 2. Many of the arguments they used quite frankly were some that you used in your first question with me. He weighed the merits and demerits of that. He said, "Sandy, I am sorry, we are going to satellites I and II." I had said that is fine, we still save $640 million.

Recognize also, sir, that when that decision was reversed by Secretary Aspin the next week, he was so impressed with the argument that I developed that he allowed the Air Force to keep the $640 million cost saving. He credited me with that cost savings, and then he turned to the Comptroller of the DOD and asked the comptroller to make that up from other sources because we presented such a convincing argument.

And what happened and as we went into the bottom-up review. Sir, we do have a process which is open and there is debate. The difficulty that I engendered was somewhat different than that which Colonel Dietz and Mr. Aru endangered. What they found is because I was so persuasive and so successful, they needed to come after me personally and take me out, and that is what they did, and I was told it was going to happen. I was told in a joking sense to start looking under my car for bombs. They were saying you had better start looking under your car for bombs Mangold because you are really making people angry.

I received a calling from a two-star general in April 1993, who told me that if I did not be quiet that I was going to—my career was over. I needed to stop. I had just put forth a recommendation to take away the mobile terminals for his system, the DSP system. I said those are cold war specific. They are costly, they are unnecessary. We can remove those at minimal impact to our Nation's defense.

When I put that option forward, that was among many options I put forward, that was probably one of the ones that they decided we need to get him out of there because he knows too much and he is too successful.

Mr. MCCANDLESS. Let me—Colonel Dietz, do you want to add anything to that?

Colonel DIETZ. I would say that maybe we weren't as successful. But maybe the same culture and values applied. Like Colonel Mangold, I was fired and moved over to another job because I did my job. The industrial program manager that worked with me, a superbly qualified lady was also suddenly reassigned, to a nonjob.

The aerospace design team that supported me in my DSP-II report had their personnel reports and potential for RIF impacted. So maybe we are seeing the same thing. It is different coasts, different reasons. I have no idea what was in people's minds. I don't think there was a conspiracy. I wouldn't know. But it is sorely disturbing that the same actions happened. When Colonel Mangold presented an unpopular conclusion or recommendation, it was dealt with in a particular manner, he was fired. Well, it seems that the same solution was used on the West Coast. Colonel Dietz had some pretty unpopular approaches and instead of dealing with it in an open technical debate, I am gone. Ms. Maguire is gone. The disturbing thought is the implication about Ms. Maguire, the TRW program manager, she was gone. Why? Because the Air Force cajoled, twisted influenced. I don't know what the terms are. It is hard to imagine she was voluntarily removed.

There is a common value somewhere or other, and I think the common ingredient is the unwillingness to discuss. Colonel Mangold suggested he was successful in his arguments. I would say I wasn't, but I was removed. That is OK. It is not a matter of winning or losing. It turns out OSD confirmed my recommendations. So the Nation is OK. But the process is still troubling.

Mr. McCandless. Let me conclude, if I may, Madam Chairman, by quoting from a letter to the Honorable Donald Atwood, Deputy Secretary of Defense, dated March 7, 1991, signed by chairman of the Senate Armed Services, Sam Nunn, and countersigned by the ranking Minority member, John Warner.

And I will paraphrase it simply by saying the Senate Armed Services Committee has reviewed the plans for the restructuring of Milstar communications system in the National Defense Authorization Act of 1991.

Congress has directed the Department to route Milstar costs substantially, increase the utility system for tactical forces and eliminate unnecessary capability for tracking nuclear war fighting. We are satisfied that the restructured program as you and your staff outlined is to us—outlined to us is designed to achieve each of these objectives.

Would you say that these Senators were misled?

Colonel Mangold. I would say, sir, that the objectives that Milstar was designed to achieve needed to be reassessed more thoroughly in the post-cold war environment.

The only dramatic reassessment that we had made in the Department of Defense after the Berlin Wall fell was to remove what we termed heroic survivability from the Milstar satellite. Many embedded cold war requirements still remained, autonomous operation on orbit without communication with the ground for extended periods of time and a number of other ones that are in fact classified.

What I advocated for, sir, was a reassessment of fundamental requirements and objectives. The decision was made not to reassess those. So in fact if you look at those requirements, Milstar satisfies them.

Make no mistake, sir, Milstar is a tribute to the American technology. If given the requirements of operating through a simulated environment in the presence of endo- and exo-atmospheric nuclear bursts and communicating with a variety of users under the most harsh conditions imaginable, American technology came through and proved to the other side that we could do it.

We not only were going to endure nuclear war, we were going to win one, and I am impressed with that technology. I was always impressed with the technical veracity of which the acquisition community approached the Milstar based on the fundamental requirements. But the difficulty is, sir, is that when you work on a program for an excess of 10 years, there is a human tendency to become wedded to that program, to believe that your solution specific answer is the only answer.

The reason I was so unpopular was because I opened up a debate to look at the requirements which would not result in that solution specific answer being the ultimate answer. So if you kept the requirements the same, the Senators were not misled. If you kept the requirements the same, I offered an opportunity in August 1992 to recognize the Berlin Wall had fallen and we needed to reassess the fundamental underlying requirements, but what that was going to do, sir, and I stated this repeatedly, that was going to put the Milstar satellite on the Mall of Washington, DC outside the Air and Space Museum where it would be a monument to the cold war. I knew that then, and I know that now.

Mr. McCandless. Thank you. Thank you, gentlemen, for your testimony. Madam Chairman, I would like to ask unanimous consent that the letter I read from the U.S. Senate's Committee on Armed Services, March 7, 1991 be entered into record.

Mrs. Maloney [presiding]. Without objection.

[The letter follows:]

United States Senate
COMMITTEE ON ARMED SERVICES
WASHINGTON, DC 20510-6050

March 7, 1991

Honorable Donald J. Atwood, Jr.
Deputy Secretary of Defense
The Pentagon
Washington, D.C. 20301

Dear Mr. Secretary:

The Senate Armed Services Committee has carefully reviewed DoD's plans for restructuring the Milstar communications system. In the National Defense Authorization Act for Fiscal Year 1991, the Congress directed the Department to reduce Milstar costs substantially, increase the utility of the system for tactical forces, and eliminate unnecessary capabilities for protracted nuclear warfighting.

We are satisfied that the restructured program as you and your staff outlined it to us is designed to achieve each of these objectives. For example, the program plan projects that life-cycle costs would be reduced twenty five percent; changes to the satellite are designed to provide operational tactical forces with much greater capacity and far cheaper and more flexible terminals; and changes to the satellites and terminals are designed to eliminate protracted nuclear warfighting features while providing necessary levels of survivability at reduced cost.

We have consulted with Committee members and, based on our recommendation, the Committee approves the requested transfer of funds. In accordance with established reprogramming procedures, and section 217(d) of the National Defense Authorization Act for Fiscal Year 1991, and the commitments expressed in the October 23, 1990, letter to the Committee from Comptroller Sean O'Keefe, the Department may transfer an additional $350 million to the Milstar program.

When this $350 million is added to the $600 million already authorized for fiscal year 1991, $950 million will be available for the Milstar program; the Department's requested allocation of these funds -- $737 million for RDT&E for satellites and terminals, and $213 million for procurement of Air Force terminals -- is approved in accordance with section 217(e) of the National Defense Authorization Act for Fiscal Year 1991.

The Committee understands that many of the specific details of the plan to restructure Milstar remain to be developed. The Committee intends to review this plan as it matures as part of the

Committee's consideration of the budget request for fiscal years 1992 and 1993.

You and your staff are to be congratulated for the Department's efforts to date to restructure the Milstar program. We look forward to working with you on this important program in the future and appreciate your cooperative approach.

Sincerely,

Sam Nunn
Chairman

John Warner
Ranking Minority Member

Mrs. MALONEY. It is a sad story in American government when two colonels and a senior research analyst testify as you are today, that they were harmed, threatened, demoted, given all types of problems for speaking up not only for the defense of the country, but for doing so in a realistic and cost-effective manner. Given your testimony, Mr. Mangold the Milstar program would cost roughly $20 billion overall.

Colonel MANGOLD. Yes, ma'am.

Mrs. MALONEY. And we are going to be sending one into space tomorrow that cost $1.4 billion. Do you think we should send this into space given the fact that it is no longer needed?

Colonel MANGOLD. No, I do not.

Mrs. MALONEY. Why not?

Colonel MANGOLD. As I indicated, ma'am, it offers minimal additional capability on orbit. The placement of that satellite is not going to dramatically enhance our war fighting capability overseas.

I am not sure of the exact level of classification for the exact placement of that satellite, so I won't get into that. You might ask the same question to my colleagues from Space Command who will be testifying momentarily as to exactly where it is going to be placed and to describe to the assembled membership why or how that is going to dramatically affect the enhanced capability on orbit—rather the enhanced war fighting capability when placed on orbit, but more specifically in answer to your question, once we have launched Milstar, we have committed 400 people who work at Fallon Air Force station to commanding and controlling that satellite to its duration of its lifetime.

Mrs. MALONEY. Which would be how long?

Colonel MANGOLD. We expect according to the chart directly to your right, ma'am, that is going to be past the turn of the century. The top line as indicated by the GAO chart will say that satellite—it is last—somewhere past the turn the century, right around the year 2000, 2001.

Mrs. MALONEY. 400 persons will be needed to watch this satellite and monitor it?

Colonel MANGOLD. Yes, ma'am.

Mrs. MALONEY. How much would that cost, roughly?

Colonel MANGOLD. I believe the GAO's on-orbit cost figures in excess of $100 million speak to the cost of operating that satellite, not only personnel costs, but of course, cost of the Command and Control equipment and the computer programs, it takes to keep that satellite operating.

You see, ma'am, the Milstar program, again, in the cold war era was a very appropriate program. And it had a very expanded mission, and it was going to give us the ability to win a nuclear war. I know the other side knew that, and it contributed a great deal to the falling of the Berlin Wall.

The unfortunate reality is that so many people are required to operate that satellite. Whether you have 1 or 20, it is the same number of people.

Mrs. MALONEY. Once it is in orbit, we have to continue those people watching it?

Colonel MANGOLD. Yes, ma'am.

Mrs. MALONEY. For the entire lifetime of it, to the tune of $100 million?

Colonel MANGOLD. Yes, ma'am.

Mrs. MALONEY. At one point, if I heard you correctly, you gained from the Air Force the belief that it was not needed and it should not go forth; is that correct? That was the Air Force decision at one point?

Colonel MANGOLD. At one point, ma'am, the argument that I used, the argument that my leadership and I used was that, again, EHF communications with all of its low probability of intercept, its antijam, the inability of an enemy to override that signal, the other attributes of Milstar are incredibly important in the 21st century battlefield.

We believe that it is an essential capability. So the argument is not against EHF. The argument is against Milstar. The satellite, the solution specific answer. So again what gave me and my team credibility was that we came forward with an alternative to the Milstar satellite which provided the same level of war fighting communications capability to the soldiers in the field in the 21st century on the 21st century battlefield.

We believed in 1992 that we could provide that at a cost savings of over $.5 billion and still get the same capability and that study so impressed the Chief of Staff that he said, you are right. Let's do this. This makes sense.

So at one time there was an Air Force decision in February/March timeframe in 1993 to cancel the Milstar program, but in the same meeting, in the same thought process, in the open debate that we have within the Pentagon, General McPeak said, no, I think we need to launch the first two. He listened to both sides and I didn't win, everything, every time, and that is fine.

But the process that Colonel Dietz spoke to in that particular instance worked. So the plan was to launch satellites 1 and 2 and allow the plan I had developed with the acquisition, the acquisition members of my team, those people that understood the way we would go out and acquire this capability using other cheaper means. He approved that plan. We sent that down to Secretary Aspin. In February/March timeframe of 1993.

Mrs. MALONEY. He overruled you and proceeded with the Milstar program.

Colonel MANGOLD. Yes, ma'am, that was part of the bottom-up review process what Secretary Aspin decided was that it was premature to terminate any specific major weapon system acquisition in isolation of a total restructuring of the Department of Defense.

He was in the process of formulating the defense planning guidance which would divide us through the rest of this century as we turned from nuclear war to tactical war orientation, so he did not want—although he believed in the merits, we were told, of what we were proposing, so much so that he allowed us to keep our $640 million, he said unfortunately this proposal, while important, would fly in the face of my overall logic, which I agreed with is that we should not terminate a system unilaterally in isolation until we look at all of them, so we started the bottom-up review process over the summer, which has received obviously a lot of press, and I know you are familiar with it, ma'am.

So that is why he reversed it. I understood, he did it and I understood what happened. I can speak to the bottom-up review process at a later time because I know we have to move on. But——

Mrs. MALONEY. You think you came here with great risk to your personal career——

Colonel MANGOLD. Yes, ma'am, I did.

Mrs. MALONEY [continuing]. To speak about what you believe. Do you think Congress should likewise take great risk in reviewing this Milstar program and cancel it if what your research and your other colleagues say is true?

Colonel MANGOLD. I would like to follow the line of logic that my two colleagues to my left have brought out. We need an open and honest debate.

We need to review the requirements in light of the evolving world situation, and make a reasoned decision as to where we think this Nation ought to go with its military technology.

Mrs. MALONEY. Specifically what should Congress do? Should we put on hold Milstar while we have a debate on the floor——

Colonel MANGOLD. Yes, ma'am.

Mrs. MALONEY. How do we suggest we go forward to correct the problem that you are courageously speaking about today. What should Congress do?

Colonel MANGOLD. I believe because of the marginal additional capability that Milstar is going to put on orbit in 72 hours, that it should be stopped, that we should in fact look at whether or not that program should continue in its present form.

What we should do this time, different than we did the bottom-up review is that we need to go back into the fundamental requirements which lie at the basis of Milstar. We need to ask "what are the requirements and what is it that we want the satellite to achieve."

Mrs. MALONEY. So you believe we should not even launch the first Milstar, we should pull it back, review it and possibly go forward with a lesser capability.

Colonel MANGOLD. I think you are starting to understand why I was the most hated man in Space Command, yes, ma'am, exactly. That was—I have been pretty strident and demonstrative on that particular subject, ma'am.

Mrs. MALONEY. My colleague, Jane Harman, has a question I want to ask one to all three of you. Do you believe that the multibillion dollar contractor business in our country has a life of its own that begins to push contracts and weapon systems that are not needed. I would like your comments on that.

Colonel MANGOLD. If I could start. I am certainly a living example of that. The allegations that have been brought forward against me were brought forward by a defense contractor who was going to lose significant bills if my proposals went forward. The defense——

Mrs. MALONEY. Who was the defense contractor?

Colonel MANGOLD. The Anser Corp.

Mrs. MALONEY. They brought charges against you?

Colonel MANGOLD. Yes, ma'am. They allege that I attempted to force them to hire an individual 7 months after the alleged incident occurred. The alleged incident occurred in the December 1992 timeframe. They felt that they needed to wait until I was named team chief for an unprecedented second year in June 1993 to come forward.

Up until that time, they continued to do business with me. They continued to work with me, and I had them conduct many of the studies which would have ultimately led to a significant reduction, not only in the overall defense base, but in their company's work as well.

When they realized that I was not going to leave as previous team chiefs had left at the end of my second total year in the Pentagon, but my 1 year as a team chief, that General Glosson had elected to keep me on because I was bringing so many cuts to the table that were successful, they realized that I needed to be removed. So, yes, ma'am, the defense contractors do have a life of their own and they do bring pressures upon the process. Sometimes positive, sometimes negative.

Right now I was on the receiving end of a negative, and it has cost me a great deal of personal money, a great deal of emotional capital, and I am not through with it yet. I will be involved in this for quite some time. Certainly beyond the life of this hearing, but that is just part of the game and the approach that each of us individually and collectively decided to take was that if we were open and we were honest is all that was required. Just be open and honest.

Sometimes we would win and sometimes we would lose, but as long as the debate was allowed to occur in an open, objective, and honest format, we were allowed to move forward with the process. Then the Nation is best served.

Mrs. MALONEY. What happened to the charges brought against you by the contractor? Where do they sit, are they live charges or——

Colonel MANGOLD. No, ma'am. The case has been closed. What occurred was that the allegations—there were never any charges, they were just allegations. The case was closed. I received a letter for instance yesterday which indicated that the case was closed, and when I come up for Brigadier General next year, I will be given a chance to comment on those allegations and based on my comments, the Secretary of the Air Force will make a decision as to whether or not he will forward the allegations as well as my comments to those allegations forward to the promotion board.

If I am able to, in the next 365 days to clear my name, then I have an opportunity to be objectively evaluated for my next rank. Again, I want to emphasize the Air Force and the Pentagon have been very fair with me.

Mrs. MALONEY. How soon after the allegations were made were you removed as team chief?

Colonel MANGOLD. Twenty-three days.

Mrs. MALONEY. Twenty-three days?

Colonel MANGOLD. Yes, ma'am. What happened is on June 1, General Glosson announced that I was going to stay on for another year. Some time between June 1, and June 23, allegations were brought forward against me. On the——

Mrs. MALONEY. How soon after that were you removed?

Colonel MANGOLD. It is my understanding that the Anser Corp. testified on June 21, and I was removed 3 days later.

Mrs. MALONEY. You were removed 3 days after the contractor alleged——

Colonel MANGOLD. Yes, ma'am. Yes, ma'am. It was directly tied, my removal was directly tied to Dr. Fabian's testimony.

Mrs. MALONEY. Thank you.

Jane Harman.

Ms. HARMAN. Thank you, Madam Chair.

I appreciate again the opportunity to be here. As you know, virtually every interest here has a presence in my congressional district, and I am extremely concerned about what has been said.

I want to make a point as a member of the House Armed Services Committee. I know that that committee, too, will be reassessing all these issues as it proceeds this year with the defense authorization bill. My colleague, Mr. Spratt, who serves on this committee as well, will be involved on that. I am guessing my colleague Mr. Kyl, who is a member of this committee will be involved, too.

I have two brief questions. One is general and one is specific. The general one is this: From your testimony and from my investigation prior to this, there is an odor here, and this relates to the DSP/FEWS issue, not to Milstar. The odor is that senior Air Force personnel decided that FEWS was what they wanted and that DSP was not, and it was either in the woodwork, in the atmosphere, or actually in direct communications that this was what they were looking for, and in fact I had my own encounter with a senior Air Force person who said, "My dear, FEWS is the future, DSP is the past."

Now, the question to you is, is this impression that there was this odor about and that frankly the Aerospace Corp. tried to please its customer, the Air Force, and this odor reached them, too. Is this impression that there was this odor correct?

Colonel MANGOLD. Why don't you guys give the West Coast version and I will give the East Coast?

Mr. ARU. I believe that impression is correct, there is something wrong, as you call it, an odor there. I would like to say that one of the events that occurred was when we briefed Major General Schnelzer who is responsible for space acquisitions in the Pentagon on the DSP upgrade concept. We briefed him on February 3, 1993, so it is almost 1 year ago to the day. An Air Force representative was also present, Lt. Col. Jeff Norton.

Several days after the meeting Brigadier General Dickman from Space Command sent a letter to Major General Schnelzer and I will quote from his letter, "You stated an Air Force position in the 3 February meeting that I would like to echo. The vice chief position was that FEWS was, and is, the Air Force and DOD ITW/AA solution of choice."

Mrs. MALONEY. Without objection, we will add that to the record.

[The information follows:]

DEPARTMENT OF THE AIR FORCE
HEADQUARTERS AIR FORCE SPACE COMMAND

FROM: HQ AFSPACECOM/DR
      1105 Vandenberg St, Ste 1105
      Peterson AFB C 80914-45909

SUBJ: Operator Comments on FEWS/ITWAA Integration Studies

TO: PEO/SPACE

1. (U) This letter describes our command's operational concerns with the "BE/ITWAA Integration Studies" you are conducting to answer Congressional concerns from the last budget cycle. I am pleased that our people were included in your latest review on 3 February and, therefore, were able to formulate these inputs to your study. I summarize many of the key issues in this letter and would be happy to speak with you in more detail if necessary.

2. ( ) First, it is absolutely essential to maintain a consistent and level playing field throughout the study tasks. In particular, the ROE that states that all "replacement system alternatives must perform the entire FEWS mission"/is critical. In that regard, the DSP and BE alternatives must address every validated FEWS mission need including:

   a. (U) On-board Data Processing down to message/information level to provide data directly to theater/worldwide users.

   b. (U) Cross-links to avoid dependency on all overseas ground stations (fixed or mobile).

   c. ( ) Worldwide collection and distribution of wide-band data back to the CONUS ground station.

   d. ( ) Full satisfaction of all threat detection requirements and report timelines including dim and short-burn missiles as well as Slow Walker detection and distribution requirements.

   e. ( ) Hardening/jamming requirements equivalent to FEWS adjusted for lower altitude:

which will be   higher at the BE altitude than for FEWS).

   f. (Collection, timing, and distribution of up to AOIs worldwide at varying revisit rates as well as sensitivities down to

3. (U) For any DSP or BE alternative, it is unacceptable to offer any "partial" solution that compromises or "trades off" our stated requirements. Such alternatives should be modified accordingly to address the full set of operational needs - and proper accounting made for increased technical risk and costs. To not address validated requirements on these DSP and BE alternatives implies that solutions providing less than the JROC-approved requirement are acceptable.

4. (U) You restated an Air Force position in the 3 February meeting that I would like to echo. The Vice Chief position was that FEWS was, and is, the Air Force and DoD ITW/AA solution of choice - supported by JROC-validated requirements, supported by full funding in the BES, supported by two Air Force Summits, and supported by a Milestone I DAB review. FEWS cannot be assumed by BE - certainly not without BE, or a BE variant, having passed the same muster.

5. (U) Your other comments are also on the mark. Specifically, we should concentrate hard on the utility of FEWS SWIR helping to offset BE requirements and satellite quantities. We should especially consider the advantages of fully integrating the two systems and, in particular, look at removing SWIR (in total) off of BE as well as the advantage (if any) of relegating the BE SWIR to an acquisition sensor vice a tracking sensor to facilitate target hand-off to the BE MWIR/LWIR. Reducing BE launch weight and complexity (a critical issue for BE) is the objective for both of these integration alternatives. An additional issue concerns using the BE Government baseline versus the BE contractor's designs for Task III (DSP & BE). Differences between using the Government and contractor concepts could have implications on acquisition sensor capabilities, timelines, hand-over, processing, and launch weight/complexity. Given that the Government describes DSP functionality and/or Aerojet provides design detail one way to Rockwell and TRW, it makes sense to change the structure of Task III to directly involve the two BE contractors and their unique designs.

6. ( ) Besides the above requirements concerns and general observations, there are a series of programmatic disconnects in the current treatment of options that need to be normalized for an apples-to-apples comparison:

    a. (U) Consistent treatment of DSP transition costs to account for lack of regional transition (vice turn-key) in low-altitude distributed alternatives.

    b. (U) Consistent treatment/quantity of Government launch reserve and growth reserve between all options (amounts up to 43 percent of recurring costs for FEWS vice as low as 20 percent for BE with no launch margin).

    c. (U) Consistent treatment of FEWS manning for any low altitude alternative. Staffing in the order of 800-900 personnel should be overlayed on such options.

d. ( ) Consistent treatment of technology assumptions (i.e. OBDP VHISC at   for FEWS vice   for BE).

e. (U) Consistent definition and treatment of Life Cycle Costs [LCC = ATP (Dem/Val) through FOC plus 10 year ops] i.e., current "LCC" for BE does not include DEM/VAL costs which contain proto-flight space vehicles amounting to over $800M in content.

f. (U) Consistent treatment of learning curve effects on LCC (i.e., FEWS at .95 and BE at .86).

g. (U) Special treatment of system availability and associated replenishment strategies and the direct implication of over-population needs on multi-plane, distributed constellations.

7. (U) I believe the requirements and programmatic adjustments outlined above will help to level the playing ground. With these changes, the study will more likely lead to answers that satisfy our operational needs. Again, I thank you for the opportunity to contribute to the ongoing study. We look forward to continuing dialogue and offer you our participation/review at any other interim and final briefings.

cc: SMC/MG
    SMC/MB
    SMC/MJ

CLASSIFIED BY: Multiple Sources

Mr. ARU. What the purpose of the congressionally mandated study was—and it was mandated in fiscal year 1992 language by the Senate Armed Services Committee—was to look at alternatives to FEWS, to look at other space programs, how they could work together; specifically the Brilliant Eyes program and other programs that fall into this.

The whole purpose was to see how other systems could work together and we put together a solution that would have saved billions of dollars in the near term and more in the long term, and that solution was rejected. In my opinion because it was a threat to the program that they had already established, the FEWS program.

Ms. HARMAN. Thank you. Any other comments on that? I have one more question.

Colonel DIETZ. Colonel Mangold was going to address that. It is interesting he had mentioned to me the other evening that for many months and on many occasions he had been looking for less expensive alternatives. He felt challenged by his leadership and by the Nation to come up with less expensive options to tailor the budget.

Surprisingly, in spite of all the effort and literally years of work in looking at lower cost options and improved DSP, he was never provided those options. I was astonished to discover that just 36 hours ago.

Colonel MANGOLD. I never saw the DSP-II report. I was the team chief, as I indicated, of Space/C3I/Nuc. I had a requirement to take several billion dollars out of the budget of fiscal year 1994 and then we were eventually going to get to fiscal year 1999, the year 2000 with $5 billion over the Reagan/Bush projections down to where President Clinton wanted us to be.

I was pushing my colleagues at Space Command and at SMC, Space and Missile Center, to come up with an alternative to FEWS because I knew that FEWS was not going to work in its present form. It was too expensive. The requirements were not well defined.

And I debated long and hard with some of the witnesses that are going to be coming forward after me sitting at these chairs and speaking at these microphones in just a few minutes.

In April when I went out to Space Command, I had a particularly acrimonious exchange with General Dickman in a conference room filled with about 30 people where he told me that I was no longer one of them. I was no longer a space person, and I needed to understand where I came from. I told him: "You are absolutely right, sir, I am an officer in the United States Air Force. First and foremost, I work for General Glosson. I will continue to bring budget cuts forward until General Glosson and General McPeak tell me to stop. I know where the money is. I know what systems don't work. I will bring them forward until I am stopped." They stopped me.

Ms. HARMAN. Thank you.

My second and last and brief question relates to something that concerns me enormously, and I think would concern the Chair. Madam Chair, you may not know that the program manager for

DSP, the Defense Support Program, at TRW is a woman, a superbly qualified lady, as Colonel Dietz has testified.

She was in charge of the visit about 6 months ago to TRW to view DSP by Vice President Gore and she did an excellent job. Just a week ago, the local press in California reported that she has been removed from her job, "in return for the reassignment of Air Force Colonel Joseph Bailey, a central figure in the controversy over a suppressed Aerospace Corporation study."

I met with Air Force personnel in my office last week and asked whether her removal had been requested. And I have written answers from the Air Force, and I would like to request unanimous consent to put those answers in the record.

Mrs. MALONEY. Without objection.

[The information follows:]

ANSWERS TO QUESTIONS FROM REPRESENTATIVE HARMAN
31 JAN 94

1. What is the Air Force's response to press reports that the TRW program manager was removed "in return" for the reassignment of the Air Force program director?

Given the recent controversy that surrounded the DSP and FEWS programs, it was concluded that the current Air Force program director was at a disadvantage in addressing future needs of the program. He is being transferred, without prejudice, to an equivalent program director's position. Even though not guilty of wrong doing, recent adversarial comments in the public forum (e.g., newspaper articles) made it increasingly more difficult for the incumbent to address fundamental program needs. <u>Please contact TRW corporate management concerning the TRW program manager,</u>

Ms. HARMAN. Thank you. On this subject, the Air Force states, "Please contact TRW corporate management concerning the TRW program manager." I would like to ask this panel whether you have any information that Ms. Maguire, a superbly qualified lady who, from my knowledge, was doing her job in the most outstanding manner, was ordered to be removed from the program by the Air Force.

Colonel DIETZ. I would like to reaffirm your observations. In my professional experience, she was superb. She had a balance between people judgment, management talent and she was a wonderful engineer. I can't tell you what was in the minds of the corporate folks.

I will suggest that it is widely discussed and almost universally believed that it was an exchange. It was to buy peace and perhaps it was. Someone quoted to me personally, it is said that her only mistake was being too close to her customer, and I was viewed as the customer. Since I had been replaced and I had been viewed as presenting controversial and unpopular approaches, she was at risk. There is a multitude of people and examinations, and maybe in this case it doesn't matter exactly why she was removed, what matters most is the perception.

It is the common perception that when dissension arrives, we handle it by removing people or firing them or hurting their performance appraisals and that sends a message to all of our professionals. There are 350 people in the immediate program office that got a message. And the message is absolutely clear, keep your mouth shut or you will lose your job. When you do that, you lose the integrity of the institution. You lose the professionalism, you lose the value of technical dialog.

I do not know why Ms. Maguire was reassigned. Everybody seems to believe that it was as an exchange.

Ms. HARMAN. Thank you, Colonel. And thank you all for your incredible courage and candor.

Thank you, Madam Chair.

Mrs. MALONEY. Thank you.

Mr. Aru, did you ever witness the passing of proprietary data?

Mr. ARU. Yes, I did, Madam Chairman. On May 21, Colonel Bailey and Mr. Parsons, the division general manager at Aerospace Corp., Colonel Bailey's counterpart, we had a meeting at 10 o'clock Friday morning where they asked me to prepare a releasable version of the DSP–II report which contained confidential, competitive sensitive data provided by Aerojet for our studies. Colonel Bailey wanted a releasable version prepared that he could give to the FEWS contractors. Later on——

Mrs. MALONEY. Why do you think he wanted to give proprietary information and competition sensitive data to——

Mr. ARU. Let me add that he asked me that at 10 o'clock. I told him we would have to have the document reviewed by the legal people within the Air Force and Aerospace and also consult with Aerojet because they provided the information.

It was a Friday, and Aerojet works a 4-day work week to comply with EPA regulations, so they are closed on Friday. That evening, after hours, at about 4:30, 5 o'clock, he had given a copy to Mr. Elliot Bailis, the TRW FEWS program manager, and subsequently they had given a copy to Mr. Wayne Craft, a retired Air Force colonel, former DSP program manager, and now an executive with Lockheed's FEWS program.

I was told subsequently in a meeting in June with the vice president of Aerospace, Mr. Dick Allman, and Mr. Parsons. When we discussed the security report that Aerospace came up with from their internal investigation, I asked Mr. Parsons, why would Colonel Bailey, why would you do such a thing as giving this out? And he stated that Colonel Bailey wanted the assistance of the FEWS contractors to refute the DSP upgrade study.

And personally, one of the things that is important to us in our business is not only the security aspects of information we deal with, but also the proprietary and competition-sensitive information of the contractors. Coming to Aerospace, it was one of the things that was impressed upon all of us that we treat that material with the utmost respect, because in government procurement that is what we depend on, our good working relationships with the contractor, and we cannot compromise those relationships.

In this case, both the Air Force and the Aerospace Corp. have tolerated it. The passing of that information was witnessed by multiple people, but unlike Colonel Mangold's case, where the charges were brought and he was immediately removed, Colonel Bailey still remains in his position. Mr. Parsons still remains in his position. And this sends a message to everyone that that was OK.

It is wrong. It is wrong.

Mrs. MALONEY. So they gave FEWS confidential information so that they could prepare their response and be more competitive—that is outrageous. That is absolutely outrageous.

Mr. ARU. Yes, it is.

Mrs. MALONEY. What other examples did you see of trying to suppress a congressionally mandated study?

Mr. ARU. Once the report——

Mrs. MALONEY. And distorts, I might add—not only suppress. This is distorting a congressionally mandated study.

Mr. ARU. Once the DSP–II report came out in May, the president of Aerospace, Mr. Aldridge, ordered it recalled almost immediately and that was after a telephone call from General Horner. General Horner also sent Mr. Aldridge a letter that said the study was found to be technically and politically and operationally flawed.

At the time, U.S. Air Force Space Command did not even have a copy of the study to come to those conclusions.

Mr. Aldridge ordered an internal Aerospace review conducted, which was headed by a gentleman by the name of Mr. Jim Slattery. Their first pass was to conclude that the study was flawed, that its conclusions about risk and cost were flawed and so forth. And that is why Mr. Aldridge, as he stated to the inspector general's investigation, affirmed his decision to recall the report.

I would like to note, at no time did Mr. Aldridge talk with anyone who helped prepare, review, or approve the report before he passed his findings. And, of course, subsequently the internal Aerospace review was shown to be flawed by the Institute of Defense Analysis and by Mr. Everett.

Also Col. Jeffrey Quirk, who is—who was, rather, the Assistant Director of Engineering for the Space-Based Early Warning System program office was responsible for providing performance and cost estimates to the bottom-up review process of Mr. Everett's committee. As Colonel Dietz spoke earlier, in his opinion and in my opinion, those performance estimates were significantly overstated for FEWS and very pessimistic for DSP, as were the cost estimates. And I would like to say that there were other people involved that tried to come forward to Colonel Quirk, one of those is Maj. Roger Hall, who works in the program office.

Major Hall made a statement that went up to General Schnelzer that said, "When there are many ways of answering questions of FEWS versus DSP, the answer chosen is usually the one which portrays FEWS to the best advantage."

He was asked to substantiate that, which he did in a memorandum to Colonel Quirk on October 12. And he summed up that memorandum with the following statement, "Space Command stated, advertised, publicized FEWS' performance as becoming more and more overstated and incredulous. [He referenced the Washington, DC, football stadium charts statements about FEWS cueing, based upon single hits and General Horner's statements related to SS-21's, clouds, and low-altitude cruise missiles.] Some of the more recent claims are probably beyond the capability and capacity of any space-based asset and may damage Space Command's credibility."

There were a lot of people that internally were trying to tell the leadership that they were wrong with the positions that were going forward—with the cost estimates and with the performance analysis. But the Air Force had an answer and the answer was FEWS, and they tried to distort the process to the senior leadership, so that the senior leadership and Air Force senior leadership would support that conclusion.

Fortunately, in this case—although it was not the result of the process, but fortunately in this case, OSD commissioned several independent reviews to find the right answer. But we cannot afford on every program to bring in separate independent teams. We have to have a process and institutions that more integrity, that won't require all these independent teams every time a decision has to be made, otherwise there is no need for the institutions like the one I work for, which is supposed to do that job in the first place.

Mrs. MALONEY. I want you to comment on one of the papers that we have. It is on a DSP misrepresentation, and the position is that some elements of the U.S. Air Force are misrepresenting Defense Support Program data to senior Air Force officers, DOD, and Congress; and in fact, they misrepresented it. I quote from one area, and I would like you to comment on it. In discussions with senior TRW executives, they asserted that they could not help because they had been threatened and intimidated by senior Air Force officers who warned TRW not to support opponents of FEWS.

Mr. ARU. Let me give a comment on that.

The distortion of information that was brought forward and examples of testimony that was previously given, that turns out to be false, I will give you an example. Major General Hard testified before the House Appropriations Committee, Subcommittee on the Department of Defense, on May 11, 1993. When questioned by Mr. Young regarding the performance of FEWS compared with DSP,

Major General Hard answered twice that, "with FEWS we can get accuracies that allow us to tell the Scud hunter in the F-16 where to look, within an area about the size of RFK Stadium instead of an area the size of Washington, DC."

That statement is incorrect. Mr. Everett validated that that was incorrect when he stated that there is "only a marginal advantage" to FEWS versus DSP. That statement is proven incorrect by DSP's real time performance in Desert Storm, which was significantly better than an area the size of Washington, DC, and it is proven wrong by an Army tactical surveillance demonstration program that has been providing operational data for almost 1 year and by the Air Forces Talon Shield program.

As far as the allegation raised by Mr. Carl Fisher, who is the president of Aerojet, I cannot comment on that specific allegation and who told him that, but I would like to comment on that the fact that the allegations he made were in a confidential letter that was sent to Major General Anderson, who was appointed by the Secretary of the Air Force to conduct an investigation. Major General Anderson's investigators took that letter that was provided in confidence and provided it to Colonel Bailey and Colonel Quirk, who were the subjects of the investigation.

Major General Anderson's staff also took material that was provided to this committee in confidence for its investigation and provided it to Colonel Quirk and Colonel Bailey, and this also sent a clear message because everyone in the program office knew that that had occurred and that had occurred on the second day of Major General Anderson's investigations. Other people that I have talked to in this program office have told me that this inhibited them from being fully open and cooperative with the investigators because they feared the loss of their anonymity. Anything they say would get back to their superior, Colonel Quirk.

Mrs. MALONEY. So our IG—in other words, the government IG took this information and gave it back to the Air Force?

Mr. ARU. Yes. The information that was provided to this committee was provided——

Mrs. MALONEY. Confidential information provided to this committee, that this committee then gave to the IG's office, the IG office then gave back?

Mr. ARU. The IG then gave it to the people that were suspects of the investigation.

Mrs. MALONEY. That is outrageous. I think we should call the IG in for some questioning.

Mr. ARU. I think questions need to be addressed to Major General Anderson and his staff as to why they would do that. And I think those actions, those specific actions have caused the IG to not be able to tell the full story because people would not talk to them. Other folks I work with have let me have information in confidence, some overtly who have told me who they are. Others haven't told me who they are.

I know others have called this committee, but they are afraid for their anonymity and they are afraid for the retribution that they know will come because of what they have seen has happened to these gentlemen and to the others that worked on the DSP-II study.

Mrs. MALONEY. In the cold war we used to fight the enemy, the military enemy. Who are we fighting now? Are we fighting our own bureaucracy that wants to do things a certain way and not listen? Who are we fighting now?

Mr. ARU. I think, as Colonel Mangold stated, there is a cancer, and the cancer is with the institutions that are responsible for the acquisition and operation of our military space systems. They have hidden under a cloak of secrecy for a very long time, not exposed to public debate, not exposed to public questioning.

I'll give you an example, I work for the Aerospace Corp. I have worked there for 6 years, and I am very proud to work there, but I am not proud of what the company's leadership has done in this case. The Aerospace Corp. was chartered by this committee, the House Government Operations Committee in 1959 with the following statement out of the hearings of 1959 that said, "the value of such an organization, [meaning Aerospace], rests on its disinterested position. The advice it gives should be based exclusively on the best interests of the government."

Two years ago after Mr. Aldridge joined the Aerospace Corp. as its president, as a former Secretary of the Air Force, he changed the vision statement for the corporation; and one of the key goals now for the corporation is, "to enhance the role of the Air Force in space." Space systems have now become more and more integrated not only throughout the military, but with civilian users, and we have to take into account—since we cannot afford to acquire every possible system, we have to take into account whether, for example, an in-theater Army radar is a better answer or a space-based IR system is a better answer.

The objectives laid out by this committee for the Aerospace Corp. in 1959 allowed us to do that. The objective of enhancing the role of the Air Force in space no longer allows us to do that because any answer that doesn't mean more money, more programs, more people for Air Force space programs is not the right answer.

Colonel MANGOLD. I find that especially true now. As I started to investigate the programs that could potentially be cut, we would look and try to hold them up to the light of day and lay them against the evolving world situation.

I chose a company which is a not-for-profit company as well. It is the Anser Corp. But what I discovered was, the answers—the responses I was getting directly affected their business base, so I saw a corrupting of the answers.

So I started to isolate them from the cost data; I started to remove them from the process. I asked for objective appraisals, but they could see me moving them out of the decisionmaking loop; and so then I was trying to develop a method to take forward decisions that basically would be isolated from the not-for-profit contractors involved in the process, because I saw they had lost their objectivity.

Coming out of that, on April 26, 1993, I wrote a letter to SMC and to the electronics system center at Hanscomb Field which said, why don't we look into a 25 percent, 50 percent, 75 percent, and 100 percent cut of the Aerospace and the Mitre Corp. engineering effort because they were not giving us what we originally intended; tell me the impacts.

That letter, over my objections, was recalled. I was then labeled "insane" by a Deputy Assistant Secretary of the Air Force. And one of my principal opponents that came out so strongly against me was an active-duty major general at that time, Maj. Gen. Donald Hard, who left the service to become a vice president of the Aerospace Corp. just a few months after I came out with this proposal. He had been opposing me for the preceding year, and when I came out with that April 26 letter, unbeknownst to me—I did not realize that is where he was intending to go work——

Mrs. MALONEY. I thought we had a revolving door law that we passed in this country so that you don't, when you leave government, go into a business that you presided over or impacted on while you were in government, so that this type of, shall we say, "friendly" deal doesn't take place.

Colonel MANGOLD. I can't speak to that, ma'am, but I can just speak to the fact that the former Assistant Secretary of the Air Force for Space went to work as a vice president of the Mitre Corp.; that when Major General Hard retired, he went to work as a vice president for the Aerospace Corp.

When I came out on April 26 of last year, recommending strongly to cut Aerospace Corp., which cost $181,000 per man-year—it is called MTS, member of the technical staff—and with Mitre Corp. at $155,000 per man-year, we spend $1 billion in not-for-profit corporations, I said, we are not getting our money's worth——

Mrs. MALONEY. $180,000 per man per year?

Colonel MANGOLD. Yes, ma'am, $181,000. Remember, it is technical staff. Mr. Aru can probably explain it in more clarity. It basically pays for that individual, the clerical support to pay the individual, his health care benefits—all of the support overhead costs are burdened on the hiring of an individual for a year. And what the charge is to the government for the Aerospace Corp. employee on April 26, was $181,000 per year. And it was—for the Mitre Corp. it was $155,000, and I said I believe that now that the cold war is over, the imperative for that type of expenditure may need to be reassessed; let's go back and reassess it.

I built a graduated scale, and I said, tell me what your level of pain will be as we reassess it. And what happened at that point was that the roof fell in on me. The letter was recalled because members of the space acquisition community demanded it be recalled. And there are many people that believed that that letter was the straw that broke the camel's back, that when I went after the FFRDCs——

Mrs. MALONEY. Could we have a copy of that letter for the record?

Colonel MANGOLD. I can get you that copy, ma'am.
Guido, did you bring the package?

Mr. ARU. I may have it. I will give it to the staff afterwards.

Colonel MANGOLD. Yes, ma'am, we will get you that letter for the record. We were just able to obtain that.

[The letter follows:]

DEPARTMENT OF THE AIR FORCE
HEADQUARTERS UNITED STATES AIR FORCE
WASHINGTON, D.C.

REPLY TO
ATTN OF: XOFS
26 APR 1993

SUBJECT: Federally Funded Research and Development Center Cost Reduction Request

TO: Associate Deputy Assistant Secretary
Management Policy and Program Integration
Assistant Secretary (Acquisition)

1. The Space and C3I team is developing options for our leadership to address new funding targets we anticipate this summer. We are considering many alternatives – nothing is off the table. As part of these deliberations, we are considering an option which reduces the allowed Federally Funded Research and Development Center (FFRDC) technical support for the Electronic System Center (ESC) and Space and Missile Systems Center (SMC) by 25%, 50%, 75% and 100%. Please provide us a projection of cost savings for each option and the impacts by 14 May 1993.

2. Our intent is not to offer options which replace the employees of these FFRDCs with government or contractor personnel, but to eliminate their positions and save $181K per Member of the Technical Staff (MTS) per year for SMC and $155K per MTS per year for ESC. POC is Maj Ivette Falto-Heck/DSN 697-5890.

SANFORD D. MANGOLD, Colonel, USAF
Chief, Space Forces Division
DCS, Plans and Operations

cc: SMC/MO (Col Randma)
ESC/MO (B. Smith)

Mrs. MALONEY. Are you implying that many people in the procurement end of the Air Force are working on their retirement—or their golden parachute—when they promote excessive contracts in weapons systems?

Colonel MANGOLD. I think it needs to be looked at, ma'am. At the time this happened to me, recognize we were working so hard to cut the budget. What I did not understand was how I had alienated many people in the blue suits and in the contractor community because of massive cuts I was proposing and the uncommon success I had in getting those proposals accepted by the senior Air Force leadership, that when I came up with a proposal to cut back the FFRDCs, I saw a level of outrage and anger and vengeance that I hadn't experienced before.

I had experienced a certain amount of acrimony as I came up with a proposal, or a general officer would call my general and say, Mangold is at it again.

But when I sent out the letter, that was the first time that any proposal that I had ever developed and formalized was ever immediately recalled.

I was told by my leadership that the principal individuals involved in recalling it were at AQS, the space acquisition leadership, that they recalled it; and I didn't understand the significance of it then. It was only after the charges were brought forward against me, I was isolated from the budget process, Major General Hard retired and went to work as a senior vice president for the Aerospace Corp. in Colorado Springs supporting Air Force Space Command.

Mrs. MALONEY. Very briefly, I am told our time is up. All of you came forward today with great risk to your personal lives and your personal career. What would you hope to accomplish?

Colonel MANGOLD. My personal view is I hope you would turn this over to the DOD IG so we get a complete reassessment of what brought us to this point.

Mrs. MALONEY. OK. Yes. I would like to hear from you.

Colonel DIETZ. I concur. Somebody asked me the other evening, was I mad? Absolutely not. I was sad. I am disappointed. I am offended. This is an institution I have worked for for 27 years, and I hold the institution to higher standards and I think we need to revisit them and get back to them.

It has nothing to do with a particular program or a particular action. It is a process. It is values. It is ethics of leadership. I would hope that somehow or other we might bring some light of day on it.

Light of day is a wonderful, wonderful cathartic. I have absolutely nothing to win from this and everything in the world to lose. Absolutely nothing good can come out of this for me personally; maybe the system will be a bit better for it.

Mr. ARU. Madam Chairman, I echo Colonel Mangold's and Colonel Dietz's hope that the DOD IG does a thorough investigation that doesn't compromise individuals and material when they conduct it.

I have also included for the record, in an area where I consider myself an expert based on 10 years' worth of work, some specific recommendations with regard to the Defense Support Program and our Nation's early warning capabilities.

I hope, as Congresswoman Harman, my Representative, said, the Armed Services Committee does look at those because that is an area where I think I have some specific expertise.

I have also offered in my written testimony, some general suggestions with regard to perhaps a time for reassessment of the FFRDCs, how they support the Air Force as opposed to supporting OSD; and maybe a reassessment, hopefully that will come internally within Aerospace, of what its vision is supposed to be.

I believe that companies like Aerospace can make a significant contribution to the national security of this Nation. We have to keep in mind budget pressures and if the track we are on is wrong.

I also hope that this committee is able to look at the broader issue of our Nation's military space institutions, the acquisition and operations arm; and perhaps have some assessment as to what is wrong that has led us to this point today.

Mrs. MALONEY. I will certainly refer this to the DOD IG, and you should all feel very good about what you have done today.

Mr. McCandless has a statement.

Mr. MCCANDLESS. Yes. Thank you, Madam Chairman.

I have some documents I would like to enter into the record.

The first is a handwritten memorandum from Mr. Aldridge to General Horner, the essence of which says: My folks are very hot about this; they see it as a shortsighted effort of the DSP SPO to sell FEWS out. I, like you, will back any scheme that makes sense. But I didn't believe we could abandon the warfighters by taking men from review. If I am wrong, educate me.

Then the letter in response to General Horner—on June 22, 1993 from Mr. Aldridge on Aerospace Corp. stationery, in which he talks about the fact that: The requirements of DSP is no excuse for the advocacy tone of the report. We in Aerospace must make sure that we retain our objectivity, independence, and freedom from conflict. The role of the program should be played, if at all, by military program offices, military services, or other government officials. If we had stayed closer to pure technical evaluation of options measured against slated requirements, we might have avoided the situation which has damaged the Aerospace people. And he goes on.

And a November 1, executive summary, titled "Review of Accusations Pertaining to the Space Based Budget Issue," it is addressed to the Air Force inspector general. Information in this particular document is now a matter in the public as a result of the inspector general's report.

And finally, a January 27 inspector general letter, memorandum for the Secretary of the Air Force, the subject of which is review of Air Force inspector general report of inquiry pertaining to Defense Support Program, Follow-On Early Warning System Program.

And Madam Chairwoman, I think it appropriate that we—for the record, that we understand that Mr. Aru worked for Aerojet prior to working for Aerospace and that the Aerojet producer produces the sensors for the DSP-II, the option that Mr. Aru's report recommends.

Thank you. I ask unanimous consent that these all be entered into the record.

[The information follows:]

June 18, 1993

Dear Pete,

Thank you for the letter on the DSP status report. I appreciate the effort it took to prepare it. I've read it and have a number of questions. I'd like to discuss them with you and the DSP Program Office staff at the earliest opportunity. Please give me a call to arrange a meeting.

Regards,
Clark

THE AEROSPACE CORPORATION

E. C. Aldridge, Jr.
President and
Chief Executive Officer

June 22, 1993

Dear Chuck,

Thanks for your note and copy of the memorandum from Jaquish to SMC and the PEOs. I share his concern and yours about this matter. I have done all I said I would do in my letter to you on May 27, 1993. A thorough independent review of the report by Aerospace confirms the overly optimistic view of the DSP follow-on, called DSP II, capabilities to meet the stated requirements. Because it did not meet the requirements DSP II was <u>rejected</u> in our internal assessment of FEWs alternatives. I have also provided the program office support for responding to inquiries about this issue and have made personal calls to John Deutch and George Schneiter to explain the situation. I have also talked to Don Hard and Gary Schnelzer to determine what else we can do to put this issue to rest.

I have tried to ascertain why such a report was written in the first place. The only "excuse" I can find is that the analysis was done <u>before</u> the final decision and it was an attempt to make the best case possible for DSP II. After the decision, the DSP program manager asked Aerospace to document the results of the effort and "file it," which they did. It was the unauthorized distribution which caused the problem, but that is no excuse for the advocacy tone of the report.

All of the Aerospace employees have been counseled on this issue. Not only have our managers and I spoke with individuals and groups about this issue, I passed the following message to <u>all</u> the Aerospace employees on Friday, June 18:

"As you know the current defense budget environment is highly uncertain and, more now than at any other time, subject to rapid and drastic adjustment by the politics of jobs in various congressional districts and by the fierce competition of those programs trying to remain in the smaller budget. Particularly at this time, we in Aerospace must make sure that we retain our objectivity, independence and freedom from conflict of interest.

There was an occasion several weeks ago, when our objectivity was challenged. We were not careful enough in our analysis and did not distinguish carefully between analysis and advocacy. The net result was that it appeared that we took on an advocacy position for a program that if accepted could have resulted in the termination of another program. The role of program advocacy should be played, if at all, by the military program office, the military services or other government officials. If we had stayed closer to pure technical evaluation of options measured against stated requirements we might have avoided this situation, which has damaged the reputation of Aerospace.

Gen. Charles A. Horner   - 2 -   June 22, 1993

While we are pursuing activities to alleviate the current problem, we must all learn from this lesson and realize that for Aerospace to do its job, we must be absolutely "pure" in our technical evaluations and avoid taking on the responsibilities which clearly rests with our customers."

On a final note, I am most disturbed about the "rumor" that Aerospace does not support FEWs. This is incorrect. I believe, as do our technical people at Aerospace, that the tactical missile threat, with the uncertainty of having nuclear or chemical/biological warheads, will be the dominant concern in any future conflict. Warning against such a threat will be a "hard" requirement. FEWs is the only system that will give us confidence in providing launch warning and tactical missile defense tip-off.

I sincerely hope that this will be behind us soon. You and your command have more important things to do.

Warmest regards,

E. C. Aldridge, Jr.

General Charles A. Horner
Commander
U. S. Space Command
Peterson AFB, CO 80914

DEPARTMENT OF THE AIR FORCE
WASHINGTON DC

OFFICE OF THE ASSISTANT SECRETARY

17 JUN 1993

SAF/AQ

MEMORANDUM FOR: COMMANDER, SPACE AND MISSILE SYSTEMS CENTER
AF PROGRAM EXECUTIVE OFFICER/SPACE PROGRAMS

SUBJECT: Acquisition Program Management, Coordination, and Approval Process for Space Programs

As you know, we are in the midst of some very difficult and important reviews of several Air Force space programs. I want to emphasize the importance of ensuring our people not go outside our existing corporate processes of coordination, review, and approval as we conduct these reviews and restructure the budget this summer and fall.

We have come a long way in refining our corporate management process for space programs. The maturation of Air Force Space Command and the implementation of Integrated Weapon System Management within Air Force Materiel Command have significantly influenced our progress. However, it appears that some of our people are not satisfied that the chain-of-command's existing corporate decision-making process produces the right answers. Hence, they do not feel bound to support the Air Force positions established by it. Recent actions of some individuals have left me seriously concerned about our people's basic understanding of their individual responsibilities to operate within our normal processes.

I suggest it is timely and appropriate to remind our people that there is a time to argue a different approach and a time to accept and support the decisions made within the corporate process by those charged with that responsibility. The strength of our process lies in giving differing views a forum in the pre-decisional stage, not in continuing to press for a particular point of view to those who were not privy to the entire deliberative process. There are already numerous vehicles (See AFR 123-11) for raising concerns if any person feels such decisions have been made in an arbitrary, capricious or fraudulent manner. It is only destructive of our process if Air Force people or support contractors advocate their personal opinions outside the corporate process, simply because the decision was not the one they wanted.

It also bears mention that higher headquarters necessarily conduct analyses from the broadest possible perspective before senior leaders form the Air Force positions which are presented to DoD and the Congress. Proposals that have not been subjected to the scrutiny of our corporate decision making process are automatically suspect, usually create unnecessary confusion and work, and often do an extreme disservice to the Air Force, DoD and, ultimately, the taxpayers. We can ill afford the expenditure of critical Air Force resources on unauthorized efforts from outside the corporate process that are intended to reverse official decisions. Those who cannot in good conscience live within such simple, but critically important, guidelines should question their own ability to make meaningful contributions to our goals.

For acquisition matters, the proper level for headquarters coordination remains the Mission Area Directors in SAF/AQ. They will work with other HQ AF offices, you, and your people. Please ensure your people understand the importance of these principles and their responsibilities to support them.

cc: AFMC/CC
AFSPACECOM/CC

JOHN E. JAQUISH, Lt Gen, USAF
Principal Deputy Assistant Secretary
of the Air Force (Acquisition)

EXECUTIVE SUMMARY

1 NOV 1993

(29 Dec 93 revision)

SUBJECT: Review of Accusations Pertaining to the Space Based Infrared Budget Issue

TO: The Air Force Inspector General
Washington, DC 20330-1000

1. Authority: An inquiry was conducted from 10-29 Oct 93 by Major General Marcus A. Anderson for the Inspector General of the Air Force, Washington DC 20330-1140 under the authority of letter of appointment, SAF/IG, dated 10 Oct 93.

2. The inquiry considered allegations from three sources. The following summarizes these allegations.

    a. The Secretary of the Air Force identified a set of five allegations in which AF officials were accused of releasing proprietary data to competing contractors, telling a contractor to "get on the FEWS team", inhibiting the flow of contractor data to OSD, suppressing information about program alternatives, and providing erroneous data to OSD.

    b. Aerojet Corporation cited several allegations surrounding an alternative to the Follow-on Early Warning System. They believed this information, in the form of an Aerospace Technical Operating Report, was suppressed and, further, given to their competitors even though it contained Aerojet proprietary data. In addition, they believed that the Air Force was not fairly evaluating cost in comparing the FEWS and DSP systems.

    c. Congressman Conyers requested that the DoD IG conduct an investigation into similar allegations. In documentation received from an unnamed source, it was claimed that senior Air Force officers suppressed information concerning a lower-cost alternative to FEWS, and that Mr Aldridge, CEO of The Aerospace Corporation, assisted in this suppression. Furthermore, it was alleged that senior AF officers passed false and misleading information to OSD decision-makers on the FEWS and DSP systems. Based on agreement between SAF/IG and DoD IG, Congressman Conyers' concerns were addressed as a part of this report.

3. Certain allegations were referred to this inquiry which suggested the possibility of misconduct by senior Air Force officials. During the course of the inquiry into these allegations, we were guided by the policy and procedures contained in AFR 120-4. Despite a vigorous inquiry involving approximately 50 hours of recorded testimony from 36 witnesses, contractor and government alike, and several hundred pages of documents, we uncovered no substantiated

ATCH 2

128

evidence of conduct which would constitute a violation of criminal law, standards of conduct, or would amount to an abuse of discretion, fraud, waste, or abuse, reprisal, or reflect adversely on a senior official's judgment. Given the above information, the following are significant findings with respect to senior Air Force officers identified from the allegations:

   a. CINCSPACE (Gen Horner) did not inhibit TRW from passing Multi-Spectral (MS) data to OSD. Although Gen Horner told TRW that he was concerned that they were sending mixed signals by proposing an MS alternative to FEWS, he did not direct TRW to withhold this data. During an interview, TRW said they made an "independent business decision" to not provide MS data to OSD/PA&E.

   b. The PEO for Space (MGen Schnelzer) did not suppress information about a lower cost alternative to the proposed $13B FEWS satellite program. While conducting a study on sensor alternatives (called Sensor Study I), MGen Schnelzer eliminated a concept called DSP-MLV since it did not meet user requirements which was a key groundrule for the OSD/Congressionally directed study. As groundrules on user requirements changed during the summer, this concept became one of several alternatives being reviewed within the Bottom-Up Review (BUR) process.

   c. Results of this inquiry reflect no wrongdoing by ▓▓▓▓▓▓▓▓▓▓▓▓ ▓▓▓▓▓▓▓▓▓▓▓. However, the allegation that ▓▓▓▓▓ provided a copy of the Aerospace TOR to Aerojet competitors was investigated by a separate inquiry which concluded that proprietary data was, in fact, inappropriately released.

4. Fifteen of the seventeen allegations noted from the three sources identified in paragraph 2 above were investigated. The two allegations not investigated deal with the release of Aerojet proprietary data to FEWS competitors which were investigated by Space and Missile Center. Of the 15 allegations reviewed, 10 are not substantiated. A summary of those substantiated in whole or in part follows:

   a. SAF-identified allegations:

      (1) "That USSPACECOM staff members told a defense contractor to "get on the FEWS team or get out of the way", is substantiated in part. While no direct statement, as alleged, could be verified, TRW got a "message" from USSPACECOM that they should pay attention to their role in the FEWS program (one of two prime competitors).

      (2) "That the briefing charts and background information for the 5 Oct 93 Space-Based IR Sensor System capabilities budget issue briefing to Mr

Deutch were released by USSPACECOM to space-based sensor competitors", is substantiated. The material was, in fact, provided to Lockheed, TRW, Gumman and Hughes; however, in the opinion of an expert witness, no proprietary data was released. On the other hand, POM data was included in the package and should not have been released. The actions were determined to be inadvertent.

b. Aerojet allegation, "That the Government attempted to discredit the Aerospace TOR" is substantiated. This is an unusual situation because the Government and the leadership of Aerospace Corporation (Mr Pete Aldridge) had good reason to discredit the report. It had not been coordinated with the user or the PEO, had been approved at an intermediate level at Aerospace, discounted JROC-validated requirements, and was written in an advocacy tone. Mr Aldridge was embarrassed with the report, as was the Air Force about the content and the way the report was coordinated and distributed.

c. Congressman Conyers-identified allegations:

(1) "That MGen Schnelzer deleted from a Congressionally-mandated study an option (DSP-MLV) identifying improvements to the existing DSP as an alternative to the FEWS that could save up to $10B" is substantiated. Like the previous allegation, MGen Schnelzer had a good reason to delete the DSP-MLV option since it didn't meet one of the key OSD/Congressional groundrules--options in the study must meet operational requirements as stated in the FEWS Operational Requirements Document.

(2) "That Mr Aldridge ordered the recall of the Aerospace TOR and assisted in the suppression of options from review by Congress. That Mr Aldridge interfered in a DoD IG investigation by requesting that the IG back-off on these issues", is substantiated in part. The part substantiated was that Mr Aldridge ordered the recall of the Aerospace TOR. He did so initially to read the report, then he affirmed the decision after review by an independent Aerospace team.

5. To summarize:

a. What brought us to this inquiry? In the space arena and perhaps across the acquisition spectrum, the intense competition for dollars in DoD and among its defense contractors ("survival" mentality) is producing distrust, suspicion, breakdowns in communications and ultimately allegations of impropriety, both from within the Air Force and from defense contractors.

(1) An event occurred in the February 1993 timeframe that was a catalyst for several of the allegations. That event was rejection of an option for Sensor Study I that had been prepared by a team from the DSP program office.

assisted by Aerospace and Aerojet. The rejection was made by MGen Schneizer (PEO for Space) who was in charge of the study. He made the decision for logical reasons, but the decision was not understood or accepted by those who had proposed the option. Thus, perceptions of favoritism toward FEWS, misleading/erroneous data being used, suppressing data in DSP, etc., ultimately became allegations in this inquiry.

        (2) Another key event was publication of the Aerospace Technical Operating Report (TOR) in April 1993. This report was purportedly done to document the results of the work done for Sensor Study I and to have an option available in case FEWS fell on hard times. In reality, the TOR became an advocacy document for those who felt "slighted" by the decision to reject a lower cost DSP option from Sensor Study I. The way in which this report was published and distributed caused a great deal of concern within the Air Force and Aerospace Corporation, and the actions taken resulted in several allegations addressed by this inquiry.

    b. Where do we go from here? There's no simple fix. Given the environment as described above, the possibility of similar allegations from defense contractors is ever-present. Good communications will help, but will not guarantee success. Within the Air Force, we must listen to those with concerns, address them and attempt to achieve consensus. If consensus is not achieved, those with dissenting opinions need to understand why their position wasn't accepted. If they continue to push their position and perceive "no one is listening", future allegations will inevitably result.

131

1 NOV 1993

REPORT OF INQUIRY

SUBJECT: Review of Accusations Pertaining to the Space-Based Infrared Budget Issue

TO: The Air Force Inspector General
Washington DC 20330-1000

1. **Authority:** An inquiry was conducted from 10-29 Oct 93 by Major General Marcus A. Anderson for the Inspector General of the Air Force, Washington DC 20330-1000 under authority of letter of appointment, SAF/IG, dated 10 Oct 93. (TAB A)

2. **Background.**

   a. This report is segmented into three separate sets of allegations. The original tasking to conduct the inquiry came from the SAF/IG letter of 10 Oct 93. After the start of the investigation, two additional sets of allegations arose that were similar in nature to those previously identified by SAF/IG and were, therefore, incorporated into this inquiry. The first of these additional allegations came from the Aerojet Corporation in a letter sent directly to the Investigating Officer (TAB B) alleging certain improprieties. The second set of additional allegations came from Congressman Conyers in a letter to the DoD Inspector General requesting an investigation. (TAB C) As a result of these new allegations, SAF/IG, in coordination with the DoD IG, concluded that the original tasking gave this inquiry team sufficient authority to address all three sets of allegations in a single report.

   b. A chronology of events and major documents bearing on the inquiry follows:

   (1) Sensor Study I - In response to questions from Congress, OSD C3I in Sep 92 began planning a study effort to review the development and integration of Brilliant Eyes (BE) with an improved space-based Tactical Warning/Attack Assessment System (TW/AA), a follow-on to the Defense Support Program (DSP). On 30 Nov 92, SAF/AQS tasked the Program Executive Officer (PEO) for Space to conduct a study. This study, known as Sensor Study I, was worked by a committee of DSP, FEWS, and Ballistic Missile Defense (BMD) system program office (SPO) personnel with support from the Aerospace Corporation and contractor inputs from Lockheed Missiles and Space Company (LMSC), TRW and Aerojet. Led by the PEO, this study was presented to OSD/C3I on 12 Apr 93 who, in turn, submitted a report to Congress in the summer of 93.

   (2) Aerospace Technical Operations Report (TOR), 93(3409)-6, "Preserving the Air Force Options", 23 Apr 93, was generated by the Aerospace Corporation in response to the DSP Program Director's Feb 93 request to consolidate work that the DSP, Aerospace, and Aerojet working group conducted to support Sensor Study I. The Sensor Study I working group addressed a DSP/BE Synergy effort, which proposed a DSP-Medium Launch Vehicle (MLV) concept and a Pre-Planned Product Improvement (P3I) of the existing DSP system. This concept was not included in the C3I

report to Congress as it did not meet the user's requirements. As a result, Aerospace was tasked by the DSP Program Director to document the concept in a TOR. This report describes a DSP variant called DSP-II, characterized by DSP plus P3I and launched on an MLV.

(3) Sensor Study II: This study, conducted between Apr-Jun 93, was a follow-on effort to Sensor Study I for presentation to Under Secretary of Defense for Acquisition and Technology (USD(A&T)). This effort focused on combining DSP and BE, and FEWS and BE satellites to satisfy both the TW/AA and BMD requirements. Due to the upcoming Bottom Up Review (BUR) in this area, the presentation was not given to USD(A&T).

(4) Bottom Up Review (BUR): The USD(A&T) directed that a study be conducted to evaluate alternative materiel solutions to the TW/AA requirement. This effort started on 24 Jun 93 and was led by ██████████████████████████████████

3. **Matters Investigated:** The following allegations were investigated:

a. SAF/IG Letter:

(1) That TRW proprietary data on a multi-spectral alternative provided in a briefing to OSD was passed by the Air Force to competitors.

(2) That USSPACECOM staff members told a defense contractor to get on the Follow-on Early Warning System (FEWS) team or get out of the way.

(3) That the CINC, USSPACECOM inhibited a defense contractor's attempts to get multi-spectral data to the Office of the Secretary of Defense (OSD).

(4) That the briefing charts and background information for the 5 Oct Space-Based IR Sensor System capabilities budget issue briefing to Mr Deutch were released by USSPACECOM to space-based sensor competitors.

(5) That data provided by the Space-Based Early Warning and Ballistic Missile Defense System Program Offices to the Commander, USSPACECOM, was erroneous.

b. Aerojet Letter:

(1) That the Air Force tried to suppress results of the Aerojet study (which eventually evolved into the Aerospace TOR of 23 Apr 93).

(2) That the Government attempted to discredit the Aerospace TOR.

(3) That the Air Force released the Aerospace TOR, which contained Aerojet proprietary data, to FEWS contractors.

(4) That the Air Force did not fairly evaluate costs in comparing FEWS and DSP systems.

(5) That the Air Force did not use accurate estimates of cost for a Shuttle launch of DSP satellites.

(6) That Senior Air Force officials threatened TRW to not provide information on Multi-Spectral technology which in turn restricted data flow from TRW to Aerojet.

c. Congressman Conyers Letter to DoD IG:

(1) That senior Air Force officials suppressed information about a lower cost alternative to the proposed $13 billion Follow-on Early Warning System (FEWS) satellite program.

(2) That General Horner as CINC, USSPACECOM made erroneous statements supporting FEWS, ordered the DSP-II report recalled and attempted to suppress discussion of technical alternatives to FEWS.

(3) That Major General Garry Schnelzer (Program Executive Officer for Space) deleted from a Congressionally-mandated study an option (DSP-II) identifying improvements to the existing Defense Support Program (DSP) as an alternative to FEWS that could save up to $10 billion.

(4) That Mr Pete Aldridge, as President of The Aerospace Corporation, ordered the recall of the Aerospace TOR and assisted in the suppression of options from review by Congress. That Mr Aldridge interfered in a DOD IG investigation by requesting that the IG back-off on these issues.

(5) That several Air Force personnel and Mr Aldridge provided false and misleading information to decision makers within OSD and Congress with regard to the cost and performance of the DSP and FEWS programs.

(6) That ███████████ provided the Aerospace TOR to Aerojet competitors, TRW and Lockheed, knowing that it contained Aerojet "competition sensitive" information.

4. Witnesses. The following individuals, in alphabetical order, were interviewed:

a. Mr Edward C. Aldridge, President, Aerospace Corporation

134

g. ████████████
h. ████████████
i. ████████████
j. ████████████
k. ████████████
l. ████████████
m. ████████████
n. ████████████
o. ████████████
p. ████████████
q. ████████████
r. General Charles A. Horner, CINC, USSPACECOM
s. ████████████
t. ████████████
u. ████████████
v. ████████████
w. ████████████
x. ████████████
y. ████████████
z. ████████████
aa. ████████████

135

ab. ████████████████████████████████████

ac. ████

ad. ████████████████

ae. Major General Garry A. Schnelzer, PEO for Space

af. ████████████

ag. ██████████

ah. ████████████████████████████

ai. ████████████████████

aj. ████████████████████████████

ak. ██████████████████████████

al. ████████████

5. SAF/IG Letter, 10 Oct 93: Facts, discussion and conclusions:

   a.   Allegation One: That TRW proprietary data on a Multi-Spectral alternative provided in a briefing to OSD was passed by the Air Force to competitors.

   1) Facts:

      a) TRW decided to withhold Multi-Spectral (MS) data to OSD/PA&E. (TAB E)

      b) Bottom Up Review directed Space-Based Early Warning System (SBEWS) System Program Office (SPO) to provide a generic Multi-Spectral briefing to the Bottom Up Review. (TAB F)

      c) SBEWS SPO constructed a Multi-Spectral briefing with inputs from The Aerospace Corporation and Lockheed Missiles and Space Company (LMSC). The Aerospace input came from a Technical Interchange Meeting between TRW and Aerospace engineers; information was passed to SBEWS SPO with a warning that it contained TRW proprietary data. The SBEWS SPO's project officer for this briefing, ████████ understood the caution and safeguarded the data. LMSC's input to the SBEWS SPO was merely a Multi-Spectral tutorial. (TABs G, H, I, J, and K)

136

███████████████

(d) On 30 Sep 93, SBEWS SPO briefed Bottom Up Review on Multi-Spectral Technology. Briefing was hand-marked as "competition sensitive". Briefer cautioned attendees that briefing contained "competition sensitive" data. (TABs F, G, and L)

(e) All witnesses denied releasing the briefing contents outside the Government. Additionally, LMSC, a FEWS competitor to TRW, denied receiving proprietary Multi-Spectral data while providing input to the SBEWS SPO. Air Force attendees of the Bottom Up Review Multi-Spectral technology briefing denied releasing the briefing or its contents outside the Air Force. (TAB M)

(2) Discussion:

(a) In Sep 93, TRW was requested in writing to brief their Multi-Spectral concept to OSD/PA&E. TRW did not brief OSD as requested because TRW made an independent business decision not to provide OSD Multi-Spectral data. As an alternative, OSD then tasked the SBEWS SPO to present a briefing on Multi-Spectral. In response to this tasking, the SPO worked with The Aerospace Corporation to obtain information to satisfy the OSD tasking. Aerospace, without SPO representation, met with TRW to discuss Multi-Spectral technology. It was made clear by TRW personnel that they regarded much of the information that was the subject of this discussion as being proprietary in nature. No charts or other documents were handed out, but it was agreed by everyone present that TRW proprietary data was discussed. After the meeting, Aerospace personnel returned to their offices, began putting thoughts on paper, and safeguarded this information as proprietary information. A memo was written by an Aerospace employee stating the specific information that was believed to be proprietary. (TAB J)

(b) Additionally, the SPO requested support from LMSC in preparing its OSD briefing on Multi-Spectral. The request was for a generic tutorial on Multi-Spectral, not a specific application. The LMSC input was faxed to the SPO in the form of a Lockheed Primer (TAB K). As part of this inquiry, the primer was later reviewed by an independent expert in the MS area, ███████████, Ph.D. Phillips Laboratory. In her opinion, the primer is generic and could have been written by anybody with a reasonable knowledge of the subject. She concluded that no TRW proprietary data was contained within the LMSC document. (TAB N)

(c) ███████ and ███████████████ with the help of Aerospace, put the OSD requested Multi-Spectral briefing together. The briefing was not originally marked proprietary. ███████ was at the Pentagon preparing to brief the Multi-Spectral concept, while ███████ was at Space and Missile Systems Center (SMC) making final preparations on the briefing charts. When ███████ finished, he faxed the unmarked charts to ███████. When ███████ received the charts at the Pentagon, he immediately marked the cover page "Competition Sensitive". ███████ later testified that he uses the terms "proprietary" and "competition sensitive" interchangeably. (TAB F)

(d) In ███████ opening remarks of the Multi-Spectral briefing to the Bottom Up Review on 30 Sep 93, he cautioned all attendees that "Competition Sensitive" data was contained in the briefing. ███████ was satisfied that all attendees understood the proprietary nature of the briefing. Copies of the briefing charts were passed out to a number of attendees, and some time after the briefing, SAF/SP was also provided a copy of the briefing. At a later date (3-4 days later), ▓▓ ▓▓ marked an additional page in the briefing as "Competition Sensitive".

(e) TRW proprietary data was contained in the briefing (TAB I); however, the briefing was not provided to TRW competitors by the Air Force.

(3) Conclusion: This allegation is not substantiated.

(a) The SPO briefing to the Bottom Up Review on Multi-Spectral was marked "competition sensitive".

(b) This briefing was prefaced by the briefer cautioning all attendees that the contents of this briefing contained proprietary information.

(c) All Air Force recepients of the briefing charts confirmed that they had not released the briefing contents outside the Government.

b. Allegation Two: That USSPACECOM staff members told a defense contractor to get on the Follow-on Early Warning System (FEWS) team or get out of the way.

(1) Facts:

(a) TRW briefed their Multi-Spectral concept to a number of organizations within the Government, including USSPACECOM. (TABs E & O)

(b) OSD/PA&E requested TRW provide information on their Multi-Spectral concept. (TAB E)

(c) CINCSPACE received a briefing from TRW on the Multi-Spectral concept. TRW briefed the concept. (TAB P).

(d) Multi-Spectral is an approach to meet the space-based early warning detection mission. (TAB L)

(e) Multi-Spectral technology is not as mature as FEWS. (TAB L)

(f) FEWS is the only system that meets all Joint Requirements Oversight Council (JROC)-validated FEWS Operational Requirement Document (ORD) requirements. (TAB Q)

(g) TRW had been briefing their Multi-Spectral concept while simultaneously being a competitor for the FEWS contract. (TAB O)

(h) CINCSPACE questioned TRW's commitment to FEWS. (TAB P)

(i) TRW said the word "told" in the allegation is too strong. (TAB E)

(2) Discussion:

(a) TRW briefed their Multi-Spectral concept to various organizations. In most cases, this briefing was unsolicited. TRW's Multi-Spectral concept was offered both as an alternative to FEWS and as a FEWS upgrade. Since TRW was also a competitor for FEWS, their Multi-Spectral briefings gave mixed signals to some military officials regarding their motivation to proffer the best possible FEWS solution.

(b) In an attempt to understand the TRW Multi-Spectral concept, as well as their motivation for offering the Multi-Spectral concept, CINCSPACE requested a briefing from TRW. After hearing the presentation, CINCSPACE questioned TRW's commitment to the FEWS program. CINCSPACE advocated FEWS as the only system that meets all the JROC-validated ORD requirements. CINCSPACE believed that the Multi-Spectral concept might be an attractive FEWS upgrade at some future time, but not now as MS technology is not as mature as FEWS.

(c) CINCSPACE's comments appeared to have an affect on TRW. Thereafter, they made a corporate decision to not provide data on Multi-Spectral that could give the appearance of advocating a position inconsistent with FEWS. (TAB P)

(3) Conclusion: This allegation is substantiated in part. Although no direct statement, as alleged, was made by CINCSPACE or the USSPACECOM staff, TRW certainly got a "message" from USSPACECOM that they should pay attention to their role in the FEWS program.

c. Allegation Three: That the Commander, USSPACECOM, inhibited a defense contractor's attempts to get Multi-Spectral data to the Office of the Secretary of Defense (OSD).

(1) Facts:

a) CINCSPACE did not support TRW providing Multi-Spectral information to OSD/PA&E; however, CINCSPACE did not direct TRW to withhold data from OSD. (TAB P)

(b) TRW made a corporate business decision to not provide Multi-Spectral information to OSD/PA&E. TRW also has a teaming arrangement with Grumman which does not permit TRW to advocate DSP upgrades that may conflict with FEWS. (TABs E & R)

(c) CINCSPACE discussed Multi-Spectral technology with  in Jul 93 and suggested that it could be appropriate technology to review for future applications (TAB P)

(d) Based on TRW's conduct, that is briefing an alternative to FEWS, it appeared to CINCSPACE that TRW was competing against itself. (TABs U & Z)

(e) All facts in Allegation Two also apply to this allegation.

(2) Discussion: CINCSPACE's primary focus is to develop a space-based TW/AA system for the next generation of warfighters. His concerns regarding the degree of TRW's commitment to meet that obligation are understandable, but he did not direct TRW to withhold data.

(3) Conclusion: This allegation is not substantiated. It was not inappropriate for CINCSPACE to expect a solid FEWS commitment by TRW, one of two contractor teams competing for the FEWS contract. TRW made an independent business decision to withhold the requested MS data from OSD/PA&E. They later provided that data to Mr Deutch, OUSD(A).

d. Allegation Four: That the briefing charts and background information for the 5 Oct 93 Space-Based IR Sensor System capabilities budget issue briefing to Mr Deutch were released by USSPACECOM to space-based sensor competitors.

(1) Facts:

(a) Bottom Up Review Briefing Charts, 5 Oct 93, with background information were released to four FEWS contractors by USSPACECOM/J5S, Space Systems Directorate. (TABs S & V)

(b) ███████████████ who released the information did not know that information contained in the package was proprietary or competition sensitive. She did remove the only chart that was marked "competition sensitive". Further, she did not know that it is inappropriate to release Government budgetary data. (TAB S)

(c) Once apprised that the briefing material was considered proprietary, ███████████ took immediate action to notify contractors receiving this information to return it. (TABs S & T)

(d) There is conflicting evidence on whether data in question is proprietary. TRW claims information within the briefing is proprietary; however, an expert witness believes the briefing contained no proprietary data, but that it did contain Government budgetary data. (TABs E & N)

(2) Discussion:

(a) Before ██████████████ gave the briefing to the contractors, she removed pages that were identified as competition sensitive. Only charts that were not marked were given to the contractors. She did not knowingly give contractors proprietary data. ████████ lack of acquisition experience and training in the handling of proprietary data may have contributed to the release of this information.

(b) Because of the apparent insufficient marking of the briefing, the suggestion that it contained proprietary data was challenged. The opinion of an independent expert suggested information contained in the briefing was not proprietary.

(c) Statutory Discussion: The "Procurement Integrity" provisions of the Office of Federal Procurement Policy Act (41 U.S.C. 423, et seq.) prohibit both contractor and government procurement officials from knowingly disclosing proprietary or source selection information to unauthorized individuals. Certain allegations of such unauthorized disclosures were referred to this inquiry:

(1) On 4 Oct 93, an officer assigned to ▓▓▓▓▓▓▓▓ released a compilation of briefing slides to contractor personnel. This information contained Program Objective Memorandum (POM) data which falls within the scope of "source selection" information (20 Public Contract Law Journal 427, at 446) and, hence, ought not to have been released.

(2) The releasor is not a procurement officer. She had no formal training or experience in the restrictions on release of information of this type. None of the slides released were marked as proprietary or competition sensitive.

(3) Also contained in this briefing was data alleged by TRW to be proprietary in nature. Although this information was released to competing contractors, our independent assessment of the information is that it did not, in all likelihood, constitute proprietary data. Futhermore, this data was not marked as proprietary or competition sensitive.

(3) Conclusion: This allegation was substantiated in part. Briefing charts were provided to LMSC, TRW, Grumman and Hughes; however, there was a conscious effort made prior to release to sanitize the briefing for competition sensitive information. Action was taken to retrieve these documents once the issue of proprietary data surfaced. The impact of release of this information is tempered by an expert witness stating that proprietary data was not in the document; however, POM values were included, and because of this, the briefing charts should not have been distributed. Thus, there is insufficient evidence to conclude that a government official knowingly released protectable data such as to constitute a violation of the Procurement Integrity Act.

e. Allegation Five: That data provided by the Space-Based Early Warning and Ballistic Missile Defense System Program Offices to the Commander, USSPACECOM, was erroneous.

(1) Facts:

(a) The Bottom Up Review set specific groundrules for the SBEWS to follow in providing comparison of all potential systems to satisfy the space-based early warning mission. (TAB W)

(b) The Bottom Up Review analyzed up to twenty alternatives to satisfy the space-based early warning mission, including several versions of DSP. (TABs X, Y, & Z)

(c) MGen Schneizer, ▓▓▓▓▓▓▓▓▓▓▓▓▓▓▓▓▓▓▓▓ were satisfied with the data submitted from the respective SPOs. (TABs X, Y, & Z)

(d) The SBEWS had a dedicated organization to provide input for Bottom Up Review-requested data. (TABs F & AT)

(e) ▓▓▓▓▓▓▓▓▓▓▓▓▓▓▓▓▓▓▓▓▓▓▓▓▓▓▓▓▓▓ believes data used to compare FEWS and DSP was erroneous. (TAB AA)

141

(f) ████████████████████ has addressed each of ████████ concerns (TABs AB & AT)

(g) Both TRW and Aerojet had expressed concerns over the validity of data; however, they have no first hand knowledge (TABs E & AC)

(2) Discussion:

(a) Prior to 1 May 93, the DSP and Follow-on Early Warning System (FEWS) were managed by two different SPOs. Both programs supported the same mission area--space-based early warning detection. As such, the two SPOs naturally competed for programmatic priority. On 1 May 93, the two SPOs were integrated into one program office, the Space-Based Early Warning SPO.

(b) ████████████████████ He has been challenged with harmonizing the two programs now under his guidance and getting his new program office pointed in one common direction. He is confident that concerns expressed by ████████ have been properly addressed. In addition to ████████ testimony, independent assessments of ████████ responses to ████████ concerns were made by an AFOTEC technical advisor. ████████████████████ His assessment endorsed ████████ response as having appropriately addressed the concerns of ████████ (TAB AD)

(c) During this investigation, the cost data provided in support of the Sensor Study I and the Bottom Up Review was reviewed by an independent team consisting of two analysts from SAF/FMCC (Directorate of Cost, DASAF for Cost and Economics) and a technical expert from AFOTEC. The team found the methodologies used to generate costs in support of the Sensor Study I to be of some concern; however, any concerns regarding the cost estimates do not negate the validity of the technical analysis performed in the Sensor Study I. In addition, changing the cost estimates would not have changed the conclusion that only the FEWS system was technically capable of meeting the users' requirements. Additionally, the team found that generally, the cost estimates prepared in support of the Bottom Up Review were done to the best quality standard that time allowed and that good tracking of cost estimates between various Bottom Up Review options exists. (see paragraph 6d and TAB AV)

(d) ████████ has been involved with the DSP, directly or indirectly, for the past 25 years. (TAB AA)

(e) In addition to ████████ TRW and Aerojet (DSP contractors) have expressed similar concerns, which are addressed later in the inquiry.

(f) Interviews with various SPO personnel in key positions, interviews with SPACECOM personnel, and interviews with recepient of the SPO-provided data, ████████ indicated confidence in the data provided. In no case, was the accuracy and validity of the data questioned. In most cases, the efforts of the SPO personnel to provide data in a timely and quality manner were highly lauded.

(3) Conclusion: This allegation was not substantiated. Data was accurate--process was sound.

6. **Aerojet Letter, 21 Oct 93**: Facts, discussion and conclusions:

   a. Allegation One: That the Air Force tried to suppress results of the Aerojet study (which eventually evolved into the Aerospace TOR).

   (1) Facts:

   (a) Sensor Study I: Congress tasked OSD to study options for a Follow-on Early Warning System to accomplish the TW/AA mission. Specifically, Congress asked for an analysis in three areas. Task 1: Report on what modifications would be needed to the BE system so that it could fulfill the requirements of the FEWS program; Task 2: Compare the FEWS design to a low altitude distributed architecture system; and Task 3: Compare the FEWS design to a combination of Brilliant Eyes and an upgraded DSP, also known as DSP/BE Synergy. MGen Schnelzer assigned ▓▓▓▓▓▓▓▓▓▓▓▓▓▓ of the BMD SPO, as the project lead with members from the DSP, FEWS and BE SPOs. The stated groundrule for this study was that each task must meet the Draft FEWS ORD requirements. The study was briefed by MGen Schnelzer on 12 Apr 93 to OSD/C3I. Thereafter, OSD/C3I submitted the required report to Congress. (TAB W & Y)

   (b) To support Task 3 of the Sensor Study I, results were briefed to the PEO for Space by then ▓▓▓▓▓▓▓▓▓▓ in a briefing entitled "DSP/BE Synergy", dated 3 Feb 93. Aerojet served as a member of a working group with DSP SPO and Aerospace membership. The solution presented was a DSP-MLV concept. The Aerojet study was their formal contribution to that working group. (TAB AE & AF)

   (c) PEO for Space rejected the DSP-MLV approach on Task 3 study since it did not meet user requirements. He included DSP++ as DSP variant closely approximating FEWS ORD requirements. (TABs Y, AG & AH)

   (d) Mr Aldridge, President of Aerospace, recalled all known copies of the Aerospace TOR, 93(3409)-6, dated 23 Apr 93. Mr Aldridge had not reviewed the TOR and wanted to conduct an assessment of this report. (TAB AI)

   (e) In response to a DOD IG hotline call in May 93 alleging that the Air Force tried to suppress the results of the Aerojet Study by recalling the Aerospace TOR, the DOD IG acquired copies of the TOR and provided it to OSD and others who requested it. (TAB AJ)

   (f) The Aerospace TOR also clearly states DSP-II does not meet all the user's requirements. (TAB AK)

   (g) The PEO for Space, MGen Schnelzer, also provided copies of the TOR to meet OSD and congressional requests. (TAB W)

143

(2) Discussion

(a) The Aerojet Study was a proposed input to the Sensor Study Task 3. It was presented to the PEO for Space in a briefing entitled, "DSP/BE Synergy", dated 3 Feb 93, by ▮▮▮▮▮. The PEO for Space rejected the Aerojet Study for inclusion in the Sensor Study I because it did not meet the groundrules established by the congressional mandate that options presented will meet the user's requirements as detailed in the draft FEWS ORD.

(b) AFSPACECOM/DRF (Directorate for Force Enhancement) first became aware of the DSP-II variant on or about 3 Feb 93 at an Space and Missile Center (SMC) briefing convened as part of the Sensor Study I. At that time, SMC/MJ (DSP SPO) surfaced DSP-MLV for consideration. AFSPACECOM/DRF questioned the obvious fact that this DSP variant did not meet certain critical ORD requirements, i.e., in the areas of detection and coverage. AFSPACECOM/DRF requested SMC/MJ to discuss the significance of these shortfalls. However, SMC/MJ declined to do so on the basis that this is a requirements issue that is more properly within the purview of the user. (TAB U) MGen Schnelzer was in attendance at this 3 Feb 93 briefing and requested an AFSPACECOM requirements analysis.

(c) DSP++ was included in the Sensor Study I, but DSP-MLV was not. DSP++ had its genesis in the FEWS COEA as a DSP variant with maximum upgrades. The Sensor Study I groundrules required all TW/AA options to comply with the FEWS ORD. Since DSP-MLV did not meet those requirements in certain critical areas, and could not be made to do so, it was determined inappropriate for inclusion in the study. DSP++, however, approximated the FEWS ORD requirements close enough to merit inclusion.

(3) Conclusions: This allegation was not substantiated. Information was provided to appropriate decision-makers and efforts to limit distribution of the study were done by the CEO of The Aerospace Corporation, owner of the study.

b. Allegation Two: That the Government attempted to discredit the Aerospace TOR report.

(1) Facts:

(a) After Mr Edward C. Aldridge recalled all known copies of the Aerospace TOR, an internal Aerospace independent analysis concluded that the DSP-II did not meet FEWS requirements, was not an apples-to-apples comparison with other TW/AA options, and contained inconsistent cost and performance comparisons. (TAB AL)

(b) Mr Aldridge claimed the TOR overstated DSP capabilities, underestimated cost, discounted JROC-validated requirements, and had an advocacy tone. (TAB AM)

(c) CINCSPACE stated the TOR was a "short-sighted" approach to the FEWS requirements (TAB AM)

(2) Discussion:

(a) The Aerospace Corporation prepared a TOR entitled, "DSP-II - Preserving the Air Force Options", 23 Apr 93. This document was approved by members of the DSP SPO and Aerospace. The genesis of this report was the Aerojet Study prepared to support the Sensor Study I effort. After being rejected by the PEO  structed Aerospace to package the Aerojet Study results in a report and file it for some possible future use. The report had distribution limited to only Aerospace and SPO addressees. However, the report found its way to a Navy office within the Pentagon, and the report was soon distributed beyond its originally intended addressees. Senior officials in the Air Force and Aerospace were upset over the way in which the TOR was coordinated and distributed.

(b) Mr Aldridge, President of Aerospace, recalled the report. Initially, his recall was intended to provide him time to review the report. Mr Aldridge had an internal Aerospace team conduct an independent analysis of the TOR. This independent analysis concluded the TOR did not meet the FEWS requirements, was not an apples-to-apples comparison, and contained inconsistent cost and performance comparisons. Mr Aldridge also claimed the TOR overstated DSP capabilities, underestimated cost, discounted JROC validated requirements, and had an advocacy tone. (TAB AM)

(3) Conclusions: This allegation is substantiated, but for logical reasons as stated in the facts and discussion paragraphs above.

c. Allegation Three: That the Air Force released the Aerospace TOR, which contained Aerojet proprietary data, to FEWS' contractors.

This allegation was investigated in a separate inquiry directed by Space and Missile Systems Center Vice Commander. That investigation concluded that Aerojet proprietary data was, in fact, inappropriately released. (TAB AN)

d. Allegation Four: That the Air Force did not fairly evaluate costs in comparing FEWS and DSP systems.

(1) Facts (supported by Inquiry Cost Team analysis):

(a) Baseline design for DSP++ assumed a Mean Mission Duration (MMD) of 8.5 years in the 1991 COEA. For Sensor Study I, MMD was estimated at 6 years. This, in turn, increased the cost of the DSP++ variant.

(b) An Aerospace risk analysis was performed for the options presented in Sensor Study I.

(c) DSP cost estimates were based on 13 satellites; FEWS cost estimates were based on 12 satellites.

145

(2) Discussion:

(a) In the course of this investigation, cost data provided by the SBEWS SPO was reviewed independently by a team consisting of two cost analysts from SAF/FMCC (Directorate of Cost Analysis, Deputy Assistant Secretary of the Air Force for Cost & Economics) and a technical expert from AFOTEC.

(b) Based on the time allotted, the SBEWS SPO performed a credible job estimating the various program option costs in support of the Bottom Up Review. However, three areas in estimating the costs for Sensor Study I options were reviewed and found to be of concern. These areas included: the addition of various "deltas" to the initial point estimates for Tasks 1 and 2 and which were eventually presented in the final version of Sensor Study I: cost risk; and an inconsistent assumption used in estimating the DSP++ option versus the FEWS baseline.

(1) Various "deltas" were added to the original point estimates for Mean Mission Duration (MMD), the Theoretical First Unit Cost (T1), and the Learning Curve (LC) due to questions regarding the systems design maturity. These deltas were accepted as a reasonable means for portraying the upper range of uncertainty about the point estimates of the various options.

(2) In the area of risk, there remains some question. A detailed analysis of risk was conducted by the Aerospace Corporation using a valid cost risk assessment methodology. Given sufficient time, a cost risk assessment of this detail is optimal. However, the Aerospace Corporation analysis was not used, and instead, a flat 15% risk factor was applied to the estimates for the Sensor Study's Task 1 and 2. We were unable to determine the reason the Aerospace risk analysis was not employed.

(3) Additionally, an assumption for estimating the DSP++ option versus the FEWS baseline in Sensor Study I was inconsistent. The number of satellites in both the FEWS and DSP++ options should have been the same. However, in the final study, the DSP++ option estimated 13 satellites and the FEWS baseline estimated only 12 satellites. This results in overstating the DSP++ option by approximately $600M. ███████████ for the technical portion of Sensor Study I - Task 3, DSP/BE Synergy, indicated this inconsistency is believed to be an inadvertent oversight.

(3) Conclusions: This allegation is not substantiated. Although questions do remain in the areas of the risk assessment and the inconsistent assumption (an extra DSP++ satellite), based on analysis of cost estimates and technical assumptions, resolution of these questions will not significantly alter the relative rankings of the DSP++ option against the FEWS baseline.

e. Allegation Five: That the Air Force did not use correct cost estimates of using a Shuttle to launch DSP satellites.

(1) Facts:

a) Aerojet was told by CINCSPACE and ███████████████████ that cost for a shuttle launch was $600-$700M. (TAB AC)

146

(b) A 5 Oct 93 paper from SMC reflects an "average total launch cost" of DSP on Titan IV and on the Shuttle to be $652M and $789M respectively, of which the "Shuttle flight" component of the total was $350M. (TAB AU)

(c) An undated point paper from SAF/AQS reflects $292M for Titan IV (with Inertial Upper Stage) and $429M for the Shuttle ($350M as "Shuttle flight" cost and the remainder for Shuttle integration, IUS hardware and IUS launch support). (TAB AU)

(d) According to Aerojet, DSP shuttle launch in 1991 cost less than $100M, when configured with an Inertial Upper Stage (IUS). (TAB AC)

(e) Aerojet stated that they had OMB data showing NASA's marginal costs for a Shuttle launch in the $50M range, but they could not confirm that figure with NASA and "marginal costs" were not defined. (TAB AC)

(f) According to AFSPACECOM, Shuttle costs are determined as a result of a complicated process that considers DoD "shuttle credits" with NASA. The cost of a shuttle launch with a shuttle credit is $350M. DoD apparently has one credit left with NASA. It is possible that this credit could be expended to launch a DSP, but this decision would ultimately depend upon other competing DoD space mission requirements. After the one shuttle credit is expended, the cost of a space shuttle launch is $650M. (TAB Z)

(2) Discussion:

It is obvious from the above range of numbers that "nailing down" a number for the cost of a Shuttle launch is extremely difficult. The common number seems to be $350M, which likely includes a credit. The marginal cost is likely the difference between a Titan IV launch and a Shuttle launch, which comes out to $137M ($789M - $652M or $429M - $292M). Bottom line -- the Air Force cost figures seem more logical and consistent.

(3) Conclusions: This allegation is not substantiated.

f. Allegation Six: That Senior Air Force officials threatened TRW to not provide information on Multi-Spectral technology which, in turn, restricted data flow from TRW to Aerojet.

(1) Facts:

(a) TRW ▮▮▮▮▮▮▮▮▮▮ declined to provide Aerojet Corporation data that Aerojet requested to support ▮▮▮▮▮ (TAB AC)

(b) CINCSPACE did not support TRW providing Multi-Spectral information to OSD/PA&E. CINCSPACE did not direct TRW to withhold data from the OSD. (TABs E & P)

(c) CINCSPACE questioned TRW's commitment to FEWS. (TAB P)

(d) TRW decided not to provide Multi-Spectral information to OSD/PA&E. (TAB E)

(2) Discussion:

(a) Discussion for allegation two and three apply here as well. Communication by CINCSPACE to TRW was not inappropriate in his role as CINC; however, his remarks were a factor influencing TRW's business decision to not submit the requested data to OSD/PA&E and to Aerojet. In TRW's testimony, it was neither stated nor implied that CINCSPACE "threatened" TRW.

(b) Aerojet testified that two TRW employees said CINCSPACE threatened TRW. Aerojet does not have first-hand knowledge of this allegation and as noted in the previous paragraph, the TRW personnel involved did not corroborate the statement.

(3) Conclusions: This allegation was not substantiated.

7. **Congressman Conyers Letter, 22 Oct 93, to DoD IG:** Facts, discussion, and conclusions:

a. Allegation One: That senior Air Force officials suppressed information about a lower cost alternative to the proposed $13 billion Follow-on Early Warning System (FEWS) satellite program.

(1) Facts (same as paragraph 6a(1)):

(a) Sensor Study I: Congress tasked OSD to study options for a Follow-on Early Warning System to accomplish the TW/AA mission. Specifically, Congress asked for an analysis in three areas: Task 1: Report on what modifications would be needed to the Brilliant Eyes system so that it could fulfill the requirements of the FEWS program; Task 2: Compare the FEWS design to a low altitude distributed architecture system; and Task 3: Compare the FEWS design to a combination of Brilliant Eyes and an upgraded DSP, also known as DSP/BE Synergy. MGen Schnelzer assigned ███████, of the BMD SPO, as the project lead with members from the DSP, FEWS and BE SPOs. The stated groundrule for this study was that each task must meet the Draft FEWS ORD requirements. The study was briefed by MGen Schnelzer on 12 Apr 93 to OSD/C3I. Thereafter, OSD/C3I submitted the required report to Congress. (TABs W & Y)

(b) To support Task 3 of the Sensor Study I, results were briefed to the PEO for Space by ███████ in a briefing entitled "DSP/BE Synergy", dated 3 Feb 93. Aerojet served as a member of a working group with DSP SPO and Aerospace membership. The solution presented was a DSP-MLV concept. The Aerojet study was their formal contribution to that working group. (TABs AE & AF)

(c) PEO for Space rejected the DSP-MLV approach on Task 3 study since it did not meet user requirements. (TABs X, Y & Z)

(d) Mr Aldridge, President of Aerospace, recalled all known copies of the Aerospace TOR, 93(3409)-6, dated 23 Apr 93. Mr Aldridge had not reviewed the TOR and wanted to conduct an assessment of this report. (TAB AI)

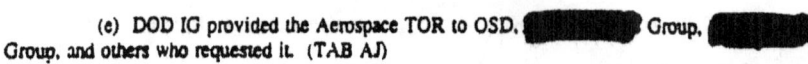

    (e) DOD IG provided the Aerospace TOR to OSD, ███████ Group, ███████ Group, and others who requested it. (TAB AJ)

  (2) Discussion: This allegation is very similar to allegation 6a, that the Air Force tried to suppress results of the Aerojet Study (which eventually evolved into the Aerospace TOR). The Aerojet Study supported the Sensor Study I, Task 3, DSP/BE Synergy. Aerojet's input helped the Government study member to develop an option which is the lower cost alternative referred to in the allegation. It is also identified as DSP-II or DSP-MLV which is the subject of the TOR. All three have been used somewhat interchangeably.

  (3) Conclusion: This allegation is not substantiated. Data did get to the decision makers. There is no evidence of attempts to suppress data.

 b. Allegation Two: That General Homer (CINC USSPACECOM) made erroneous statements supporting FEWS, ordered the DSP-II report be recalled and attempted to suppress discussion of technical alternatives to FEWS.

  (1) Facts:

   (a) Mr Aldridge ordered the TOR recalled; the TOR was not recalled by CINCSPACE. (TAB AI)

   (b) Gen Homer presented a FEWS-DSP Briefing to CSAF and the Vice Chairman of the JCS in July that Aerojet alleges was erroneous. (TAB AC)

   (c) ███████ and ███████ Aerospace, claimed CINCSPACE made erroneous statements. (TABs AA & AO)

   (d) Facts from paragraphs 5e, 6a and 7a apply here as well concerning the general allegation that Gen Homer suppressed discussion of technical alternatives to FEWS.

   (e) In the mid-Jul 93 time frame, CINCSPACE presented a FEWS briefing to CSAF and VCJCS. This briefing was prepared for the CINC's use by USSPACECOM/CX. It was compiled from sources already within the headquarters, to wit, the Sensor Study I, a USSPACECOM/J5 Study, and AFSPACECOM/DRF information. It is possible that other sources, including contractor source information were utilized. The briefing was styled and presented as an advocacy presentation. Because of the short period of time available to prepare the briefing, USSPACECOM/CX did not coordinate their final product with AFSPACECOM although it was reviewed by USSPACECOM/J5S. USSPACECOM has not received any challenges to the accuracy of the information contained in the briefing. (TAB AP)

   (f) During discussion with ███████ 27 Oct 93, concerning the Gen Homer briefing, he indicated the SPO had developed a response for MGen Schnelzer with copies to USSPACECOM that would update USSPACECOM information from the Jul 93 briefing. (TAB AQ)

149

(2) Discussion: This allegation has three parts:

(a) The first part of this allegation claims that Gen Horner made erroneous statements. There is mixed sworn testimony for this allegation. Additionally, an independent space expert from AFOTEC reviewed the briefing presented by Gen Horner to CSAF. Within this briefing, were a mix of conservative and optimistic statements about DSP and FEWS performance. Specific assessment of these statements, none of which were ajudged to be erroneous, are identified in a classified exhibit to this report. (TAB AR)

(b) The second part alleges that Gen Horner ordered that DSP-II report (TOR) be recalled. Mr Aldridge testified that Gen Horner did not order the recall. The TOR is an Aerospace document and Mr Aldridge ordered the recall.

(c) The third part of the allegation alleges that Gen Horner attempted to suppress discussions of technical alternatives to FEWS. Gen Horner has stated a preference for FEWS as the only system that meets JCS validated TW/AA requirements. Gen Horner was concerned that TRW, one of the two competing contractors for FEWS, by offering a multi-spectral alternative to FEWS, was unnecessarily confusing the issue. Gen Horner communicated his concern to TRW, and although his remarks, in all likelihood, had an affect on TRW, TRW testified that they made an independent business decision not to present their data to OSD. Gen Horner did not act inappropriately as CINC.

(d) To assist MGen Schneizer and USSPACECOM in providing current information and avoid possible use of outdated information, the SPO provided information on 16 Sep 93 which updated launch point accuracy determination and mean mission duration confidence. This represents a conscientious effort by all parties to ensure the most current and accurate information is provided to decision makers.

(3) Conclusion: All three parts of this allegation were not substantiated.

c. Allegation Three: That Major General Garry Schneizer (Program Executive Officer for Space) deleted from a Congressionally-mandated industry study an option (DSP-II) identifying improvements to the existing Defense Support Program (DSP) as an alternative to FEWS that could save up to $10 billion.

(1) Facts:

a) OSD/Congressional guidelines drove Sensor Study I. (TAB W)

(b) ▓▓▓▓ briefed the PEO for Space on a "DSP-II type" option. Briefing entitled, "DSP/BE Synergy", dated 3 Feb 93. (TAB AF)

(c) AFSPACECOM/DR sent a letter to MGen Schneizer stating the need for Sensor Study I alternatives to address every validated FEWS mission need and proceeded to list these needs. (TAB AG)

150

  (d) The PEO for Space rejected the DSP-II type option (DSP/BE synergy) based on ground rules (did not meet user requirements). DSP++ was included in the Sensor Study I since it was determined that it approximated the FEWS ORD requirements. (TAB Y)

  (e) ▇▇▇▇ briefing claimed DSP/BE met user requirements. (TABs AE & AF)

  (f) AFSPACECOM/DR Ltr, 10 Feb 93, to the PEO for Space identified DSP-II type option as not meeting user requirements. (TAB AG)

  (g) The Aerospace TOR contents indicate that DSP-II does not meet ORD requirements. (TAB AK)

  (h) OSD/C3I ▇▇▇▇ submitted the required report to Congress. (TAB Y)

 (2) Discussion:

▇▇▇▇ briefed the PEO for Space on the DSP/BE synergy concept on 3 Feb 93. In his briefing, ▇▇▇▇ believed this concept met the user's requirements. On 10 Feb 93, HQ AFSPACECOM/DR (Directorate of Requirements) sent a letter to the PEO for Space, stating that the concept that goes forward must meet all user requirements and that the DSP/BE synergy concept did not, in fact, do so. Thereafter, the PEO for Space rejected the DSP/BE synergy option from further consideration.

 (3) Conclusions: This allegation was substantiated, but for the reason stated in subparagraph (d) above.

 d. Allegation Four: That Mr Pete Aldridge, as President of The Aerospace Corporation, ordered the recall of the DSP-II report and assisted in the suppression of options from review by Congress. That Mr Aldridge interfered in the DoD IG's investigation by requesting that the IG back-off on these issues.

 (1) Facts:

  (a) Mr Aldridge initially recalled the TOR in order to review it, as it had been published without review by senior Aerospace officials. (TAB AI)

  (b) Mr Aldridge did not think the TOR was up to the standards of professional work products typically produced by Aerospace. It lacked objectivity and, as a result, he decided to retain the document and disapprove its distribution. (TAB AI)

  (c) Mr Aldridge denied suppressing data. (TAB AI)

  (d) Mr Aldridge talked to DoD IG about the TOR. He stated it was not being suppressed. It was for internal use, and no one associated with it would suffer reprisals. (TAB AI)

(e) ███████ said that he had suffered no reprisal action resulting from his participation in the Aerospace TOR. (TAB AO)

(2) Discussion:

(a) In an interview with Mr Aldridge, he stated that it was he who ordered recall of the TOR. He had not yet reviewed the document and needed time to do so. Mr Aldridge also had an independent Aerospace team analyze the TOR. Overall, it was determined that it had inconsistent cost and performance comparisons and lacked objectivity.

(b) Based on Mr Aldridge's perception that the TOR did not meet Aerospace's standards, he did not allow distribution. He retained it in-house for internal use. According to Mr Aldridge and confirmed by ███ no one associated with this product suffered reprisal.

(c) Mr Aldridge communicated with the DoD IG about the TOR. He stated he was not suppressing the data. There is no available information corroborating the allegation that Mr Aldridge interfered in any way with the DoD IG.

(3) Conclusions: This allegation is substantiated in part.

(a) The allegation that Mr Aldridge recalled the TOR was substantiated. By his own testimony, Mr Aldridge stated that he directed the TOR to be recalled.

(b) The allegation that Mr Aldridge suppressed options was not substantiated. Mr Aldridge recalled the Aerospace TOR, but did not, nor cannot, prevent flow of Air Force information to other organizations within the Air Force and to OSD.

(c) The allegation that Mr Aldridge interfered with the DoD IG was not substantiated. Neither Mr Aldridge, nor the DoD IG, felt that Mr Aldridge interfered with the proceedings of the DOD IG.

e. Allegation Five: That several Air Force personnel and Mr Aldridge provided false and misleading information to decision makers within OSD and Congress with regard to the cost, performance and capabilities of the DSP and FEWS programs

(1) Facts:

(a) FEWS evolved over time from the Boost Surveillance Tracking System (BSTS) to the Advance Warning System (AWS) and, ultimately, FEWS. This system was subjected to two summits during which TW/AA mission requirements were critically reviewed. The summit processes considered the present state of world affairs as it impacts on threat assessment and TW/AA mission requirements. As an example, at the beginning of the Summit process, the FEWS space platform under consideration weighed approximated 12,000 pounds. FEWS, today, weighs approximates 4,000 pounds. This reflects the rigor of the requirements review applied by the Summit process. (TAB AS)

(b) At Milestone I (Dec 91) of the FEWS program an AF-validated SORD was presented. At that time, AFSPACECOM was directed to convert this document to an ORD. This was accomplished without any substantive change to the SORD. The JROC-validated ORD is presently pending CSAF approval. (TAB Z)

(c) CINC USSPACECOM presented a briefing to the CSAF and Vice Chairman of the JCS advocating FEWS. (TAB AP)

(d) Briefing contained some statements which were a mix of conservative and optimistic statements about DSP and FEWS performance, none of which were ajudged to be erroneous. (TAB AR)

(e) ▆▆▆▆▆ and ▆▆▆▆▆ were satisfied that data received from the program offices was accurate. (TAB X)

(f) Cost data was reviewed by an independent team of two cost analysts and one technical advisor and was determined to be appropriately developed. (Supported by Inquiry Cost Team analysis and TAB AV)

(g) Mr Aldridge stated that Aerospace must provide good technical products and any advocacy should be left to customers. (TAB AI)

(h) SPO rebuttal to specific alleged false technical data was reviewed by an independent AFOTEC Technical Advisor and determined to appropriately address the technical data concerns. (TAB AR)

(2) Discussion:

(a) Cost data was reviewed and determined to be adequate.

(b) Alleged false technical data was responded to by the SBEWS program office. This rebuttal was reviewed by an independent techical advisor and found to be a valid response. (TAB AD)

(3) Conclusion: This allegation was not substantiated.

f. Allegation Six: ▆▆▆▆▆▆▆▆▆▆ knowingly provided the DSP-II report, which contained "competition sensitive" information provided by Aerojet, to Aerojet competitors TRW and LMSC.

This allegation has been investigated in another inquiry conducted at the direction of Space and Missile Center Vice Commander (SMC/CV). That investigation concluded that Aerojet proprietary data was, in fact, inappropriately released. (TAB AN)

8. To summarize:

a. What brought us to this inquiry? In the space arena and perhaps across the acquisition spectrum, the intense competition for dollars in DoD and among its defense contractors ("survival" mentality) is producing distrust, suspicion, breakdowns in communications and ultimately allegations of impropriety, both from within the Air Force and from defense contractors.

(1) An event occurred in the February 1993 timeframe that was a catalyst for several of the allegations. That event was rejection of an option for Sensor Study I that had been prepared by a team from the DSP program office, assisted by Aerospace and Aerojet. The rejection was made by MGen Schnelzer (PEO for Space) who was in charge of the study. He made the decision for logical reasons, but the decision was not understood or accepted by those who had proposed the option. Thus, perceptions of favoritism toward FEWS, misleading/erroneous data being used, suppressing data in DSP, etc., ultimately became allegations in this inquiry.

(2) Another key event was publication of the Aerospace Technical Operating Report (TOR) in April 1993. This report was purportedly done to document the results of the work done for Sensor Study I and to have an option available in case FEWS fell on hard times. In reality, the TOR became an advocacy document for those who felt "slighted" by the decision to reject a lower cost DSP option from Sensor Study I. The way in which this report was published and distributed caused a great deal of concern within the Air Force and Aerospace Corporation, and the actions taken resulted in several allegations addressed by this inquiry.

b. Where do we go from here? There's no simple fix. Given the environment as described above, the possibility of similar allegations from defense contractors is ever present. Good communications will help, but will not guarantee success. Within the Air Force, we must listen to those concerns, address them and attempt to achieve consensus. If consensus is not achieved, those with dissenting opinions need to understand why their position wasn't accepted. If they continue to push their position and perceive 'no one is listening', future allegations will inevitably result.

MARCUS A. ANDERSON
Major General, USAF
Inquiry Officer

2 Atch
1. Exhibit Index
2. Exhibits*

*CLASSIFIED EXHIBITS FILED IN SEPARATE BINDER

INDEX OF EXHIBITS

	EXHIBITS
Appointment Letters	A
GenCorp Aerojet Corporation Letter, 19 Oct 93	B
Congressman Conyers Letter, 12 Oct 93	C
Witnesses Interviewed	D
Interview of TRW	E
Testimony of ▓▓▓	F
Testimony of ▓▓▓	G
Interview of Aerospace Employee ▓▓▓	H
Interview of Aerospace Employee ▓▓▓	I
Memorandum, The Aerospace Corporation, 27 Sep 93	J
Lockheed Primer, 19 Sep 93	K
Briefing, "Assessment of Multi-Spectral Systems for TW/AA", 30 Sep 93	L
Memorandum for Record, Release of TRW MS Proprietary Data, 1 Nov 93	M
Statement from Expert Witness - ▓▓▓	N
TRW Chronology, 5 Oct 93	O
Testimony from General Charles A. Horner (Secret)*	P
Testimony from ▓▓▓ (Unclas & Secret)*	Q
Memorandum for Record, TRW Telecon with ▓▓▓ 1 Nov 93	R
Testimony from ▓▓▓	S
Testimony from ▓▓▓	T
Memorandum for Record from ▓▓▓ 7 Jun 93	U
Bottom Up Review Briefing, 5 Oct 93 (Secret)*	V
OSD Letter, 24 Sep 93 and SAF/AQS Letter, 30 Nov 93	W
Interview of ▓▓▓ and ▓▓▓	X
Testimony of Major General Garry A. Schneizer	Y
Testimony of ▓▓▓ (Secret)*	Z
Testimony of ▓▓▓ (Secret)*	AA
SMC/MT Letter, 13 Oct 93	AB
Interview of GenCorp Aerojet Corporation (Secret)*	AC
Statement by Expert Space Witness ▓▓▓, 29 Oct 93	AD
Testimony of ▓▓▓	AE
Briefing, "Task 3 - DSP/BE Synergy" (Secret)*	AF
AFSPACECOM/DR Ltr, 10 Feb 93 (Secret)*	AG
FEWS Operational Requirements Document, 6 May 93 (Secret)*	AH
Interview of Mr Edward C. Aldridge	AI
Memorandum for Record, Telecon with DoD IG ▓▓▓	AJ
Aerospace Technical Operations Requirement, 23 Apr 93	AK
Analyses of Aerospace TOR (Aerospace and Air Force) (Secret)*	AL
General Horner Memorandum to Mr Aldridge, 24 May 93 and return letter from Mr Aldridge, 22 Jun 93	AM

*NOTE: CLASSIFIED INFORMATION FILED IN SEPARATE BINDER

Space and Missile Systems Center Report, 27 Oct 93	AN
Interview of ▮▮▮▮ (Secret)*	AO
Testimony of ▮▮▮▮ (Secret)*	AP
MGen Schneizer's Question and Answers, Undated	AQ
Memorandum for Record, Comments on Gen Horner Briefing, 1 Nov 93 (Secret)*	AR
Summit Charts (Secret)*	AS
Testimony of ▮▮▮▮ (Secret)*	AT
SMC Letter, 5 Oct 93 and Related Documents	AU
Analysis of Cost Information	AV

*NOTE: CLASSIFIED INFORMATION FILED IN SEPARATE BINDER

INSPECTOR GENERAL
DEPARTMENT OF DEFENSE
400 ARMY NAVY DRIVE
ARLINGTON, VIRGINIA 22202-2884

JAN 27 1994

MEMORANDUM FOR SECRETARY OF THE AIR FORCE

SUBJECT: Review of Air Force Inspector General Report of Inquiry Pertaining to Defense Support Program/Follow-On Early Warning System Program

We have reviewed the report of inquiry pertaining to the Defense Support Program (DSP)/Follow-On Early Warning System (FEWS) Program forwarded by your memorandum of January 7, 1994.

During our review, in addition to the report of inquiry, we also considered two volumes of transcripts of interviews, statements of witnesses and relevant documents; the legal review performed by the Chief, General Law Division, Office of the Air Force Judge Advocate General; and the separate report of investigation into the unauthorized release of proprietary data in connection with the DSP-II Technical Operating Report. We did not conduct additional interviews of witnesses or assemble additional documentary evidence.

We found that the inquiry adequately addressed the issues raised within the Air Force as well as those presented by a contractor and Chairman John Conyers. While we identified several concerns with respect to investigative actions and practices, we view those issues as without consequence with respect to the ultimate conclusions of the investigation and minor in the context of an unusually complex subject. We will discuss those concerns with the Air Force Inspector General to assist in his continuing improvements to the investigative program.

I agree with the actions proposed in your memorandum to provide the results of the inquiry and our review to Chairman Conyers, other interested Members of Congress and the media.

Finally, I request that you advise Air Force personnel, at all levels, involved in the inquiry as well as appropriate contractor officials of the need to avoid acts of reprisal or the appearance of retaliation in connection with testimony before the investigating officer or in other protected forums.

Should you have any questions, please contact me or Mr. Michael B. Suessmann, Assistant Inspector General for Departmental Inquiries, at (703) 697-6582.

Derek J. Vander Schaaf
Deputy Inspector General

Mrs. MALONEY. Would you like to respond?

Mr. ARU. I certainly would. General Horner, along with that handwritten note, sent a letter to Mr. Aldridge which he did not sign, but it was on his four star flag stationery. That challenged my integrity by saying the DSP–II report was "flawed technically, operationally, and politically, compiled with the help and input of Aerojet by an ex-Aerojet member of your technical staff."

A member of the Senate Armed Services Committee staff told me he was told that I was an ex-Aerojet executive that had left a few months ago and went to Aerospace to sabotage the FEWS program for the DSP program. I left Aerojet Electrosystems over 6 years ago and have been with Aerospace for 6 years. And I was a junior person at Aerojet. I have no financial interests or affiliation with Aerojet Electrosystems.

In the previous assignment to doing this report, I was the project engineer for a program known as system one. And I was asked by Colonel Dietz' boss, Col. John Kidd, to make an assessment of that program.

It was a multihundred million dollar program of which another part was a significant hardware contract to upgrade the hardware at DSP ground stations. I recommended that that program be terminated. Aerojet was a major subcontractor on that program.

I have never, ever allowed any affiliation or association to affect my integrity and my decisions and my recommendations to the Air Force. And General Horner's letter to me was personally offensive.

He summed it up with a statement that I would also like to read and make for the record. It says, "this kind of, quote, 'work,' unquote, is unprofessional and is not representative of the type of government industry team I want, especially when it ends up in Washington in the Navy staff, exclamation mark. Please help."

I thought General Horner was a unified CINC and he worked with the Navy; and as Colonel Dietz once remarked as they were trying to recall the report, it was as if it got passed to the Romanian navy instead of the United States Navy.

But that ending statement of General Horner's, that it "is not representative of the type of government industry team I want," I believe, if I was on the receiving end of that letter, is a direct threat; and I do not appreciate the General or anyone impugning my integrity.

Mr. MCCANDLESS. Madam Chairman, I appreciate the comments with respect to the items that I request to be entered into the record. Obviously, the gentleman is entitled to his comments and I respect them.

Mrs. MALONEY. Thank you very much, gentlemen.

Without objection, we will keep the record open until February——

Mr. MCCANDLESS. May I ask, did we get these entered into the record?

Mrs. MALONEY. Yes. Without objection. All the documents are in the record and we will keep the record open until February 18, 1994, for additional questions.

The chairman has asked me to read this, and we thank you for your testimony; and we are calling the next witnesses. And as they come forward, I am going to read into the record an item from the chairman.

> Last night—late last night, the subcommittee received a report from the Air Force Inspector General on the FEWS DSP controversy. It appears that findings of this report were publicly released earlier that day. I am troubled by both the timing and the substance of this report.
>
> First, the Air Force IG concluded, and I quote, the Aerojet allegation that the government attempted to discredit the Aerospace technical operating report is substantiated.
>
> Second, the Air Force IG concluded, and again I quote, the allegation that, quote, Major General Schnelzer deleted from a congressionally mandated study an option DSP-MLV identifying improvement to the existing DSP as an alternative to the FEWS that can save up to 10 billion, is substantiated.
>
> Third, the Air Force IG concluded that Aerospace Corporation President Pete Aldridge had, in fact, quote, ordered the recall of the Aerospace technical operating report, end quote.
>
> Despite these and equally troubling findings, the Air Force IG has publicly stated that there was no, quote, conduct that could constitute a violation of criminal law in the FEWS DSP affair. I must point out that criminality is not the issue. The factual findings speak for themselves. There was an effort to suppress a congressionally mandated study. Such actions by senior Air Force officers are deeply troubling.
>
> This morning the subcommittee was informed that the Department of Defense Inspector General is still reviewing allegations of retaliation in connection with the FEWS DSP report and in connection with actions taken against Colonel Mangold. I intend to monitor this matter closely and to carefully review the results of these ongoing investigations.
>
> Thank you.

Our final witness today is Dr. Thomas Quinn, the Deputy Assistant Secretary of Defense for Command, Communications and Computer Systems Directorate of the Joint Chiefs of Staff. Joining Dr. Quinn are Maj. Gen. David Kelley, Col. Steven Stadler, William Schepens, and Brent Collins.

Major General Kelley is the Vice Director of the U.S. Army Command, Control Communications, and Computer Systems Directorate of the Joint Staff; and Col. Steven Stadler is Deputy Chief of Staff for Requirements of the Air Force Space Command. Col. William Schepens is the Director of Inspections for the Air Force inspector general's office; and Col. Brent Collins is Deputy Director for Space Programs and Assistant Secretary of the Air Force Acquisition.

Gentlemen, we welcome you. As is our practice, I will swear you in.

[Witnesses sworn.]

Mrs. MALONEY. Dr. Quinn, you may proceed.

STATEMENT OF THOMAS P. QUINN, Ph.D., DEPUTY ASSISTANT SECRETARY OF DEFENSE, COMMAND, CONTROL, COMMUNICATIONS AND INTELLIGENCE ACQUISITION, ACCOMPANIED BY MAJ. GEN. DAVID KELLEY, DEPUTY DIRECTOR, DEFENSE-WIDE COMMAND, CONTROL, COMMUNICATIONS, AND COMPUTERS SUPPORT FOR THE JOINT STAFF, U.S. ARMY; COL. STEVE STADLER, DEPUTY CHIEF OF STAFF, REQUIREMENTS, AIR FORCE SPACE INSPECTIONS, INSPECTOR GENERAL'S OFFICE, U.S. AIR FORCE, AND COL. BRENT COLLINGS, DEPUTY DIRECTOR, SPACE PROGRAMS

Dr. QUINN. Thank you, Madam Chairman. Members of the committee, I have submitted a written statement for the record. I would like to now briefly summarize this statement in my opening remarks. Then I will be happy to answer your questions.

It is my privilege to speak to you today on the Defense Support Program or DSP and its follow on system which was formerly called the Follow-On Early Warning System known as FEWS and about the Milstar program.

Let me first discuss the background of the DSP and the FEWS programs and bring you up to date on the current plans for these systems and recent departmental decisions. Following this discussion I will address the Milstar program.

As you know, the DSP is our primary system for providing the first warning of ballistic missile launches worldwide. It is a constellation of satellites in geosynchronous orbit that detect infrared radiation. The detected data is broadcast to ground stations where it is processed to determine if the data represents a missile launch. Once a launch is identified, tactical parameters, such as the launch point, launch time, heading, and missile class are calculated, and a warning message is sent to users.

DSP was developed in the late 1960's to address the threat to the United States from inter continental and submarine-launched ballistic missiles. Since that time, the Department has made block changes to the satellite. These upgrades have provided improvements in sensor performance, satellite hardening, and longevity.

In 1985, the Department decided to develop a new surveillance system capable of supporting active strategic defense. This new system was called the boost surveillance and tracking system or BSTS and it would replace DSP. However, the Brilliant Pebbles and the Brilliant Eyes programs were later initiated to reflect a restructured ballistic missile defense architecture, and the BSTS program was terminated. FEWS was then established to support the early warning mission and to place more emphasis on detecting tactical ballistic missiles. Tactical ballistic missiles now represent the greatest threat, because they are dim, short burning, and therefore hard to detect, and they are proliferating. FEWS was designed to cope with that threat.

Before we decided on the FEWS program, the Department considered additional upgrades to DSP, but it determined that these upgrades were not a cost-effective solution to satisfy current requirements and would not provide a flexible platform that could accommodate threats that might develop in the future. FEWS also offered other advantages over DSP. One of the advantages was its ability to process infrared data on the satellite instead of sending the data to the ground for processing. This capability would allow the satellite to send warning messages directly to the tactical user and avoid the roundabout routing that was necessary during Desert Storm. This capability would also require less manpower by eliminating the need for overseas ground processing centers.

However, with the collapse of the Soviet Union and attendant changes in threat from strategic ballistic missiles, it once again became necessary to reexamine our early warning systems. These systems and our plans were examined in an internal DOD review conducted last summer.

Because of the national security issues at stake in the early warning mission, the Department also convened an independent study group, in parallel with the Department's internal review. This study group consisted of members from federally funded research and development centers. Their charter was to examine the issues associated with this mission. This group was chaired by Mr. Robert Everett from the Mitre Corp. and included representatives from the Institute for Defense Analyses, the Aerospace Corp., MIT Lincoln Labs, and the Johns Hopkins Applied Physics Laboratory.

The study group examined several alternatives for satisfying the early warning mission. These alternatives included the existing DSP, a lightweight DSP, the current FEWS design, a lightweight FEWS design, and a new satellite design developed by the study group. The group recommended that the Department should: Continue the block buy of three DSP satellites because of the near-term considerations, terminate the FEWS program because it was intertwined with nuclear war fighting and the strategic defense initiative and, therefore, was not responsive to current DOD needs.

It further advised the Department to acquire a better surveillance capability than DSP and advised that a better system could be acquired for less cost than DSP and could be available on the FEWS schedule. The Department accepted some of these recommendations and incorporated them into our plans.

In our internal review, both the Department and the independent study group examined the DSP II option. This option was first documented in a technical report by the Aerospace Corp. The Aerospace report suggested modifications to the DSP platform to reduce weight and improve sensor performance. Neither the Department's internal review nor the independent study group found advantages to this concept that outweighed the advantages of a competitive effort for a new early warning system.

Accordingly, our bottom-line conclusions are that the FEWS program as configured is unaffordable, but a new early warning system is still needed. As a result, we are in the process of canceling the FEWS program, and plan to start a new program to replace DSP with a system that will have less onboard data processing than FEWS, but better detection performance than DSP and especially against tactical ballistic missiles. The cost of this program will be less than continuing with DSP and we will be able to boost it into orbit on a medium launch vehicle or MLV instead of a Titan IV. The Air Force is reviewing the requirements for worldwide early warning in order to construct a new program that is affordable. Next year we plan to start contractor efforts on a new design for the DSP follow-on program.

In addition to interest in the current status of the DSP and FEWS program, the committee has expressed concern over alleged misconduct by Air Force and contractor personnel involved in the DSP/FEWS program. This issue was investigated by the Air Force inspector general, was reviewed by the DOD inspector general, and a report on the matter has been forwarded to Congress. I would like to submit a copy of the DOD inspector general's assessment of the report for the record. Colonel Schepens from the Office of the Air Force Inspector General will address the report after the conclusion of my opening remarks.

Now, let's consider the Milstar program.

The Milstar satellite system is planned to provide operational forces, especially highly mobile tactical units, with secure, survivable, flexible communications on a worldwide basis. The Milstar system operates in the extremely high frequency or EHF, a previously unused part of the radio spectrum. This attribute plus some other design features, like advanced signal processing, provide unique mission capabilities required by today's war fighters for power projection into possible theater conflicts around the globe.

While the Milstar program has focused on satisfying needs identified at its inception in the early 1980's—providing secure, survivable, flexible communications for both tactical and strategic users—the world situation has changed dramatically and so has the scope and application of the Milstar program. Although the threat of protracted nuclear war is reduced, the threat of regional conflicts has risen dramatically. During this time, the Milstar program has not been static. It has been revised and restructured several times in harmony with the force structure to meet the changing threat.

The Department restructured the Milstar program extensively 3 years ago, at congressional urging, to reduce costs and to account for changes in the international and national security environments. Requirements for a classified payload were deleted. "Heroic" survivability features envisioned for the cold war environment were eliminated. The number of satellites and ground control elements were reduced commensurate with the threat and force structure reductions.

A higher capacity, medium data rate or MDR payload was planned for a second generation Milstar II satellite which expanded its tactical utility. This MDR payload will greatly increase communications capacity compared to the low data rate or LDR capabilities on the initial Milstar I satellites. Use of both LDR and MDR will greatly enhance the utility of Milstar II satellites in a wide range of future potential scenarios.

The restructured Milstar program also reduced the numbers of strategic terminals and defined new mobile terminals for tactical uses. It reduced program life cycle costs by 25 percent and the terminal costs by 35 percent.

The Department reviewed requirements and tailored the unique capabilities of the Milstar system to provide "flexible" and protected communications for mobile forces. It addresses many of the deficiencies observed during Desert Storm when U.S. ground forces outran their communications support. These changes exploited many of the new technologies integrated into the EHF packages on the Navy's ultra-high frequency follow-on satellites. The Department also incorporated new technologies into terminal designs for mobile platforms, man portable and tactical applications. At the time, the restructured program gained congressional support for reducing program costs and increasing its tactical orientation.

In 1993, the Department further scrutinized MILSATCOM programs as a part of the bottom up review of military forces and major defense programs. The review evaluated numerous alternatives to Milstar while considering an updated threat estimate, operational requirements, cost effectiveness tradeoffs, risk, and affordability. The review emphasized LDR and MDR capabilities for

U.S. tactical forces. It focused specifically on providing lower cost alternatives to the baseline Milstar program.

Similar to DSP and FEWS, a select group of technical experts known as the "Technical Support Group" reviewed the MILSATCOM programs. The group was headed by Dr. Bob Everett from Mitre, and members from the Aerospace Corp., MIT Lincoln Laboratories, and the John Hopkins Applied Physics Laboratory. The group recommended that the Department pursue a "cost constrained" EHF system for protected connectivity by limiting the size of the communications payload so it would fit on a medium-launch vehicle.

The baseline Milstar program examined in the bottom up review included the launch of two, nearly complete Milstar I satellites in fiscal years 1994 and 1995, development and launch of nine Milstar II satellites in fiscal years 1999 to 2011. After considering various alternatives, the review ultimately examined four principal options to this baseline—all with the objective of obtaining cost reductions. All four options would launch the first two Milstar I satellites. All four also included a transition to a lower weight, lower-cost EHF satellite which would fit on a medium launch vehicle delivered at different times and with different capabilities. The selected option called for four Milstar II's followed by the development and launch of an advanced EHF LDR MDR satellite not later than the year 2006. It was selected because it best met military requirements and provided the most capability at the earliest date. All the other options were higher risk and offered the potential for additional cost savings only by deferring delivery of needed operational capability. The selected option represented the best means of achieving needed capability while reducing long term costs. It is the strategy we are now implementing.

Under our current plans the first Milstar I satellite with LDR-only capability is scheduled for launch later this month. The second Milstar I satellite will be delivered in time to support a scheduled launch in fiscal year 1995. The MDR payload development is on track for a first Milstar II launch in fiscal year 1999. The technology assessment for an advanced EHF system has begun and an advanced EHF satellite is currently planned to be available for launch after the Milstar 6 satellite. At the time of the review, the selected option was assessed by the Department to save approximately $3 billion in program life cycle costs. After further examination we now believe we can save almost $4 billion in life cycle costs compared to the baseline Milstar program. These savings have been made possible through a combination of measures—improved efficiencies in program execution and the transition to a lower cost, lower weight advanced EHF satellite design.

We recognize that developing an advanced EHF satellite will require ingenuity within the Department and industry and it is not without risk. Reducing the weight of the current Milstar II payload by a factor of 3 or 4 and providing a sufficient number of narrow beam EHF antennas to connect the tactical forces needed to fight a regional conflict is a higher risk but potentially lower cost approach than the continued development of the Milstar II satellites. The Department is currently examining a wide range of potentially applicable technologies. The review will provide the foundation for the technology development necessary to support concept definition and development of a future, lower cost EHF satellite design.

Wherever possible the Department intends to continue identifying cost-effective reductions as a part of its overall SATCOM investment strategy—in line with current and potential future force structure decisions. The bottom-up review confirmed with independent technical assessments that a processed EHF satellite system provides great promise for meeting current requirements to provide protected connectivity to mobile forces. It validated the Milstar II approach as the lowest risk near term solution and it identified the need to transition to a lower cost lower weight EHF alternative. The bottom-up review was not, however, the final word on cost savings. While the Department has made progress in reducing SATCOM costs—we do not plan to rest. We are expanding our focus beyond reducing the cost of the Milstar program.

The Department will continue reviewing requirements for communications—inserting new technologies—and using commercial systems to supplement core military capabilities wherever these steps are proven as cost-effective measures. Affordability will continue to be a principal criterion used to determine the best mix of providing military and commercial SATCOM systems and services.

In conclusion, the Department has reviewed and restructured the DSP/FEWS and Milstar programs over the past few years in response to the changing threat and national security posture. We are in the process of terminating the FEWS program and are working to define an affordable, follow-on system to DSP. Similarly, we have reviewed, restructured, and reduced the cost of Milstar and have begun technology development for a follow-on advanced EHF system. Risk and affordability have been integral elements of the Department's decisions. We will continue reviewing operational requirements and cost-effective solutions appropriate to meet essential military needs.

This completes my opening remarks. Major General Kelley from the Joint Staff, J-6, has a few brief remarks on joint requirements, and he will be followed by Colonel Schepens who will address the Air Force inspector general's DSP FEWS report.

Thank you.

[The prepared statement of Dr. Quinn follows:]

PREPARED STATEMENT

by

DR. THOMAS P. QUINN

DEPUTY ASSISTANT SECRETARY OF DEFENSE

COMMAND, CONTROL, COMMUNICATIONS AND INTELLIGENCE ACQUISITION

to the LEGISLATION AND NATIONAL SECURITY SUBCOMMITTEE

of the COMMITTEE ON GOVERNMENT OPERATIONS

U.S. HOUSE OF REPRESENTATIVES

February 2, 1994

Mr. Chairman. Distinguished Members. Thank you for the opportunity to represent the Department of Defense and speak to you today on the development and deployment plans of the DSP/FEWS and Milstar programs -- programs which have been extensively reviewed by the Department under both the previous and current Administrations. These reviews have focused on tailoring these systems to the new national security realities. In fact, we have based our budget decisions on two principal criteria -- applicability to meet the tactical theater threats we will most likely face in the post-Cold War environment and careful consideration of affordability. I have here with me today members of the Office of the Secretary of the Air Force, the Air Force Space Command, and the Joint Chiefs of Staff, who as representatives of the Department, are ready to support me in responding to any detailed questions you may have concerning the numerous requirements reviews, assessments, and technical evaluations of these important programs. Let me speak first to the Defense Support Program (DSP) and to the Follow-On Early Warning System (FEWS) and bring you up to date on the current plans for these systems and recent Departmental decisions.

EARLY WARNING SYSTEMS

As you know, the Defense Support Program (DSP) is our primary system for providing the first warning of ballistic missile launches worldwide. DSP is a constellation of satellites in geo-synchronous orbit that detect infrared radiation. This infrared data is broadcast to ground stations where it is processed to determine if detected data represents a missile launch. Once a launch is identified, tactical parameters, such as launch point, launch time, heading and missile class are calculated, and a warning message is sent to users.

DSP was developed in the late 1960s and became an operational system in the early 1970s. At that time, the threat to the US was inter-continental and submarine-launched ballistic missiles which DSP is very capable of detecting. In 1985, the Department began planning the Strategic Defense Initiative and decided to develop a new surveillance system because, DSP did not provide timely or sufficiently accurate tactical parameters to support the active defensive mission. The Strategic Defense Initiative Organization (SDIO) (Since redesignated the Ballistic Missile Defense Organization or "BMDO") initiated the Boost Surveillance and Tracking System (BSTS) for this mission. This new system would also support the early warning mission and would replace DSP.

In 1990 and 1991, the SDIO restructured the ballistic missile defense architecture and initiated the Brilliant Pebbles and Brilliant Eyes programs and terminated the BSTS program. The early warning mission was transferred back to the Air Force. Consequently, the Air Force modified the BSTS program by eliminating the requirement for post-boost vehicle tracking and removing the battle management capabilities, and called the new program the Follow-on Early Warning System (FEWS). In response to Desert Storm, however, more emphasis was placed on reliably detecting tactical ballistic missiles.

One of the advantages of FEWS over DSP was to be its ability to process infrared data on the satellite platform instead of sending all data to the ground for processing. This capability would allow the satellite to send warning messages directly to the tactical user and avoid using the circuitous routing that was necessary during Desert Storm. This capability would also eliminate the need for overseas ground processing centers which would significantly have reduced manpower requirements.

In the latest round of program re-examinations, we took into account that the threat has dramatically changed. The Soviet Union no longer exists and the threat from strategic ballistic missiles is greatly reduced. Tactical ballistic missiles now represent the greatest threat, because they are dim, short-burning and therefore hard to detect, and they are proliferating. FEWS was designed to detect these missiles, but we decided the program as configured was unaffordable and we are in the process of cancelling it.

This decision to cancel FEWS is represented in our FY1995 budget request. Our new plan is to start a program to replace DSP that will have more modest performance in the area of on-board data processing than FEWS, but have better detection performance than DSP especially against tactical ballistic missiles. The unit cost of this program will be less than DSP and we'll be able to boost it into orbit on a medium launch vehicle instead of a TITAN IV. The Air Force is still developing the details of this plan.

Because of the national security issues at stake in the early warning mission, the Department convened an independent study group, in parallel with the Department's internal review. This study group consisted of members from Federally Funded Research and Development Centers, and their charter was to examine the issues associated with this mission. This group was chaired by Mr. Robert Everett from the MITRE Corp. and included representatives from the Institute for Defense Analyses, Aerospace Corp., MIT Lincoln Labs, and Johns Hopkins Applied Physics Lab.

The study group examined several alternatives for satisfying the early warning mission. These alternatives included the existing DSP, a light-weight DSP, the current FEWS design, a light-weight FEWS design, and a new satellite design developed by the study group. The group recommended that the Department should: 1) continue the block buy of three DSP satellites because of near-term considerations and 2) terminate the FEWS program because it was intertwined with nuclear war-fighting and the Strategic Defense Initiative and therefore not responsive to current DOD direction. It further advised the Department to acquire a better surveillance capability than DSP, and that a better system than DSP could be acquired for less cost than DSP and could be available on the FEWS schedule. The Department accepted some of these recommendations and incorporated them into our plan that is represented in our FY1995 budget request.

With regard to DSP upgrades, the Department has made block changes to the satellite several times since 1970. These upgrades have provided improvements in sensor performance, satellite hardening, and longevity. In 1991 before we decided on the FEWS program, the Department considered additional upgrades to DSP, but determined that these upgrades were not a cost effective solution to satisfying current requirements and would not provide a flexible platform that could accommodate threats that might develop in the future. Consequently, the FEWS program was initiated in lieu of upgrading DSP.

In our latest review, both the Department and the independent study group examined the DSP II option as described in the Aerospace technical report. The report suggests modifications to the DSP platform for light-weighting and improved sensor performance. Neither the Department's internal review nor the independent study group found advantages to this concept that outweighed the advantages of a competitive effort.

In fiscal year 1994, the Air Force will review the requirements for worldwide early warning and construct a new program that is affordable. Our FY1995 request represents the funding we need to start contractor efforts on a new design for the DSP Follow-on program.

Now, consider the Milstar program.

Milstar PROGRAM

BACKGROUND

The Milstar satellite system is planned to provide operational forces -- especially highly mobile tactical units -- secure, survivable, flexible communications on a world-wide basis. The Milstar system operates in a previously unused part of the radio spectrum -- Extremely High Frequency (EHF). This attribute plus other design features, like advanced signal processing and crosslinks, provide unique mission capabilities -- capabilities required by today's warfighters for power projection into possible theater conflicts around the globe.

While the Milstar program has focused on satisfying needs identified at its inception in the early 1980s -- providing secure, survivable, flexible communications for both tactical and strategic users -- the world situation has changed dramatically and so has the scope and application of the Milstar program. While the threat of protracted nuclear war is greatly reduced, the threat of regional conflicts has risen dramatically. During this time, the Milstar program has not been static -- it has been revised and restructured several times in harmony with the force structure to meet the changing threat.

THE RESTRUCTURED MILSTAR PROGRAM

The Department restructured the Milstar program extensively three years ago, at Congressional urging, to reduce costs and to account for changes in the international and national security environments. Requirements for a classified payload were deleted. "Heroic" survivability features envisioned for the Cold War environment were eliminated. The number of satellites and ground control elements were reduced commensurate with the threat and force structure reductions.

A higher capacity, Medium Data Rate or MDR payload was planned for a second generation Milstar II satellite which expanded its tactical utility. This MDR payload will greatly increase communications capacity compared to the Low Data Rate (LDR) capabilities on the initial Milstar I satellites -- use of both LDR and MDR will greatly enhance the utility of Milstar II satellites in a wide range of future potential scenarios.

The restructured Milstar program also reduced the numbers of strategic terminals and defined new mobile terminals for tactical uses. It reduced program life cycle costs by 25 percent, FYDP costs by 30 percent, and terminal costs by 35 percent.

The Department reviewed requirements and tailored the unique capabilities of the Milstar system to provide "flexible" and protected communications for mobile forces -- redressing many of the deficiencies observed during Desert Storm when U.S. ground forces outran their communications support. These changes exploited many of the new technologies integrated into the EHF packages on the Navy's Ultra-High Frequency (UHF) Follow-On satellites. The Department also incorporated new technologies into terminal designs for mobile platforms, man portable and tactical applications. At the time, the restructured program gained the support of the four principal Congressional defense committees for reducing program costs and increasing its tactical orientation.

THE 1992 DEFENSE ACQUISITION BOARD REVIEW

In 1992, the Joint Requirements Oversight Council (JROC) reviewed and approved a new set of Milstar requirements based on global military needs as part of a new National Military Strategy, with special emphasis on how Milstar would support a potential future South West Asian theater conflict. In October 1992, a Defense Acquisition Board (DAB) review resulted in Departmental approval of the restructured Milstar program, its acquisition strategy, and the development of the MDR payload.

Affordability was one of four principal criteria examined at that time. The Department considered Milstar program costs against those of the other major defense acquisition programs, compared them to the DoD investment in the forces it supported, and assessed affordability relative to the overall DoD budget. The Department made its recommendations on the Milstar program while considering over twenty different payload and architecture alternatives which had been completed over the previous two years and careful consideration of the risks associated with the MDR payload development. Projected program costs were further reduced during this period by introducing plans for a smaller, more affordable Milstar polar adjunct to satisfy high latitude requirements, additional reductions in requirements for Command

Post Terminals, and by deferring requirements to integrate Milstar terminals into a number of airborne platforms.

MILSATCOM BOTTOM UP REVIEW

In 1993, the Department further scrutinized MILSATCOM programs as part of the Bottom Up Review of military forces and major defense programs -- consistent with a military strategy focused on theater conflict. The Review evaluated numerous alternatives to Milstar while considering an updated threat estimate, operational requirements, cost-effectiveness tradeoffs, risk, and affordability. The review emphasized LDR and MDR capabilities for U.S. tactical forces. It focused specifically on providing lower cost alternatives to the baseline Milstar program.

As part of this review, a select group of technical experts -- known as the "Technical Support Group", headed by Dr. Bob Everett with members from MITRE, Aerospace Corporation, MIT Lincoln Laboratories, and John Hopkins Applied Physics Laboratory -- also reviewed MILSATCOM programs. The Technical Support Group recommended that the Department pursue a "cost-constrained" EHF system for protected connectivity by limiting the size of the communications payload so it would fit on a medium lift launch vehicle (MLV).

The "baseline" Milstar program, examined in the Bottom Up Review, was the program reviewed by the DAB in October 1992. It included launch of two, nearly complete Milstar I satellites in

FYs 1994 and 1995, development and launch of nine Milstar II satellites in fiscal years 1999-11. The review ultimately examined four principal options to this baseline -- all with the objective of obtaining cost reductions. All four options would launch the first two Milstar I satellites. All four also included a transition to a lower weight, lower cost EHF satellite which would fit on an MLV, delivered at different times with different capabilities. The options included:

-- Option 1: Four Milstar IIs, followed by the development and launch of an advanced EHF LDR/MDR satellite not later than FY 2006

-- Option 2: Cancel Milstar II and replace it with an MDR only EHF satellite in FY 2000; replaced in turn by advanced LDR/MDR satellites in FY 2007

-- Option 3: Cancel Milstar II and deploy an advanced EHF LDR/MDR satellite in FY 2003

-- Option 4: Similar to Option 3, but launch an advanced EHF LDR/MDR satellite in FY 2000

Of these alternatives, Option 1 was selected because it best met military requirements and provided the most capability at the earliest date. All other options were higher risk and offered the potential for additional cost savings only by deferring delivery of needed operational capability. The Department decided that Option 1 represented the best means of achieving needed capability while reducing long-term costs. It is the strategy we are now implementing.

THE FY 1995 PROGRAM

The first Milstar I satellite, with LDR only capability, is scheduled for launch later this month. The second Milstar I satellite will be delivered in time to support a scheduled launch in FY 1995. The MDR payload development is on track for a first Milstar II launch in FY 1999. Technology assessment for an advanced EHF system has begun.

At the time of the review, Option 1 was assessed by the Department to save approximately $300 million within the FYDP and about $3 billion in program life cycle costs. After further examination, we now believe we can save almost $1 billion in the FYDP and almost $4 billion in life cycle costs, compared to the baseline Milstar program. These savings have been made possible through a combination of measures -- improved efficiencies in program execution and the transition to a lower cost, lower weight advanced EHF satellite design. An advanced EHF satellite is currently planned to be available for launch after Milstar satellite #6, as identified by the General Accounting Office in their July 9, 1993 Report: GAO/NSIAD-93-216, "MILITARY SATELLITE COMMUNICATIONS: Opportunity to Save Billions of Dollars".

We recognize that developing an advanced EHF satellite will require ingenuity -- within the Department and industry -- and is not without risk. Reducing the weight of the current Milstar II payload by a factor of three to four and providing a sufficient number of narrow beam EHF antennas to connect the tactical forces needed to fight a regional conflict is a higher risk, but potentially lower cost, approach than the continued development of Milstar II satellites. The Department is currently examining a wide range of potentially applicable technologies -- inflatable antennas, carbon-carbon structures, light weight beam forming networks, advanced technology cross-links, digital electronics, inflatable solar arrays, high energy batteries, integrated electronics, etc. The review will provide the foundation for the technology development necessary to support concept definition and development of a future, lower cost EHF satellite design.

The current budget request includes funding to begin evaluating concepts and to assess the development risks a possible lower cost EHF system design. The FY 1995 budget request also reduced the level of RDT&E funding for Milstar satellites -- made possible, in part, by using funds appropriated in FY 1993 for Milstar but made available as a result of implementing the Bottom Up Review decision.

Additionally, the FY 1995 budget request reflects the further reductions in SATCOM investment by delaying the replacement of MILSATCOM capabilities and by the expanded use of commercial SATCOM services. In developing the FY 1995-1999 program, the Department further assessed the services provided by the Defense Satellite Communications System (DSCS-III) satellites. We now plan to stretch out the launches of the six remaining DSCS-III satellites currently in storage. With the anticipation of having five operationally "green" DSCS-III satellites on-orbit by May of 1994, this action allows us to delay the decision for follow-on Super High Frequency (SHF) service until FY 1996. This decision also provides additional time to implement a planned modification of the DSCS-III beam forming network on the last four satellites. These modifications directly expand the tactical utility of the DSCS-III system by incorporating state-of-the-art technology improvements into a system which was designed in the mid-1970s.

Similarly, the Department has re-examined the timing of its need to replace aging Ultra High Frequency (UHF) on-orbit capabilities and was able again to defer the decision to begin development of a Milstar-compatible polar adjunct until FY 1997. Both program adjustments will save additional cost within the FYDP and afford the Department the opportunity to further examine needs for follow-on MILSATCOM services in conjunction with expanding utilization of commercial services.

COMMERCIAL SERVICES

On November 8, 1993, the Department promulgated new policy guidance for the use of commercial satellite communications. This policy was an outgrowth, in part, of the Congressionally-mandated Commercial Satellite Communications Initiative (CSCI) studies and the demonstrable benefits available from an increased use of commercial SATCOM for military applications. The CSCI studies demonstrated the applicability of commercial SATCOM to a variety of command, control, communications and intelligence missions. The new policy guidance establishes the framework to integrate the Department's efforts for implementing commercial capabilities and will guide the resulting commercial service investment strategy to ensure a cost-effective augmentation of military satellite capabilities by the Department.

The policy states: to the extent operationally and fiscally practical, the DoD will augment its military SATCOM capability with both domestic and international commercial services. To ensure maximum savings are achieved through economies of scale, all acquisition of commercial SATCOM services shall be consistent with the approved Defense Information Services Network (DISN) acquisition strategy and shall be acquired through the auspices of the Defense Commercial Communications Office (DECCO) of the Defense Information Systems Agency (DISA), as a single manager.

As the use of commercial SATCOM increases throughout the Department, basic interoperability among Fixed Satellite Service (FSS) terminals will be established and maintained through the use of appropriate standards, and in a manner consistent with advancing commercial technology. To the maximum extent practical, all new military transportable FSS earth terminals shall be acquired with the ability to access both the commercial C and Ku frequency bands.

In support of this tasking, the Department recently hosted a Defense-wide Commercial SATCOM Conference which allowed for the exchange of ideas on the use of commercial satellite systems. DISA will capture this information into a program plan and for the first time, fully lay out a comprehensive Departmental commercial SATCOM strategy.

THE ARCHITECTURE

When the Department restructured the Milstar program in 1991, it also updated the MILSATCOM Architecture -- the framework used to manage, organize, and evaluate MILSATCOM systems relative to other satellite and terrestrial communications systems. At that time, Milstar and the DSCS were identified as the programs satisfying core military requirements, with UHF satellite and commercial systems providing unprotected service. Technology investments were made by the Advanced Research Projects Agency (ARPA) to reduce the size and weight of EHF communications payloads. The architecture provided a framework within which MILSATCOM cost reduction decisions have been evaluated -- the restructured Milstar program in 1991, the 1992 DAB review, the 1993 Bottom Up Review, etc -- resulting in a net reduction in life cycle costs of almost $20 billion dollars.

The 1991 architecture study identified numerous combinations of alternatives: existing systems with either enhanced or reduced capabilities, advanced technology proposals, and extensive use of commercial satellites. The DoD selected the baseline architecture of currently approved and ongoing systems -- including: MILSTAR; the Defense Satellite Communications System (DSCS); Ultra High Frequency (UHF) Follow-On.

Cost estimates for the 1991 architecture were developed for relative comparison of alternatives. There was a wide variance of quality among the various estimates and high potential for cost risk with less mature satellite concepts and technologies considered within the study. Costs for the baseline architecture were based on mature system designs with existing spacecraft or developed hardware. In some cases, new parametric estimates were developed using only satellite weight as a measure of system cost. The major reasons for selecting the baseline over the other alternatives was better schedule performance and lower technology risk. The baseline represented the lowest risk approach to meeting stated requirements. The cost uncertainty of relatively new concepts was carefully considered by the Department in its decision.

The content of the baseline architecture used in the 1991 study has changed substantially over the past three years. While this 1991 architecture served the Department well, it is currently considerably out of date. With the series of program changes discussed above and the increased use of commercial systems to supplement military capabilities, we plan a comprehensive update of the architecture -- a new DoD SATCOM Architecture for FY 1996. To support that update, the Department is currently conducting a review and recertification of requirements, identifying the mix of long haul and tactical transmission services which should be allocated to military and commercial systems, and identifying which communications networks could cost effectively transition from long haul SHF service to commercial SATCOM or fiber optic cable. This extensive review of communications needs and systems solutions should be available for a full evaluation of the FY 1996 budget request next year.

CONTINUED SCRUTINY

Wherever possible, the Department intends to continue identifying cost-effective reductions as a part of its overall SATCOM investment strategy -- in line with current and potential future force structure decisions. The Bottom Up Review confirmed, with independent technical assessments, that a processed EHF satellite system provides great promise for meeting current requirements to provide protected connectivity to mobile forces. It validated the Milstar II approach as the lowest risk, near term solution and it identified the need to transition to a lower cost, lower weight EHF alternative. The Bottom Up Review was not, however, the final word on cost savings. While the Department has made progress in reducing SATCOM costs -- we do not plan to rest. We are expanding our focus beyond reducing the cost of the Milstar program.

The Department will continue reviewing requirements for communications -- inserting new technologies -- and using commercial systems to supplement core military capabilities wherever these steps are proven as cost-effective measures. Affordability will continue to be a principal criteria used to determine the best mix of providing military and commercial SATCOM systems and services.

SUMMARY

Over the past several years, the Department has reviewed and restructured the DSP/FEWS and Milstar programs in response to the changing threat and national security posture. We are in the process of terminating the FEWS program and are working to define an affordable, follow-on system to DSP. Similarly, we have reviewed, restructured, and reduced the cost of Milstar and have begun technology development for a follow-on advanced EHF system. Risk (operational, technical, programmatic) and affordability have been integral elements of the Department's decisions. We will continue reviewing operational requirements and cost-effective solutions appropriate to meet essential military needs.

General KELLEY. Good afternoon. I am Maj. Gen. David Kelley. I have been the Deputy Director for Defense-Wide Command, Control, Communications and Computer Support for the Joint Staff since April 1993. I am here today representing the chairman of the Joint Chiefs of Staff.

During my career, I have had six commands, including 1 year of command in Vietnam and 2 years as a signal brigade commander in Europe. I also served as Director of Combat Developments, U.S. Army Signal School. I am here today to speak about the warfighter requirements.

Milstar was originally designed to satisfy a combination of strategic and tactical requirements. Based on direction in the fiscal year 1991 appropriations conference report, the program was restructured in 1991 to eliminate "unnecessary capabilities for protracted nuclear warfighting, increase tactical utility, and reduce costs." This was accomplished; key warfighting requirements were validated by the Joint Requirements Oversight Council, and the triservice program was approved by the Defense Acquisition Board.

The restructured Milstar is now primarily designed to satisfy tactical maritime, land, and special operations forces requirements which will enable our CONUS-based projection military to deploy overseas and win. Milstar will eliminate deficiencies encountered during Desert Storm where jamming could have denied or severely limited U.S. use of satellite communications and where U.S. ground forces outran their communications support.

Critical warfighter requirements satisfied by Milstar include essential satellite coverage and capacity when and where combat forces need it, antijam capability, covertness, deployability, and mobility. These requirements are essential for successful conduct of a Desert Storm-type war; satisfying them is a war-winning endeavor and an absolute necessity.

As we look to the future, Milstar is the only current program which adequately meets these requirements. The DOD bottom-up review revalidated critical warfighter requirements and the Milstar program as the best near-term solution to those requirements. We support the bottom-up review conclusions and will continue to exploit new technology and additional opportunities for economies.

Now, I would like to speak to the lesson we took from Desert Storm. Success of the Defense Support Program [DSP], to provide Scud warning during the Gulf war is well chronicled. However, conditions were ideal during that conflict, and we can't always be assured of such ideal conditions in future warfighting environments.

Additionally, with the proliferation of newer generation tactical ballistic missiles throughout the world, the need for improved space based sensor for launch detection has become even more critical. Key performance parameters, increased coverage and detection, for advanced space based tactical warning and attack assessment were also validated by the Joint Requirements Oversight Council in 1991. The warfighters need a solution to this critical requirement.

Thank you. That concludes my statement.

[The prepared statement of General Kelley follows:]

Statement for J61 at Congressman Conyers' Hearing

Good morning. I am Major General David Kelley. I have been the Deputy Director for Defense Wide Command, Control, Communications and Computers Support for the Joint Staff since April 1993. I am here today representing the Chairman of the Joint Chiefs of Staff. During my career, I have had six commands, including a year of command in combat and two years as a signal brigade commander in Europe. Also, I have served as Director of Combat Developments, United States Army Signal School. I am here today to speak about warfighter requirements.

Milstar was originally designed to satisfy a combination of strategic and tactical requirements. Based on direction in the FY91 Appropriations Conference Report, the program was restructured in 1991 to eliminate "unnecessary capabilities for protracted nuclear warfighting", increase tactical utility, and reduce cost. This was accomplished, key warfighting requirements were validated by the Joint Requirements Oversight Council, and the Tri-Service program was approved by the Defense Acquisition Board.

The restructured Milstar is now primarily designed to satisfy TACTICAL maritime, land, and special operations forces (SOF) requirements which will enable our CONUS-based force projection military to deploy overseas and win. Milstar will eliminate deficiencies encountered during DESERT STORM where jamming could have denied or severely limited US use of satellite communications and where US ground forces out ran their communications support.

Critical warfighter requirements satisfied by Milstar include essential satellite coverage and capacity when and where combat forces need it, antijam capability, covertness, deployability, and mobility. These requirements are essential for successful conduct of a DESERT STORM type war, satisfying them is a war-winning endeavor and an absolute necessity. Milstar is the only current program which can adequately meet these requirements. The DoD Bottom-Up Review revalidated critical warfighter requirements and the Milstar program as the best near-term solution to those requirements. We support the Bottom-Up Review conclusions and will continue to exploit new technology and additional opportunities for economies.

Now, I would like to speak about a DESERT STORM lesson. Success of Defense Support Program (DSP) to provide SCUD warning during the Gulf War is well-chronicled. However, conditions were ideal for warning during that conflict and we can't always be assured of such an ideal warning environment. Additionally, with the proliferation of newer generation Tactical Ballistic Missiles throughout the world, the need for an improved spaced based sensor for launch detection has become even more critical. Key performance parameters, increased coverage and detection, for Advanced Spaced Based Tactical Warning and Attack Assessment were also validated by the Joint Requirements Oversight Council in 1991. The warfighters need a solution to this critical requirement.

Mr. CONYERS [presiding]. Colonel Schepens.

STATEMENT OF COL. WILLIAM SCHEPENS, DIRECTOR, INSPECTIONS, INSPECTOR GENERAL'S OFFICE, U.S. AIR FORCE

Colonel SCHEPENS. I am Col. William Schepens, Director of Inspections, in the Air Force inspector general's office.

During October 1993, the Air Force inspector general investigated 17 allegations of misconduct and mismanagement relating to the DSP and FEWS acquisition programs.

On November 1, the IG reported inquiry results. Seven allegations were substantiated in part or in whole. The Air Force began the internal inquiry immediately identifying five allegations. GenCorp Aerojet then made six related allegations to the Air Force. Representative Conyers reported six additional related allegations to DOD IG which the Air Force incorporated into its ongoing inquiry. In general, there were three categories of allegations: improper release of contractor-owned proprietary data to competitors; false, misleading, or erroneous data being provided to OSD and Congress; and data being suppressed.

The results of the inquiry follow.

I would like to make a note that some of the information has been paraphrased to protect the identity of witnesses and subjects, as required by the Privacy Act.

An Air Force Materiel Command investigating officer substantiated two very similar allegations from Aerojet and Representative Conyers. The allegations were that the Air Force released an Aerospace Corp. technical operating report [TOR], which contained proprietary data belonging to GenCorp Aerojet, to Aerojet's competitors. The investigating officer found that a Federal acquisition regulation had been violated by the failure of a member of the Air Force to give proper instructions and to personally ensure that competition sensitive/proprietary data was removed from the TOR. The member's supervisor has taken appropriate corrective action.

The IG substantiated two other allegations: First, Aerojet allegation, "That the government attempted to discredit the Aerospace Technical Operating Report (TOR)." The Government and leadership of Aerospace Corp. had good reason to discredit the report. It had not been properly coordinated, approved, or distributed; it discounted validated requirements; and it was written with an advocacy tone.

Second, Representative Conyers-reported allegation: That a member of the Air Force deleted from a congressionally mandated study an option identifying improvements to the existing DSP as an alternative to FEWS that could save up to $10 billion. The member had good reason to delete the option because it did not satisfy the key DOD and congressional groundrule that it meet operational requirements.

The IG substantiated three other allegations in part: One, an Air Force-identified allegation, "That USSPACECOM staff members told a defense contractor to get on the FEWS team or get out of the way." That statement was not verified, but TRW understood from U.S. Space Command that it should pay attention to its role on the FEWS program.

Second, an Air Force-identified allegation, "That the briefing charts and background information for the 5 Oct 93 Space-Based Infrared Sensor system capabilities budget issue briefing to Mr. Deutch were released by USSPACECOM to space-based sensor competitors." Government budget data were inadvertently released, but the material did not include proprietary information, as alleged.

Third, a Representative Conyers-reported allegation: That a contractor ordered the recall of the Aerospace TOR; assisted in the suppression of options from review by Congress; and interfered in a DOD IG investigation by requesting that the IG back off on these issues. The part substantiated was that the contractor ordered the recall of the TOR in order to read the report for the first time. Then, after review by an Air Force/Aerospace Corp. team, the recall decision was affirmed.

The IG did not find misconduct by general officers. Specifically, general officers did not suppress data, did not inhibit TRW, and did not make erroneous statements supporting FEWS, as alleged in Representative Conyers' letter to DOD IG. The Air Force Judge Advocate General and the Air Force general counsel concurred in the IG's finding of no misconduct.

The IG reached two general conclusions from this investigation. First, intense competition for defense dollars is producing distrust, breakdown in communications, and allegations of impropriety. Second, the Air Force must listen to all concerns and clearly communicate why dissenting positions are not accepted. Doing so will help avoid future allegations and perceptions that "no one is listening."

In early January, following a briefing by the IG, the Secretary of the Air Force studied the IG's report of inquiry in depth and provided the inquiry results to the Department of Defense inspector general. The DOD IG reviewed the report and found that the inquiry adequately addressed the issues. Yesterday the Secretary provided the results and DOD IG's comments to congressional committee chairmen. Following this hearing, the Secretary will release inquiry results to the media and the public.

Mrs. MALONEY [presiding]. Thank you very much.

Colonel Schepens or Dr. Quinn, do you believe the Aerojet study was technically flawed?

Dr. QUINN. I wouldn't say it was technically flawed. I am not sure what you mean by that. The aerospace study——

Mrs. MALONEY. It was in the letter. Horner alleged it was in the letter that was discussed earlier; that it was "technically flawed" was his term.

Where is that letter?

Dr. QUINN. Perhaps the representative of the Space Command would like to comment on that.

Colonel STADLER. The review?

Mrs. MALONEY. He says, and I quote from General Charles, USA Commander, it was "flawed technically, operationally and politically."

What does he mean "politically flawed"?

Colonel STADLER. I will attempt to shed some light on that.

The report came out after we had already evaluated the DSP-I requirements earlier and found them to be not responsive to the needs for particularly the detection of theater missiles. The report came out in such a manner as without prior review, without an opportunity for the Air Force to assess the findings of the report. Again we had already assessed the concept and found it wanting once, and the report came out again and we found it wanting, but we were not given the opportunity to do that before it received wide distribution in the Washington area.

That precipitated the comment for "politically" because we knew that the reported solution of our requirements by this system would get wide play and cause more and increased confusion relative to the ongoing FEWS program.

Mrs. MALONEY. But a decision to recall it, in effect, to suppress it, if you disagreed with it, why not relet it and have another analyst review it, but by just pulling it back from public review, congressional review, and anyone else's view, in a sense, that is suppressing it.

Colonel STADLER. We did not attempt to suppress the report. The reason the report was recalled was to perform the analysis of what the report was advocating and to then provide a level playing field assessment of the capabilities of DSP-II to satisfy the requirements.

Mrs. MALONEY. Yet Congress did not have an opportunity to see this report because you recalled it to assess what the report said? Maybe other people would have liked to have assessed—weighed what the report said.

Colonel SCHEPENS. I think I can address that. The IG looked into whether the report was suppressed or not and found that the report in its original format made it to Dr. Schneiter's committee, Dr. Everett's group, and also to Congress.

In the meantime, the person who was responsible for the report, Mr. Aldridge, the CEO of Aerospace Corp., had not seen the report. He felt it was within his prerogative as the CEO to look at the report and comment on it. He put together a team within his corporation to evaluate what was in the report, and decided he was not happy with the report when the evaluation was complete.

Likewise, the Air Force formed a separate team and made an evaluation of the report. However, to reemphasize, the report in its original format, did make it to the right decisionmakers in order for them to assess what was in that report.

Mrs. MALONEY. There has been allegations that you attempted to discredit—I am reading from your report to us early this morning or last night, the Air Force concluded, and I again quote, that General Schnelzer—that the government attempted to discredit the aerospace technical operating report and it says you substantiated the government attempted to discredit the report.

Colonel SCHEPENS. Well, the reason we said they discredited it was: one of the ground rules for the space based sensors study was each system had to meet FEWS requirements. The report's option DEPII did not meet the FEWS requirements. Therefore, it was discredited.

Mrs. MALONEY. GAO earlier testified that there were no validated FEWS requirements.

Colonel STADLER. That is incorrect. We have a documented set of requirements that have been approved both by the joint requirements oversight——

Mrs. MALONEY. Especially for FEWS?

Colonel STADLER. Yes, ma'am.

Mrs. MALONEY. When?

Colonel STADLER. Those were done in 1991, that is when the approval of the Joint Requirements Oversight Council, the operational requirements document was done, and that is the document that we have been using to support the demonstration and validation phase of the FEWS program.

We are also, up until the time that Dr. Deutch terminated the FEWS program in November, we were drafting the second iteration of that document, it is called a FEWS operational requirements document which was incorporated within that document——

Mrs. MALONEY. Was that document issued?

Colonel STADLER. No, ma'am, it was not.

Mrs. MALONEY. It was not?

Colonel STADLER. Because it was prepared for the Milestone II decision.

Mrs. MALONEY. So there were no FEWS requirements?

Colonel STADLER. No, ma'am, that is not correct. The FEWS requirements are on the street, and the first article is the FEWS SORD.

Mrs. MALONEY. Could I see the FEWS requirements that are validated?

Colonel STADLER. Yes, ma'am. I don't have them with me, but we can provide that.

[The information follows:]

[redacted]

DSP FOLLOW-ON PROGRAM KEY REQUIREMENTS
(VALIDATED BY THE JOINT REQUIREMENTS OVERSIGHT COUNCIL - JROC)

	THRESHOLDS	OBJECTIVES
COVERAGE	DELETED DELETED	DELETED DELETED
PROBABILITY OF DETECTION		
– ICBM	DELETED	DELETED
– SLBM	DELETED DELETED	DELETED
– SS-1C	DELETED DELETED	DELETED

REQUIREMENTS SOURCE: AFSPACECOM SORD FOR THE ADVANCED SPACE-BASED TW/AA SYSTEM, 9 AUG 91, SIGNED BY USAF/CV. THESE KEY REQUIREMENTS WERE VALIDATED BY JROC ON 18 OCT 91

[redacted]

[redacted]

Mrs. MALONEY. Earlier you said you did not release the report because they didn't meet the FEWS requirements. Is that correct what you said earlier in your statement on the IG's report? You didn't release the——

Colonel SCHEPENS. I think the allegations was the Air Force did not include the DSP-II alternative to FEWS in the sensor I study. The reason they didn't include it in their submission to Congress was primarily it didn't meet the ground rules, which was it had to meet the FEWS requirement. That is why it was discounted.

Mrs. MALONEY. Yet, hasn't there been a—wasn't there another option that also did not meet the FEWS requirement?

Colonel SCHEPENS. I think what you are referring to is the DSP plus, plus. That was included in the sensor I study which was submitted to OSD and Congress, and that was the closest DSP alternative that met the FEWS requirement. It came close to, but did not meet the requirement.

Mrs. MALONEY. In your testimony, you stated it came close to, but did not meet the FEWS requirement. You released that, but you did not release the other.

Colonel SCHEPENS. Maybe you should handle this.

Colonel COLLINS. As part of the study that the Air Force was doing for——

Mrs. MALONEY. Excuse me, I add for the record, was not the one you released much more expensive and therefore not a threat for a change in the program as opposed to the alternative that the auditor or the research analyst put forward that would have saved $10 billion for the Government.

Colonel COLLINS. There was a slightly higher cost to the DSP, plus, plus.

Mrs. MALONEY. How much higher?

Colonel COLLINS. I would have to get that precise number for the record, but it was not a great deal higher than the FEWS program.

But it was higher than the——

Mrs. MALONEY. We would like that number.

Colonel COLLINS. Yes, ma'am.

[The information follows:]

During the Sensor Integration Study, the FEWS Life Cycle Cost was estimated at $13.1 Billion. The cost of the DSP++ concept was estimated between $13.8 Billion for a 6 year mean mission duration and $16.2 Billion for an 8.5 year mean mission duration. Please note that the DSP++ concept does not meet the FEWS ORD requirements.

Mrs. MALONEY. May I—I was disturbed by some of the earlier testimony, actually, of former Air Force dignitaries becoming contractors dealing with the Air Force. And as you know, President Clinton issued an Executive order that forbids senior officials from becoming contractors with the agency they headed. So how could former Air Force Secretary Pete Aldridge become a principle at first McDonnell-Douglas and later president of Aerospace or General Ramhard, a vice president of Aerospace?

How did he do that? Does it not violate the Executive order on the revolving door?

Dr. QUINN. I can't answer that directly, but we can certainly provide the answer for you.

In the case of Mr. Aldridge, however, he had intermediate employment before he went to Aerospace.

Mrs. MALONEY. McDonnell-Douglas. Again, a major contractor with the Air Force and the Government.

Dr. QUINN. Yes. I don't know that the prohibition is that they cannot work at all for a major contractor. It is a matter of how much interface there is with the government and things of that nature, which we would have to get legal counsel to give you an answer on.

Mrs. MALONEY. He was president of the company both times and we have correspondence back and forth to the military from his position as president of both companies.

Dr. QUINN. It is a legal counsel issue and we would have to get you a formal answer.

Mrs. MALONEY. We request a formal answer.

[The information follows:]

United States
Office of Government Ethics
Suite 500, 1201 New York Avenue, N.W.
Washington, D.C. 20005-3917

January 22, 1993

MEMORANDUM

TO: Designated Agency Ethics Officials

FROM: Stephen D. Potts
Director

SUBJECT: President Clinton's Executive Order Entitled "Ethics Commitments by Executive Branch Appointees"

On January 20, 1993, President Clinton signed Executive Order 12834, "Ethics Commitments by Executive Branch Appointees." See 58 Fed. Reg. 5911-5916 (Jan. 22, 1993). The Executive order requires certain persons appointed on or after January 20, 1993, to sign a pledge which establishes a contractual commitment regarding their activities after they have been employed as "senior appointees" or after they have participated personally and substantially in trade negotiations.

A copy of the Executive order is attached. The activities which will be restricted by the pledges are set forth in section 1 of the Executive order.

Who Must Sign a Pledge

"Senior appointees" and "trade negotiators," who are appointed on or after January 20, 1993, must sign a pledge. Under the terms of the Executive order, "senior appointee" means "every full-time, noncareer Presidential, Vice-Presidential or agency head appointee in an executive agency whose rate of basic pay is not less than the rate for level V of the Executive Schedule (5 U.S.C. 5316) but does not include any person appointed as a member of the senior foreign service or solely as a uniformed service commissioned officer." "Trade negotiator" means "a[ny] full-time, non-career Presidential, Vice-Presidential or agency head appointee (whether or not a senior appointee) who personally and substantially participates in a trade negotiation as an employee of an executive agency." The Executive order does not cover career officials at any level, or those officials of President Bush's Administration who are staying on in President Clinton's Administration for a period of time without receiving a new appointment.

DO-93-003

OGE-106
October

Forms of Pledges

Senior appointees will sign a "Senior Appointee Pledge." Trade negotiators who are not senior appointees (and who therefore will not have signed a "Senior Appointee Pledge") will sign a "Trade Negotiator Pledge." This Office has developed forms for these pledges, based upon language provided in the Executive order. A copy of each pledge form is attached to this memorandum for local reproduction and immediate use. The Executive order is incorporated by reference in both pledges, so senior appointees and trade negotiators must be given a copy of the Executive order to read before signing a pledge.

When a Pledge Must Be Signed

A senior appointee must sign the pledge "upon becoming" a senior appointee, i.e., at the time that person is appointed to a position that meets the terms of the Executive order. A person who is being paid less than the rate for level V of the Executive Schedule, but who otherwise meets the terms of the Executive order, must sign the pledge when his or her rate of basic pay is raised so that it equals or exceeds the rate for level V of the Executive Schedule (for example, a person in the Senior Executive Service whose rate of basic pay changes to ES-5 from ES-4.)

A non-career trade negotiator who is not a senior appointee must sign the pledge prior to personally and substantially participating in a "trade negotiation," which the Executive order defines as "a negotiation that the President determines to undertake to enter into a trade agreement with one or more foreign governments, and does not include any action taken before that determination." This Office will, after consultation with the White House, notify Designated Agency Ethics Officials of any negotiation which the President determines to be a "trade negotiation" for purposes of requiring a pledge under the terms of the Executive order. Until such notification, agencies need not collect any trade negotiator pledges; but agencies should be prepared to collect such pledges promptly.

A person who has signed a senior appointee pledge does not have to sign another pledge if that person changes senior appointee positions, unless there was a period of time between those positions during which that person was not a senior appointee. Similarly, a trade negotiator who is not also a senior appointee and who has signed a trade negotiator pledge once does not have to sign the pledge again for other trade negotiations in which that person will be participating personally and substantially, unless prior to the person's personal and substantial participation in those other trade negotiations there was a period of time during which the person was not employed in the executive branch.

Collection of the Pledges

A senior appointee is to submit his or her signed pledge to the head of his or her agency upon becoming a senior appointee. A trade negotiator who is not a senior appointee is to submit his or her signed pledge to the head of his or her agency prior to participating personally and substantially in a trade negotiation. At the Executive Office of the President, pledges are to be submitted to the White House Counsel or other official(s) to whom the President delegates that responsibility.

Signed pledges will be placed in the senior appointee's or trade negotiator's Official Personnel Folder or equivalent personnel file.

Waivers

Only the President can grant a waiver of any of the restrictions contained in a pledge. A request for a waiver should be submitted to the head of the affected agency for submission to the President through the Counsel to the President. A waiver requires the President's written certification, and publication in the Federal Register, that it is in the public interest for the waiver to be granted.

Enforcement

The Executive order specifies that the contractual commitments established by the pledges will be enforced by any legally available means, including debarment proceedings within the affected agency, or judicial or civil proceedings brought by the Attorney General for declaratory, injunctive, or monetary relief.

Further Guidance

This Office will assist Designated Agency Ethics Officials in providing advice to current or former senior appointees and trade negotiators regarding the application of the pledges. In providing this assistance, this Office will consult with the Attorney General or Counsel to the President when appropriate. In addition, within the next six months, the Attorney General will be publishing in the Federal Register a "Statement of Covered Activities" regarding the restriction on a former senior appointee's activities on behalf of a foreign government or foreign political party.

Attachments (3)

SENIOR APPOI... PLEDGE

As a condition, and in consideration, of my emp... t in the United States Government in a senior appointee position invested with the public trust, I ... myself to the following obligations, which I understand are binding on me and are enforceable u... w:

1. I will not, within five years after the termin... my employment as a senior appointee in any executive agency in which I am appointed to serve, lo... y officer or employee of that agency.

2. In the event that I serve as a senior appoin... he Executive Office of the President ("EOP"), I also will not, within five years after I cease to be a ... appointee in the EOP, lobby any officer or employee of any other executive agency with respect to ... I had personal and substantial responsibility as a senior appointee in the EOP.

3. I will not, at any time after the termination o... nployment in the United States Government, engage in any activity on behalf of any foreign governm... foreign political party which, if undertaken on January 20, 1993, would require me to register und... Foreign Agents Registration Act of 1938, as amended.

4. I will not, within five years after termination... y personal and substantial participation in a trade negotiation, represent, aid or advise any foreig... ernment, foreign political party or foreign business entity with the intent to influence a decision o... officer or employee of any executive agency, in carrying out his or her official duties.

5. I acknowledge that the Executive order ent... "Ethics Commitments by Executive Branch Appointees," issued by the President on January 20, 19... ch I have read before signing this document, defines certain of the terms applicable to the foregoing o... ons and sets forth the methods for enforcing them. I expressly accept the provisions of that Executiv... order as a part of this agreement and as binding on me. I understand that the terms of this pledge are in ad...tion to any statutory or other legal restrictions applicable to me by virtue of Federal Government service.

_____   _____ 19___
Signature   Date

_____
Print or type your full name (Last, first, middle -- spell out each fully)

Privacy Act Statement

Executive Order 12834 entitled "Ethics Commitments by Executive Branch Appointees," issued by the President on January 20, 1993 (and published at 58 Federal Register 5911-5916 on 1/22/93), requires every senior appointee in every executive agency appointed on or after January 20, 1993 to sign this pledge upon becoming a senior appointee. This pledge establishes a contractual commitment regarding your post-employment activities and your activities after your personal and substantial participation in a trade negotiation has ceased. If there is a violation or apparent violation of this pledge, this pledge may be disclosed to the Department of Justice or any other appropriate Federal agency charged with the responsibility of investigating, prosecuting, enforcing or implementing the Executive order. Disclosure of this pledge can also be made to another Federal agency, a court or a party in court litigation or an administrative proceeding when the Government is a party as well as to another Federal agency in connection with your hiring when the pledge is relevant and necessary thereto. Further, this pledge may be disclosed to the Executive Office of the President and the Office of Government Ethics to enable them to carry out their responsibilities under Executive Order 12834 and other ethics oversight authorities. This pledge will be filed for permanent retention in your official personnel folder or equivalent folder. Your signing this pledge is a condition, and in consideration, of your employment as a senior appointee, or your receiving a pay raise that will make you a senior appointee, as defined in the Executive order.

OGE Form 203
Jan. 1993

Presidential Documents

Title 3—

The President

Executive Order 12834 of January 20, 1993

Ethics Commitments by Executive Branch Appointees

By the authority vested in me as President of the United States by the Constitution and laws of the United States of America, including section 301 of title 3, United States Code, and sections 3301 and 7301 of title 5, United States Code, it is hereby ordered as follows:

Section 1. *Ethics Pledges.* (a) Every senior appointee in every executive agency appointed on or after January 20, 1993, shall sign, and upon signing shall be contractually committed to, the following pledge ("senior appointee pledge") upon becoming a senior appointee:

"As a condition, and in consideration, of my employment in the United States Government in a senior appointee position invested with the public trust, I commit myself to the following obligations, which I understand are binding on me and are enforceable under law:

"1. I will not, within five years after the termination of my employment as a senior appointee in any executive agency in which I am appointed to serve, lobby any officer or employee of that agency.

"2. In the event that I serve as a senior appointee in the Executive Office of the President ('EOP'), I also will not, within five years after I cease to be a senior appointee in the EOP, lobby any officer or employee of any other executive agency with respect to which I had personal and substantial responsibility as a senior appointee in the EOP.

"3. I will not, at any time after the termination of my employment in the United States Government, engage in any activity on behalf of any foreign government or foreign political party which, if undertaken on January 20, 1993, would require me to register under the Foreign Agents Registration Act of 1938, as amended.

"4. I will not, within five years after termination of my personal and substantial participation in a trade negotiation, represent, aid or advise any foreign government, foreign political party or foreign business entity with the intent to influence a decision of any officer or employee of any executive agency, in carrying out his or her official duties.

"5. I acknowledge that the Executive order entitled 'Ethics Commitments by Executive Branch Appointees,' issued by the President on January 20, 1993, which I have read before signing this document, defines certain of the terms applicable to the foregoing obligations and sets forth the methods for enforcing them. I expressly accept the provisions of that Executive order as a part of this agreement and as binding on me. I understand that the terms of this pledge are in addition to any statutory or other legal restrictions applicable to me by virtue of Federal Government service."

(b) Every trade negotiator who is not a senior appointee and is appointed to a position in an executive agency on or after January 20, 1993, shall (prior to personally and substantially participating in a trade negotiation) sign, and upon signing be contractually committed to, the following pledge ("trade negotiator pledge"):

"As a condition, and in consideration, of my employment in the United States Government as a trade negotiator, which is a position invested with the public trust, I commit myself to the following obligations, which I understand are binding on me and are enforceable under law:

"1. I will not, within five years after termination of my personal and substantial participation in a trade negotiation, represent, aid or advise any foreign government, foreign political party or foreign business entity with the intent to influence a decision of any officer or employee of any executive agency, in carrying out his or her official duties.

"2. I acknowledge that the Executive order entitled 'Ethics Commitments by Executive Branch Appointees,' issued by the President on January 20, 1993, which I have read before signing this document, defines certain of the terms applicable to the foregoing obligations and sets forth the methods for enforcing them. I expressly accept the provisions of that Executive order as a part of this agreement and as binding on me. I understand that the terms of this pledge are in addition to any statutory or other legal restrictions applicable to me by virtue of Federal Government service."

Sec. 2. *Definitions.* As used herein and in the pledges:

(a) "Senior appointee" means every full-time, non-career Presidential, Vice-presidential or agency head appointee in an executive agency whose rate of basic pay is not less than the rate for level V of the Executive Schedule (5 U.S.C. 5316) but does not include any person appointed as a member of the senior foreign service or solely as a uniformed service commissioned officer.

(b) "Trade negotiator" means a full-time, non-career Presidential, Vice-presidential or agency head appointee (whether or not a senior appointee) who personally and substantially participates in a trade negotiation as an employee of an executive agency.

(c) "Lobby" means to knowingly communicate to or appear before any officer or employee of any executive agency on behalf of another (except the United States) with the intent to influence official action, except that the term "lobby" does not include:

(1) communicating or appearing on behalf of and as an officer or employee of a State or local government or the government of the District of Columbia, a Native American tribe or a United States territory or possession;

(2) communicating or appearing with regard to a judicial proceeding, or a criminal or civil law enforcement inquiry, investigation or proceeding (but not with regard to an administrative proceeding or with regard to an administrative proceeding to the extent that such communications or appearances are made after the commencement of and in connection with the conduct or disposition of a judicial proceeding;

(3) communicating or appearing with regard to any government grant, contract or similar benefit on behalf of and as an officer or employee of:

(A) an accredited, degree-granting institution of higher education, as defined in section 1201(a) of title 20, United States Code; or

(B) a hospital; a medical, scientific or environmental research institution; or a charitable or educational institution; provided that such entity is a not-for-profit organization exempted from Federal income taxes under sections 501(a) and 501(c)(3) of title 26, United States Code;

(4) communicating or appearing on behalf of an international organization in which the United States participates, if the Secretary of State certifies in advance that such activity is in the interest of the United States;

(5) communicating or appearing solely for the purpose of furnishing scientific or technological information, subject to the procedures and conditions applicable under section 207(j)(5) of title 18, United States Code; or

(6) giving testimony under oath, subject to the conditions applicable under section 207(j)(6) of title 18, United States Code.

(d) "On behalf of another" means on behalf of a person or entity other than the individual signing the pledge or his or her spouse, child or parent.

(e) "Administrative proceeding" means any agency process for rulemaking, adjudication or licensing, as defined in and governed by the Administrative Procedure Act, as amended (5 U.S.C. 551, et seq.).

(f) "Executive agency" and "agency" mean "Executive agency" as defined in section 105 of title 5, United States Code, except that the term includes the Executive Office of the President, the United States Postal Service and the Postal Rate Commission and excludes the General Accounting Office. As used in paragraph 1 of the senior appointee pledge, "executive agency" means the entire agency in which the senior appointee is appointed to serve, except that:

(1) with respect to those senior appointees to whom such designations are applicable under section 207(h) of title 18, United States Code, the term means an agency or bureau designated by the Director of the Office of Government Ethics under section 207(h) as a separate department or agency at the time the senior appointee ceased to serve in that department or agency; and

(2) a senior appointee who is detailed from one executive agency to another for more than sixty days in any calendar year shall be deemed to be an officer or employee of both agencies during the period such person is detailed.

(g) "Personal and substantial responsibility" "with respect to" an executive agency, as used in paragraph 2 of the senior appointee pledge, means ongoing oversight of, or significant ongoing decision-making involvement in, the agency's budget, major programs or personnel actions, when acting both "personally" and "substantially" (as those terms are defined for purposes of sections 207(a) and (b) of title 18, United States Code).

(h) "Personal and substantial participation" and "personally and substantially participates" mean acting both "personally" and "substantially" (as those terms are defined for purposes of sections 207(a) and (b) of title 18, United States Code) as an employee through decision, approval, disapproval, recommendation, the rendering of advice, investigation or other such action.

(i) "Trade negotiation" means a negotiation that the President determines to undertake to enter into a trade agreement with one or more foreign governments, and does not include any action taken before that determination.

(j) "Foreign Agents Registration Act of 1938, as amended" means sections 611–621 of title 22, United States Code.

(k) "Foreign government" means "the government of a foreign country," as defined in section 1(e) of the Foreign Agents Registration Act of 1938, as amended (22 U.S.C. 611(e)).

(l) "Foreign political party" has the same meaning as that term in section 1(f) of the Foreign Agents Registration Act of 1938, as amended (22 U.S.C. 611(f)).

(m) "Foreign business entity" means a partnership, association, corporation, organization or other combination of persons organized under the laws of or having its principal place of business in a foreign country.

(n) Terms that are used herein and in the pledges, and also used in section 207 of title 18, United States Code, shall be given the same meaning as they have in section 207 and any implementing regulations issued or to be issued by the Office of Government Ethics, except to the extent those terms are otherwise defined in this order.

Sec. 3. *Waiver.* (a) The President may grant to any person a waiver of any restrictions contained in the pledge signed by such person if, and to the extent that, the President certifies in writing that it is in the public interest to grant the waiver.

(b) A waiver shall take effect when the certification is signed by the President.

(c) The waiver certification shall be published in the Federal Register, identifying the name and executive agency position of the person covered by the waiver and the reasons for granting it.

(d) A copy of the waiver certification shall be furnished to the person covered by the waiver and filed with the head of the agency in which that person is or was appointed to serve.

Sec. 4. *Administration.* (a) The head of every executive agency shall establish for that agency such rules or procedures (conforming as nearly as practicable to the agency's general ethics rules and procedures, including those relating to designated agency ethics officers) as are necessary or appropriate:

(1) to ensure that every senior appointee in the agency signs the senior appointee pledge upon assuming the appointed office or otherwise becoming a senior appointee;

(2) to ensure that every trade negotiator in the agency who is not a senior appointee signs the trade negotiator pledge prior to personally and substantially participating in a trade negotiation;

(3) to ensure that no senior appointee or trade negotiator in the agency personally and substantially participates in a trade negotiation prior to signing the pledge; and

(4) generally to ensure compliance with this order within the agency.

(b) With respect to the Executive Office of the President, the duties set forth in section 4(a), above, shall be the responsibility of the White House Counsel or such other official or officials to whom the President delegates those duties.

(c) The Director of the Office of Government Ethics shall:

(1) subject to the prior approval of the White House Counsel, develop a form of the pledges to be completed by senior appointees and trade negotiators and see that the pledges and a copy of this Executive order are made available for use by agencies in fulfilling their duties under section 4(a) above;

(2) in consultation with the Attorney General or White House Counsel, when appropriate assist designated agency ethics officers in providing advice to current or former senior appointees and trade negotiators regarding the application of the pledges; and

(3) subject to the prior approval of the White House Counsel, adopt such rules or procedures (conforming as nearly as practicable to its generally applicable rules and procedures) as are necessary or appropriate to carry out the foregoing responsibilities.

(d) In order to promote clarity and fairness in the application of paragraph 3 of the senior appointee pledge:

(1) the Attorney General shall, within six months after the issuance of this order, publish in the Federal Register a "Statement of Covered Activities," based on the statute, applicable regulations and published guidelines, and any other material reflecting the Attorney General's current interpretation of the law, describing in sufficient detail to provide adequate guidance the activities on behalf of a foreign government or foreign political party which, if undertaken as of January 20, 1993, would require a person to register as an agent for such foreign government or political party under the Foreign Agents Registration Act of 1938, as amended; and

(2) the Attorney General's "Statement of Covered Activities" shall be presumed to be the definitive statement of the activities in which the senior appointee agrees not to engage under paragraph 3 of the pledge.

(e) A senior appointee who has signed the senior appointee pledge is not required to sign the pledge again upon appointment to a different office, except that a person who has ceased to be a senior appointee, due to termination of employment in the executive branch or otherwise, shall sign the senior appointee pledge prior to thereafter assuming office as a senior appointee.

(f) A trade negotiator who is not also a senior appointee and who has once signed the trade negotiator pledge is not required to sign the pledge again prior to personally and substantially participating in a subsequent trade negotiation, except that a person who has ceased employment in the executive branch shall, after returning to such employment, be obligated to sign a pledge as provided herein notwithstanding the signing of any previous pledge.

(g) All pledges signed by senior appointees and trade negotiators, and all waiver certifications with respect thereto, shall be filed with the head of the appointee's agency for permanent retention in the appointee's official personnel folder or equivalent folder.

Sec. 5. *Enforcement.* (a) The contractual, fiduciary and ethical commitments in the pledges provided for herein are enforceable by any legally available means, including any or all of the following: debarment proceedings within any affected executive agency or judicial civil proceedings for declaratory, injunctive or monetary relief.

(b) Any former senior appointee or trade negotiator who is determined, after notice and hearing, by the duly designated authority within any agency, to have violated his or her pledge not to lobby any officer or employee of that agency, or not to represent, aid or advise a foreign entity specified in the pledge with the intent to influence the official decision of that agency, may be barred from lobbying any officer or employee of that agency for up to five years in addition to the five-year time period covered by the pledge.

(1) The head of every executive agency shall, in consultation with the Director of the Office of Government Ethics, establish procedures to implement the foregoing subsection, which shall conform as nearly as practicable to the procedures for debarment of former employees found to have violated section 207 of title 18, United States Code (1988 ed.), set forth in section 2637.212 of title 5, Code of Federal Regulations (revised as of January 1, 1992).

(2) Any person who is debarred from lobbying following an agency proceeding pursuant to the foregoing subsection may seek judicial review of the administrative determination, which shall be subject to established standards for judicial review of comparable agency actions.

(c) The Attorney General is authorized:

(1) upon receiving information regarding the possible breach of any commitment in a signed pledge, to request any appropriate federal investigative authority to conduct such investigations as may be appropriate; and

(2) upon determining that there is a reasonable basis to believe that a breach of a commitment has occurred or will occur or continue, if not enjoined, to commence a civil action against the former employee in any United States District Court with jurisdiction to consider the matter.

(d) In such civil action, the Attorney General is authorized to request any and all relief authorized by law, including but not limited to:

(1) such temporary restraining orders and preliminary and permanent injunctions as may be appropriate to restrain future, recurring or continuing conduct by the former employee in breach of the commitments in the pledge he or she signed; and

(2) establishment of a constructive trust for the benefit of the United States, requiring an accounting and payment to the United States Treasury of all money and other things of value received by, or payable to, the former employee arising out of any breach or attempted breach of the pledge signed by the former employee.

Sec. 6. General Provisions. (a) No prior Executive orders are repealed by this order. To the extent that this order is inconsistent with any provision of any prior Executive order, this order shall control.

(b) If any provision of this order or the application of such provision is held to be invalid, the remainder of this order and other dissimilar applications of such provision shall not be affected.

(c) Except as expressly provided in section 5(b)(2) of this order, nothing in the pledges or in this order is intended to create any right or benefit, substantive or procedural, enforceable at law by a party against the United States, its agencies, its officers, or any person.

THE WHITE HOUSE,
January 20, 1993.

[FR Doc. 93-1871
Filed 1-21-93; 12:20 pm]
Billing code 3195-01-M

DEPARTMENT OF THE AIR FORCE
WASHINGTON DC

OFFICE OF THE GENERAL COUNSEL

AUG 27 1993

MEMORANDUM FOR MAJOR GENERAL DONALD G. HARD, USAF, RETIRED

SUBJECT: 10 U.S.C. § 2397b Opinion and Other Post-Government Employment Restrictions

Opinion

This responds to your request for an opinion concerning the applicability of 10 U.S.C. § 2397b to your post-government employment (Attachment 1). Pursuant to my delegated authority from the Air Force Designated Agency Ethics Official, i.e., the General Counsel, to render post-government employment opinions, 10 U.S.C. § 2397b will not apply to your employment with any defense contractors. My reasoning, based on the information that you have provided, follows.

10 U.S.C. § 2397b
Two-Year Employment Bar

As we have discussed, this two-year employment restriction applies to procurement officials who have:

1. Spent the majority of their working days during the last two years of DoD service at a defense contractor's plant or site;

2. Performed on a majority of their working days during the last two years of DoD service a procurement function relating to a major defense system, and participated on any occasion in decision-making responsibilities regarding the major defense system through contact with the defense contractor; or,

3. Acted as a primary representative of the government during the last two years of DoD service in negotiating a contract or settling a claim in excess of $10 million with a defense contractor.

The threshold 10 U.S.C. § 2397b determination is your last two years of DoD service. It covers the period August 1, 1991, to August 1, 1993.

The next issue involves an analyses of the three above 10 U.S.C. § 2397b categories to your post-government employment. My determination of the non-applicability of the three 10 U.S.C. § 2397b categories to your post-government employment takes into consideration the following factors:

1. The first category of 10 U.S.C. § 2397b does not apply to you. It only covers former government employees who spent the majority of their working days during the last two years of their DoD service at a defense contractor's plant or site. Your principal place of employment, however, as the Director of Space Programs during the period August 1, 1991, to August 1, 1993, was at the Pentagon -- not at any sites or plants of defense contractors.

2. The second category of 10 U.S.C. § 2397b also does not apply to you. It targets former government employees who spent a majority of their working days on a major defense system and who participated in decision-making responsibilities regarding the system through contact with the prime defense contractor. If such is the case, then the former government employee would be barred from employment with the prime defense contractor for two years after leaving DoD.

Your duties as the Director of Space Programs were broad scope. As a result, you have advised me that you did not spend a majority of your working days during the period August 1, 1991, to August 1, 1993, on any major defense system (Attachment 1). Or, in other words, although a former government employee's duties may relate to a number of major defense systems, such as in your case, if he or she works on none of those individual systems for a majority of working days during the two-year period prior to leaving DoD, then the former employee does not fall within the ambit of the second 10 U.S.C. § 2397b category.

3. The third category covers former government employees who acted as one of the primary government representatives in negotiating a contract or settling a claim in excess of $10 million with a defense contractor. This category is strictly interpreted as requiring personal and substantial participation in the contract negotiation or claim settlement process by personal presence, telephone conversation, or similar personal involvement with representatives of a defense contractor.

For example, if a contracting officer had been the person conducting all negotiations with a defense contractor, but a superior intervened directly in the negotiation process to make a decision and there was personal contact with representatives of the defense contractor, then the superior would be deemed to be one of the primary representatives for the contract negotiation.

Your duties as the Director of Space Programs did not involve personal and substantial participation in contract negotiations or claim settlements. Rather, these types of duties were generally performed by other offices within the Air Force acquisition system. And, you have confirmed that you did not perform such duties during your last two years of DoD service. Thus, this third statutory category is not applicable to your post-government employment.

In addition to 10 U.S.C. §2397b, there are a number of other restrictions that possibly could apply to your post-government employment. They are summarized below.

Procurement Integrity
41 U.S.C. § 423(f)

In contrast to the 10 U.S.C. § 2397b employment bar, these restrictions do not preclude employment with any entity. Rather, they only restrict certain activities on behalf of prospective employers regarding certain procurements. Stated otherwise, the Procurement Integrity post-government employment restrictions are contract specific.

These restrictions preclude both "behind-the-scenes" assistance rendered at corporate offices and representational contacts, i.e., making telephone calls, attending meetings or writing letters, to government personnel.

The Procurement Integrity restrictions only come into play if you participated personally and substantially in "pre-award activities," defined below, during an agency procurement. If such is the case, then you cannot:

1. Participate in any negotiations involving the procurement; or,

2. Be involved in the performance of the contract.

The above prohibitions last for two years after your participation in the procurement as a government official.

The "pre-award activities" that trigger the Procurement Integrity restrictions are:

-- Drafting or reviewing and approving a specification or statement of work;

-- Preparing or developing a procurement or purchase request;

-- Preparing or issuing a procurement solicitation;

-- Evaluating bids or proposals or selecting sources;

-- Negotiating the price or terms and conditions of a contract or contract modification; or,

-- Reviewing and approving the award, modification or extension of a contract.

18 U.S.C. § 207
Five Possible Restrictions

Three of these restrictions preclude representational contacts with government officials. The three restrictions are: (1) the lifetime representational bar relating to official matters in which you had personal and substantial participation; (2) the two-year official responsibility ban; and, (3) the one-year "cooling-off" period.

You have stated that your post-government employment will probably not involve any representational contacts with government officials. Rather, it will only consist of "behind-the-scenes" duties not involving any contact with government officials. Thus, the three representational restrictions should not impact your post-government employment.

The 18 U.S.C. § 207 trade or treaty restriction lasts for one year after leaving government service. It targets former employees who personally and substantially participated in trade or treaty negotiations within the last year of government service and who, consequently, learned of information exempt from disclosure under the Freedom of Information Act (FOIA). Such employees are barred from representing, aiding or advising any person regarding the ongoing trade or treaty negotiations on the basis of the FOIA exempt information.

It is my understanding that your post-government employment will not involve any representing, aiding or advising on ongoing trade or treaty negotiations in which you participated as a government official. Hence, this restriction will not affect your employment activities after your retirement from the Air Force.

The fifth 18 U.S.C. § 207 restriction prohibits representing, aiding or advising foreign governments or foreign political parties with the intent to influence the official actions of an employee of a department or agency of the United States. It lasts for one year. Thus, you must be careful to avoid such activity for foreign governments or foreign political parties for one year after leaving the Air Force.

Foreign Government Employment
All Retired Military Personnel

The U.S. Constitution prohibits employment of all retired military personnel by a foreign government unless first approved by the Secretary of State and, for Air Force members, the Secretary of the Air Force. Therefore, before accepting employment with any entity owned, operated or controlled by a foreign government, you should contact me.

Foreign Agents Registration Act (FARA)

A former government official desiring employment by a foreign government, foreign political party or any foreign business must also consider whether such employment would require registration under the Foreign Agents Registration Act. This Act requires anyone who engages in certain activities as an agent of a foreign principal to file a registration statement with the Attorney General.

Mr. Joseph Clarkson, a lawyer with the FARA Registration Unit, Department of Justice, is available to answer questions in this area. His telephone number is (202) 514-1231.

Inside Information

There are a number of criminal and civil laws and regulations that preclude the release of government "inside information" to private sector entities. The term, "inside information," has been generally defined in the DoD Standards of Conduct directive as information: (1) not available to the public, and (2) obtained by reason of one's DoD duties. Some examples include classified materials and procurement sensitive matters, such as proprietary and source selection information and non-public budget information.

It is my understanding that your post-government employment duties will not involve any "inside information" issues. Therefore, this restriction should not cause any difficulty.

Post-Government Employment Reports

The DD Form 1787 must be filed if you are employed within two years of leaving DoD by a defense contractor that received $10 million or more in defense contracts the past fiscal year and you are paid at the rate of $25,000 per year or more (about $12 per hour). (Copy at Attachment 2.)

In addition you will have to file a DD Form 1357 (Attachment 3) and a termination SF 278 Report (Attachment 4) within 30 days of your retirement.

The above reports should be mailed to me at the following address:

SAF/GCA
1740 Air Force Pentagon
Washington, D.C. 20330-1740

Please ensure these reports are timely filed. Otherwise, there may be monetary fines that you will have to pay.

18 U.S.C. § 281 and 37 U.S.C. § 801
Selling and Claims Restrictions

Combining the two above statutory prohibitions, retired military officers cannot engage in "selling" for three years after retirement to any DoD component or agency, the Coast Guard, the National Oceanic and Atmospheric Administration, or the Public Health Service.

"Selling" is broadly defined. It includes the following activities:

- Signing a bid, proposal or contract;

- Negotiating a contract;

- Contacting an officer or employee of the above departments or agencies for the purpose of:

    - Obtaining or negotiating contracts;

    -- Negotiating or discussing changes in specifications, price, cost allowances, or other terms of a contract;

    -- Settling disputes concerning performance of a contract; or,

- Any other liaison activity with a view toward the ultimate consummation of a sale although the actual contract is subsequently negotiated by another person.

The Comptroller General has held that:

- Contacts made for the purpose of promoting goodwill which may lead to future sales are tantamount to "selling."

- A presumption will be applied that pre-contract contacts by retired military officers with DoD personnel are for the purpose of prohibited selling activity. The burden is on the officer to demonstrate "clearly and adequately" that such contacts are made for some purpose other than "selling," such as social activity. (Note: Even if a contact is made after contract award, you must be able to satisfy this burden.)

The criminal law, 18 U.S.C. § 281, also restricts retired military officers from representing others on claims against the U.S. involving the military department from which they retired or involving any matter with which they were directly connected while on active duty.

Applying the above "selling" restrictions to your post-government employment, you must be very cautious whenever you have any contact with DoD or Air Force personnel for three years after your retirement date. In this regard, you have advised me that your post-government employment will not involve such contact for three years after your retirement date. Rather, you will probably be involved in "behind-the-scenes" employment. Hence, the "selling" restrictions should not present any problems.

I trust the foregoing information will be useful. If you have any questions, please do not hesitate to call me on (703) 695-6552.

Roger T. McNamara
Roger T. McNamara
Ethics Official
Office of the General Counsel

Attachments
1. Your memo of
   August 11, 1993
2. DD Form 1787
3. DD Form 1357
4. SF 278

cc w/ atchs to:
Ms. Druyun
Mr. Willson
Mr. Janecek

DEPARTMENT OF THE AIR FORCE
WASHINGTON, D.C. 20330-1000

OFFICE OF THE GENERAL COUNSEL

September 26, 1988

MEMORANDUM FOR MR. ALDRIDGE, SAF/OS

SUBJECT: Request for a 10 U.S.C. §2397b Opinion Letter

This is in response to your inquiry regarding employment restrictions under section 2397b, Title 10, United States Code, in connection with post-government service employment with defense contractors.

You have requested advice as provided by 10 U.S.C. §2397b(e), and I am responding in my capacity as the Designated Agency Ethics Official of the Department of the Air Force. Based on our discussions, I conclude that you have not, within the past two years: (1) performed, on a majority of your working days during the last two years, a procurement function relating to a major defense system, or (2) acted as one of the primary representatives of the United States in the negotiation of a contract or the settlement of a contractual claim in excess of $10,000,000. Accordingly, it is my opinion that your post-government service employment by any defense contractor is not subject to the two-year employment bar imposed by 10 U.S.C. §2397b(a).

This opinion is specifically limited to the application of 10 U.S.C. §2397b to your proposed employment. I am separately providing you a memorandum concerning other statutory and regulatory restrictions on your future employment. I will be glad to answer questions you may have regarding any conflict of interest or post-employment provisions.

Anne N. Foreman
General Counsel

DEPARTMENT OF THE AIR FORCE
WASHINGTON, D.C. 20330-1000

OFFICE OF THE GENERAL COUNSEL

September 26, 1988

MEMORANDUM FOR MR. ALDRIDGE, SAF/OS

SUBJECT: Post-Government Service Conflict of Interest Restrictions

This is in response to your request for advice concerning conflict of interest restrictions which will apply to you in seeking private employment and after you leave the Air Force. Two statutes, 18 U.S.C. § 208 and 10 U.S.C. § 2397a, apply to your employment discussions while you remain in office, and two principal kinds of restrictions apply to your post-government work: those applicable to all former government officers and employees under 18 U.S.C. §207 and those applicable to certain DOD officials under 10 U.S.C. §2397b. The latter statute will be addressed in a separate memorandum.

I. **Seeking Private Employment**

A. **18 U.S.C. §208**

This criminal statute requires that all government employees and military members not participate in any particular matter in which any person or organization with whom he or she is negotiating for future employment has a financial interest. You can avoid violating this statute by disqualifying yourself in writing from participating in any matters in which a person or company with whom you are negotiating has a financial interest. The statute requires disqualification when you begin "negotiating" for future employment. Since exactly what constitutes negotiating is not always clear, you should disqualify yourself any time there is any contact between you and any company employee concerning the possibility of some future job unless the contact is initiated by the company employee and you immediately reject it.

B. **10 U.S.C. 2397a**

This statute adds reporting and disqualification requirements for certain DOD personnel (GS-11/0-4 or higher) who seek future employment while still working for the government. It requires that if you have participated in a procurement function in connection with a DOD contract and you contact, or are contacted by, the DOD contractor to whom the contract was awarded regarding future employment, you must report the contact (unless it was a rejected first contact by the contractor) to me, as the Designated Agency Ethics Official for the Air Force, and disqualify yourself from participating in any procurement functions relating to contracts of that contractor. The term "procurement function" includes (1) negotiation, award, administration, or approval of a contract, (2) selection of a contractor, (3) approval of changes in the contract, (4) quality assurance, operation and developmental testing, the approval of payment, or auditing under the contract, and (5) management of the procurement program. The required report should be in writing and include the name of the contractor, the date of each contact, and a brief description of the substance of the contact. This provision would apply, for example, if you are contacted by a company which was awarded an Air Force contract for which you were the Source Selection Authority. Violation of these requirements may bring an administrative penalty of up to $10,000 and up to a 10-year bar on working for the contractor involved. At Attachment 1 are a sample report and disqualification memorandums and Enclosure 9 to DoD Directive 5500.7, which implements the statutory requirement.

II. <u>Post-Government Service Restrictions</u>

  A. <u>18 U.S.C. §207</u>

There are four prohibitions contained in 18 U.S.C. §207, all of which apply to you. These prohibitions are stated in summary form in the matrix at Attachment 2 and are explained in detail in the regulations of the Office of Government Ethics (5 CFR Part 737) at Attachment 3. This regulation contains numerous examples; we have highlighted the ones of particular interest to you. The applicable prohibitions are explained briefly below.

    1. <u>Sec. 207(a)</u>

This is a lifetime bar on acting as attorney or agent for, or otherwise representing, any other person in any formal or informal appearance or, with intent to influence, making any oral or written communication to or before any Government agency or employee thereof in connection with a <u>particular matter involving specific parties</u> in which you participated personally and substantially for the Government. This restriction, and the other restrictions discussed below, apply only to certain representational activities, <u>viz.</u>, appearing before or communicating with Government officials. The restrictions do not apply to advising an employer or client where there is no direct contact with the Government. See 5 CFR 737.5(b)(6). In addition, communications without an "intent to influence" are not prohibited, <u>e.g.</u>, asking about the status of a matter, requesting publicly available documents, or imparting purely factual information not in connection with an adversary proceeding. See 5 CFR 737.5(b)(5).

The restrictions in §207(a) (and also in §207(b) described below) apply only to particular matters involving a specific party or parties. Various particular matters are identified in the statute: "judicial or other proceeding, application, request for a ruling or other determination, contract, claim, controversy, investigation, charge, accusation, arrest." A particular matter does not involve rulemaking, *e.g.*, drafting a regulation or FAR provision, nor does it involve work on legislation or formulation of general policy. See 5 CFR 735.5(c)(1). Section 207(a) also applies only to those matters in which you had personal and substantial participation exercised "through decision, approval, disapproval, recommendation, rendering of advice, investigation or otherwise." There are no very precise guidelines for determining what is "personal and substantial." It is certainly a greater degree of participation in a matter than merely having the matter pending under your official responsibility (see discussion of §207(b)(i) below). The OGE regulations state that "substantially" means that involvement must be "of significance to the matter or form a basis for a reasonable appearance of such significance." It is more than knowledge, perfunctory involvement, or involvement in an administrative or peripheral issue. See 5 CFR 737.5(d). For example, your action as a Source Selection Authority in *any given procurement* would result in a lifetime bar on representing the selected contractor before any Government agency on any matter connected with *that* procurement.

2. Sec. 207(b)(i)

This is a restriction that differs from §207(a) in only two respects: it is a bar for only two years after leaving Government service (rather than for life), and it applies to matters pending under the individual's official responsibility within a period of one year prior to the termination of such responsibility (rather than personal and substantial involvement). All other aspects of §207(a) are also applicable to §207(b)(i), *e.g.*, representation by personal appearance or communication with intent to influence, in connection with a particular matter involving specific parties. Section 202(b) of title 18 defines "official responsibility" as "the direct administrative or operating authority, whether intermediate or final, and either exercisable alone or with others, and either personally or through subordinates, to approve, disapprove, or otherwise direct Government actions." Ordinarily, official responsibility would include areas assigned to a position by regulation, job description, or delegation of authority. It would also include any matter in which one of your immediate subordinates actually participated. See 5 CFR 737.7(b).

3. **Sec. 207(b)(ii)**.

This is a two year bar applicable to a "senior employee" (which includes all Presidential appointees) who "knowingly represents or aids, counsels, advises, consults, or assists in representing any other person (except the United States) by personal presence at any formal or informal appearance" before a Government agency in connection with a particular matter involving specific parties in which he participated personally and substantially as an employee of the Government. The intent of this provision is to go slightly beyond §207(a) and prohibit in certain circumstances assisting in representing as well as representing itself. As a practical matter, in your case, it is unlikely that a situation would arise where §207(b)(ii) would prohibit actions not prohibited by §207(a).

4. **Sec. 207(c)**.

This is a one year bar on acting as agent or attorney for, or otherwise representing, anyone in any formal or informal appearance before or, with intent to influence, making any oral or written communication to the agency in which the former senior employee served, in connection with any rulemaking or any particular matter which is pending before such agency or in which such agency has a direct and substantial interest. Like the other prohibitions, §207(c) applies to certain representational activities (i.e., making an appearance or a communication). Unlike other restrictions, however, it applies only to the agency in which the senior employee served. Because you served as Secretary of the Air Force, the applicable agency is the entire Department of Defense. (For other Air Force senior employees, the agency is the Air Force.) Unlike the other restrictions, §207(c) applies to rulemaking as well as to particular matters, and specific parties are not necessary. It also applies to any matter pending before the Department of Defense or in which the Department of Defense has a direct and substantial interest, rather than being limited to matters in which the senior employee had previously had some kind of involvement. This prohibition does not apply to appearances or communications concerning matters of a personal and individual nature, nor does it prohibit providing a statement based on special knowledge in the particular area, provided no compensation is received other than that regularly provided for witnesses. §207(i). Also see 5 CFR 737.11.

To illustrate the restrictions of 18 U.S.C. §207 assume you become an employee of Company X, a major DoD contractor:

(1) At any future date Company X asks you to represent it in dealing with Executive branch officials on an aircraft production contract. As Secretary you were the source selection authority who chose Company X for the contract. You could not represent Company X because section 207(a) prohibits you for life from representing anyone on a particular matter (the contract) involving specific parties (Company X and the Air Force) in which you participated personally and substantially (as source selection authority) for the Air Force.

(2) Within two years of your resignation, Company X asks you to represent it in dealing with Executive Branch officials concerning a missile contract with the Air Force. During your last year as Secretary, the Assistant Secretary (Acquisition) was heavily involved in decisions concerning this contract and you were occasionally briefed on developments and approved the general approach taken by the Air Force. You could not represent Company X because section 207(b)(i) prohibits you for two years after your resignation from representing anyone on a particular matter (the contract) involving specific parties (Company X and the Air Force) which was under your official responsibility (oversight but less than personal and substantial involvement) during your last year in office.

(3) Within one year of your resignation Company X asks you to represent it in dealing with Navy officials concerning a proposed new Navy policy with which you had no involvement as Secretary of the Air Force. You could not do so because section 207(c) prohibits you from representing anyone before any DoD component on a particular matter (the policy) which is pending before the DoD component or in which the DoD component has a direct and substantial interest.

B. **10 U.S.C. §2397b**

In addition to the restrictions discussed above, a two-year prohibition on accepting employment with certain DOD contractors became effective April 16, 1987. The applicability of this statute to you will be addressed in a separate memorandum.

C. **Reporting Requirements - 10 U.S.C. §2397**

Finally, if during the two years after the termination of your government service you are employed by a defense contractor who was awarded $10 million or more in defense contracts in a year and if you are paid at a rate of $25,000 a year or more for services rendered to that contractor, you must file DD Form 1787, a copy of which is at Attachment 4, by mailing it to AFAFC/RPCR, Denver, Colorado 80279.

If specific questions arise ... e you are seeking or after you begin your p st-serv... employ...t, I will be happy to discuss them with you.

Anne N. Foreman
General Counsel

Attachments

REPORT OF POTENTIAL EMPLOYMENT CONTACTS

A. PERSONNEL REQUIRED TO FILE

Under 10 U.S.C. 2397a (reference (f)), "covered defense officials" (as defined in E.1., below) who participated in the performance of a procurement function in connection with a contract awarded by any DoD Component, who contacts, or is contacted by, any representative of that contractor regarding his or her future employment with that defense contractor, shall file reports and disqualifications.

B. CONTENT OF REPORT

1. **Reports of Contact.** "Covered defense officials" shall promptly report the contact describes in A. of this enclosure, above, to the supervisor or superior, and the Designated Agency Ethics Official (DAEO) or designee of the DoD Component. Reports of contact shall include the following:

    a. the name, title, agency address and telephone number of reporting official,

    b. the name of the defense contractor concerned,

    c. the date of each contact covered by the report, and

    d. a brief description of the substance of each contact.

2. **Disqualifications.** "Covered defense officials" shall disqualify themselves from all participation in the performance of procurement functions relating to contracts of the defense contractor, for any period for which future employment opportunities for the official have not been rejected by the official or the defense contractor. Such disqualification shall be in writing and shall be filed with the supervisor or superior, the immediate subordinates, and the DAEO or designee. Reports of disqualification shall accompany reports of contacts and shall include the following:

    a. the name of contractor,

    b. extent of disqualification (this may be a description of duties the official may not perform as a result of the disqualification),

    c. identification of the individual or office that shall handle duties during disqualification period, and

    d. an explanation of any other steps required to avoid potential conflict of interest.

3. <u>Cancellations.</u> Disqualifications are considered to remain in effect until canceled in writing. Such cancellations shall include:

    a. a copy of the original disqualification,

    b. an explanation of the reason for the cancellation, and

    c. the effective date of the cancellation.

4. <u>Limited Exception</u>. A defense official is not required to report the first contact initiated by a defense contractor regarding employment or to disqualify him or herself, if the official terminates discussion immediately. If an additional contact of the same or similar nature is made by or with the contractor, the official shall report the contact and all contacts of the same or similar nature by or with the contractor during the 90-day period ending on the date the additional contact is made.

C. SUBMISSION AND REVIEW OF REPORTS

1. <u>Time of Filing</u>. Reports of contact and disqualifications shall be filed immediately after the contact and disqualifications. Cancellations shall be filed when applicable.

2. <u>Submission</u>. The original of reports of contact, disqualifications and cancellations shall be filed with the supervisor or superior, the immediate subordinates, and the DAEO or designee.

3. <u>Review</u>

    a. The reviewing official shall review each report of contact disqualification and cancellation to determine that the document contains all required information.

    b. The date and time of receipt shall be noted on each report.

    c. The DAEO or designees shall counsel DoD officers and employees and provide guidance in specific instances regarding the need for reports or disqualification action.

    d. If a written opinion of the DAEO or designee is desired, it shall be given in response to a written request from the officer or employee. Such request for an opinion shall contain a full account of the relevant facts.

    e. There shall be a rebuttable presumption in favor of a covered defense official that failure to report a contact with a defense contractor, or failure to disqualify himself from participation in the performance of certain procurement functions, is not a violation if the defense official has received an opinion in writing from the DAEO stating that a report or disqualification by the official was not necessary.

D. REMEDIAL ACTION

1. Supervisors and DAEO's or designees taking remedial actions in connection with any report shall keep a brief record of such action with each report.

2. The Head of each DoD Component shall establish procedures to identify persons who fail to file required reports or to take necessary disqualification action, shall establish procedures for agency hearings, and shall establish other implementing regulations as required by 10 U.S.C. 2397a (reference (f)).

E. SPECIAL DEFINITIONS

For purposes of this enclosure, terms used shall have the following meanings (see the basic Directive for other definitions):

1. Covered Defense Official. Any individual serving as a civilian officer or employee of the Department of Defense in a position for which the rate of pay is equal to or greater than the minimum rate of pay for GS-11 or any officer on active duty in the Armed Forces in a pay grade of O-4 or higher.

2. Defense Contractor. An individual or business entity that provides services, supplies, or both (including construction) to any component of the Department of Defense under a contract directly with the Department of Defense. Individuals and business entities holding contracts with a combined net cost of not more than $25,000 in any calendar year shall not be considered defense contractors, during such year.

F. PENALTIES

1. Administrative Penalties. Penalties that may be imposed pursuant to component regulations may include the following:

 a. prohibition of employment with the defense contractor for up to 10 years from date of separation from employment or service with the Department of Defense,

 b. administrative penalty not to exceed $10,000 under 10 U.S.C. 2397a (reference (f)).

2. Criminal Liability. Any individual who knowingly or willfully falsified information on a report required to be filed under this enclosure may also be subject to criminal prosecution under 18 U.S.C. 1001 (reference (p)).

SAMPLE DISQUALIFICATION MEMORANDUM

MEMORANDUM FOR THE SECRETARY OF DEFENSE

SUBJECT: Disqualification

This is to advise you that I am beginning discussions concerning future employment with the following companies: _____. Accordingly, I am disqualified from participating in any matter relating to or having an impact on any of these companies.

If any matter relating to or having an impact on these companies would normally require my consideration, it will be referred to the Under Secretary of the Air Force.

cc: Mr. McGovern, SAF/US
    Mrs. Foreman, SAF/GC
    Brig Gen Reynolds, SAF/OS

POST EMPLOYMENT RESTRICTIONS
(18 U.S.C. 207)
Ethics in Government Act of 1978, as amended by P.L. 6-28, 22 June 79

Provision	Persons Covered	Representational Activities Covered	To or Before	In Connection With	Comments
Lifetime Bar (18 USC 207(a))	Any officer or employee (including a special Government Employee)	Acts as agents or attorney for, or otherwise represents another, in any formal or informal appearance or with intent to influence, makes any oral or written communication to:	Any Government department, agency, court, office, officer, or employee thereof	Any particular matter involving specific parties in which you participated personally and substantially for the Government.	None
"Regular" 2-yr bar (18 USC 207(b)(i)). Runs from termination of position.	Any officer or employee (including a special Government Employee)	Acts as agent or attorney for, or otherwise represents another, in any formal or informal appearance, or with intent to influence, makes any oral or written communication to:	Any Government department, agency, court, office, officer, or employee thereof	Any particular matter involving specific parties which was pending under your official responsibility within 1 year prior to the termination of such responsibility.	None
"Special" 2-yr bar against "aiding and assisting" (18 USC 207(b)(ii)). Runs from termination of position.	(1) a statutory appointee, (2) a military officer 0-9 or above, or (3) a military officer 0-7 or 0-8 or a civilian in a GS-17 or above position or an SES position, who has significant decision making or supervisory responsibility, as designated by the Office of Government Ethics	Represents, aids, counsels, advises, consults, or assists in representing another by personal presence at any formal or informal appearance.	Any Government department, agency, court, office, officer or employee thereof	Any particular matter involving specific parties in which you participated personally and substantially for the Government.	Coverage of 0-7's and 0-8's not automatic. Covered representational assistance now limited to personal appearance at meetings with Government officials.
One year "no contact" bar (18 USC 207(c)). Runs from termination of service in department.	(1) a statutory appointee, (2) a military officer 0-9 or above, or (3) a military officer 0-7 or 0-8 or a civilian in a GS-17 or above position or an SES position, who has significant decision making or supervisory responsibility, as designated by the Office of Government Ethics.	Acts as agent or attorney for, or otherwise represents anyone, in any formal or informal appearance, or with an intent to influence, makes any oral or written communication to:	Ones former department, or officer or employee thereof	Any rule making or any particular matter which is pending before your agency or in which your agency has a direct and substantial interest.	Coverage of 0-7s and 0-8s not automatic. The military departments are separate agencies; designated 0-7s and 0-8s, civilian in an SES position (GS-17 or above) may be restricted only from contacts with specified offices or positions rather than with entire agency.

Exemptions:
1. Prohibitions do not apply to communications for the purpose of furnishing scientific or technological information.
2. Prohibitions do not apply when the agency head certifies that the former officer or employee has outstanding scientific or technological qualifications and that the national interest would be served by participation in a particular matter.
3. Prohibitions of Section 207(c) do not apply to former officers who are elected State or local Government officials or whose principal occupation or employment is with a State or local Government agency or instrumentality, an accredited, degree-granting institution of higher education or a hospital or medical research organization. NOTE: Prohibitions of 207(c) do not apply to contacts of a personal and individual nature such as personal income taxes or pension benefits.

DEPARTMENT OF THE AIR FORCE
WASHINGTON, D.C. 20330-1000

OFFICE OF THE GENERAL COUNSEL

November 7, 1988

MEMORANDUM FOR SECRETARY ALDRIDGE

SUBJECT: Post-Employment Restrictions

As you know, I have previously given you a detailed memorandum concerning the post-employment representational restrictions of 18 U.S.C. §207 and a separate memorandum that concludes that your future employment by any defense contractor is not subject to the two-year employment bar imposed by 10 U.S.C. §2397b(a). This memorandum is to advise you of two new pieces of legislation concerning post-employment restrictions which were passed by the Congress but are not yet signed by the President.

Post-Employment Restrictions Act of 1988

First is the Post-Employment Restrictions Act of 1988 which revises 18 U.S.C. §207. This Act will take effect nine months after it is signed by the President. It contains an explicit provision that it will apply only to former Government employees who terminate their Government service on or after the effective date. Thus assuming you leave Government within the next nine months, you will not be affected by this Act. You will, however, still be covered by the previous version of 18 U.S.C. §207, described in my earlier memorandum.

Office of Federal Procurement Policy Act Amendments of 1988

The second new Act is the Office of Federal Procurement Policy Act Amendments of 1988. It contains a post-employment restriction in its section on "Procurement Integrity." The restriction and one relevant definition are attached. The post-employment provision takes effect 180 days after the date of enactment. There is no provision that specifically exempts persons who leave Government service before the effective date from being affected by the post-employment restriction. Since post-employment restrictions normally do contain such a provision, the absence of such a provision in this Act would indicate that the post-employment restriction will apply to those who leave Government before the effective date and even to those who left prior to its enactment. Although it is possible that the Department of Justice or OFPP, which will issue implementing regulations in the Federal Acquisition Regulation, could interpret the Act to apply only to persons who leave Government service after the effective date, absent such an interpretation, it appears to apply to you.

The substance of this provision is that if you have participated personally and substantially in the conduct of a procurement (from the development of the solicitation through the award of the contract) or have personally reviewed and approved the contract award, modification or extension, you may not _for two years after such action_ (1) participate on behalf of a contractor in any negotiations leading to the award, modification, or extension of a contract for such procurement, or (2) participate personally or substantially on behalf of the contractor in the performance of such contract. The exact scope of these two restrictions will be more precisely defined in implementing regulations, but they are clearly more restrictive than the old version of 18 U.S.C. §207 which will apply to you. For example, if you were the source selection authority for a contract, you could accept a job with the successful bidder but you could not participate personally and substantially in the performance of such contract for two years after the date of the source selection. This restriction would appear to preclude any kind of personal and substantial work pertaining to the contract.

If you have any questions about these new Acts, I will be happy to try to answer them. I will also keep you advised of any new developments.

Anne N. Foreman
General Counsel

Attachments

EXCERPT FROM THE OFFICE OF FEDERAL PROCUREMENT POLICY ACT

AMENDMENTS OF 1988

(e) RESTRICTIONS ON GOVERNMENT OFFICIALS AND EMPLOYEES. No Government official or employee, civilian or military, who has participated personally and substantially in the conduct of any Federal agency procurement or who has personally reviewed and approved the award, modification, or extension of any contract for such procurement shall

(1) participate in any manner, as an officer, employee, agent, or representative of a competing contractor, in any <u>negotiations</u> leading to the award, modification, or extension of a contract for such procurement, or

(2) participate personally and substantially on behalf of the competing contractor in the <u>performance</u> of such contract

during the period ending 2 years after the last date such individual participated personally and substantially in the conduct of such procurement or personally reviewed and approved the award, modification, or extension of any contract for such procurement. (emphasis added)

The term "conduct of any Federal agency procurement" is defined as the "period beginning with the development, preparation, and issuance of a procurement solicitation, and concluding with the award, modification, or extension of a contract, and includes the evaluation of bids or proposals, selection of sources, and conduct of negotiations."

DEPARTMENT OF THE AIR FORCE
WASHINGTON, D.C. 20330-1000

OFFICE OF THE GENERAL COUNSEL

December 15, 1988

Pete

MEMORANDUM FOR SECRETARY ALDRIDGE

SUBJECT: Post-Employment Restrictions

Now that you have accepted a position with McDonnell Douglas, I thought it might be helpful to review again the post-employment restrictions with particular attention to your past participation in matters involving McDonnell Douglas. I will first discuss the restrictions in 18 U.S.C. §207* and then the new restriction in the Office of Federal Procurement Policy Act Amendments. Previous explanations of these statutes were in my memoranda to you dated September 26, 1988 and November 7, 1988.

I. <u>18 U.S.C. § 207</u>

The restriction of 18 U.S.C. §207(c) has no particular relationship to matters you have worked on for the Air Force; it prohibits you for one year from representing McDonnell Douglas in any formal or informal appearance before, or with intent to influence making any oral or written communication to, the DoD on <u>any matter</u> pending before the DoD or in which DoD has a direct and substantial interest. The other restrictions of 18 U.S.C. §207 concern <u>particular matters</u> involving <u>specific parties</u> which (1) you participated in personally and substantially at any time during your Government service, or (2) were pending under your official responsibility during your last year as Secretary.

A. Personal and Substantial Participation.

18 U.S.C. §207(a) creates a lifetime bar on your representing McDonnell Douglas in any formal or informal appearance before, or making with the intent to influence any oral or written communication to, any Government department or agency in connection with a <u>particular matter</u> involving McDonnell Douglas in which you participated <u>personally</u> and <u>substantially</u> for the Government at any time during your Government service. Section 207(b)(ii) prohibits you from assisting someone else by personal presence at an appearance before a Government department or agency in connection with a particular matter involving McDonnell Douglas in which you participated personally and

---

*As you know, the recent amendments to 18 U.S.C. §207 passed by the Congress were pocket-vetoed by the President.

substantially for the Government. Personal and substantial participation may be exercised "through decision, approval, recommendation, rendering of advice, investigation or otherwise" (§207(a)(3)). Substantial participation means involvement of significance to the matter and is more than mere knowledge, perfunctory involvement, or involvement in an administrative or peripheral issue (5 CFR 737.5(d)). One clear example of personal and substantial participation would be acting as a Source Selection Authority. For example, if you were the Source Selection Authority for a procurement and selected McDonnell Douglas, you could never represent McDonnell Douglas before any Government department or agency concerning that contract. I understand that one program for which you were the Source Selection Authority was the Advanced Tactical Fighter (ATF). Since McDonnell Douglas was one of the losing competitors, normally no restriction on representing McDonnell Douglas based on 18 U.S.C. §207 would arise. Similarly, the fact that McDonnell Douglas is an ATF subcontractor normally would not create a restriction since the Air Force does not select subcontractors or deal directly with them. The ATF procurement was unique because I understand that the Air Force knew that Northrop planned to "team" with McDonnell Douglas if Northrop was awarded one of the two prime contracts. The teaming arrangement, however, was not part of Northrop's official proposal nor was it identified in your decision document selecting Northrop. Thus if you think you might ever be called upon to represent McDonnell Douglas before any Government department or agency concerning its work on the ATF, the possible application of 18 U.S.C. 207(a) should be explored in more depth. Whether you could represent McDonnell Douglas in the future on some follow-on ATF contracts would also depend on the precise facts at that time and should also be carefully examined by appropriate corporate and Government attorneys.

Acting as a Source Selection Authority is not the only way in which you may have participated personally and substantially in a particular matter involving McDonnell Douglas. You may have approved the award of a contract even though someone else was the Source Selection Authority. Approval of a contract award could be personal and substantial participation or it could be merely a matter under your official responsibility (see discussion below) depending on the nature and extent of your involvement. In addition, I understand you have personally approved indemnifying McDonnell Douglas for unusually hazardous risks in connection with the Medium Lift Vehicle Delta II contract. You need to think back over the last seven years to determine if there were any other matters involving McDonnell Douglas in which you participated personally and substantially, such as the F-15 program, the C-17 program, and classified programs. If you are unsure whether your participation in any situation was personal and substantial, I would be happy to review the specific facts and assist in that determination.

B. Official Responsibility.

18 U.S.C. §207(b)(i) prohibits you _for two years_ from _representing_ McDonnell Douglas in any formal or informal appearance before, or with intent to influence making any oral or written communications to, any Government department or agency in connection with a _particular matter_ involving McDonnell Douglas which was _pending under your official responsibility within your last year as Secretary_. Official responsibility is defined as "the direct administrative or operating authority, whether intermediate or final, and either exercisable alone or with others, and either personally or through subordinates, to approve, disapprove, or otherwise direct Government actions" (18 U.S.C. §202(b)). Matters under your official responsibility are obviously matters in which your involvement is less than personal and substantial. They would often be matters in which one of the Assistant Secretaries participated substantially; you might have received occasional briefings or discussed the matter at meetings, and you would normally have at least implicitly approved a general course of action. Recent actions concerning the C-17 production might fit in this category, and there may be matters involving McDonnell Douglas classified contracts that also were pending under your responsibility. In thinking about matters that are subject to this two-year restriction, you need only consider matters that arose _during the last year_.

II. OFPP Act Amendments

The Act containing this new post-employment restriction was signed by the President on November 17, 1988, and becomes effective on May 16, 1989. Assuming that the Act will apply to persons who leave Government service before the effective date (see the attached copy of my November 7, 1988 memorandum), it would apply to you if you have participated personally and substantially in the conduct of an Air Force procurement in which McDonnell Douglas competed or if you personally reviewed and approved the award, modification, or extension of a McDonnell Douglas contract for such a procurement. The term conduct of any procurement is defined as the "period beginning with the development, preparation, and issuance of a procurement solicitation, and concluding with the award, modification, or extension of a contract, and includes the evaluation of bids or proposals, selection of sources, and conduct of negotiations." The Act contains two prohibitions which would have this effect on your proposed employment: (a) you could not participate on behalf of McDonnell Douglas in any negotiations leading to the award, modification or extension of a contract for such procurement, and (b) you could not participate personally and substantially on behalf of McDonnell Douglas in the _performance_ of such a contract. The restrictions apply for _two years after the last date_ you participated for the Air Force in the conduct of the procurement.

In applying this restriction, you need to consider whether you participated in the conduct of any procurements in which McDonnell Douglas competed during about the last 19 months you were Secretary. Actions prior to that time would not create a restriction since the restrictions last for only two years and the Act does not go into effect until May 16, 1989. If you were a Source Selection Authority or otherwise participated personally and substantially in the conduct of a procurement in which McDonnell Douglas was a competing contractor, the restrictions would apply.

You also need to be aware that these restrictions are broader than the representational restrictions of 18 U.S.C. §207. The first restriction applies to participation <u>in any manner</u> in negotiations; presumably this includes internal company advice and planning. The second restriction applies to personal and substantial participation in the <u>performance of the contract</u>. This would seem to preclude participating in any significant corporate decisions relating to the contract. If it becomes necessary, McDonnell Douglas attorneys can assist you in developing procedures to isolate you from participating in any matters that would create a violation of the statute. We will advise you of any Government-wide interpretations or implementations of this statute when they occur.

Anne N. Foreman
General Counsel

Attachment

Mrs. MALONEY. I have more questions, but Mr. McCandless is here.

Dr. QUINN. Before we leave the report, if we could, I would like to make it clear that the DSP–II report was indeed made available to the Everett committee and the committees that worked on the assessments in the bottom-up review. So that regardless of what the history of it was, it was indeed available to all the people that made the assessments later on and they compared the different alternatives that finally were considered in the recommendations to Dr. Deutch.

Mrs. MALONEY. But that happened only after the IG came and got copies.

Dr. QUINN. Yes. I just want to make clear that there might have been an impression that the report never saw the light of day or it never was considered by the people advising Dr. Deutch, and it was.

Mrs. MALONEY. But was it not the Department of Defense IG who made public the inquiry and secured copies?

Dr. QUINN. It was made available to the committee working for the bottom-up review, the Schneiter committee that was mentioned by the program office. Somebody in the Air Force provided it back in the summer of 1993.

Mrs. MALONEY. Mr. McCandless.

Mr. MCCANDLESS. Thank you, Madam Chairman.

In my opening remarks I discussed these programs in the text that we need to focus on the basic issues here. The key questions of why do we need these systems, what are the requirements that determine this need, what determined these requirements, and are these requirements still valid in light of recent criticism.

Dr. Quinn, I pose the questions to you in very simple terms. Maybe we can get simple answers from you and/or the panel.

Dr. QUINN. There is a formal requirements process and the requirements are constantly under review, but the requirement to be able to detect ballistic missiles certainly does continue to exist and the details of that detection and so on are what is in the requirements document that has been referred to. But I would defer to General Kelley if he would like to address that as a requirements issue.

General KELLEY. Yes, sir. As Dr. Quinn indicated, the Joint Requirements Oversight Council received both programs, Milstar and DSP in 1991, and validated the critical military requirements. That committee consists of the vice chief of each service, as well as the vice chairman of the Joint Chiefs of Staff, and they look in detail at the military requirements and there is an extensive scrubbing process that it goes through before a requirement makes it through the wicket. By the time it gets to that point, it has been through a pretty rigorous process.

I don't know if that answers you or do you want me——

Mr. MCCANDLESS. Fine. We need the systems for self-defense. You touched on the missile aspect of it. What are the other requirements that determine the need?

Dr. QUINN. I am sorry?

Mr. MCCANDLESS. What are the requirements that determine the need?

General KELLEY. I will do Milstar; you do DSP.

Colonel STADLER. The requirements for a space-based early warning system are based upon what you perceive to be the threat.

Mr. MCCANDLESS. Sorry?

Colonel STADLER. What you perceive to be the threat, against what you are defending. In the case of strategic, as you well know, our DSP system has been serving us well for the last 25 years or so in watching for, detecting, and giving us some idea in which direction ICBMs and sea-launched ballistic missile may be headed and in particular those that may be targeted or headed for the United States. So that we can carry out our mission within the Unified Space Command and NORAD and our support of that, Air Force Space Command, to warn the President that the Nation is under attack.

Now, with the end of the cold war you can discuss the intent of a superpower, in this case the Russians, to use those missiles, but you cannot deny at the point that they still have the capability inherent in their missile fleet to threaten the United States; although the threat, you may question the intent.

In the case of theater warning, the DSP system was never sized to detect missiles much below the smallest of our sea-launched ballistic missiles that we see as threatening. What we saw in Desert Storm, however, was that the missiles that were actually threatening U.S. forces and their allies abroad, such as in the desert, were a much shorter burning, much dimmer target for which DSP had never been sized.

With DSP, we got lucky in the desert. Certain very positive environmental conditions and things like that enabled us to use the DSP system against the Scuds. However, the future bodes a proliferating threat of more missiles around the world in Third World nations, as well as a further deterioration in the IR, low Earth signatures and shorter burn times and DSP will not be capable of reporting inbound ballistic missiles to the war zone.

Colonel STADLER. It is to that requirement, then, that we pose the requirements of our Follow-On Early Warning System and we will continue to advocate for systems that will follow the FEWS program now that Dr. Deutch has canceled it.

We believe that going into battle without something that tells the forces commander on the ground that he is under attack is not reasonable. We would not believe in going into a theater without an air surveillance radar to detect inbound enemy aircraft that may be bombing our positions. The same is true for ballistic missiles in the future.

Mr. MCCANDLESS. Are these viable in light of the recent criticism?

Colonel STADLER. Sir, I am not sure what criticism you are speaking of.

Mr. MCCANDLESS. We have had most of the morning and part of the afternoon criticizing the current status quo. My question centers around the fact that the systems have been criticized by those who have had a great deal to do with their evolvement and operation.

And so my question pointed in that direction: Are these requirements still valid in light of recent criticism.

Dr. QUINN. I think General Kelley can answer that.

General KELLEY. Sir, the requirements are still valid. As I indicated in my opening remarks, the Joint Requirements Oversight Council reviewed both DSP and Milstar, and validated the key war fighting requirements once again. I would add to what has been said on DSP, that from a Milstar perspective some of the requirements are threatening.

For example the antijam requirement. None of our satellite capacity has the capability to withstand jamming and allow us to remain effective. We were lucky in Desert Storm, but I think a lot of people took lessons from that war. The Milstar system will give us that antijam capability.

Other requirements are driven by lessons we learned from the past. For example, interoperability. We remember the stories that came out on that when we could not interoperate between our forces. That concern is being answered in large part by Milstar where it is a triservice program and the terminals that each service gets will in fact fully interoperate with each other.

Those are two examples for the requirements of Milstar. Yes, they are still valid today and more so after Desert Storm where our potential foes had an opportunity to go to school on us and see where our weaknesses lay.

Mr. McCANDLESS. One thing keeps gnawing at me here. We talk about the post-cold war period. I realize we are talking about systems and their capability, not necessarily policy of—with respect to international regions, but we have a number of countries out there that are either nuclear capable or coming close to it.

And one is left with the impression, after listening to the testimony, that we no longer need anything in the way of a means by which to detect nuclear activity in this form.

Do these systems have the capability that we talked about as being our capability prior to the cold war in terms of Soviet missile capability?

Dr. QUINN. You will find they have the ability to detect missiles that are capable of carrying nuclear weapons?

Mr. McCANDLESS. We got some wild person out who says, OK, I have got a megaton of something or other and I am not willing to sacrifice the country for some cause. It has nothing to do with rationale, logic, or anything else, unless the world community provides me with the following list of whatever it is the demands would be.

Now, we are between the rock and a hard spot here as well as the nations involved. Do we have the capability of detecting if that missile is really fired as we would have if we are talking about the post—pre-cold war, pre-Berlin Wall capability?

Dr. QUINN. I think you are asking whether we could detect whether the nuclear event actually occurred, and the answer is yes. Not necessarily with this system. There are other systems to do that. This system is designed to detect the boosters, the vehicles that would deliver whatever the weapon is, nuclear or otherwise, from their launch point and to provide a tracking to get back to the launcher as well as to attack the missile.

But there are systems that can detect whether or not a nuclear event actually occurred on the Earth or near the Earth's surface as well. Yes, we can do that.

Mr. MCCANDLESS. During our previous testimony, a great deal was talked about in terms of people who spend their life developing the basis for information and knowledge which results then in capabilities to develop, to monitor, to make recommendations to command relating to systems, relating to the various types of products such as we are talking about here—Milstar and so on and so forth—and that the system appears to be breaking down or has broken down.

With respect to those people who have spent their life developing this knowledge and advising senior policymakers, that in that process their knowledge and ability to advise is somewhat sidetracked on occasions by third parties such as possibly defense manufacturers who are involved.

Do you have any response to that, Dr. Quinn.

Dr. QUINN. Yes. I do not think that the system has broken down. I think there is a system in place which is a system capable of thoroughly examining the systems that might meet the requirements that are current and that process is used to make the various assessments that I alluded to earlier.

Now, the difficulty I think that is occurring here, and it was also mentioned earlier, is that as the defense budget is shrinking, then the opportunities for solutions and alternatives to actually be pursued beyond a paper thinking stage are also diminishing.

And what happens is, there are disappointments and people feel that their particular solution should be pursued and will argue and frequently believe in it within their heart that it is the right thing, but when measured against other solutions against the same requirement, it doesn't measure up and, therefore, it is not pursued and results in a disappointment.

Now, frequently what happens is that person will then take some other avenue to get this particular alternative reconsidered if possible, and that is not unusual. It has gone on in the past and will continue to go on in the future. But I think you have to agree that if we are going to compare things in a sensible, responsible, objective way, then there has to be some metric, some measure against which they can be weighed.

And that is why we refer to these requirements which are stated in a way that you can compare the capability of different systems to meet that same requirement. If we allow anyone that has a proposal for a particular system solution to also decide what requirements it will meet, well then the system would break down if we allowed that, and we would have chaos in what systems were pursued.

I think the responsible people who have to deliver these systems and the military people who have to operate them are using a responsible system. They are the ones that are going to be out there on the battlefield using the systems, and if they don't work, they and the managers and the tens of people who have been involved in this are the ones that who are going to be called to account, not the people who have done a little study and say my solution is better than any of the ones that you have.

I think we bend over backwards to look at as many solutions and entertain as many ideas and suggestions as possible. We are indeed interested in getting the best solution at the lowest cost, but we do want a solution that the military people can rely on. And when it comes time to respond to a threat that actually occurs, we want them to be able to do that with confidence.

And I think if you ask any of the Commanders in Chief or the military people whether they agree with cheaper, lesser solutions that don't do the job, you will find out they don't agree. So I think the difficulty is, we have to have a way to measure one system against another. The only way you can do that is to have an agreed-upon set of requirements and a set of system parameters that derive from that and then you can fairly and objectively compare system A with system B.

If everyone is free to decide what requirements his system will meet, then the ability to make a judgment on which one is best is very difficult if not impossible.

Mr. McCandless. Thank you.

General Kelley, you mentioned in your comments that the Joint Chiefs of Staff have done a rather extensive scrubbing job—I think that was the term you used—with respect to systems such as those under discussion here.

Could you very quickly elaborate on what you mean by scrubbing and how that would apply to what it is we are talking about here?

General Kelley. Yes, sir. I will use Milstar as an example. I didn't mean to imply or suggest to the Joint Chiefs it is in the process excelling to the Joint Chiefs that a lot of scrubbing gets done. Milstar was a system designed to the nuclear environment, primarily strategic heavy emphasis.

That requirement, after 1991, was reevaluated. The services involved looked at it and reoriented the program to be tactical. In that reorientation, we took what was at one time primarily a strategic system. It is now only 11 percent strategic, that is for the National Command Authority conferencing for emergency action messages and for missile warning. All of the other functions of that system are now related to CINC support, CINC warfighting, or for ships that happen to be at sea so that the CINC can talk to his component commanders.

That goes back to my interoperability point, all of these requirements. For example, there is a requirement for Earth coverage in the old Milstar. That technical requirement was then translated into narrow beam coverage so that you could better effect an environment where you are going to be jammed, so it took weight off the satellite. It reduced the cost.

These are the kinds of tradeoffs that are gone through and they get very complex. All of the services play in them so that there is not an opportunity or a chance where we would ignore, for example, the Navy's requirement to contact submarines that operate throughout the oceans. How do we bring them into the net?

That requirement bubbles up through this process. That is why we have agile beam antennas on the Milstar satellite, to make sure we bring in the submarines. That is the kind of process it goes through so that nobody we need to bring into this warfighting net to be effective is left out.

Mr. McCandless. Thank you. Final question, Madam Chairman. Colonel Schepens—am I pronouncing——

Colonel Schepens. Schepens.

Mr. McCandless. Thank you. You represent the IG's office. Your statement addressed the issue of the IG's report. Are you satisfied that what the report has given the committee and those who ask for it is objective in any detail and recommends to the best of your knowledge the facts in the issue and that we don't have something here that was swept under the rug or in some way averted in order to embarrass or in some other way compromise the command system?

Colonel Schepens. I think our IG system is designed around the very things you talked about: impartial and fair. We sent out an investigating officer in this particular case who was a two star at that time he is now a three star. That was not part of the process in any way, form, or fashion. We picked a couple of officers from our inspection agency that did not have an agenda, and also a lawyer.

Anytime we ran into cost data, we used cost analysts who were not part of either the AQ or the material of the Command organizations. And we started investigating in September, and it took us until December to finish the process.

In the meantime, we had two different legal reviews: One with our Air Force Judge Advocate General and the other by the Air Force general counsel. And finally, the DOD IG took the last 4 weeks reviewing the report. Also, we were in contact with the DOD IG throughout the investigation to make sure they knew what was going on. So I would say, I don't know how you can get it any more impartial or fairer than that, sir.

Mr. McCandless. Thank you.

Thank you, Madam Chair.

Mrs. Maloney. Mr. Schepens, you have testified, Colonel, earlier that proprietary information was passed by the Air Force to the FEWS contractor, Lockheed, correct?

Colonel Schepens. That was the finding of a separate investigation. There were two different allegations within our purview. One occurred at Space Command. We looked at that and it was an inadvertent release primarily of Air Force budgetary data. There was no proprietary data released in that particular case.

The second investigation was conducted by the Space and Missile Center in Los Angeles and in that particular one, there was a release of proprietary data.

Mrs. Maloney. There was. Who passed the information and what action was taken against the person who did it?

Colonel Schepens. Based on proprietary—I mean, on the Privacy Act, I can't release the name of the individual in this forum. I think it is in the report we provided to you, but the action was the appropriate command action and, again, that goes through the command channels.

Mrs. Maloney. What was the appropriate command action?

Colonel Schepens. Again, in this forum, I am not at liberty to say.

Mrs. MALONEY. There is no privacy protection. There is privacy for an individual's name but not for the, quote, appropriate action that was taken. Was there any action taken.

Colonel SCHEPENS. Yes, there was action taken.

Mrs. MALONEY. What was it?

Colonel SCHEPENS. I might refer that to the—the action was, he received a letter of reprimand and that was the initial action taken on it.

Mrs. MALONEY. Was there any other?

Colonel SCHEPENS. I would say there was also some concern, I think, within the Air Force about whether he should retain his current position.

Mrs. MALONEY. But he has retained it?

Colonel SCHEPENS. He has not retained it.

Mrs. MALONEY. What is it now.

Colonel COLLINS. If I could, ma'am, I could speak to that. He has been reassigned to another position as a program director in a different program within the Air Force.

Mrs. MALONEY. Well, that is not much of a demotion. Will he handle proprietary information in his new position?

Colonel COLLINS. Yes, ma'am. There will be proprietary information, I would expect, involved and if that comes up, he would have access to that.

Mrs. MALONEY. He will. Has he indicated if he will continue handing out proprietary information? Has he given any indication that he will improve his performance in protecting proprietary information of the military?

Colonel COLLINS. As officers, we all understand what our responsibilities and obligations are in handling that kind of material.

Mrs. MALONEY. Well, he apparently didn't the first time.

Colonel COLLINS. Well, ma'am, as Colonel Schepens mentioned, he received proper actions for that. We have no reason to believe that that would be a recurring event.

Mrs. MALONEY. Why was Colonel Mangold relieved of his responsibilities and this particular gentleman was not?

Colonel COLLINS. Ma'am, the personnel in the chain of command of Colonel Mangold are not here with us. I have no—I am not prepared to address that in any manner.

Mrs. MALONEY. Will Colonels Mangold and Dietz have reason to be deeply concerned about the future of their careers as a result of these hearings today?

Dr. QUINN. Others will have to address that.

Colonel COLLINS. Ma'am, I know of no—no continuing action within the Air Force. That would obviously be something that would be included in their evaluations in the normal process of the evaluations of officers for promotion.

Mr. MCCANDLESS. Would the chairlady yield?

Mrs. MALONEY. Yes.

Mr. MCCANDLESS. Do I understand correctly that we still have an ongoing investigation relative to this issue and that the IG is involved in it, or am I misled somewhere along the line.

Colonel SCHEPENS. Well, the DSP/FEWS investigation has terminated, and in that particular investigation, I can say very clearly that one of the concerns that General Anderson had as the investigating officer was reprisal against Colonel Dietz or anybody in the Aerospace Corps who worked on or released the technical operating report. In his discussions with the various people involved, there was no one who indicated that any reprisal had taken place.

Now, the other investigation has to do with Milstar and some of its activities. I know within the Air Force IG, there is a couple of letters which have been sent to General Anderson, and we are in the process of a legal review to determine what action needs to be taken.

Mr. MCCANDLESS. Thank you.

Mrs. MALONEY. Are you still advocating the FEWS program? Did I hear you correctly, are you still advocating the FEWS program?

Dr. QUINN. No, ma'am, we are not. The FEWS program is in the process of being terminated. The work has actually been stopped on the program and the process has begun to terminate the program formally.

Mrs. MALONEY. OK. The space representative, do you agree?

Colonel STADLER. Yes, ma'am, I do agree. We are terminating the FEWS program as Dr. Quinn said. I will say, however, that the requirements are not terminated necessarily. We still have an ongoing need to detect ballistic missiles launched against——

Mrs. MALONEY. So the requirements are there—a FEWS by any other name——

Colonel STADLER. Eventually——

Dr. QUINN. No, that is not quite what is being said. The FEWS program—did indeed meet the requirements. It was a way to do it. It was designed for that purpose and was developed to accomplish that. It was a very expensive program and it was determined after recommendation by a number of people, that it was not affordable within the Department's constrained budget environment, so the FEWS program, as such, was terminated.

Now, as has been stated, there is still a requirement to detect ballistic missiles that is still on the books. The DSP program is based on that and has been with us for 25 years. And we are now up to DSP No. 23, and what we do beyond DSP, is an open question. We have asked, in light of the new technologies that are available and new launch vehicles to examine how best to meet that requirement at the least cost and hopefully to get a solution that can be launched, as I mentioned earlier, on a medium launched vehicle. That is one of the major contributors to the high cost. So the FEWS program, as it was constituted is in the process of being terminated. That program will not be revitalized.

Mrs. MALONEY. But I would like to hear from Colonel Stadler who has online responsibility in the space program, the FEWS. The requirements are still there and you are still going to be trying to achieve those requirements; is that correct, Colonel? I wanted to hear what you had to say or what you were attempting to say.

Colonel STADLER. I agree with Dr. Quinn that the reason the FEWS program was terminated was due to costs. That did not, however, cancel the requirements to continue the—to continue to detect both strategic and theater missiles. We will continue to work within the guidance that the Department has given us to develop ongoing programs, possibly not as sophisticated as the FEWS program. We haven't made those determinations yet, to achieve those requirements some time in the outyears.

Mrs. MALONEY. I would like to ask General Kelley, when you were talking about Milstar and how it had changed and the needs, you were constantly incorporating the needs for various defense—with various departments. But as you explained we are now progressing with Milstar. In a sense, we have outgrown the Milstar. We are getting ready to launch; is that not correct?

If that is true, why are we then committing what will be roughly $100 million to a system that has now—in your own words, we are building in other items that we need that we have learned are more important and that many of the items in the Milstar that we are about to launch in 72 hours are basically obsolete.

Did I not hear you correctly? Would you clarify?

General KELLEY. I did not say that. The requirements I alluded to are the requirements process that we normally go through, and these antennas, for example, that I am speaking about will be on the Milstar that will be launched, and can bring submarines into communications as an example. So there is not a situation where the satellite that we are going to launch will not provide the capability that we need. It will definitely be a step forward.

Mrs. MALONEY. And you believe we need to launch Milstar?

General KELLEY. That is correct.

Mrs. MALONEY. Thank you very much. Would you like to——

Mr. MCCANDLESS. We have some additional questions, but rather than take the time of panel and members of the subcommittee, we will submit those.

[The information follows:]

Minority Questions for the Record For the Department of Defense for MILSTAR/DSP/FEWS Oversight Hearing Held on February 2, 1994

(1) Questions have been raised about "launching 2,000 pounds of sand" as ballast for the MILSTAR satellite. Please explain as fully as possible the reasons for launching the satellite with this ballast. Does this design, in fact, cut costs, and if so how ? Please be as specific as possible. Why not completely re-design the satellite; how much additional time and money would that have required?

(2) How important is the MILSTAR program to the overall defense planning strategy for our country over the next ten years. Hasn't the Bottom Up Review confirmed that MILSTAR should remain a key component of The Defense Planning Guidance, the primary document that sets out our nation's military planning for the next decade ?

(3) How much would it cost taxpayers not to launch the first two MILSTAR satellites. Won't it cost approximately $40 million/year just to store the satellites in addition to the lost investment, i.e. "sunk costs ?" How much are the sunk costs ?

(4) Please describe the tactical capability the first two MILSTAR satellites would give our country's military forces. Wouldn't these be available immediately upon launch; and why are they important, i.e., how can they help our forces in foreseeable conflict scenario's in the near future ?

Answers to these questions must be submitted no later than February 18, 1994. Please call L. Stephan Vincze of the minority staff at telephone (202) 225-2738 if you have any questions. Answers may be faxed on telephone (202) 225-5127.

Minority Questions for the Record -- February 2, 1994 Hearing

1. Questions have been raised about "launching 2,000 pounds of sand" as ballast for the Milstar satellite. Please explain as fully as possible the reasons for launching the satellite with this ballast. Does this design, in fact, cut costs, and if so how? Please be as specific as possible. Why not completely re-design the satellite; how much additional time and money would that have required?

ANSWER:

The satellites do not use 2,000 pounds of sand as ballast. Satellite #1, launched February 7, 1994, carries a deactivated, classified payload that is no longer required. The deactivated payload weighs 878 pounds. Satellite #2, scheduled for launch in 1995, will carry 878 pounds of solid aluminum to simulate the weight of the cancelled payload. The ballast is necessary to ensure dynamic balance for the satellite while on orbit -- similar to that often contained in ballistic missiles or aircraft to ensure stable performance.

The deactivated payload on satellite #1 and the aluminum on satellite #2 add nothing to the cost of launching either satellite. The size of the spacecraft bus and the Low Data Rate (LDR) Extremely High Frequency (EHF) payload all Milstar satellites will carry, require a Titan IV launch vehicle. The use of the Titan IV booster establishes the cost of the launch.

In its FY 1991 language, Congress directed the DoD to decrease Milstar program costs and to increase its tactical utility. A number of options were studied to carry out that direction. The alternative selected by the DoD and approved by Congress retained the basic Milstar design, but deleted the classified payload in favor of a Medium Data Rate (MDR) EHF communications package with a modified suite of antennas. By integrating the payload onto the current Milstar satellite design, the DoD was able to meet an operational need date of 1999 for MDR service. Other alternatives were assessed at the time to have delayed delivery of MDR service by four to seven years and were judged to be higher risk developments.

Launch of satellites #1 and #2 as scheduled allows the DoD to establish required, initial EHF communications service for operational forces. Incorporation of the MDR payload onto these satellites would have delayed fielding initial capability by more than five years. Modification of these satellites, well into the fabrication and test cycle at the time of the 1991 restructure, would also have been more expensive than purchasing two additional newly-built satellites. Redesign would have been more expensive and would have also further delayed delivering needed capability.

2. How important is the Milstar program to overall defense planning strategy for our country over the next ten years. Hasn't the Bottom Up Review confirmed that Milstar should remain a key component of the Defense Planning Guidance, the primary document that sets out our nation's military planning for the next decade?

ANSWER:

The Milstar system supports a fundamental requirement contained in the Defense Planning Guidance to provide integrated connectivity to all theater and tactical elements through a modernized, jam-resistant telecommunications network in support of operational forces.

The Bottom Up Review reaffirmed the need for a processed EHF satellite system to meet this essential requirement. The Defense Planning Guidance reflected the results of the Bottom Up Review by directing the DoD to proceed with the launch of Milstar I satellites in fiscal years 1994 and 1995, followed by a constellation of four Milstar II satellites with a first launch in fiscal year 1999 and a transition to a lower-cost, lower weight advanced EHF satellite system with a first launch no later than fiscal year 2006. The first Milstar I satellite was launched on February 7, 1994.

3. How much would it cost taxpayers not to launch the first two Milstar satellites? Won't it cost approximately $40 million/year just to store the satellites in addition to the lost investment, i.e. "sunk costs?" How much are the sunk costs?

ANSWER:

The first Milstar I satellite was launched on February 7, 1994 and has been performing well in its initial testing on-orbit.

Currently, all subsystems have been activated. The Mission Control Element (MCE) has been checked out and is processing telemetry and commands on EHF links. Connectivity has been exercised with AF-to-AF and AF-to-Navy terminals. Connectivity has been tested with an Airborne Command Post at Wright-Patterson Air Force Base. Reportback has been exercised. Checkout is proceeding by exercising teletype and voice links; various earth coverage, agile and spot beam antennas; and assessing satellite subsystem performance.

Milstar satellite #2 is on track for a scheduled 1995 launch. Not launching this satellite would significantly degrade EHF coverage and capability for the operational forces. It would also preclude operational use of Milstar crosslinks to connect two satellites -- a key element in establishing EHF connectivity from the CONUS into a potential theater of conflict.

Additionally, it would require storage of the satellite at additional cost to the Milstar development program. The first year of storage would be approximately $5 million. After the first year, storage costs increase because of the more extensive monitoring and retest required to activate the satellite.

The "sunk costs" of the Milstar space segment as it is defined today are a total of $5.8 billion through FY 1994. Additional funds have been invested by all three services for development and initial fielding of terminals.

4. Please describe the tactical capability the first two Milstar satellites would give to our country's military forces. Wouldn't these be available immediately upon launch; and why are they important, i.e. how can they help our forces in foreseeable conflict scenarios in the near future?

ANSWER:

Current plans call for extensive on-orbit testing of each of the first Milstar satellites following launch, but contingency requirements could dictate use of a satellite after an abbreviated series of initial functional and calibration tests. The first two Milstar satellites will provide theater command and control, unscheduled service for submarines and special operations forces, and support strategic warning and nuclear deterrence missions.

Milstar will satisfy many key requirements essential to the military operations of a power-projection force:

- Anti-jam: Milstar communications cannot be disrupted by the enemy

- Interoperability: Army, Navy, Air Force, and Marines -- Milstar will enable immediate communications between the Services

- Mobility: Milstar terminals will move with front-line forces

- Covert Operations: Communicating via Milstar will not compromise the location of users to enemy listening systems

- Reachback: Milstar will enable communications out of theater without reliance on foreign-based ground relays vulnerable to destruction, sabotage, or host nation policy restrictions

The first two Milstar satellites will enable efficient synchronization of combat power and are not vulnerable to enemy efforts to deny U.S. forces this capability. As the number of tactical ground terminals expands; the first two satellites, coupled with additional satellites to form a complete constellation, will provide all the above capabilities.

With the addition of satellites #3 and beyond, Milstar will add capability to provide more data, faster to combat commanders. It will also enable the Army's Mobile Subscriber Equipment (MSE) to provide global communications to combat commanders on the move. No other planned or existing satellite system can provide the flexibility and assurance of uninterrupted communications available from Milstar.

Mrs. MALONEY. Thank you. We are going to keep the record open until February 18 if there are other questions and other items that anyone would like to submit.

I thank you very much for coming. The meeting is adjourned.

[Whereupon, at 1:50 p.m., the subcommittee adjourned, to reconvene subject to the call of the Chair.]

APPENDIX

MATERIAL SUBMITTED FOR THE HEARING RECORD

CAROLYN B. MALONEY
14TH DISTRICT, NEW YORK

COMMITTEE ON BANKING, FINANCE
AND URBAN AFFAIRS

COMMITTEE ON
GOVERNMENT OPERATIONS

CONGRESSIONAL CAUCUS
ON WOMEN'S ISSUES
EXECUTIVE COMMITTEE

CONGRESSIONAL ARTS CAUCUS
EXECUTIVE COMMITTEE

Congress of the United States
House of Representatives
Washington, DC 20515-3214

WASHINGTON OFFICE
1504 LONGWORTH BUILDING
WASHINGTON, DC 20515-3214
(202) 225-7944

DISTRICT OFFICES
950 THIRD AVENUE
19TH FLOOR
NEW YORK, NY 10022
(212) 832-6531

28-11 ASTORIA BLVD
ASTORIA, NY 11102
(718) 932-1804

619 LORIMER STREET
BROOKLYN, NY 11211
(718) 349-1260

OPENING STATEMENT

Subcommittee on National Security & Legislation
HEARING ON STRATEGIC SATELLITE SYSTEMS
February 2, 1994

Thank you Mr. Chairman. I am pleased that you have convened this important oversight hearing on two satellite systems -- Milstar and the Follow-On Early Warning System -- that have been seriously plagued by budget overruns and technological failures.

I, for one, have serious doubts about the need and effectiveness of these Cold War relics.

In today's international climate, spending billions of scarce taxpayer dollars to build Milstar seems like a misplaced priority -- to put it mildly.

Do we really need a communications satellite system capable of surviving not just a nuclear war, but a protracted nuclear war?

And does anyone seriously believe that anything or anyone can survive such a war?

The Follow-On Early Warning System is another relic of the mistaken SDI program.

Once again, the Pentagon seems intent on developing a phenomanally expensive system that sounds as exciting as a video game, but serves no practical purpose and is not technologically feasible.

The major improvement of FEWS is to detect the launch of ground-based tactical nuclear missiles, missiles which are launched in close proximity to US borders.

One can only wonder if the Pentagon anticipates an impending war with our NAFTA partners Mexico and Canada.

We are also here today to examine an even more troubling development than spending billions to defend the US from Canada's military might.

Serious allegations have been that senior Air Force officials may have suppressed information about lower-cost alternatives to these two troubled satellite systems.

If these allegations are true, we have an extremely dangerous and potentially criminal situation.

Withholding information vital to Congressional decisions is a violation that I view with the utmost concern and I hope that we can shed some light on these allegations.

Again, my thanks to the Chairman for scheduling these significant hearings.

PRINTED ON RECYCLED PAPER

Remarks of
Congressman Norm Dicks
Committee on Government Operations
Legislation and National Security Subcommittee
February 2, 1994

Strategic Satellites in the Post Cold War

Thank you Mr. Chairman for giving me this opportunity to appear before your distinguished Committee.

As Vice Chairman of the House Defense Appropriations Subcommittee, I have witnessed the development and deployment of many our Nation's important military programs. One such program is the MILSTAR program. I have supported this program since its origin, and would like to express this support in my statement today.

Since the end of Operation Desert Shield/Desert Storm, there have been a number of publications made available portraying various accounts and incidents during the Gulf War. These publications range from an individual soldier's account, to the Department's report, Conduct Of the Persian Gulf War.

It was widely known that the U.S. troops experienced difficulty receiving real time information, intelligence, and communications from the satellite capabilities. The dissemination of information to the tactical units was also difficult, and there were many incidents where mobile units were unable to communicate with the commands in the rear.

I would like to read some excerpts from an article: Desert Storm and Deterrence in the Future:

"...For the first time in a war, the U.S. made effective use of all of its satellite systems to support field commanders. Most of these systems were designed to support national objectives--not military operations....

...During Desert Storm, all of these systems plus weather satellites were dedicated to the support of coalition forces...Also in Desert Storm, the data from satellites were subject to communication delays in getting to military commanders. All of these factors adversely affected the timeliness of data necessary for the planning of military operations or targeting...

...Some of the intelligence data collected was processed at sites in the United States. Therefore it was necessary to make extensive use of satellite communications systems for communicating large volumes of data, ...from the U.S. to the theater daily. Most of this traffic was carried by the Defense Satellite Communication System, which was operating at capacity, and because of the heavy load, still had to be supplemented with commercial satellites and couriers...

"...Because the U.S. C³I is so significant, it will be carefully studied by other nations, not only to learn how to emulate it, but to learn how to counter it. Many of the C³I systems used in Desert Storm could be degraded by foreseeable countermeasures. In addition, most of the communication systems were already stretched beyond their capacity; response to countermeasures would have reduced the capacity further...

...because of the shock effect of coalition air raids in the first week, the Iraqis never mounted a meaningful countermeasure program, even though their forces were equipped,...As a result, the U.S. C³I systems got a 'free ride' to some extent, which is unlikely to happen again.

Therefore a critically important part of the U.S. future defense program should be dedicated to the hardening of these C³I systems..."

In case you do not recognize the author of this article, he is Dr. Bill Perry, our Secretary of Defense designee. All of the incidents in Dr. Perry's article, and the other articles, provide tangible reasons why the Military Strategic and Tactical Relay or MILSTAR program is so important.

The MILSTAR program began in the early 1980s, with the Full Scale Development beginning in 1983. The initial mission requirements were to provide both strategic and tactical military forces the essential communications capability, and the original design provided a number of unique capabilities that included the survivability of the system to operate during a nuclear conflict.

In FY1991, the Congress directed the Department to reduce the MILSTAR costs substantially, to increase the utility of the systems for tactical forces and to eliminate unnecessary capabilities for protracted nuclear war-fighting. The Department worked hard to present a revised program to the Congress that next year.

Changes were made to provide the operational tactical forces with a much greater capability at a greatly reduced cost [overall costs were reduced by 30 percent], and changes were also made to eliminate unnecessary nuclear war-fighting features, without jeopardizing survivability. This now multi-service program was successfully restructured to meet third world and conventional contingencies, and provided the essential command, control and communications [C³] capability for our tactical and strategic forces. The Milstar system will provide the anti-jam, inter-operable communications and the flexibility to adjust and meet the range of operational requirements, thereby ensuring the tactical commanders the access to battle management data in a jamming environment.

The threat of global nuclear war as we once knew it has dramatically changed. Today, instead of a single, threatening and relatively predictable adversary, we are now in a world where uncertainty and instability are increasingly more and more common.

But even before the break up of the Soviet Union, the increased importance of supporting Joint Task Forces was recognized. Even then, the focus of our national security interests was changing from a superpower conflict to the many regional and ethnic conflicts.

This program is not a Cold War Dinosaur. The restructured MILSTAR program effectively made the post Cold War transition from a primarily strategic/nuclear program to a tactical/ conventional program----even before the Cold War was over. This program is responsive to the user's needs, it is responsive to the new World Order, and it is responsive to our new Nation's Military Strategy.

And while Desert Storm did prove that the U.S. military was technologically superior, the command, communications, and control necessary for quick, reactive deployment is still not in place today. The lack of C^3I capability was cited as an important "lesson learned". MILSTAR was immediately identified as the resolution to this problem. But it was also a lesson learned by our adversaries, many who know that jamming the tactical communications is a key to success.

One of MILSTAR's most important features is the capability to resist jamming. In Desert Storm, our military was extremely lucky in that Saddam had no jamming capability. We may not be so lucky the next time.

In his testimony before the Congress last year, General Horner, the CINC-Space testified: "...Any officer with more than a month in uniform understands that the single most important requirement of the battlefield commander is assured communications....MILSTAR will ensure that critical command and control connectivity is maintained through all levels of conflict. There is no other communications satellite that will serve our nation's future war-fighting needs better than MILSTAR."

Over the past few years, we have heard comments from many individuals who have testified on behalf of the importance of this system before the various Committees of Congress. The Chief of Staff of the Army, The Chief of Naval Operations, Secretaries of the Army and Navy, CINCS of Space Command, Joint Chiefs of Staff, Assistant Secretaries, etc., all of whom share the credible concern and communicate the ultimate message, that we must have MILSTAR.

Secretary of Defense Les Aspin, in his Bottom Up Review, provided an exhaustive research and review of this system. This review involved great scrutiny by the Department and the MILSTAR community for performance, cost, schedule and risk implications. Four options were evaluated that considered changes to the system to reduce weight, to reduce costs. The review looked at terminating the system, adding or subtracting capabilities, changing the type of launch vehicles, etc.

During this review process, I personally recommended to the Department that the MILSTAR program continue with the initial constellation of the two Low Data Rate and four Medium Data Rate satellites, also known as Option I. Of the four options considered, only one remained acceptable. The Bottom Up Review indicated the Option I represented "...the best means of achieving a needed military communications capability in the near term while potentially reducing long term costs associated with sustaining this capability".

The recent Rand report, entitled "Whither MILSTAR?" offers no new information to any of us: If anything, it provides to us a rather closed-minded view of military requirements and operations. This report focuses substantially on costs and limiting capabilities. However I think it is important to note the statement in the Bottom Up Review referring to MILSTAR: "...the system should be designed to meet our military requirements, not to cost or weight limits."

GAO believes that DOD could consider inserting new technologies. This assumption comes from an assessment by the Mitre Group. Mitre was one of two groups tasked by Dr. Deutch as part of the Bottom Up Review on MILSTAR. Mitre's assessment indicated that an advanced design could be deployed on a medium launch, and could be available for launch by 2004--two years after the DOD-predicted launch date of MILSTAR II #6. Mitre also proposed to reduce the weight of the satellite by 40 percent, ultimately requiring the development an entirely new antenna system that would be condensed to meet such weight reductions. It is well known in the scientific community that this magnitude of reduction would be no easy chore.

It is extremely important to understand that many of these technologies being proposed to achieve cost savings and weight reductions (and not limit the capabilities) are merely paper designs: no hardware exists. This undoubtedly was a major factor in the Department's decision to pursue Option I in the Bottom Up Review. Any immediate conversion to smaller satellites on medium launch vehicles is a major technological risk.

The requirement for spaced-based communications remains a priority in the Department to Defense. The changes and progress of this system will continue beyond the initial six satellites. I have also recommended that follow-on technologies should be researched and developed, concurrently with the progress and launch of the six satellites. MILSTAR II provides the evolution for technology insertion on smaller future satellites.

Many say, why not terminate the program now and restart this entire endeavor? This is not realistic. The systems that are being developed today are a direct result of a decade of tremendous scientific and technological advancement.

All of our military's weaponry have significant mission requirements thus demanding the most advanced technology and capability. This country's military superiority did not develop overnight, nor was it developed for free. These technologies take time and investment, and must remain our priority.

In summary, Mr. Chairman, the MILSTAR program:

o   Is critical to the post Cold-War mission requirements;
o   Has been scaled back already to eliminate unnecessary costs and features; and it
o   Ensures mobile, real time, anti-jammable communications in the field.

Thank you, Mr. Chairman, again, for the opportunity to speak on behalf of the merits of this program. I understand you have a number of distinguished witnesses here to day, who will be able to comment even further on the merits and requirements of this program.

OFFICE OF THE SECRETARY OF DEFENSE
WASHINGTON, DC 20301-1000

1 FEB 1994

Honorable John Conyers, Jr.
Chairman, Subcommittee on Legislation and National Security
Committee on Government Operations
U. S. House of Representatives
Washington, D. C. 29515 - 6035

Dear Mr. Chairman:

I have been asked to respond on behalf of Secretary Aspin to your letter of January 26 which requested that Colonel Sanford Mangold and Colonel Edward Dietz present testimony at the Subcommittee's February 2 hearing on the Defense Support Program/Follow - on Early Warning System. The Department has no objection to Colonels Mangold and Dietz presenting testimony to the Subcommittee in their personal capacity. While we will not compel their presence in that they will not be testifying on behalf of the Department, should either or both wish to appear, the Department of the Air Force has been instructed to take whatever steps are necessary to facilitate their appearance.

The Department is also fully prepared to provide appropriate witnesses to address the issues raised in your letter of January 11. Our point of contact on this issue is Ms. Rossie Payne who may be contacted at 703 - 695 - 5497.

Sincerely,

Sandra K. Stuart
Assistant to the Secretary
(Legislative Affairs)

THE AEROSPACE CORPORATION

 Mail Log. No.

E. C. Aldridge, Jr.
*President and
Chief Executive Officer*

February 1, 1994

Congressman John Conyers, Jr.
Chairman
Subcommittee on Legislation and National Security
House of Representatives
Washington, D.C. 20515-2214

Dear Mr. Chairman:

The purpose of this letter is to place on the record the significant facts surrounding The Aerospace Corporation's Technical Operating Report, entitled "DSP-II: Preserving the Air Force's Options," dated April 23, 1993. Your Subcommittee is holding a hearing on issues related to this report on February 2, 1994.

Since its publication, the DSP-II Report has been the subject of several press articles and controversy within the government and industry. Given the condition of the Defense Budget, one can understand the enormous economic impact on the defense contractor community and the tremendous competition among the contractors to win a large space program for our future missile warning capability. Because of this environment, there have been numerous allegations implying suppression of data and inappropriate pressure on The Aerospace Corporation to ignore valid solutions. <u>None of these allegations are true.</u>

I first heard of the DSP-II Report and the concerns of the Air Force on May 21, 1993, shortly after the report was distributed. I directed that the report be recalled until the corporation's management and I had a chance to review the report and determine the subsequent and appropriate distribution. I also initiated an independent review of the technical and cost data presented in the report. On May 24, 1993, I received an "informal" hand-written note from General Chuck Horner, Commander of the U. S. Space Command, stating his concern and asking me to help him "get this thing back on track."

I replied to General Horner's informal note on May 27, 1993, with a letter that is attached to this correspondence. My letter explains why such a report was written and what actions the Corporation has undertaken to avoid future occurrences of this type. General Horner sent me another handwritten note on

An Affirmative Action Employer
Corporate Offices: 2350 East El Segundo Blvd., El Segundo, CA 90245-4691/Mail: P. O. Box 92957, Los Angeles, CA 90009-2957/Phone: (310) 336-5672

Congressman John Conyers
Page Two
February 1, 1993

June 18, 1993, thanking me for the May 27 letter. There has been no other official correspondence from General Horner on this matter.

I have personally reviewed the DSP-II Report and the independent assessment and decided that the report as written did not represent a balanced, fully coordinated technical assessment of the DSP-II option and was not representative of the type of report which should be developed and distributed externally by The Aerospace Corporation. I decided that the report should be recalled on a permanent basis for the following reasons:

- --The report was written for internal Air Force/Aerospace use only and had not been coordinated with other affected programs and agencies. It did not have the proper management coordination and approval for external distribution beyond that originally intended.

- --The report had a tone of advocacy for a specific design solution and inappropriately attacked operational requirements. It is the proper role of the Air Force Space Command to establish operational requirements and not the role of The Aerospace Corporation to challenge these requirements in an external forum.

- --Finally, the report as written, and unchallenged, could have misled Air Force and Office of the Secretary of Defense (OSD) decision makers into accepting a design solution that was implied to have more capability to meet validated requirements than was possible.

While the report was recalled, due to the deficiencies noted above, the system performance and technical and cost data on the DSP-II concept was provided to an independent team formed by OSD to reassess requirements and technical solutions to meet these requirements. At no time was the DSP-II data denied or suppressed from those needing and having valid access to this information. The Air Force and OSD are currently evaluating alternative design solutions to meet the mission needs.

I hope this factual information on the circumstances surrounding the DSP-II Report controversy is useful to the Subcommittee in accomplishing it's oversight responsibilities.

Sincerely,

E. C. Aldridge, Jr.
President and CEO

THE AEROSPACE
CORPORATION

E. C. Aldridge, Jr.
*President and
Chief Executive Officer*

May 27, 1993

General Charles A. Horner
Commander
Air Force Space Command
Peterson AFB, CO 80914

Dear Chuck:

As you know, for over thirty years The Aerospace Corporation has maintained the tradition of objective, independent, and comprehensive technology and engineering analyses of all aspects of our government space programs. We have taken pride in our products, our contributions to mission success, and our support to the Air Force and other national security space missions. While we are asked often for our technical assessment of spacecraft or launch vehicle system alternatives, it is not the policy of Aerospace to advocate one solution over another or to "sell" a particular system at the expense of another.

On a recent occasion we were asked to document for internal use only a study of an Air Force option for ballistic missile early warning using a derivative of the Defense Support Program (DSP). This DSP option had been considered in the Sensor Integration Study, but rejected because it did not meet the operational requirements. The objective of the Aerospace effort was to provide the documentation to the DSP System Program Office (SPO) for such an Air Force back-up option should: a) the Follow-on Early Warning System (FEWS) be delayed or terminated by the Department of Defense or Congress and b) near-term performance improvements to DSP be needed prior to FEWS full operational capability. Overall, this is certainly an appropriate request by the SPO and activity for Aerospace.

Aerospace clearly understands the operational needs of FEWS, has supported its development, and has established that the FEWS capability and design is the only concept that satisfies the needs of the operational commander. Unfortunately, too much program "advocacy" crept into the report and its Executive Summary in support of the DSP alternative. This led to the mistaken conclusion by many that Aerospace supported a DSP derivative over FEWS. I want to emphasize that this is not the position of The Aerospace Corporation, or any member of our management or staff.

THE AEROSPACE CORPORATION

E. C. Aldridge, Jr.
President and
Chief Executive Officer

May 27, 1993

General Charles A. Horner
Commander
Air Force Space Command
Peterson AFB, CO 80914

Dear Chuck:

As you know, for over thirty years The Aerospace Corporation has maintained the tradition of objective, independent, and comprehensive technology and engineering analyses of all aspects of our government space programs. We have taken pride in our products, our contributions to mission success, and our support to the Air Force and other national security space missions. While we are asked often for our technical assessment of spacecraft or launch vehicle system alternatives, it is not the policy of Aerospace to advocate one solution over another or to "sell" a particular system at the expense of another.

On a recent occasion we were asked to document for internal use only a study of an Air Force option for ballistic missile early warning using a derivative of the Defense Support Program (DSP). This DSP option had been considered in the Sensor Integration Study, but rejected because it did not meet the operational requirements. The objective of the Aerospace effort was to provide the documentation to the DSP System Program Office (SPO) for such an Air Force back-up option should: a) the Follow-on Early Warning System (FEWS) be delayed or terminated by the Department of Defense or Congress and b) near-term performance improvements to DSP be needed prior to FEWS full operational capability. Overall, this is certainly an appropriate request by the SPO and activity for Aerospace.

Aerospace clearly understands the operational needs of FEWS, has supported its development, and has established that the FEWS capability and design is the only concept that satisfies the needs of the operational commander. Unfortunately, too much program "advocacy" crept into the report and its Executive Summary in support of the DSP alternative. This led to the mistaken conclusion by many that Aerospace supported a DSP derivative over FEWS. I want to emphasize that this is not the position of The Aerospace Corporation, or any member of our management or staff.

General Charles A. Horner
Page Two
May 27, 1993

I am most distressed that a report on such a critical Air Force mission took on this advocacy tone for support of a particular solution and then was approved and released outside of its intended channels without sufficient and appropriate coordination and review. I am taking immediate action to: a) withdraw from distribution the existing report as written, b) initiate an independent technical review of the content of the report, c) have the Aerospace staff participate with the Air Force to "clear the air," and d) review the processes and procedures to ensure that this is a one-time, anomalous event for Aerospace. In addition, I will counsel my staff on the proper role of Aerospace in support of our customers.

I want to assure you and the rest of your Command that The Aerospace Corporation, and I personally, will remain an objective member of the Air Force team and will continue to be dedicated to the successful support of your mission.

Sincerely,

E. C. Aldridge, Jr.

MEMORANDUM FOR CORRESPONDENTS

No. 024-M
February 1, 1994

Secretary of the Air Force Sheila Widnall today announced the results of an Air Force Inspector General inquiry into allegations of wrongdoing and mismanagement in two space-based early warning system programs -- the Follow-on Early Warning System (FEWS) and the Defense Support Program (DSP). The Air Force initiated the internal inquiry during October. The Air Force IG inquiry did not substantiate any misconduct or wrongdoing by Air Force general officers.

The Department of Defense Inspector General reviewed the results of the Air Force inquiry and found that it adequately addressed the issues raised within the Air Force as well as those presented by a contractor and Rep. John Conyers, Jr., (D-Mich.), chairman of the House Government Operations Committee.

The allegations dealt with obstruction, suppression or restriction of contractor data, studies or options; release of contractor proprietary data; providing erroneous data, estimates and statements; making unfair or biased cost comparisons; and providing false or misleading information to DoD and Congress.

Investigators substantiated two allegations. They found that the government took exception to an Aerospace Corporation report about upgrading the Defense Support Program system, as asserted by a contractor. This was done because the report discounted validated requirements, contained inconsistent cost and performance comparisons, and had an advocacy tone. The report was recalled by Aerospace senior management.

Investigators also found that information on an alternative DSP system was deleted from a Congressionally-mandated study, as alleged. This was done because the system did not satisfy the DoD and Congressional ground rule that it meet validated operational requirements.

Investigators verified three allegations in part.

First, US Space Command officials released charts containing budgetary data to competing sensor contractors. However, the charts did not include contractor proprietary data, as alleged.

Second, TRW understood from US Space Command that TRW should pay attention to its role in the FEWS program. This was done because TRW was simultaneously involved in the DSP, FEWS, Brilliant Eyes and Multi-Spectral system programs. Space Command officials questioned whether TRW was supporting FEWS appropriately.

Third, investigators found that the Aerospace Corporation did recall a DSP report, as alleged. It was recalled to confirm the accuracy of the data, since it had not been properly coordinated. After further review, the company reaffirmed its recall decision. The report, in its original form, was given to Congress and the Department of Defense.

All other allegations investigated by the Inspector General were not substantiated.

(MORE)

A separate investigation conducted earlier by Air Force Materiel Command addressed two allegations of inappropriate release of proprietary information by a member of the Air Force. These allegations were substantiated by the separate investigation, and administrative action has been taken. Further, to help prevent the unauthorized release of information in the future, the Air Force is developing additional guidance on marking and protecting contractor proprietary data.

A background briefing by a member of the Air Force Inspector General staff will be held in Room 2E776 at 4 p.m. on Tuesday, Feb. 1. Interested media should contact Major Dave Thurston, Air Force Press Desk, at (703) 695-0640, or Major Linda Leong, Air Force Public Affairs, at (703) 695-3063.

-END-

NORM DICKS
6TH DISTRICT, WASHINGTON

COMMITTEES:
SELECT COMMITTEE ON
INTELLIGENCE
APPROPRIATIONS

SUBCOMMITTEES:
DEFENSE
INTERIOR
MILITARY CONSTRUCTION

2467 RAYBURN HOUSE OFFICE BUILDING
WASHINGTON, DC 20515-4706
PHONE: (202) 225-5916

Congress of the United States
House of Representatives

DISTRICT OFFICES:
SUITE 2244
1717 PACIFIC AVE.
TACOMA, WA 98402-3234
PHONE: (206) 593-6536

SUITE 301
500 PACIFIC AVENUE
BREMERTON, WA 98310-1904
PHONE: (206) 479-4011

1.28.94

January 27, 1994

The Honorable John Conyers, Jr.
Chairman
Committee on Government Operations
2157 Rayburn House Office Building
Washington, DC 20515

Dear Mr. Chairman:

I am respectfully requesting the opportunity to appear before the Legislation and National Security Subcommittee of the Committee on Government Operations on Thursday, at the hearing on Strategic Satellite Systems in the Post Cold War Environment, February 2, 1994.

As Vice Chairman of the House Defense Appropriations Subcommittee, I have closely followed the development of the MILSTAR program. In my statement, I would like to briefly summarize the importance of the military requirement, continued development and support of this program.

Thank you for your utmost consideration.

Sincerely,

NORM DICKS
Member of Congress

NDD:cmk

ONE HUNDRED THIRD CONGRESS

Congress of the United States
House of Representatives
COMMITTEE ON GOVERNMENT OPERATIONS
2157 RAYBURN HOUSE OFFICE BUILDING
WASHINGTON, DC 20515-6143

October 12, 1993

Mr. Derek J. Vander Schaaf
Inspector General
Department of Defense
400 Army-Navy Drive, Room 1000
Arlington, Virginia 22202-2884

Dear Mr. Vander Schaaf:

   The Subcommittee has recently received information alleging that senior Air Force officials <u>suppressed</u> information about a lower cost alternative to the proposed $13 billion Follow-on Early Warning System (FEWS) satellite program. If true, this would be an extremely serious -- and possibly criminal -- withholding of information vital to Congressional deliberations. I would like you to investigate this matter and report to the Subcommittee as soon as possible.

   Specifically, the Subcommittee possesses memoranda (enclosed) from Air Force Colonel Edward Dietz warning that statements supporting FEWS made by General Charles Horner, chief of U.S. Space Command, are erroneous and based on "data to support a pre-selected answer, and worse yet suppressing discussion of technical alternatives."

   Documents (enclosed) from other defense officials allege that Major General Garry Schneizer <u>deleted</u> from a Congressionally-mandated industry study an option identifying improvements to the existing Defense Support Program (DSP) as an alternative to FEWS that could save up to $10 billion. If these allegations are unfounded, they should be resolved in order to preserve the careers of the officers involved.

   Please have your staff contact Subcommittee Deputy Staff Director Joseph Cirincione, at (202) 225-5147, to coordinate your response to this request.

Sincerely,

John Conyers, Jr.
Chairman
Legislation and National Security
Subcommittee

Mr. Joe Cirincione, Professional Staff Member
Subcommittee On Legislation And National Security
House Committee On Government Operations
Rayburn House Office Building, Room B-373
WASHINGTON, DC 20515-6149

September 21, 1993

Dear Mr. Cirincione:

Thank you for taking the time to investigate the procurement integrity issues related to the Defense Support Program (DSP) and the Follow-On Early Warning System (FEWS) programs.

As we discussed yesterday, I am sending you several attachments to this letter as follows:

1. A summary of the issues we discussed over the telephone.
2. Several memoranda from Col. Ed Dietz, DSP Program Manager, to Col. Joe Bailey, Space Based Early Warning Systems Program Director, and others discussing Col. Dietz's concerns with regard to the cost and performance estimates for DSP and FEWS.
3. Correspondence between General C. Horner, CINC USSPACECOM, and Mr. Pete Aldridge, President of The Aerospace Corporation.
4. Several articles which have appeared in Defense News, Space News, Inside The Air Force, and other periodicals.

I have substantially more documentation on these issues, most of which has already been given to the DoD Inspector General's Office. My point of contact in that office was ▇▇▇▇▇▇▇▇. I could mail copies of this documentation to you, or I could travel to DC and go over it with you in person. If the DoD IG is going to be asked to investigate, it may be more appropriate for me to review the documentation with their office. Please let me know what you prefer.

▇▇▇▇▇▇▇ is also willing to discuss these issues with you. You can reach him at his office ▇▇▇▇▇▇▇ or at home ▇▇▇▇▇▇▇. I believe it would be beneficial for you to talk with ▇▇▇▇▇▇▇ before going to the Staff Director or Chairman to ask for the IG investigation because he could give you additional insight based on his Air Force background and his personnel interaction with the other Air Force officers involved.

Again, thank you for your time.

Sincerely,

~~COMPETITION SENSITIVE~~

DSP MISREPRESENTATION

Position: Some elements of USAF are misrepresenting Defense Support Program (DSP) data to Senior Air Force Officers, DoD and Congress.

Background: For the last several years the Nation has been deciding if a new early warning system was necessary to replace the DSP. Although independent assessments made by non-profit organizations such as the Institute for Defense Analysis, and Aerospace Corp. as well as the Defense Science Board, have recommended continuing DSP or upgrading DSP, these assessments have been suppressed and not fully disclosed.

Prior to the now well known Aerospace Report (known as the Aerospace TOR or DSP-II), the Air Force funded Aerojet and their subcontractor TRW to accomplish a study on DSP and Brilliant Eyes synergy options, which was in response to FY92 Congressional direction. <u>Data from the study results was not included in the Air Force report to Congress and the data was suppressed.</u> Some Air Force personnel, notably the DSP SPO, believed the data from the Brilliant Eyes synergy study was important. They commissioned a team of Air Force and Aerospace personnel to perform additional studies using the Brilliant Eyes "Synergy Study" material as a back drop. That group produced the TOR Report. The Space Based Early Warning System Program Office, which has responsibility for the Follow on Early Warning System (FEWS) as well as DSP and a new tactical ground system called Talon Shield, responded adversely to the release of that Aerospace Corp. report. <u>They launched an effort to discredit the study.</u> To aid them in their rebuttal, Aerojet DSP data,

COMPETITION SENSITIVE

COMPETITION SENSITIVE

specifically marked Competition Sensitive and Proprietary, was released from the Program Office to the FEWS prime contractors TRW and Lockheed. Aerojet has protested this impropriety and can provide details about this improper and illegal release.

Aerojet asserts that Air Force cost estimating for FEWS employs biased cost assumptions. Inconsistent comparisons were made that unfairly made DSP look expensive when compared with FEWS. For example, FEWS was assumed to: (1) be launchable on a medium launch vehicle, (2) have no cross links, and (3) have the advantage of low cost ground station while DSP was constrained to (a) be launched on an expensive launch vehicle Titan IV or a cost inflated shuttle, (b) have laser cross links, and (c) never achieve the benefit of a low cost ground station. In addition to making inappropriate comparisons, the data supplied decision makers was further skewed by being extremely optimistic with regards to FEWS and extremely pessimistic for DSP options.

Aerojet would like to amplify its concern on the issue of biased costing. The access to space for DSP is currently on the Titan IV booster or the Shuttle. Since the Titan failure in early August, the necessity of DSP shuttle launches to replenish the constellations has been apparent. This replenishment is mandatory for supplying war fighters unequivocal warning of tactical missiles for two geographically distributed regional conflicts. The marginal costs of shuttle launches for NASA is estimated in the $50M range, and

COMPETITION SENSITIVE

264

COMPETITION SENSITIVE

civilian personnel at OSD PA&E believe NASA owes the Air Force a launch. Senior Air Force officers in Colorado Springs, however, estimate shuttle costs at over $600M which could deprive the DSP launches so desperately needed.

Earlier misrepresentation of the DSP involving the issue of roles and missions among the services surfaced to Aerojet in 1988. More information on these differences which adversely affected DSP and improvements thereto can be obtained by reviewing Aerojet's report #237 and the background data combined therein submitted in February 1992 to the DoD Inspector General under the Voluntary Disclosure Program. The statements alleged by senior Air Force personnel and General Officers, which are detailed in attachments to Aerojet's report, are truly startling.

In the recent months, Aerojet was requested to supply data to the Everett Committee on DSP. To do this job properly, Aerojet required the assistance of TRW. However, TRW refused to help. In discussion with senior TRW executives, they asserted that they could not help because they had been threatened and intimidated by senior Air Force officers who warned TRW not to support opponents of FEWS. Aerojet's response to the Everett Committee was thus less than that committee deserved. Use of intimidation to suppress information unfairly tipped the playing field in favor of FEWS.

With regards to alleged disclosure of TRW proprietary data on the Multi-Spectral Scanner (MSS) to Lockheed, Aerojet has no first hand information. Such behavior is, however, entirely consistent with the behavior exhibited with the handling of Aerojet's proprietary data.

COMPETITION SENSITIVE

3

~~COMPETITION SENSITIVE~~

Summary: Aerojet believes DSP data has not been fairly evaluated by the Air Force and there has been suppression and biasing of data as well as skewed analysis to mislead decision makers. In addition, Aerojet is seriously concerned that unauthorized disclosure of competition sensitive data may adversely impact or compromise our current and future position on competitive acquisitions. Aerojet strongly believes that senior Air Force, DoD and congressional decision makers deserve accurate and complete information on which they can base their decisions. Aerojet also believes that information provided to the Air Force that is competition sensitive or proprietary must be protected so that business can be conducted on a open and fair basis. Aerojet would be glad to discuss these matters in more detail at the government's convenience. Aerojet's point of contact is Dr. Philip A. Buckley, Vice President, Space Surveillance, on (818) 812-1951.

Summary of
Defense Support Program (DSP) And Follow-On Early Warning System (FEWS) Procurement Integrity Issues

September 21, 1993

Background:

FY 92 Congressional language directed the Air Force to examine issues with regard to the acquisition of the Defense Support Program (DSP), Follow-On Early Warning System (FEWS) and Brilliant Eyes (BE) to determine if a lower-cost alternative to these multiple space-based IR programs is feasible and could meet the Tactical Warning / Attack Assessment (TW/AA) and Global Protection Against Limited Strike (GPALS) surveillance requirements. The Air Force tasked The Aerospace Corporation to conduct a series of trade studies in response to the Congressional language -- these studies became collectively known as the Air Force Sensor Integration Study. One of these studies, known as Task III or the DSP/BE Synergy Study, examined the potential for a synergistic DSP and BE system to meet the TW/AA and GPALS requirements. At the direction of the Air Force, Aerojet and Aerospace worked together to define this concept. Aerojet was funded for $300,000 and Aerospace expended approximately $200,000 on this activity.

The conclusions of the DSP/BE synergy study were published by Aerojet on February 10, 1993. This report, "DSP/BE Synergy Study Task III Final Briefing (U)", Report No. 10168, provided the technical details of the synergistic DSP/BE concept. Tecolote, an Air Force contractor tasked with performing cost analysis for the Space And Missile Systems Center (SMC), prepared the cost estimates for all of the Air Force Sensor Integration Studies, including Task III. Tecolote's analysis showed that the Task III concept was the lowest cost alternative considered, with project savings of over $3B in the FYDP (95-99) and approaching $10B life-cycle through 2015 as compared with the baseline Air Force plan of separate FEWS and BE acquisitions. An independent engineering team from The Aerospace Corporation (independent from the Aerospace personnel directly supporting the Air Force Sensor Integration Studies) reviewed all of the concepts including Task III. They concluded that the DSP/BE synergistic system was technically feasible.

Major General Garry Schnelzer, AFPEO/SP, was briefed on the progress of the Sensor Integration Studies on a weekly basis. In late February, Maj. Gen. Schnelzer and Lt. Col. Jeff Norton, Air Force Space Command (AFSPACECOM/DR) were briefed specifically on the DSP/BE study results. They rejected the study's conclusions with the stated reason that the proposed DSP system (known as DSP-II) did not employ crosslinks nor on-board processing which were "Air Force requirements". Maj. Gen. Schnelzer ordered that the DSP-II concept be replaced with a two-year-old DSP concept known as DSP++ and that an option of continuing DSP "as is" (known as DSP-26) with no life-extension or other improvements also be considered. Neither of these two options met the "Air Force requirements", but their cost was comparable to the FEWS costs. The DSP++ and DSP-26 options were presented to Congress, but the DSP-II option was not.

On February 23, 1993, Col. John Kidd, then DSP Program Director, and Col. Ed Dietz, then Deputy DSP Program Director, directed Aerospace to prepare a report documenting the DSP-II concept to include a pre-planned product improvement (P'I) and technology insertion approach building on the existing DSP spacecraft and ground processing systems. This report, "DSP-II: Preserving The Air Force's Options (U)", Report No. TOR-93(3409)-6, was published on April 23, 1993.

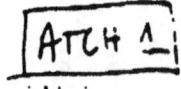

On May 20, 1993, Gen. Horner, CINC USSPACECOM, heard of the DSP-II report and its conclusions with regard to the cost of DSP-II versus FEWS. He and Mr. Pete Aldridge, President of The Aerospace Corporation, ordered that the report be recalled. On May 21 and May 22 (late Friday and on Saturday), Col. Bailey, Space Based Early Warning System (SBEWS) Program Director, gave copies of the DSP-II report, which contained Competition Sensitive Information (provided by Aerojet) and was so marked, to the FEWS contractors TRW and Lockheed. There were multiple witnesses to this. On May 26, two agents from the DoD IG's office seized a copy of the DSP-II report from the SBEWS program office. In early June, the DoD IG met with Mr. Aldridge. After this meeting, the IG has not taken any action despite repeated hot-line calls from multiple people.

Since May, two committees have been convened to review the DSP-II report and the issues related to DSP, FEWS and BE. One is the Schnieter Committee (Dr. George Schnieter is the Director of Space and Strategic Systems in OSD), and the other is the Technical Support Group appointed by Mr. John Deutch which is headed by Mr. Robert Everett (also known as the Everett Committee). The Air Force, Lt. Col. Norton, Col. Jeff Quirk, Col. Bailey, Maj. Gen. Schnelzer, Maj. Gen. Don Hard, and Gen. Horner have continued to provide false and misleading data to these committees to substantiate the need for FEWS. They consistently understate DSP performance, understate FEWS program cost and risk, overstate DSP costs, and overstate FEWS performance and capability.

Col. Ed Dietz has written several "I am concerned" memoranda to Col. Quirk, Col. Bailey, Maj. Gen. Schnelzer and the Aerospace Corporation. In August, he brought his concerns directly to Lt. Gen. Ed Barry, Commander Space And Missile Systems Center. Rather than take any corrective measures, Lt. Gen. Barry, who was forced to recuse himself from direct oversight of acquisition programs as a result of his involvement in the C-17 program, ordered Col. Dietz reassigned to the TQM support office. This reassignment is effective October 1, 1993.

Issues Which Should Be Investigated:

1. Did Maj. Gen. Garry Schnelzer commit acquisition fraud by deleting the DSP-II option from the Sensor Integration Study presented to Congress? He replaced the low-cost DSP-II with two other DSP concepts (DSP++ and DSP-26) which were significantly higher cost and had poorer performance than DSP-II.

2. Did Col. Joe Bailey violate the Trade Secrets Act by providing the DSP-II report which contained Competition Sensitive Information provided by Aerojet to Aerojet's competitors TRW and Lockheed? He did this knowingly and there are multiple witnesses.

3. Did Mr. Pete Aldridge, as President of The Aerospace Corporation, act improperly in ordering the recall of the DSP-II report and assisting in the suppression of options from Congress? Did Mr. Aldridge interfere in the DoD IG's investigation by requesting that the IG back-off on these issues?

4. Are Lt. Col. Jeff Norton, Col. Jeff Quirk, Col. Joe Bailey, Maj. Gen. Garry Schnelzer, Maj. Gen. Don Hard, Gen. Chuck Horner, and Mr. Pete Aldridge guilty of continuing to provide false and misleading information to the decision makers within OSD and Congress with regard to the cost, performance, and capabilities of the DSP and FEWS programs? Are they guilty of conspiracy to defraud the acquisition process with their actions?

GenCorp Aerojet

Carl C. Fischer
President
Aerojet Electronic Systems

Electronic Systems Division

P.O. Box 296
1100 West Hollyvale Street
Azusa, CA 91702

Tel: (818) 812-2201
Fax: (818) 812-2792

FACSIMILE TRANSMISSION SHEET

NUMBER OF PAGES INCLUDING TRANSMISSION SHEET   6

TO: Major General Marcus Anderson   DATE: 10/19/93

        Headquarters AFOTEC/CC

        Kirtland, New Mexico 87177   FAX: (505) 846-9726

FROM: Carl Fischer

TELEPHONE: (818) 812-2201

MESSAGE:

**PROGRAM MANAGER, DEFENSE SUPPORT PROGRAM
SPACE BASED EARLY WARNING SYSTEMS**
HEADQUARTERS SPACE AND MISSILE SYSTEMS CENTER
LOS ANGELES AIR FORCE BASE, CALIFORNIA

DATE 28 SEP 93

MEMORANDUM FOR: Joe Batty
John Parsons

I've tried to get together with, one last time, but with, death, travel etc it's not worked yet. I think I have some time (with y) next week. I'm truly concerned we have a broken "process," and we're tolerating it. It has nothing to do with requirements or politics, that job belongs in Co., we're putting out material that violates good sense, and in some cases is wrong, and we know in some cases it's wrong, and haven't encouraged the folks or teams to resolve it. This is no fun, but I am [illegible].

Ed [signature]

RETYPED FOR CLARITY BY SUBCOMMITTEE STAFF

MEMORANDUM FOR: Joe Bailey
John Parsons

I've tried to get together with you one last time, but with death travel etc. it's not worked yet. I think I have some time with you next week. I'm truly concerned <u>we</u> have a broken "process," and we're tolerating it. It has nothing to do with requirements or politics, that job belongs in Colorado. We're putting out material that violates good sense, and in many cases is wrong and we know it. In some cases it's wrong, and we haven't encouraged the engineering debate to resolve it. This is not fun, "but I am concerned."

Ed Dietz

**PROGRAM MANAGER, DEFENSE SUPPORT PROGRAM
SPACE BASED EARLY WARNING SYSTEMS**
HEADQUARTERS SPACE AND MISSILE SYSTEMS CENTER
LOS ANGELES AIR FORCE BASE, CALIFORNIA

DATE 7 Sep 93

MEMORANDUM FOR: Colonel Bailey

SUBJECT: "I am Concerned"

General Horner, his staff, and AFSPACECOM are clearly misinformed re: FEWS' and DSP's attributes. The errors are favorable to FEWS, giving the appearance of bias.

Gen Horner erroneously believes FEWS is cheaper, ten time more accurate, capable of detecting cruise missiles and SS-21's, etc., and DSP current life expectancy is 7-8 years.

Gen Horner's memo to Gen McPeak, briefing to Gen McPeak and recent Aviation Week article demonstrate this.

SMC is responsible for these errors and we are subject to criticism because:

- SMC documentation is the original source of the errors, and subsequent SMC material (i.e. Gen Cairn's Chart) reinforces the errors, and could appear to intentionally mislead.

- SMC has done nothing substantial nor formal to correct these errors.

Recent USAF experience with DoD IG, OSD, and congressional oversight demand absolute candor. I believe corrections to these and other errors should be provided to AFSPACECOM.

EDWARD R. DIETZ, Col, USAF   cc: John Parsons
Program Manager

TO: Joseph A. Bailey, Colonel, USAF

SUBJ: "I am Concerned"

FROM: Edward R. Dietz, Colonel, USAF

1. I am concerned about the "conditions" imposed on the DSP options costed and presented to higher Headquarters. They are illogical and reflect poor program management judgment. These conditions give the appearance of bias towards a FEWS solution, and are obvious enough that observers such as OSD will discover them and question SMC's integrity and motives.

2. These concerns, and others, were discussed with you previously and in your Friday, 13 Aug review with your 3 letters, but they were tabled and no action was directed. Some of these concerns are:

    A. DSP Block 26 costs include $1.5 billion for LCS, though we're in the process of deleting LCS from all future DSP's.

    B. DSP on MLV costs are about $2B too high because we haven't deleted Block 23 and T IV from the model as we did for FEWS.

    C. DSP P^3I Program, as suggested by recent OSD policy has been precluded, increasing cost as much as $1 billion, and delaying implementation of improvements.

    D. About $4 billion has been added to DSP to insure availability of detailed signatures. However, 18 months ago AFSPACECOM ceased funding the 1 Man/Yr necessary to insure collection and delivery of this data to in analysts.

    E. FEWS performance estimates exceeds the specification, and contractors are unlikely to spend much money attempting to exceed the specification.

    F. FEWS cost is based upon an assessment of the risk of meeting the specification, but performance quoted exceeds the specification. The cost of exceeding the specification, and meeting our performance expectations/goals, could be very high.

    G. DSP accuracy performance quoted is limited to that already demonstrated rigorously, even though small procedural changes at sites, or modest investments in software ($50-$100M) would yield major improvements in accuracy.

    H. FEWS optimizes their hypothetical orbits and performance. But DSP quoted performance is limited by current satellite locations, chosen for different reasons. Optimizing DSP configuration will improve quoted performance.

    I. The quoted DSP detection performance against the SCUD is significantly lower than that demonstrated during Desert Storm.

    J. FEWS attitude and ephemeris data is incorrectly presumed better than DSP's.

K. For years DSP has proposed investing in life extension and producibility for cost reduction. It has always been rejected because FEWS was planned to replace DSP in the near future. However, due to the budget environment, small investments in DSP to yield large life cycle costs reductions would be prudent. Block 26 should reflect these savings. It is unethical to use the higher cost basis.

L. Etc, etc, see notes from 13 Aug Meeting.

3. Modeling and comparison conditions such as these conflict with our stated objectives of rigor and impartiality.

cc: Ev Bersinger
John Parsons

FROM: Dietz, Edward R., COL\MTP
DATE: 06/17/93   17:04
TO: Quirk, Jeffrey A, COL

C: Heydinger, Gerard N., GM15\MTP
   Planeaux, James B., CAPT\
   Ching, Barbara   SEO
   Leuthauser, Paul R., MAJ\MTE

SUBJECT: New FEWS TMD & TWAA Rqmts
PRIORITY:
ATTACHMENTS:

I've been thinking some more about the strange set of TMD & TWAA requirements we were working this Thursday. With additional thought I'm convinced we're not giving a completely honest answer.

The answer we're going to give is wrong, we're giving an answer we think they want........The truth is that if we want theater support (presuming it is needed or valuable) in the areas and manners described......FEWS is not a reasonable way to do this job, nor are the orbits correct....it was designed for a different job. DSP is not right for the job either untill we make a few improvements, but it is in the right orbit.

We're focusing on the number of satelites that are required, and where they should be put, but we should be considering what type of a satelite is needed. This can't be done in 36 hours......but we could give the boss the right answer.....FEWS is not the right system to do the job proposed...... by failing to tell them this we're failing to help them when they need it most.

Painfull as it may seem, let's tell them in big print and a loud voice....

**FEWS IS NOT A THEATER SUPPORT SYSTEM
NAVY & ARMY DON'T CURRENTLY WANT OVERHEAD SUPPORT
PAYOFF FOR OVERHEAD SUPPORT MAY BE SMALL
IF YOU WANT A STOPGAP, DSP IS GOOD ENOUGH WHILE WE DECIDE**

and while we're demonstrating our new found integrity, let's also tell them that their requirements and conditions are inconsistent, and perhaps illogical.

Paul Leuthauser

- FYI & limited circulation
- I am concerned, I told the boss, he feels obliged to follow SpCmd and USAF party line
- Don't get me in trouble!

ED

(T...9.)

the credibility of SMC,

ing the central issue and

DSP, downsized DSP, or modest
M is unwilling to consider anything
udent because it's inconsistent with
FSPACECOM

tion and requirements allocaton is that
d and downsized, and BE downsized to
cted in the options presented.

n and unchanged" is contrary to the
a system with high and low altitude

nd not well justified in terms of Military

- This issue and AFSPACECOM unwillingness to consider anything but a 100% solution highlights SMC's lack of cross system system engineering and may compromise our credibility in the eyes of OSD and Congress. Worse yet we may be jeopardizing FEWS and BE.

I am concerned the be synergy study will compromise the credibility of SMC, Aerospace, and PEO office.

- We are focusing on answering the mail, but missing the central issue and jeopardizing the Air Force's credibility

- The options being addressed ignore unchanged DSP, down sized DSP, or modest DSP upgrades. This is because AFSPACECOM is unwilling to consider anything but 100% solutions. This is wrong, and imprudent because it's inconsistent with budget options being addressed by AQ and AFSPACECOM

- The conclusion of the study of sensor interaction and requirements allocaton is that if BE exits, FEWS/DSP should be combined and downsized, and BE downsized to a lesser extent. This conclusion is not reflected in the options presented.

- The implied ground rule, "FEWS is chosen and unchanged" is contrary to the objective of understanding, the nature of a system with high and low altitude components.

- Requirements and desires are confused and not well justified in terms of Military Utility

- This issue and AFSPACECOM unwillingness to consider anything but a 100% solution highlights SMC's lack of cross system system engineering and may compromise our credibility in the eyes of OSD and Congress. Worse yet we may be jeopardizing FEWS and BE.

FROM: Dietz, Edward R
DATE: 05/11/93
TO: Parsons, John

Cole, David F.   MJP
Glaze, Orville B.   MJG
Hall, Roger L.   MJI
Leuthauser, Paul R.   MJI
Pesapane, John   Col
Bailey, Joseph A.   Col.
Turelli, Robert R, Col AFPEOSP/WASHDC

SUBJECT: DSP Costing
PRIORITY:
ATTACHMENTS:
....

Last friday costing was requested and provided on a DSP program option. I am concerned that the costs do not reflect what you think they do. You had requested DSP life cycle costs based upon Block 23 contract values. This presumed no performance or MMD improvements. For years we have been advocating MMD improvements, but they have been declined because FEWS is just around the corner and we don't want to improve the old system. It is unreasonable to imagine a large purchase of DSP satelites without MMD improvements. The costing ground rules precluded MMD improvements and made the life cycle cost of DSP appear more expensive than FEWS. I am concerned that this inappropriately distorts the cost comparisons. I believe the ground rules of this DSP life cycle cost deserve a little more discussion in house, although I understand the numbers were already sent to D.C.

I've put these concerns on Voice Mail for Gen S, Col Bailey, Col Mitchel, Col Pesapane.

Paul Leuthauser, please pass to Col Quirk, he's not on my E-Mail, and his Voice Mail with Aerospace doesn't work.

```
FROM: Dietz, Edward R.                    MJ
DATE: 05/27/93       08:04
TO: Margullis, Mary E.            MJ


SUBJECT: Follow Up
PRIORITY:
ATTACHMENTS:
------------------------------------------------------------------------
    Please print 2 copies
------------------------------------------------------------------------
FORWARDED FROM: Dietz, Edward R.           MJ        MJ
FROM: Dietz, Edward R.           MJ
DATE: 05/25/93      18:09
TO:
CC:
SUBJECT: Follow Up
PRIORITY:
ATTACHMENTS:
------------------------------------------------------------------------
```

Gen S' speech to us today (Tues) and events of the last few days suggest a few comments to you.

Watch out for your people. Protect them.
A witch hunt will begin, and the hunters have have the wrong target.

Your people did what John & I told them, and they did it well. Not perfectly, but within the scope of the BE study effort. The language is inflamatory and unfortunate. It's outrageous that somebody leaked it. But we did it publically, openly, and we briefed it to all, including Gen Schnelzer. We did it we ought to, what was reasonable, what was directed, and everybody knew exactly what we were doing. Your people deserve no criticism.

Today the Gen said I was dead wrong! Gen S made it clear he feels it's inappropriate for us to look at anything less than full satisfaction of customer requirements. I know Col Bailey believes this, and I've heard Gen S say it before, but I thought I misunderstood him. This adds new meaning to System Engineering, Requirements Analysis, the Aerospace Corp's most important strengths. I may have erred, but your people did not. I hope you're able to provide your people some top cover, they feel very vulnerable.

ANOTHER UNSOLICITED COMMENT
As you know I've given Gen Schnelzer my "I am concerned" speech enough so that he recognizes the preamble. I continue to be concerned for the integrity of the USAF And Aerospace Corp. We have avoided dealing with a number of fundamental challenges to our organizational reasons for existance. We continue to appear to be trying to provide data to support a pre selected answer, and worse yet supressing discussion of technical alternatives.
The anxious call I gave you 6-8 weeks ago was prompted by the same concerns.
The quality and impartiality of the BE Study was not up to our normal standards, it still isn't and we still appear to be avoiding answering the central questions of the Congress and OSD re the 3 surveillance programs.

Suggested Congressional Language: (SMC/MT)

The Follow-On Early Warning System (FEWS) is a vitally needed replacement for the Defense Support Program (DSP) in response to the changing World-wide missile threat. The FEWS development schedule is longer than necessary in order to limit annual funding requirements. This schedule increases total program cost since the procurement of additional DSP satellite and continued operation of the DSP overseas ground stations is required. The committee supports the FEWS program and directs the DoD to accelerate the program. The DoD is directed to adjust the FEWS FYDP and program schedules to achieve launch of the first satellite, IOC, and FOC one year earlier than currently planned. The committee increases FY94 funding for FEWS by 85 $20M to begin implementation of the accelerated program and intends to increase FY95 funding by $100M to continue its first full year. The DoD is directed to restructure the DSP and FEWS program to provide the funding necessary for the accelerated FEWS program in the remainder of the FYDP.

Ed Quirk

I believe this is ill advised. It will infer that SMC believes this can and should be done. Implied requirements are inconsistent and illogical. Gap charts suggest a disaster, and worse yet I can't believe that canceling DSP 23-25 will save enough $ to fund FEWS, and the FEWS acceleration! This is not plausible!

This note duplicates the voice mail I left you Fri.

Ed Dietz

**PROGRAM DIRECTOR
DEFENSE SUPPORT PROGRAM**
HQ SPACE AND MISSILE SYSTEMS CENTER
LOS ANGELES AIR FORCE BASE, CALIFORNIA

DATE: 20 July

MEMORANDUM FOR: Joe Bailey

Attached items are not new, but I just reviewed Gen Heiner's memo to Gen McPeak and his briefing. They are logical and reasonable, but based upon factual errors (B.S.) from his staff. His material was very disheartening as an Air Force officer. He's making decisions on the wrong data..... maybe the right decision... but he deserves the facts.

Ed

DEFENSE SUPPORT PROGRAM
INTEROFFICE MEMO
(Dietzgram)

TO: Col Bailey

SUBJECT: Support of Senior Management

FROM: COL DIETZ

DATE: 20 July 93

I am concerned, we've discussed all of the following, but I'm concerned!

Cost comparisons (Gen Horner) exclude consideration of DSP-2

DSP performance assessments are perjorative, while FEWS is presumed to perform better than specification.

DSP-26 costs are inflated and do not reflect good engineering and programatic judgement

Components of DSP-26, included by direction, are useless, but expensive

Costs of "A" ($2B) are added to all DSP options, but none of the FEWS options

It has been widely, and incorrectly, stated that FEWS is cheaper than DSP

The types of tactical targets that DSP can not see is widely and incorrectly quoted, as are the conditions under which DSP performance is degraded

The DSP mean mission duration is generally over stated

The FEWS launch point and azimuth accuracy is alleged to be substantially better than DSP

DEPARTMENT OF THE AIR FORCE
HEADQUARTERS UNITED STATES AIR FORCE
WASHINGTON, D.C.

REPLY TO
ATTN OF: XOFS

26 APR 1993

SUBJECT: Federally Funded Research and Development Center Cost Reduction Request

TO: Associate Deputy Assistant Secretary
Management Policy and Program Integration
Assistant Secretary (Acquisition)

1. The Space and C3I team is developing options for our leadership to address new funding targets we anticipate this summer. We are considering many alternatives -- nothing is off the table. As part of these deliberations, we are considering an option which reduces the allowed Federally Funded Research and Development Center (FFRDC) technical support for the Electronic System Center (ESC) and Space and Missile Systems Center (SMC) by 25%, 50%, 75% and 100%. Please provide us a projection of cost savings for each option and the impacts by 14 May 1993.

2. Our intent is not to offer options which replace the employees of these FFRDCs with government or contractor personnel, but to eliminate their positions and save $181K per Member of the Technical Staff (MTS) per year for SMC and $155K per MTS per year for ESC. POC is Maj Ivette Falto-Heck/DSN 697-5890.

SANFORD D. MANGOLD, Colonel, USAF
Chief, Space Forces Division
DCS, Plans and Operations

cc: SMC/MO (Col Randms)
ESC/MO (B. Smith)

MEMORANDUM TO: Eric Thorson   3 Feb 94

FROM: Col Sanford D. Mangold

SUBJECT: Additional Material Requested by Govt Ops Subcommittee

1. Attached is the 26 Apr 93 letter I sent to Mr. Blaise Durante (SAF/AQX - SES-1 and former USAF Colonel). Upon receipt of this letter, Blaise told my action officer (Major Falto-Heck) that I was "insane" and, in conjunction with Maj Gen Hard (then SAF/AQS, now and Aerospace VP in Colo Spgs, supporting Space Command) pressured my leadership to withdraw the letter.

2. So far everything remains calm over here in light of the testimony. I will keep you informed as events unfold.

SANFORD D. MANGOLD
Colonel, USAF

ATCH
26 Apr 93 letter

For O. Use Only

Aerospace Re[
TOR-93(3-...6
AS-93-00386 Copy No.

DSP-II
"Preserving The Air Force's Options" (U)

Prepared by

Guido W. Aru and Carl T. Lunde
DEFENSE SUPPORT PROGRAM
Space Program Operations

23 April 1993

Programs Group
THE AEROSPACE CORPORATION
El Segundo, CA 90245

Prepared for

SPACE AND MISSILE SYSTEMS CENTER
US AIR FORCE MATERIEL COMMAND
Los Angeles Air Force Base
Los Angeles, CA 90009-2960

Contract No. F04701-88-C-0089

COMPETITION SENSITIVE INFORMATION -- Secondary distribution authorized to U.S. Government agencies and The Aerospace Corporation only: For Official Use Only: 23 April 1993. Other requests shall be referred to SMC/MJ.

DESTRUCTION NOTICE - For classified documents, follow the procedures in DoD 5200.22-M, Industrial Security Manual, Section 9.10 or DoD 5200.1-R, Information Security Program Regulation, Chapter IX. For unclassified, limited documents, destroy by any method that will prevent disclosure of contents or reconstruction of the document.

CLASSIFICATION MARKING NOTICE - Some pages within this document are classified SECRET due to the compilation and association of data contained on the given page. Individual paragraphs, tables, and charts are not commonly marked.

UNCLASSIFIED

Aerospace Report
TOR-93(34

DSP-II - "Preserving The Air Force's Options" (U)

Prepared by:

Guido W. Aru, Project Manager
System Analysis
Defense Support Program

Carl T. Lunde, Engineering Specialist
Electronic Systems Department
Electronics And Sensors Division

Approved by:

Barbara K. Ching, Assoc. Principal Director
Systems Engineering
Defense Support Program

Everitt V. Bersinger, Principal Director
Defense Support Program
Space Program Operations

Paul R. Leuthauser, Major, USAF
Director For System Engineering
Defense Support Program

John R. Kidd, Colonel, USAF
System Program Director
Defense Support Program

NOTICE. The information in a Technical Operating Report is developed for a particular program and is therefore not necessarily of broader technical applicability.

UNCLASSIFIED

Abstract (U)

(U) The Air Force is committed to the development of the Follow-on Early Warning System (FEWS) to replace the Defense Support Program (DSP). Potential technical risks lie ahead -- few, if any, programs have ever become cheaper, lighter, or faster during EMD. In addition, fiscal uncertainties lie ahead -- these are particularly vexatious since they are subject to higher-level DoD, Congressional, and Executive polices, priorities, and direction. As a result, DSP will likely be around longer than anticipated. It is prudent, then, to fully explore, understand, and consider the alternatives available to the Air Force should the FEWS program experience technical or programmatic delays, redirection, or cancellation.

(U) It is within this context, as well as Aerospace's role as general systems engineer for the Air Force, that this report has been prepared -- exploring potential evolutionary upgrades to the DSP which preserve the Air Force's options for space-based Tactical Warning and Attack Assessment (TW/AA). These upgrades are designed to enhance the DSP's capabilities to meet the post-Cold War New World Order requirements while simultaneously reducing life-cycle costs in-line with the President's proposed budget reductions. Technology insertion and Pre-Planned Product Improvement (P^3I) options are explored which, if exercised, provide near-term enhancements and cost savings prior to FEWS FOC or a low-cost and low-risk alternative should the FEWS program be canceled. If the evolutionary DSP upgrade program outlined herein as DSP-II is pursued, it will require approximately $1 billion in funding through FY99 versus $5 billion for FEWS. In addition, DSP-II offers the potential for over $10 billion in total life-cycle cost savings through 2015.

UNCLASSIFIED

Preface (U)

(U) The purpose of this Technical Operating Report (TOR) is to explore alternatives and methods to preserve the Air Force's options for Space-Based Tactical Warning and Attack Assessment Systems. Although the Air Force, specifically Air Force Space Command (AFSPACECOM) and the Air Force Program Executive Office for Space (AFPEO/SP), is committed to the development of the Follow-on Early Warning System (FEWS) to replace the existing Defense Support Program (DSP), there are potential technical risks and fiscal uncertainties which may adversely impact the schedule or the very future of the FEWS program. The fiscal uncertainties are particularly troublesome in that they are outside the direct control of the Air Force and are driven by higher-level DoD, Congressional, and Executive policies and budget priorities. As a result, it is prudent to fully explore and understand the alternatives available to the Air Force should the FEWS program experience delays or face cancellation. It is within this context, as well as within Aerospace's role as general system engineer for the Air Force, that this report is prepared.

(U) There are two principal objectives of this report: the first is to examine the role of DSP as a safety net for FEWS in the event of FEWS schedule slips or program cancellation as discussed above, and the second is to examine the benefit from potential near-term enhancements to the DSP to provide improved interim capabilities prior to FEWS. Both of these objectives are accomplished by examining the application of Pre-Planned Product Improvements (P^3I) and Technology Insertion options to upgrade the DSP. In order to control cost and risk, while simultaneously providing for near-term performance enhancements, alternatives are delineated for progressive P^3I and technology insertion retrofits to DSP-I Satellites 21 through 25, culminating with the advent of DSP-II as Satellite 26. Evolutionary enhancements to the DSP ground segment are also examined. Options are provided for near-term centralization of processing to reduce Operations and Maintenance (O&M) costs using System 5 for the Global Mission (Strategic) and Talon Shield for the Theater Mission (Tactical).

(U) In considering the type of evolutionary upgrades to apply to DSP-I, the Draft FEWS Operational Requirements Document (ORD), dated October 1992, was used as the source requirements document. The performance requirements and design/implementation specified in the Draft FEWS ORD were balanced against military utility, cost, risk, and schedule. Integrated Weapons System Management (IWSM) concepts, which encourage consideration of other than 100% solutions (i.e., cost-effective methods to provide the 80% to 90% solution), were also applied in the development of the DSP upgrades. Options for additional DSP performance enhancements to approach the 100% solution (as defined by the Draft FEWS ORD) are provided along with their Life-Cycle Cost (LCC) impact and risk.

(U) Many of the concepts presented within this report were an outgrowth of the DSP/Brilliant Eyes Synergy Study conducted between November, 1992 and February, 1993 in response to tasking from the Office of the Secretary Of Defense (OSD) and SAF/AQ to examine synergy issues and concepts between DSP, FEWS, and Brilliant Eyes. The results of the DSP/BE synergy study were rejected by the study's Steering Committee and the AFPEO/SP because the synergistic DSP/BE system failed to meet all of the design and implementation detail specified by the Draft Follow-on Early Warning System (FEWS) Operational Requirements Document (ORD). In particular, the synergistic DSP/BE system failed to provide crosslinks between all satellites and on-board mission processing on all satellites. In the proposed concept, only Brilliant Eye's satellites had crosslinks and on-board mission processing. Thus, these results were not carried forward to AFSPACECOM, SAF/AQ, nor the OSD. They are documented herein, however, so that when a re-evaluation of the protracted nuclear warfighting survivability requirements driving crosslinks and on-board mission processing is conducted -- in light of budget priorities and the New World Order -- these ideas will have been preserved and available for further study and/or implementation.

UNCLASSIFIED

Acknowledgements (U)

(U) This Technical Operating Report (TOR) is the result of many thousands of man-hours spent since November developing, analyzing, and assessing various potential evolutionary upgrades to the Defense Support Program (DSP). These studies involved not only Aerospace Corporation personnel, but also personnel from Aerojet Electronic Systems Division, TRW, Tecolote, and the US Air Force.

(U) The authors wish to thank all of those who contributed to this study. In particular, the following people are recognized for their significant contributions to this effort:

(U) The Aerospace Corporation: Lou Bodnar for his analysis of the DSP-II weights and volumetric envelopes; Charlie Dippel for his support to the sensor studies; Patricia Enns for her analysis of spacecraft sub-systems; Tony Gregory for his invaluable insight into Brilliant Eyes in support of the DSP/BE synergy study; Mike Jacobs for his critiques of DSP/BE synergistic system performance; Kam Lee and Paul Montag for their satellite GAP availability analyses; Benjamin Savagian for his analyses of SGLS/SDLS uplinks/downlinks and future crosslink concepts; Ted Stindt for conducting reviews of the DSP and FEWS requirements; Tom Stocker for his support of the performance analysis; David Truong for his work on launch vehicle interfaces; and Allen Tungseth for his analysis of the attitude control and propulsion systems.

(U) Aerojet Electronic Systems Division: For their analysis of DSP evolutionary concepts and potential DSP synergy with Brilliant Eyes, the following people are recognized: Bill Mullooly, DSP Program Manager; Harvey Clouser, DSP/BE Synergy study leader; Dick Castleberry, Cal Chastain, John Conklin, Gene Dryden, Martha Fortson, Gunars Grabis, Dick Lehmann, Ellen Linder, Ken Marks, and Amiel Shulsinger.

(U) TRW: Arnold Galloway and Art Terry for their evaluation of the DSP spacecraft section of the DSP/BE synergy study.

(U) Tecolote: Linda Huang for her contributions to DSP/BE synergy study cost analysis of DSP-II.

(U) Atlas Launch Vehicle SPO: Colonel Mark Lacaillade, Program Manager Atlas II; Major Milt Tucker, Deputy Program Manager Atlas II; and Captain Bailey for their help in understanding the capabilities, volumetric constraints, and limitations of the Atlas IIAS launch vehicle.

(U) The authors also recognize Roger Hall, Major (sel.), USAF, for his outstanding effort in leading the DSP/BE synergy study. He suffered many grueling late-night and weekend hours helping develop the concepts presented herein. Of even greater significance, Major (sel.) Hall endured presenting some of these concepts to less-than-receptive audiences while managing to not become a friendly-fire statistic.

UNCLASSIFIED

Report Outline (U)

(U) This Technical Operating Report (TOR) is divided into seven sections, including the Executive Overview, the main body, and five appendices.

(U) The *Executive Overview* is 27 pages in length and provides a top-level review of the DSP evolutionary upgrade program known as DSP-II. The cost, risk, performance, and schedule of the DSP-II program is summarized here. Top-level comparisons to the FEWS program are also provided.

(U) The main body of the report, *DSP-II - Preserving The Air Force's Options*, is 113 pages in length. It provides a detailed description of the DSP-II program, including the satellite, launch vehicle, and ground processing sub-systems. Options for transitioning from today's DSP-I system to the DSP-II system are also reviewed here.

(U) Appendix A - *DSP-II Space Segment Details* provides a low-level description of the DSP-II satellite and launch vehicle. The technology insertion and Pre-Planned Product Improvement (P^3I) approach employed to create the DSP-II satellite is also delineated.

(U) Appendix B - *DSP-II Ground Segment Details* provides a thorough description of the DSP-II Global and Theater Systems as well as a description of the ground segment transition approach.

(U) Appendix C - *DSP-II Cost And Schedule* presents the DSP-II program schedule, life-cycle cost estimates, and the methodology behind the cost estimates. Details of Tecolote's and Aerospace's quasi-independent cost estimates are delineated.

(U) Appendix D - *DSP-II Capabilities And Performance* describes the performance analysis used to estimate DSP-II system performance. In addition, a summary of system performance is presented along with the deviations from the draft FEWS ORD.

(U) Appendix E - *DSP-II / Brilliant Eyes Synergy* presents a potential concept for a synergistic DSP-II / BE system. The operational concepts, cost, performance, and schedule are reviewed. The topic of DSP-II / BE synergy is not discussed in any of the other sections of this report.

UNCLASSIFIED

UNCLASSIFIED

Table Of Contents (U)

Abstract (U) v

Preface (U) vii

Acknowledgements (U) ix

DSP-II Executive Overview (U) EX-1

DSP-II "Preserving The Air Force's Options" (U) 1
    Purpose (U) 3
    DSP-II Concept Overview (U) 11
    DSP-II Space Segment And Transition Options (U) 19
    DSP-II Ground Segment And Transition Options (U) 55
    DSP-II Cost And Schedule (U) 71
    DSP-II Capabilities And Performance (U) 79
    Comparative Assessment Of FEWS And DSP-II (U) 93
    Conclusions (U) 107

Appendix A - DSP-II Space Segment Details (U) A-1
    DSP-II Space Segment Overview (U) A-3
    DSP-II Sensor (U) A-11
    DSP-II Spacecraft (U) A-35
    DSP-II Launch Vehicle (U) A-65
    Transition Options And Schedules (U) A-77

UNCLASSIFIED

Table Of Contents (Continued) (U)

Appendix B - DSP-II Ground Segment Details (U) B-1

    DSP-II Ground Segment Overview (U) B-3
    Mission Processing Architecture (U) B-11
    Risk Assessment (U) B-39
    Transition Options And Schedules (U) B-43
    Ground System Survivability Issues (U) B-49

Appendix C - DSP-II Cost And Schedule (U) C-1

    DSP-II Schedule (U) C-3
    DSP-II Life Cycle Costs (U) C-7
    DSP-II Cost Estimation Details (U) C-19

Appendix D - DSP-II Capabilities And Performance (U) D-1

    DSP-II Capabilities Overview (U) D-3
    Performance Analysis (U) D-9
    DSP-II Performance Summary (U) D-29
    DSP-II Deviations From Draft FEWS ORD D-39

Appendix E - DSP-II / Brilliant Eyes Synergy (U) E-1

    Executive Summary (U) E-3
    Potential BE Enhancements To Maximize Synergy (U) ... E-15
    DSP-II / BE Synergistic System Operational Concept (U) . E-29
    Performance Assessment (U) E-45
    Cost Assessment (U) E-71
    Potential BE Cost And Risk Reductions (U) E-75
    Summary (U) E-81

UNCLASSIFIED

DSP-II
"Preserving The Air Force's Options"
EXECUTIVE OVERVIEW (U)

April 23, 1993

Presented By

Guido W. Aru

And

Carl T. Lunde

Presented To

Colonel John Kidd

(U) The purpose of this Technical Operating Report (TOR) is to explore alternatives and methods to preserve the Air Force's options for Space-Based Tactical Warning and Attack Assessment Systems. Although the Air Force, specifically Air Force Space Command (AFSPACECOM) and the Air Force Program Executive Office for Space (AFPEO/SP), is committed to the development of the Follow-on Early Warning System (FEWS) to replace the existing Defense Support Program (DSP), there are potential technical risks and fiscal uncertainties which may adversely impact the schedule or the very future of the FEWS program. The fiscal uncertainties are particularly troublesome in that they are outside the direct control of the Air Force and are driven by higher-level DoD, Congressional, and Executive policies and budget priorities. As a result, it is prudent to fully explore and understand the alternatives available to the Air Force should the FEWS program experience delays or face cancellation. It is within this context, as well as within Aerospace's role as general system engineer for the Air Force, that this report is prepared.

(U) There are two principal objectives to this report: the first is to examine the role of DSP as a safety net for FEWS in the event of FEWS schedule slips or program cancellation as discussed above, and the second is to examine the benefit from potential near-term enhancements to the DSP to provide improved interim capabilities prior to FEWS. Both of these objectives are accomplished by examining the application of Pre-Planned Product Improvements (P^3I) and Technology Insertion options to upgrade the DSP. In order to control cost and risk while simultaneously providing for near-term performance enhancements, alternatives are delineated for progressive P^3I and technology insertion retrofits to DSP-I Satellites 21 through 25, culminating with the advent of DSP-II as Satellite 26. Evolutionary enhancements to the DSP ground segment are also examined, providing options for near-term centralization of processing to reduce Operations and Maintenance (O&M) costs using System B for the Global Mission (Strategic) and Talon Shield for the Theater Mission (Tactical).

(U) In considering the type of evolutionary upgrades to apply to DSP-I, the Draft FEWS Operational Requirements Document (ORD), dated October 1992, was used as the source requirements document. The performance requirements and design/implementation specified in the Draft FEWS ORD were balanced against military utility, cost, risk, and schedule. Integrated Weapons System Management (IWSM) concepts, which encourage consideration of other than 100% solutions (i.e., cost-effective methods to provide the 80% to 90% solution), were also applied in the development of the DSP upgrades. Options for additional DSP performance enhancements to approach the 100% solution (as defined by the Draft FEWS ORD) are provided along with their Life-Cycle Cost (LCC) impact and risk.

(U) This report also compares the cost, risk, performance, and schedule of the FEWS program with the upgraded DSP program (DSP-II). The two programs are also considered in the context of the "Changing Acquisition Environment" as defined by the report: "DoD Space Investment Strategy - A Report To The SAF/AQ", prepared by: AFMC Space And Missile System Center and AFSPACECOM. The nature of the changing acquisition environment and the priority of the system development factors is discussed on the following page.

DSP II Executive Overview · April 1993

UNCLASSIFIED

Page EX-2

Purpose (U)

Explore Alternatives And Methods To Preserve The Air Force's Options For Space-Based Tactical Warning And Attack Assessment Systems

- **Examine The Role Of DSP As A Safety Net For FEWS In The Event Of FEWS Schedule Slips Or Program Cancellation**
    - Evaluate Near-Term DSP-I Enhancements To Provide Improved Interim Capabilities
    - Assess Continuation Of An Evolving DSP As An Alternative To FEWS (Safe Exit)
    - Apply IWSM Concepts To Evaluate Other Than 100% Solutions

- **Evaluate Evolutionary Upgrades To DSP-I**
    - Examine Pre-Planned Product Improvement (P^3I) And Technology Insertion Options
    - Provide Near-Term Performance Enhancements Through Satellite 21-25 Retrofits
    - Balance Performance And Risk Against Cost And Schedule

- **Compare FEWS With Upgraded DSP-I (DSP-II)**
    - Compare Cost, Risk, Performance, And Schedule
    - Provide Options For Additional DSP Performance Enhancements
    - Evaluate Programs Within The Context Of The Changing Acquisition Environment

Changing Acquisition Environment
Priority Of System Development Factors Reordered (U)

From: "DoD Space Investment Strategy - A Report To The SAF/AQ"
Prepared By: AFMC Space And Missile System Center and AFSPACECOM

Cold War Cost Drivers For Space Systems

(U) "The Cold War has made space systems expensive for several reasons. First, for the past thirty years or so, we have been building systems that have never been built before. Whole new technologies have had to be invented to make today's space systems possible. Microelectronics is perhaps the most profound example. Second, the threat driving space systems development was so unacceptable that cost was not an obstacle. We built systems to do the job regardless of cost. We could not afford to consider cost. Performance was the primary driver. Nuclear survivability of spacecraft was an especially difficult requirement that had a significant impact on cost. Third, time was of the essence as space systems were the key to our deterrence capability; to have them in place as soon as possible was essential to our national security. Fourth, security needs forced program development into rigid security compartments."

(U) "The result was a crisis-driven acquisition process. Technology was developed concurrent with system procurement, with resulting delays and redesign. The threat was expanding and system designs were seldom stable. The result was constant redesign to meet the expanding requirement. In addition, security barriers discouraged efforts for commonality across systems or sharing of resources."

Cold War Procurement Rationale No Longer Applies

(U) "Today, we have breathing room for the first time in thirty years. We are now able to look at the threat today, and our systems in context and proceed on a more ordered and efficient path. We can now allow technology to mature to the level where no additional development is needed after a full-scale engineering development has begun. The relaxation of security compartments now allow much cross-program sharing to occur in technologies, standards, and common resources (e.g., common satellite control systems)."

UNCLASSIFIED

UNCLASSIFIED

Changing Acquisition Environment
Priority Of System Development Factors Reordered (U)

Defense Support Program

From: "DoD Space Investment Strategy - A Report To The SAF/AQ"
Prepared By: AFMC Space And Missile Systems Center And AFSPACECOM

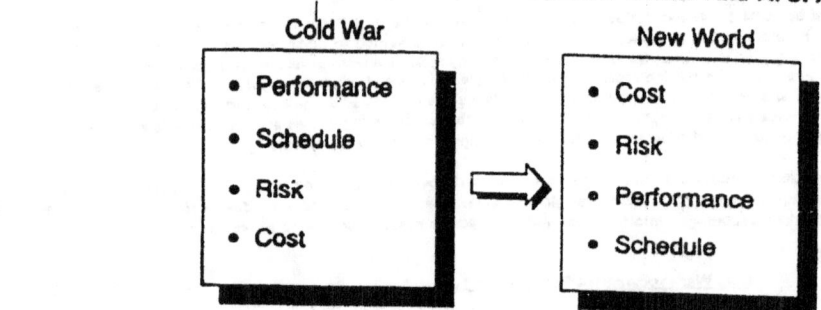

Cold War
- Performance
- Schedule
- Risk
- Cost

New World
- Cost
- Risk
- Performance
- Schedule

Cold War Cost Drivers For Space Systems

"...the threat driving space systems development was so unacceptable that cost was not an obstacle. We built systems to do the job regardless of the cost. We could not afford to consider cost. Performance was the primary driver. Nuclear survivability of spacecraft was an especially difficult requirement that had a significant impact on cost."

Cold War Procurement Rationale No Longer Applies

"Today, we have breathing room for the first time in thirty years. We are now able to look at the threat today, and our systems in context and proceed on a more ordered and efficient path."

UNCLASSIFIED

DSP-II - Executive Overview - April, 1993

DSP History (U)

(U) The Defense Support Program (DSP) has undergone a continuous evolution since its beginnings in the late 1950s. DSP itself evolved from the MIDAS and Program 461 satellite series of the 1960-to-1968 period. The capabilities and performance of both the space- and ground-segments have been continuously evolving to meet the changing threats and user needs of the Cold War era. The satellite constellation has also grown from supporting only surveillance of the eastern hemisphere to providing world-wide coverage, including significant dual- and triple-coverage.

(U) The trend in the evolution of the DSP space segment has been towards larger and more capable satellites with increased Mean Mission Duration (MMD). The latest DSP satellite, DSP-I, is significantly larger and requires significantly more power than its predecessor - the Sensor Evolutionary Development (SED) satellite. SED was actually a retrofit to the Phase II satellites numbers five and six (i.e., 5R and 6R). The increased weight and power of DSP-I is principally to accommodate the LASER Crosslink Subsystem (LCS), Advanced RADEC-I (AR-I), as well as an improved IR sensor which includes Above-The-Horizon (ATH) and Medium Wavelength IR (MWIR) capabilities. These enhancements, plus radiation hardening of the spacecraft, were added to provide the capability for survivability in a massive protracted nuclear war with the Soviet Union.

(U) The DSP ground segment has also evolved during the history of the program. Initially, a single Overseas Ground Station (OGS) was built in Australia to provide processing of the single eastern hemisphere satellite. A few years later, the CONUS Ground Station (CGS) was constructed to support the expanding satellite constellation. In the mid-1980s a third site was built, the European Ground Station (EGS). Also, the Mobile Ground Segment (MGS) was developed to provide ground system survivability. Most recently, in reaction to the tactical missile threat, a new DSP ground station (Talon Shield) is being readied at the National Test Facility (NTF) to provide a prototype for a dedicated DSP tactical processing system.

Aside from growth in the number of ground stations, the ground stations have also grown in their functions and capabilities. The initial monocular processing capabilities of the OGS were expanded at the CGS in the mid-1970s to include "DUAL" processing which provided for the capability to fuse data from two satellites for improved performance against short-duration / low-intensity events. At that time, the short-duration / low-intensity event of concern was the Cold War ████████████████████ the US coast. Today, that threat is gone, but it has been "replaced" with the tactical missile threat. ██
████████████████████████ The Slow Walker m ████████ was fostered by the Navy in the late 1970s and became operational in the early 1980s.

In the late-1980s, the Army became interested in the use of DSP data for tactical missile warning -- due in part to the demonstrated capabilities of the DSP to detect these missiles during the Iran-Iraq "war of the cities". In 1990, the Army embarked on the Tactical Surveillance Demonstration (TSD) program to develop a prototype dedicated DSP tactical processing system. With the enormous success of DSP in providing warning of all Iraqi Scud missile attacks against the allied forces in Desert Storm, the Air Force also became interested in the tactical mission. This interest has been manifested in the Talon Shield effort which builds on the Army's TSD program. Talon Shield also builds on the Navy TENCAP's Radiant Ivory effort to provide multi-source data fusion to enhance ████████████████
████████████

DSP-II - Executive Overview - April 1993

Page EX-6

UNCLASSIFIED

Defense Support Program

DSP History (U)

DSP Has Continuously Evolved For Over Twenty Years Adapting To Changing Threat And New Mission Requirements

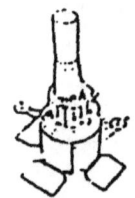

Phase I
- Sats 1-4
- 907 Kgs
- 400 W
- 1.25 Years
- BTH SWIR

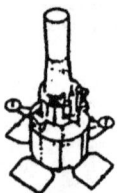

Phase II
- Sats 5-7
- 1043 Kgs
- 480 W
- 2 Years

MOS/PIM
- Sats 8-13
- 1170 Kgs
- 500 W
- 3 Years
- Multi-Orbit Capability

SED
- Sats 5R/6R
- 1685 Kgs
- 664 W
- 3 Years
- Expand BTH
- Adv. RADEC
- Hardening

DSP-I
- Sats 14-22
- 2348 Kgs
- 1225 W
- 5 Years
- ATH
- BTH MWIR
- LCS & MDM

('70s)   ('90s)

- Strategic Ground Processing
- Improved Strategic Capabilities
- Evolving Tactical Systems
  - Army TSD
  - Talon Shield
  - IR&D Efforts

UNCLASSIFIED

DSP-II - Executive Overview - April 1993

DS.
Continuation Of DSP's Evolution (U)

(U) The DSP-II concept is to continue the evolution of the DSP program in order to preserve the Air Force's options for space-based Tactical Warning and Attack Assessment capabilities in the event of technical or fiscal problems with the development of the Follow-on Early Warning System (FEWS). As with any new program of the size and scope of FEWS, there are many technical challenges which can greatly delay the program. Examples of programs which have suffered technical problems and schedule delays include: Milstar, Teal Ruby, DSM, C-17, etc. Also, because of the significant expense associated with a new program start, national budget priorities, as dictated by the President and Congress, may result in schedule extensions or program cancellation in favor of a less-costly alternative.

(U) The Defense Support Program (DSP) has remained in a "holding pattern" for some time now because of the Air Force's interest in pursuing a replacement early warning system. In the early-1980's, the replacement program was known as the Advanced Warning System (AWS). With the advent of SDI, the Boost Surveillance and Tracking System (BSTS) was created to provide Ballistic Missile Defense (BMD) surveillance capabilities. When the BMD goals were abandoned in the late-1980s, the replacement program became known as AWS again. In the early 1990s, the program name was changed to FEWS. As a result, no significant investments have been made in Pre-Planned Product Improvements (P^3I) or technology insertion for the DSP satellite since the development of the DSP-I Satellite 14 in the early 1980s. The Air Force is currently going on contract for "cookie-cutter" DSP-I Satellites 23-25. This lack of investment is resulting in the use of obsolete technology in the production of the DSP satellite, and actually results in higher-than-necessary production costs due to the materials and processes involved (e.g., PbS detectors, off-focal plane multiplexing, outdated electronics, etc.).

(U) Because of the very real technical and fiscal threats to fielding a new early warning system within projected schedules, it is prudent to examine both near- and long-term methods to continue the DSP to provide a viable national capability well into the future. The evolutionary upgrades to DSP described within this report are designed to reflect the new National priorities as defined by: (1) budget realities which will mandate continued reductions in defense spending for the foreseeable future; (2) the post-Cold War New World Order which dictates new defense strategies based on regional conflicts and limited nuclear war potential, and not the massive protracted nuclear war with the now non-existent Soviet Union; and, (3) the evolving threat which is characterized by a proliferation of tactical missiles to third world countries which can threaten US and allied forces.

(U) The evolutionary DSP concept addresses the budget realities by employing Technology Insertion and Pre-Planned Product Improvements (P^3I) to control cost and risk. Progressive retrofits to existing and planned satellites (21 through 25) can be made to provide near-term performance improvements and life extension prior to FEWS. Because of the New World Order which changes the threat from protracted nuclear war-fighting, which requires significant expense to achieve survivability (e.g., on-board processing, LASER crosslinks, etc.), to regional conflicts and limited nuclear war potential, changes to the satellite can be made to significantly reduce weight and power requirements. These changes would enable the use of a smaller launch vehicle, which could save approximately $150 Million per launch. As a direct result of these investments in P^3I and technology insertion, the life expectancy, or Mean Mission Duration (MMD), can also be increased from 5 years to 8.5 years. Thus, if FEWS is significantly delayed or canceled, this evolutionary approach will result in near-term performance improvements and life-extension as well as a low-cost, in-place program for DSP Satellites 26 and beyond.

UNCLASSIFIED

DSP-II
Continuation Of DSP's Evolution (U)

**Continue DSP Evolution To Reflect
Budget Realities, New World Order, And Evolving Threats**

- **Preserve The Air Force's Options**
    - Potential For Problems And Delays In FEWS
    - Budget Priorities May Force Cancellation Of FEWS

- **Provide A Viable DSP Program For The Future**
    - Employ Technology Insertion And P^3I To Control Cost And Risk
        - Implemented Through Evolutionary retrofits To Existing Satellites
    - Reduce Satellite Weight To Enable Utilization Of The Atlas IIAS Medium Launch Vehicle (MLV) For Significant Reduction In DSP Launch Costs
    - Evolve The Ground Segment To Centralize Operations And Reduce O&M Costs

- **Enhance DSP System Performance In Critical Areas**
    - Tactical Missile Performance
    - Tactical Parameter Accuracy
    - "All-Source" Data Fusion To Fully Exploit All National Capabilities

DSP-II Concept

(U) The DSP-II satellite concept is illustrated on the opposite page. It is an evolutionary approach, building on existing DSP sensor and spacecraft designs. Pre-Planned Product Improvements (P³I) and technology insertion are employed to provide a cost-effective and low-risk approach to provide improved performance and increased Mean Mission Duration (MMD). This evolutionary approach also results in a significant weight reduction which enables the utilization of the Atlas II AS Medium Launch Vehicle (MLV), reducing launch costs by approximately $150 Million per launch. Combined with reduced manufacturing costs and the improved MMD, the life-cycle costs of the DSP program are significantly reduced.

(U) The DSP-II spacecraft reuses the GED 5R/6R spacecraft structure which is significantly smaller and lighter than the DSP-I spacecraft structure. The larger DSP-I spacecraft structure was built to accommodate the LASER Crosslink Subsystem (LCS), AR-I (power requirements), and Mission Data Message (MDM) payloads to support the survivability requirements of the Cold War era. In the New World Order, where survivability is no longer paramount, the functions of these payloads can be accomplished via alternative means, specifically: bent-pipes can be used to relay data to the CONUS for consolidated processing at significantly less cost than crosslinks; the GPS endo-atmospheric NUDET detection capability can be used in place of the DSP-based AR-I capability; and, Milstar and other communication systems can be used in place of the Mission Data Message (MDM) subsystem.

(U) The electronic subsystems of the spacecraft will be based on DSP-I electronics. Technology insertion will be applied, however, to update and redesign (for parts obsolescence) the electronics to increase their life, decrease power requirements, and improve manufacturability. The Si solar cells will also be replaced with GaAs/Ge solar cells to improve power generation and end-of-life performance, and a NiH$_2$ battery will also replace the three NiCd batteries used today.

(U) An SDLS is added to the DSP-II spacecraft. This link will be combined with an on-board representative return processor to provide a jam resistant / survivable downlink at the 64Kbps data rate. This link can support Global (strategic) and Theater (tactical) missions, and also (when combined with the on-board representative-return processor) provides a future growth-path for an on-board mission processor and low data rate crosslink should a high-level of survivability become a requirement to counter a future protracted nuclear war threat.

(U) The DSP-II sensor builds on the DSP-I sensor. P³I and technology insertion are used to upgrade specific subsystems such as the focal plane and the thermal control system to improve manufacturability and performance. For example, the current DSP-I focal plane employs PbS detectors and off-focal plane multiplexing. PbS detectors are no-longer manufactured, and off-focal plane multiplexing results in a tedious and costly manufacturing and assembly process. Low-risk technology exists to employ HgCdTe detectors and provide on-focal plane multiplexing to greatly reduce costs and improve performance.

(U) The upgrades to the DSP satellite would be accomplished in an evolutionary manner. Phased upgrades would begin with DSP Satellite 21 and culminate with DSP-II Satellite 26. This phased program provides for a low-risk approach to achieving reduced life-cycle costs and improved performance. An evolutionary approach to improving the ground segment would also be employed, providing near-term cost reduction through centralization of processing within the CONUS. The Global (strategic) mission would be accomplished using an upgraded System 8, and the Theater (tactical) mission would be performed with Talon Shield. In the long-term, a new generation Global and Theater ground system would be developed as an evolutionary growth from both System 8 and Talon Shield. The performance capabilities of the combined space and ground segments would approach the FEWS requirements as defined by the October 1992 Draft FEWS ORD.

UNCLASSIFIED

DSP-II - Executive Overview - April, 1993

UNCLASSIFIED

Defense Support Program

DSP-II Concept (U)

Technology Insertion And P³I Improve Performance While Controlling Cost And Risk
Weight Reductions Enable Utilization Of Atlas IIAS To Significantly Reduce Launch Costs

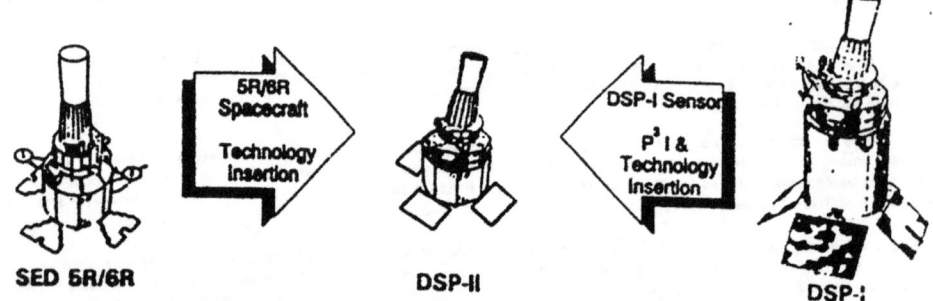

SED 5R/6R → 5R/6R Spacecraft Technology Insertion → DSP-II → DSP-I Sensor P³I & Technology Insertion → DSP-I

- DSP-II Uses 5R/6R Spacecraft Structure
  - DSP-I LCS And MDM Removed
  - SDLS Added
  - Low-Risk Technology Insertion
    - GaAs/Ge Solar Cells
    - NiH₂ Battery
    - Electronics Parts Obsolescence
  - 10-Year Design Life

- Weight Savings Enables Use Of Atlas IIAS Medium Launch Vehicle (MLV)

- DSP-II Builds On DSP-I Sensor
  - AR-I Removed
  - Rep-Return Processor Added
  - P³I Improvements
    - Upgraded Focal Plane
    - Passive Thermal Control
  - Phased Upgrades Begin With Sat 21 And Culminate With Sat 26

- Approaches FEWS ORD Performance

UNCLASSIFIED

DSP II - Executive Overview - April 1993

DSP-II System Overview

An overview of the DSP-II system is illustrated on the opposite page. [redacted] would employ four or five geo-synchronous orbit DSP satellites with coverage augmentation provided by [redacted]. The constellation size would be determined by an assessment of the threat. Remembering that the Earth's surface is 78% water, a properly positioned four-satellite constellation with [redacted] provides for stereo coverage of [redacted] threat regions, and monocular coverage of all possible SLBM areas. The use of geosynchronous orbits enables the [redacted] four-satellite constellation (i.e., the capability for tactical and strategic coverage as discussed above). Use of inclined orbit [redacted] requires five satellites to provide similar coverage. otherwise, predictable [redacted].

The DSP-II system would provide the capability to support all missions: Integrated Tactical Warning and Attack Assessment (ITW&AA), Theater Missile Defense (TMD) surveillance, [redacted]. The performance of the system would meet the vast majority of the FEWS requirements as defined in the Draft FEWS ORD dated October 1992.

(U) From an operational perspective, the system will provide centralized processing within the CONUS. This will eliminate the need for overseas ground stations which have significant operating and personnel expenses. Data from all overseas DSP satellites would be relayed to the CONUS via redundant bent-pipes, just as is done today with data for one of the DSP satellites. The relay stations would be established at existing US facilities overseas, thus requiring only minimal expense in additional manpower for antenna and communication equipment maintenance. It is currently envisioned by AFSPACECOM and the DSP SPO that this connectivity will be established in the next one or two years to eliminate the European Ground Station (EGS) and potentially the Australian Overseas Ground Station (OGS) for a substantial near-term savings in DSP O&M costs.

The current generation survivable Mobile Ground System (MGS) [redacted]. This could also be accomplished in the very near-term, resulting in an additional significant savings in O&M costs. In the [redacted] Theater System (MTS) would be developed to provide an organic in-theater DSP processing capability. This system would permit fusion of DSP data with other organic surveillance systems for improved mission performance and military utility. The [redacted] would be based on a ruggedized version of the Global in-CONUS processing system, with commonality of [redacted]. The MTS DOOR, therefore, serve in a dual role as a "survivable" ground system. Although not [redacted] nuclear exchange, [redacted] could operate through limited nuclear strikes [redacted] capability in-line with the potential future third-world nuclear threat, at significantly [redacted] more expensive survivable system employing crosslinks and on-board mission processing.

DSP-II - Executive Overview - April 1993

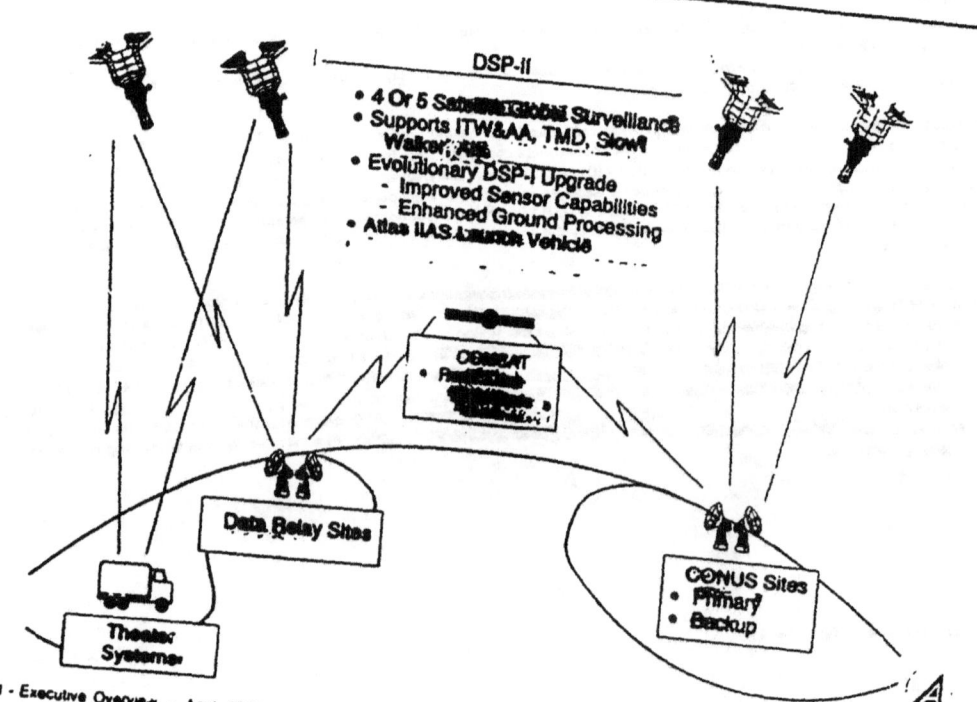

DSP-II System Capabilities (U)

) The evolved DSP system provides considerable mission capabilities to support the needs of the strategic, tactical, and ▬▬▬▬. The combined space and ground segment evolution are specifically designed to support the threat posed in the post-Cold War New World Order. This threat is dominated by an increasing ▬▬▬▬▬ of tactical missiles throughout the third world, particularly in the eastern hemisphere, and by a decreasing emphasis on engagement in a protracted massive global nuclear war with the now non-existent Soviet Union. The evolutionary approach also provides a path for future growth to provide increased survivability by employment of crosslinks and on-board mission processing -- through the SDLS uplink/downlink and the on-board representative-return processor -- without requiring any significant investment at this time.

) DSP-II provides for maximum exploitation of other national capabilities through data fusion. The Global System, which supports all missions, provides for in-CONUS fusion of DSP data with ▬▬▬▬ and All-Source data. The Theater System, which supports the tactical mission and provides a "survivable" backup to the Global System, provides in-theater DSP fusion with organic system assets to maximize military utility to the theater users. Thus, the system capitalizes on the nation's significant investment in national and theater-organic systems through a modest investment in ground processing systems.

) As was demonstrated during Desert Storm, the existing DSP system (without the benefit of Talon Shield) offers significant capability to support theater users. With the addition of capabilities already ▬▬▬▬ by the Army's Tactical Surveillance Demonstration (TSD) and being developed under Talon Shield, DSP's performance will be improved further as shown in the table below. With the envisioned enhancements to the ground segment (including ▬▬▬ and All-Source fusion), and the evolution of the DSP sensor's capabilities (improved sensitivity and Area-Of-Interest (AOI) processor, etc.), DSP-II provides for a cost-conscious, low-risk evolutionary path to achieve the majority of, and in some cases exceed, the performance requirements specified in the FEWS Operational Requirements Document (ORD).

Parameter	▬▬▬	▬▬▬	▬▬▬ TSD	▬▬▬ Talon Shield
Launch Point (CEP)*				
Launch Azimuth (68%ile)				
Launch time (68%ile)				
Initial alert sent (90%ile)				
Man-validated report sent (90%ile)				

DSP-II - Executive Overview - April 1993

DSP-II System Capabilities (U)

- **Supports ITW&AA Mission Requirements**
  - Assured And Timely Global Tactical Warning (TW)
  - Unambiguous And Accurate Attack Assessment (AA)
  - Indefinite Survivability Through HEMP-, Small-, And Medium-Attacks
  - All-Source Fusion Maximizes Exploitation Of National Capabilities

- **Meets Theater Missile Defense Surveillance Needs**
  - Assured And Timely Theater Detection For Warning
  - Accurate State Vector Information For Active Defense
  - Accurate Launch Point Information For Counter-Strike Operations
  - Provides In-Theater Data Fusion With Organic Systems To Maximize Capabilities

- **Supports Slow Walker Mission Requirements**

  - All-Source Fusion Maximizes Capabilities

DSP-II Schedule (U)

The DSP-II schedule through 2006 is shown on the opposite page. The satellite launch dates are derived from the Option 1 space segment transition approach as described in Appendix A - DSP-II Space Segment Details. These dates are based on a satellite GAP availability of 0.9. For the period through 2003, the current three-plus-one-satellite constellation is assumed. For the period beyond 2004, a four-satellite constellation is assumed. The actual constellation size (4, 5, 6) would be determined by an assessment of the threat. Remembering, however, that the Earth's surface is 78% water, a properly positioned four-satellite constellation w[ill p]rovides for stereo coverage of all current tactical missile threat regions, and monocular coverage of all possible SLBM areas. The use of geosynchronous orbits enables the effective use of a four-satellite constellation (i.e., the capability for tactical and strategic coverage as discussed above). [A] three [or] five satellite constellation [would provide similar] coverage, otherwise, predictable coverage gaps would exist. inclined orbits.

(U) Because of the retrofits to DSP-I Satellites 21 through 25, a four-satellite constellation with virtually all DSP-II capabilities (excluding the on-board representative-return processor and the SDLS) would be available in 2003. If a five-satellite DSP constellation is desired, the Satellite 26 launch date could be move to the left one year by providing ATP for DSP-II in early 1997 vice early 1998 as shown.

(U) The sensor and spacecraft retrofit schedules for DSP-I satellites 21 through 25 are also shown. The details of the retrofits are discussed in the "DSP-II Space Segment and Transition Options" section as well as in Appendix A - "DSP-II Space Segment Details".

(U) The Global and Theater System schedules shown are based on the vision that the DSP-II system will achieve operational capability with the launch of the retrofitted Satellite 25, which provides a four-satellite constellation. If required, a five-satellite constellation would become operationally available with the accelerated launch of Satellite 26 in 2004 as discussed above. Because of the evolutionary approach in developing the DSP-II, the evolved existing DSP ground system (System 8 and Talon Shield) will be able to support the DSP-II satellites. Also, the DSP-II Global and Theater Systems will be able to supported the retrofitted DSP-I satellites. Therefore, the schedule for the DSP-II ground segment can be adjusted to the right as dictated by budget priorities without causing a gap in the Global or Tactical missions. Of course, delaying the DSP-II ground segment acquisition will delay new features and enhancements such as the capability for in-theater processing and organic system fusion for the Theater (tactical) mission.

DSP-II - Executive Overview - April 1993

UNCLASSIFIED

DSP-II Schedule (U)

Defense Support Program

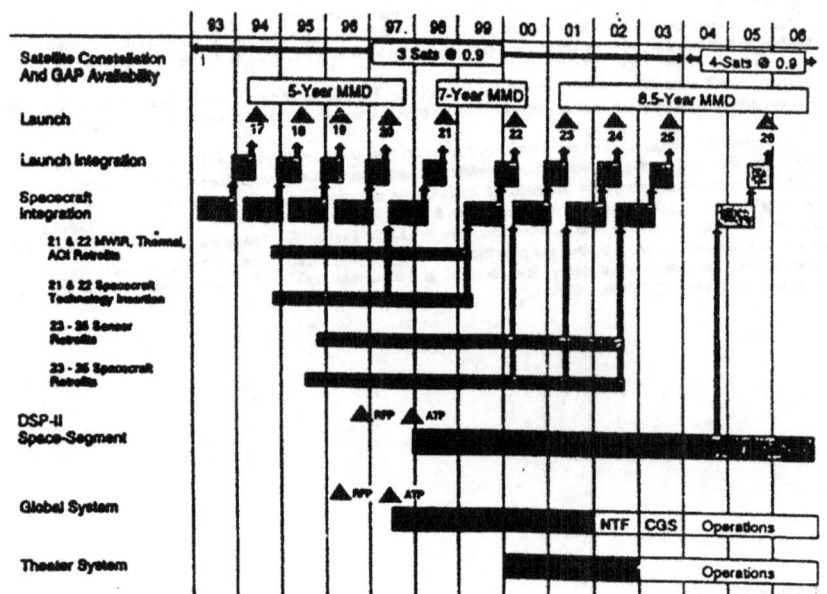

* DSP-II Space-Segment Assumes Satellite 21-25 Technology Insertion And P³I Implemented. Without These, The DSP-II Space-Segment Schedule Must Be Adjusted To The Left Two Years.

UNCLASSIFIED

DSP-II · Executive Overview · April, 1993

Summary Of DSP-II Life Cycle Costs To 2015 (U)

(U) The DSP-II Life-Cycle Costs (LCC) were derived from quasi-independent assessments by The Aerospace Corporation and Tecolote (some specific sensor retrofit and RDT&E costs were also independently estimated by Aerojet Electronic Systems Division). In all instances, the worst-case estimates were used. For example, Aerospace estimated DSP-II spacecraft RDT&E at $200 Million since a previous design was being used (i.e., 5R/6R), but Tecolote estimated $300 Million. As is shown in the table opposite, the $300 Million figure is utilized.

(U) The table shows life-cycle costs for either a four- or five-satellite DSP-II constellation. The number of satellites required is derived by a GAP analysis assuming a point availability of 0.9 for the specified constellation (this is the GAP availability assumed by FEWS). It should be noted that significantly fewer DSP-II satellites are required than for a comparable FEWS constellation through the same timeframe. This is because the retrofitted DSP-I satellites 21 through 25, which have comparable capabilities to DSP-II, are available with this approach.

(U) Operations and Maintenance (O&M) costs are shown from 2003 through 2015. These costs are assessed at about $150 Million/year and become effective with the activation of the DSP-II Global and Theater Systems which centralize operations within the CONUS and provide a mobile theater system. This is a conservative estimate based on today's costs of maintaining three DSP ground stations (two overseas) and an autonomous survivable Mobile Ground System (MGS) with different hardware and software than the fixed ground systems. The DSP-II ground system provides standardization between the Global and Theater system hardware and software. An additional $200 Million is added for a five-satellite constellation in order to be extra conservative.

(U) The life-cycle costs also assume that the Option 1 space segment transition approach as described in Appendix A - Space Segment Details is utilized. If another approach is used, it can impact the transition costs. Selection of another transition approach could also impact the DSP-II RDT&E costs and risks.

(U) The life-cycle costs are controlled by early identification and consideration of the DSP system cost drivers as shown in the figure on the right. In considering the type of evolutionary upgrades to apply to DSP-I, the performance requirements and design/implementation specified in the Draft FEWS ORD were balanced against military utility, cost, risk, and schedule. Integrated Weapons System Management (IWSM) concepts, which encourage consideration of other than 100% solutions (i.e., cost-effective methods to provide the 80% to 90% solution), were also applied in the development of the DSP upgrades. Options for additional DSP performance enhancements to approach the 100% solution (as defined by the Draft FEWS ORD) are provided along with their Life-Cycle Cost (LCC) impact and risk in a subsequent section.

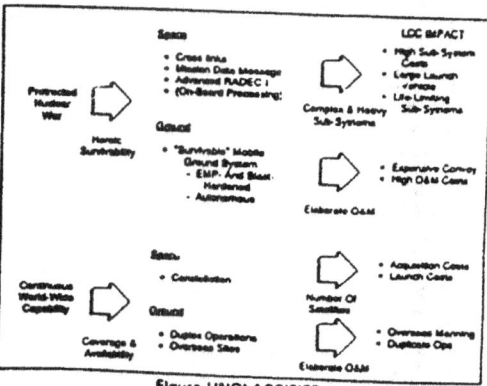

Figure UNCLASSIFIED

UNCLASSIFIED

Summary Of DSP-II Life Cycle Costs To 2015 (U)

Subsystem		3-Sat DSP-II Constellation	5-Sat DSP-II Constellation
No Of DSP-II Satellites[1]	--	7	11
Spacecraft			
Non-Recurring (RDT&E)	300	300	300
Average Unit Cost	80	560	880
Sensor			
Non-Recurring (RDT&E)	250	250	250
Average Unit Cost	140	980	1,540
Launch Segment			
Launch Vehicle	110	770	1,210
Payload Launch Services	40	280	440
Ground Segment (Non-Recurring)			
Software & Integration	400	400	400
Global System	200	200	200
Theater System	150	150	150
O&M (2003 Thru 2015)	--	2,000	2,200
Transition (DSP-I To DSP-II)[2]	3,720	3,720	3,720
Total LCC (FY93 $ Mil)	--	9,610	11,290

[1] Number of DSP-II satellites required beyond Satellite 25 for 0.9 GAP Point Availability Through 2015
[2] Assumes Space-Segment Transition Option 1 (Maximum cost using Option 3 is $4,440 Mil)

Comparison Costs Of FEWS And [DSP-II] Satellites (U)

(U) The costs of the DSP-I, DSP-II, and FEWS satellites are shown in the chart on the opposite page. This chart also illustrates the cost and weight history of the DSP satellites. The FEWS costs shown are from: "The Cost and Operational Effectiveness Analysis (COEA) for the Advanced Space-Based Tactical Warning And Attack Assessment System", prepared by: Space-Based Warning Division Directorate of Aerospace Control and Force Application, Deputy Chief Of Staff/Plans, Air Force Space Command; dated 17 September 1991. The costs from this document in FY91 dollars were adjusted to FY93 dollars. Launch costs shown are based on Titan IV/IUS for DSP-I, Atlas IIAS/Star 48B-18 for DSP-II, and Titan IV (with no upper stage) for FEWS. Included in the launch costs for each satellite is $40 Million in contractor payload launch services. This is based on DSP experience.

(U) As is shown in the chart opposite and the table to the right, the cost of a DSP-II satellite on-orbit is approximately 40% less than the cost of a FEWS satellite on-orbit ($390 Mil versus $680 Mil). This is due to the reduced complexity of the DSP-II satellite compared with FEWS and the savings from the use of the Atlas IIAS versus the Titan IV.

(U) As is illustrated by the DSP cost and weight history graphs, the DSP-II cost estimates are consistent with past DSP experience. The estimates of FEWS satellite cost as shown in $K/Kg is also consistent with DSP history and the increased complexity of the FEWS satellite compared with DSP.

(U) Costs can also be evaluated in terms of dollars per Satellite-Year On-Orbit as show in the table to the right. Because of the improved Mean Mission Duration (MMD) of DSP-II and the reduced launch costs, DSP-II provides a 62% savings in life-cycle costs compared with DSP-I -- as measured in terms of the costs per satellite-year on-orbit ($46 Mil versus $120 Mil). DSP-II also provide a 42% savings compared with FEWS ($46 Mil versus $80 Mil).

	DSP-I	DSP-II	FEWS
Satellite MMD	5 Years	8.5 Years	8.5 Years
Dry Weight (Kgs)	2188 Kgs	1546 Kgs	2700 Kgs
Avg. Unit Cost (FY 93 $Mil)	290	220	420
Launch Cost (FY93 $Mil)	310	150	260
Avg. Unit Cost/Kg (FY93 $K/Kg)	133	142	156
Cost Per Sat On-Orbit (FY93 $Mil)	600	390	680
Cost Per Sat-Year On-Orbit (FY93 $Mil)	120	46	80

Table UNCLASSIFIED

UNCLASSIFIED

Comparative Costs Of FEWS And DSP-II Satellites (U)

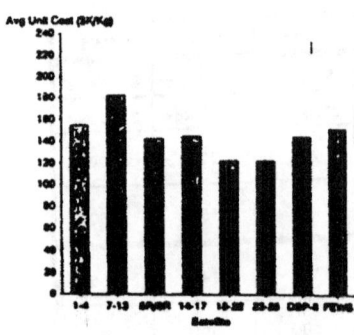

	DSP-I	DSP-II	FEWS
Dry Weight (Kgs)	2186	1546	2700
Avg. Unit Cost (FY 93 $Mil)	290	220	420
Launch Cost (FY93 $Mil)	310	150	260
Avg. Unit Cost/Kg (FY93 $K/Kg)	133	142	156
Cost Per Sat On-Orbit (FY93 $Mil)	600	390	680

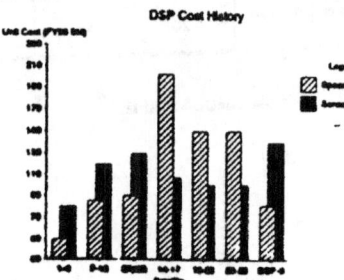

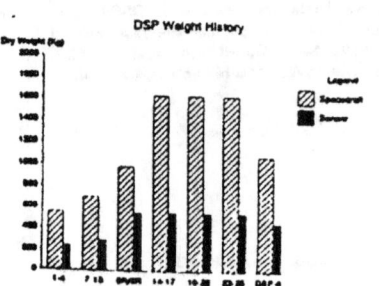

DSP-II Executive Overview - April, 1993

UNCLASSIFIED

Page EX-21

Comparative Summary FEWS And DSP-II (U)

(U) A comparative summary of FEWS and DSP-II is shown in the table on the opposite page. FEWS cost, risk, performance, and schedule are compared with various-sized constellations of DSP-II satellites, with and without ____. The life-cycle cost data for DSP-II were derived from quasi-independent assessments by The Aerospace Corporation and Tecolote (some specific sensor retrofit and RDT&E costs were also independently estimated by Aerojet Electronic Systems Division). The cost analysis is discussed in Appendix C - DSP-II Cost And Schedule. The ____ costs, $1.1 Billion LCC, were derived from the FEWS COEA. The FEWS costs are also obtained from the FEWS COEA (adjusted to FY93 dollars). It should be noted that DSP-II life-cycle costs are for operations through 2015; the FEWS costs are for operations through only 2010 as specified in the FEWS COEA. No effort was made herein to project these costs through 2015. However, it is obvious that substantial addition satellite procurement and O&M costs can be expected for FEWS to operate through 2015.

(U) The 95-99 Five Year Defense Plan (FYDP) costs for DSP-II are based on the DSP-II schedule and cost previously described on pages EX 16 through EX-19 and as described in Appendix C - DSP-II Cost And Schedule. The FEWS 95-99 FYDP costs are from the FEWS program plan dated February 1993. The by-year 95-99 FYDP costs are shown in the table below along with the savings from DSP-II. This table assumes a four-satellite DSP constellation. For a five-satellite DSP-II constellation, $0.1 Billion must be added to the FYDP. Whether or not ____ is to be included does not impact the 95 - 99 FYD. ____. If 1994 costs are included, DSP-II will save an additional $ 225 Million compared with FEWS.

FEWS Versus Four-Satellite DSP-II Constellation 95-99 FYDP (U)

	FY 95	FY 96	FY 97	FY 98	FY 99	Total
FEWS ($ Million)	$ 365	$ 890	$ 1,042	$ 1,202	$ 1,370	$ 4,869
DSP-II ($ Million)	$ 80	$ 120	$ 180	$ 340	$ 280	$ 1,000
Savings ($ Million)	$ 285	$ 770	$ 862	$ 862	$ 1,090	$ 3,869

Table UNCLASSIFIED -- FOR OFFICIAL USE ONLY

(U) The overall risk of the DSP-II is assessed as low due to the evolutionary approach to the development of both the space and ground segments. Pre-Planned Product Improvements (P³I) and technology insertion are applied to phase-in improvements via retrofit to DSP I Satellites 21 through 25. The DSP-II ground segment is an evolutionary development based on System 8 and Talon Shield. FEWS technical risks are from the COEA and are discussed in the main section of the report on pages 96 and 97.

(U) The performance assessment for DSP-II is based on the analysis described in detail in Appendix D - DSP-II Performance Assessment. The FEWS performance assessment of 99% of the ORD requirements is based on the inability of the competing designs to meet the following ORD specified requirements:

Comparative Summary
FEWS And DSP-II (U)

Characteristics	5 DSP-II + OTHER	4 DSP-II + OTHER	5 DSP-II	4 DSP-II	FEWS
Life Cycle Cost (FY 93 Dollars)	$ 12.4 (Bil) (To 2015)	$ 10.7 (Bil) (To 2015)	$ 11.3 (Bil) (To 2015)	$ 9.6 (Bil) (To 2015)	$ 18.4 (Bil)[1] (To 2010)
95 - 99 FYDP[2] (FY 93 Dollars)	$1.1 (Bil)	$1.0 (Bil)	$1.1 (Bil)	$1.0 (Bil)	$4.9 (Bil)
Technical Risk	Low	Low	Low	Low	Med-High
~ % Of The Draft FEWS ORD Satisfied	98%	95%	88%	85%	99%
Schedule For FOC	2004	2003	2004	2003	

[1] FEWS Cost (LCC To 2010) FEWS COEA Dated 17 September 1991 (Adjusted For FY 93 Dollars)
[2] The 1995 to 1999 Five Year Defense Plan (FYDP) costs are the required deltas to the existing DSP budget-line

Conclusions (U)

(U) As is illustrated throughout this report, significant value can be received from the investment in DSP technology insertion and Pre-Planned Product Improvement (P³I) regardless of the destiny of FEWS. The implementation of evolutionary retrofits to the DSP-I satellites will provide significant return on investment. Retrofits to DSP-I Satellites 21 through 25 will provide 14.5 years of DSP MMD extension to provide a cushion for technical or fiscal delays in FEWS. The retrofits will also provide near-term performance improvements, especially for the tactical mission. Furthermore, the retrofits may provide risk reduction for FEWS by providing empirical data on low-intensity MWIR events and Earth background, for example.

(U) Upgrades to the DSP System 8 and Talon Shield ground processing systems also provide near-term performance improvements and cost savings. Continuing Talon Shield to its logical conclusion -- an operational system -- will provide significant capabilities to support the theater users. Centralization of DSP ground processing within the CONUS will result in substantial savings in O&M costs by enabling the closure of overseas ground stations.

(U) The implementation of Pre-Planned Product Improvements (P³I) and technology insertion to provide enhanced capabilities while controlling cost and risk is the type of continuous process and product improvement envisioned by Integrated Weapon System Management (IWSM) and Total Quality Management (TQM). The DSP program has suffered for almost a decade from the overriding principle that it is to be replaced "soon": in the early-1980s it was the Advanced Warning System (AWS), in the mid-1980s it was the Boost Surveillance and Tracking System (BSTS), in the late-1980s the Advance Warning System (AWS) reemerged as the replacement, and today the DSP replacement is the Follow on Early Warning System (FEWS). During this time, the successful evolutionary upgrade approach which had been followed since the DSP's beginnings in late 1960s was abandoned. DSP still has a significant future regardless of the destiny of FEWS - DSP will remain the nation's principal early warning system for a minimum of ten to fifteen years. If the potential for technical and fiscal problems with FEWS is considered, a viable DSP program will be required for many more years. In this light, beginning the process of implementing P³I and technology insertion to DSP seems prudent and within the national interest.

(U) While the Follow-on Early Warning System offers the potential for greater performance than possible with the proposed DSP-II program, particularly with respect to mass-attack survivability provided by the use of crosslinks and on-board mission processing, DSP-II is a feasible alternative to FEWS. DSP-II reflects the budget realities dictated by the changing national priorities and policies established by the President and Congress. It also reflects the post-Cold War New World Order which is no longer dominated by the prospect of a protracted nuclear war with the non-existent Soviet Union. If the world order again changes, DSP-II offers growth alternatives to provide additional capabilities (such as increased survivability to support a protracted nuclear war) without requiring any significant investment at this time.

UNCLASSIFIED

Conclusions (U)

- **Significant Value In DSP Technology Insertion And P³I Investment Regardless Of FEWS Destiny**

    - $180 Million Investment Returns 14.5 Years Of DSP MMD Extension By Sat 25
        - Provides Continuation Of Early Warning Capabilities If FEWS Delayed
        - Provides Near-Term Enhancements For Global And Theater Missions

    - Provides Low-Cost Program For Satellites 26+ If FEWS Is Significantly Delayed
        - Technical Problems
        - Program Stretch-Out Due To Budget Priorities

- **DSP-II Is A Feasible Alternative To FEWS**

    - Near-Term Savings Of ~ $4 Billion In 95-99 FYDP
    - Potential For > $10 Billion Savings In Life-Cycle Costs Through 2015
    - Low-Risk Solution To Meet Global And Theater Requirements
    - Consistent With Budget Realities And Post-Cold War New World Requirements
    - Growth Paths Available To Address Future Threats

DSP-II Reflects The Changing Acquisition Environment (U)

(U) As is discussed in "DoD Space Investment Strategy - A Report To The SAF/AQ", the Cold War procurement rationale no longer applies. Performance is no longer paramount - cost and risk are now the principal factors. The continued evolution of the Defense Support Program and the DSP-II concept reflect this principal tenet. The evolutionary approach for upgrading the DSP system provides for a cost-conscious, low-risk program to simultaneously achieve significant budget savings and performance improvements in-line with the post-Cold War world. If the world again changes, DSP-II provides growth alternatives to support additional capabilities (such as increased survivability to support a protracted nuclear war) without requiring any significant investment at this time.

(U) As illustrated in the figure on the right, the DoD RDT&E budget planned by the Bush Administration had a steady decrease to provide a total DoD budget reduction of approximately $50 billion through 1998. The Clinton Administration, however, is calling for significantly larger reductions as shown in the table below. When the recent pay freeze and alternative inflation adjustments are considered, the Administration projects an $88 to $100 billion cut through 1998. The Air Force share can be assumed to be on the order of $20 to $30 billion. The cost difference between DSP-II and FEWS represents approximately 15% of the total required Air Force reductions.

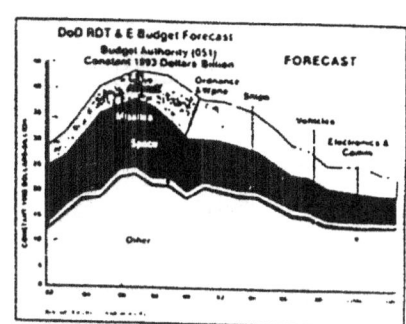

Figure UNCLASSIFIED

Proposed DoD Budget Reductions And FEWS Versus Four-Satellite DSP-II Constellation (U)

	FY 94	FY 95	FY 96	FY 97	FY 98	FY 99	Total
Proposed DoD Budget Reduction ($ Billion)	$11.6	$16.1	$24.8	36.8	39.8	?	$129.1
FEWS ($ Million)	$226	$365	$890	$1,042	$1,202	$1,370	$5,094
DSP-II ($ Million)	$0	$80	$120	$180	$340	$280	$1,000
Savings ($ Million)	$225	$285	$770	$862	$862	$1,090	$4,094

Table UNCLASSIFIED -- FOR OFFICIAL USE ONLY

UNCLASSIFIED

UNCLASSIFIED

DSP-II Reflects The Changing Acquisition Environment (U)

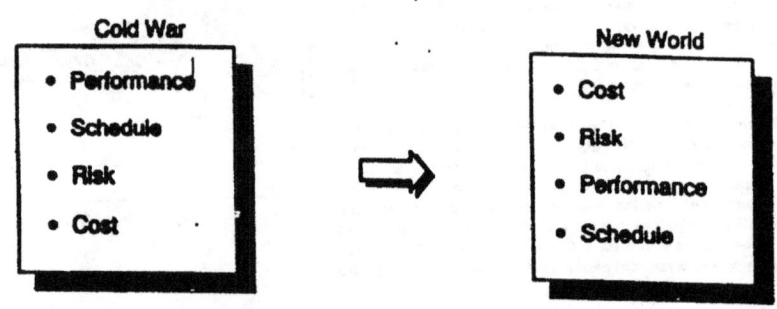

Cold War
- Performance
- Schedule
- Risk
- Cost

⇒

New World
- Cost
- Risk
- Performance
- Schedule

- Potential For > $10 Billion Savings
- Low Technical Risk
- 85% To 98% Solution
- Low-Risk Schedule

UNCLASSIFIED

APPENDIX E

DSP-II / Brilliant Eyes Synergy (U)

April 23, 1993

UNCLASSIFIED

Defense Support Program

Agenda (U)

- Executive Summary

- Potential BE Enhancements To Maximize Synergy

- DSP-II / BE Synergistic System Operational Concept

- Performance Assessment

- Cost Assessment

- Potential BE Cost And Risk Reductions

- Summary

UNCLASSIFIED

Purpose And Background (U)

(U) The purpose of the DSP / Brilliant Eyes synergy study is to explore alternatives to the current Air Force plan of acquiring separate FEWS and Brilliant Eyes systems. FY92 Congressional language has directed the Air Force to examine its approach to determine if it is the most cost-effective solution in the light of the post-Cold War New World Order and then-President Bush's proposed defense budget reductions. Since that time, President Clinton has called for even deeper defense budget cuts, thus greatly increasing the importance of these issues.

(U) The DSP / BE Synergy concepts presented within this appendix were an outgrowth of the DSP/Brilliant Eyes Synergy Study conducted between November, 1992 and February, 1993 in response to tasking from the Office of the Secretary Of Defense (OSD) and SAF/AQ to examine synergy issues and concepts between DSP, FEWS, and Brilliant Eyes. The results of the DSP/BE synergy study were rejected by the study's Steering Committee and the AFPEO/SP because the synergistic DSP/BE system failed to meet all of the design and implementation detail specified by the Draft Follow-on Early Warning System (FEWS) Operational Requirements Document (ORD). In particular, the synergistic DSP/BE system failed to provide crosslinks between all satellites and on-board mission processing on all satellites. In the proposed concept, only Brilliant Eye's satellites had crosslinks and on-board mission processing. Thus, these results were not carried forward to AFSPACECOM, SAF/AQ, nor the OSD. They are documented herein, however, so that when a re-evaluation of the protracted nuclear warfighting survivability requirements driving crosslinks and on-board mission processing is conducted -- in light of budget priorities and the New World Order -- these ideas will have been preserved and available for further study and/or implementation.

(U) The DSP-II / BE Synergy concept presented herein was jointly developed by personnel from The Aerospace Corporation and Aerojet Electronic Systems Division. Cost analysis was conducted by Aerospace, Aerojet, and Tecolote. The detailed study report "DSP/BE Synergy Study Task III Final Briefing (U)", Report No. 10168, dated 10 February 1993, is available from Aerojet. The point of contact is Mr. Bill Mullooly, DSP Program Manager. The address is:

Aerojet Electronic Systems Division
1100 W. Hollyvale
P.O. Box 296
Azusa, CA 91702

UNCLASSIFIED

Purpose And Background (U)

- **Examine Potential Synergy Between DSP-II and Brilliant Eyes**
  - Provide A Synergistic System Which Meets FEWS And GPALS Requirements
  - Exploit Synergistic Capabilities Where Possible To Control Cost And Risk

- **Study Conducted In Response To FY92 Congressional Language**
  - Why Multiple Space-Based IR Systems (DSP, FEWS, And BE)?
  - Can We Save Money By Combining Functions?

- **Conclusions Of DSP-II / BE Study Rejected By AFPEO/SP**
  - Did Not Meet All Draft FEWS ORD Design/Implementation Specifications
    - Crosslinks Between All Satellites
    - On-Board Mission Processing On All Satellites

- **Synergy Study Results Preserved Herein For Future Evaluation**
  - DSP-II / BE Is A Viable Option When Survivability Requirements Are Re-Evaluated
    - "Heroic" Survivability Drives Crosslinks And On-Board Processing
    - Is This Required In The Post-Cold War New World Order?

DSP-II / BE Synergy Concept Overview (U)

The proposed DSP-II / BE concept is designed to exploit the inherent synergistic features of the two systems to maximize performance while simultaneously maintaining reasonable costs and technical risks. To accomplish this, the concept relies on the fundamental intrinsic characteristics of both systems. Specifically, the high-altitude segment (DSP-II) is relied upon to provide survivable global surveillance from geosynchronous orbit. From its _____ BE is relied upon to provide highly-accurate tracking throughout a missile's powered flight as well as tracking of the _____ rvents. Although not as survivable in low-Earth orbit as DSP-II in geosynchronous orbit, the BE data would be available during the most critical decision making time - the transition from peace-time (pre-attack) to global nuclear war (trans-attack).

The proposed DSP-II constellation will consist of four geosynchronous orbit DSP-II satellites. This constellation will provide monocular geometric coverage of the earth and _____ -stereo coverage. DSP-II polar coverage will be accomplished using Above The Horizon (ATH) detectors, and f _____ DSP-II will also host the exo-atmospheric _____ On-board data processing would be employed to reduce the down link data rate to ≈ 64 Kbit for transmission via SDLS. If survivability concerns dictate, the SDLS data could be relayed from overseas mobile relay terminals via MILSTAR to the CONUS for survivable mission processing. The 1.5 Mbit S-band down link is also retained to provide data to support all mission requirements during _____ band data is also relayed from overseas to the CONUS for processing.

The proposed Brilliant Eyes constellation is the government baseline configuration of _____ in each of _____. The altitude of the constellation is _____ a. BE will provide surveillance of the polar region as well as theater regions, fixed-site ICBMs, mobile ICBM bases, submarine patrol regions, and areas in which DSP-II suffers solar degradation. BE will also accept cuing from DSP-II to other areas where targets are detected. Minor modifications to the government baseline system are made to enable the BE to process up to _____ targets for enhanced Attack Assessment information. An additional modification is made to the starring sensor to add a SWIR linear array focal plane to support the FEW _____ quirements for _____ second revisit rate / high-sensitivity Area-Of-Interest (AOI) surveillance. It is recommended, however, that the FEWS _____ requirements be re-examined in the context of the DSP-II / BE capabilities to determine if this modification is actually required.

Ground processing for all of the missions is accomplished in the CONUS as well as in-theater for the tactical missions. The ground processing segment consists of two fixed-sites (primary and backup) as well as five mobile theater systems to provide tactical mission processing as well as a dual-use survivable backup to the Global System. Centralized data fusion of DSP-II and BE will maximize the performance of the system.

(U) Technical risks are controlled through the implementation of only minor modifications to the baseline DSP system (DSP-I) and the government baseline BE system. Cost control is accomplished through DSP weight reductions which enable utilization of the Atlas MLV which reduces launch costs by approximately $150 Million per launch. Because BE is not required to be survivable, additional shielding is not required. This maintains BE satellite weight near the government baseline which enables launch of four BE satellites on a Delta.

Appendix E · DSP II / Brilliant Eyes Synergy   April 1993

Page E 6

DSP-II / BE Synergy Concept Overview (U)

Defense Support Program

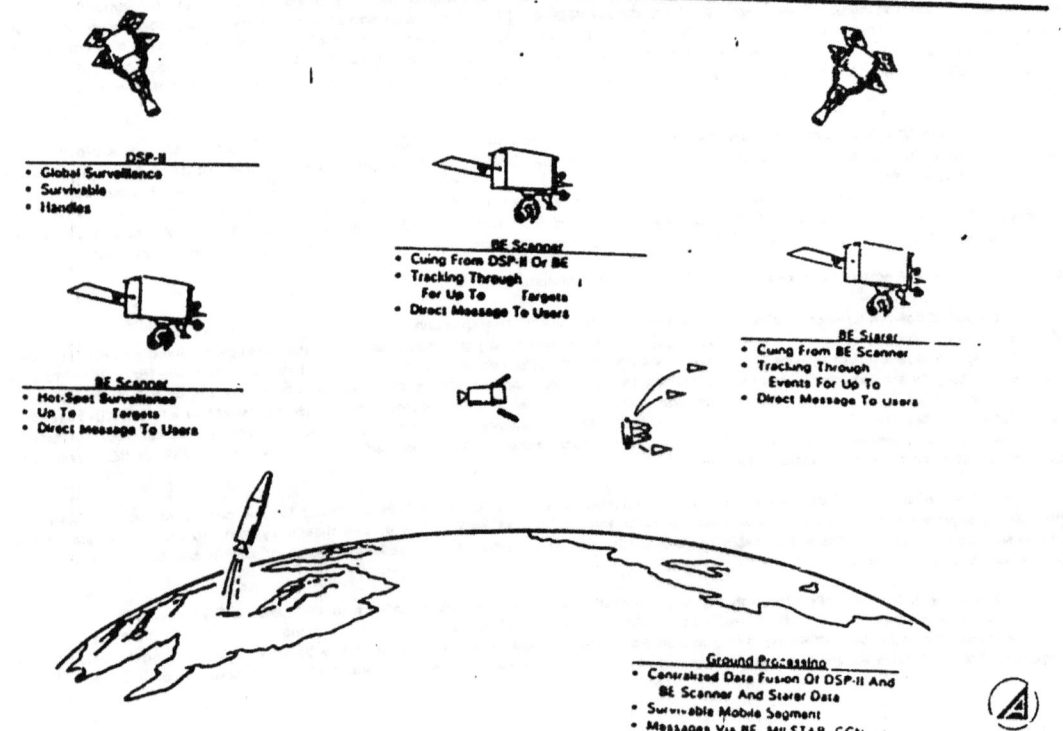

Appendix E - DSP-II / Brilliant Eyes Synergy - April, 1993

DSP-II / BE S[ynerg]y Overview - Missile Detectio[n a]nd Tracking (U)

The synergistic characteristics of the DSP-II and BE systems are exploited to provide missile detection and tracking as shown in the illustration. DSP-II, which provides global surveillance, has primary responsibility for initial detection of a missile launch to provide Tactical Warning (TW). BE has primary responsibility to track the missile through burn-out, and also to detect and track _____ events to provide Attack Assessment (AA) information.

DSP-II has a secondary responsibility to provide data through that segment of a missile's flight which is observable by the DSP-II sensor. This data is combined with BE observations to enhance Attack Assessment (AA) capabilities

BE also has secondary responsibilities which include missile detection in areas of degraded DSP-II coverage as well as providing DSP-II missile detection conformation and additional IR observations to enhance tactical parameter accuracy.

DSP-II / BE Synergy Overview - Missile Detection And Tracking (U)

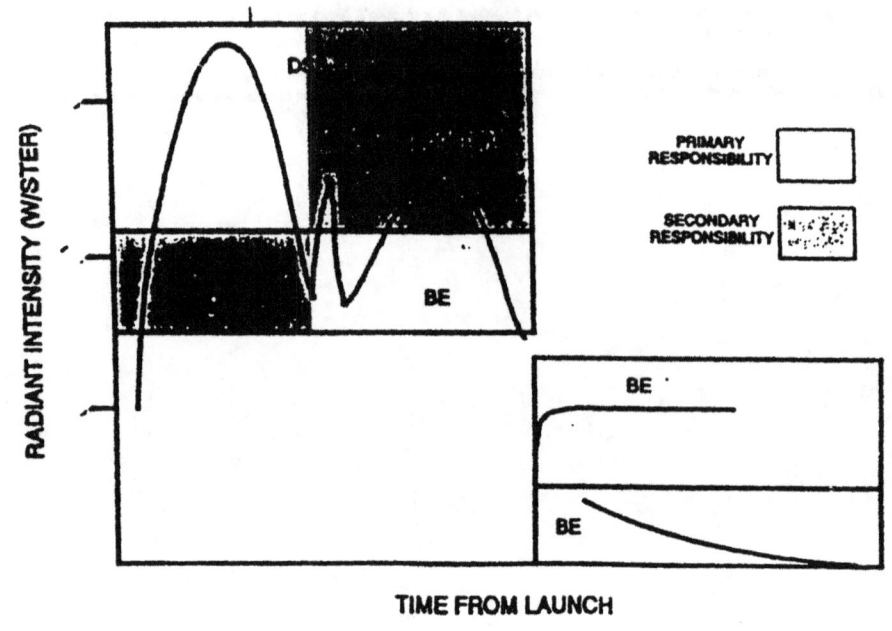

Appendix E - DSP-II / Brilliant Eyes Synergy - April, 1993

DSP-II / BE Synergistic System Overview (U)

The characteristics of the DSP-II and BE systems are delineated in the illustration. The DSP-II constellation will consist of four geosynchronous orbit satellites. This provides for monocular geometric coverage of _____ of the earth and _____ stereo coverage. Modifications to the baseline DSP system (DSP-I) are minimized to control cost and risk as described in the previous sections of this report.

The BE system closely follows the government baseline with a few minor changes which include: additional signal processing to enable processing of 200 targets and a linear array SWIR focal with the BE staring sensor to provide additional TI and MASINT capabilities. The _____ satellite BE constellation combined with the 4-satellite DSP-II constellation provides _____, monocular and stereo coverage of the earth.

(U) The ground segment combines DSP-II and BE data processing to fully exploit the synergistic capabilities of the system. The DSP-II data processing will be an evolution of current DSP ground processing programs (System 8, Talon Shield, and MGS) and will also incorporate lessons learned from System 1. Centralized data fusion will merge the DSP-II and BE data to maximize system performance. A mobile theater processing system provides for enhanced tactical mission support as well as a dual-use system to provide a survivable backup to the Global System.

(U) The combined system provides the capability to meet all FEWS mission performance requirements as defined in the draft FEWS Operational Requirements Document (ORD). Specific system design delineated in the draft ORD, such as on-board mission data processing and the utilization of crosslinks, is not necessarily implemented (BE provides on-board mission processing and crosslinks, DSP-II does not). This design direction, however, does not appear appropriate for a requirements document. Such issues should be addressed through system design studies which assess the cost and risk of alternatives for implementing the actual mission requirements (timeliness, accuracy, etc.). Furthermore, in order to exploit the synergistic features of the DSP-II/Brilliant Eyes system, it is necessary to utilize ground-based processing. This is because of the extreme difficulty, if not impossibility, of implementing crosslinks between the low-Earth orbit (LEO) BE constellation and the geosynchronous-orbit DSP-II constellation (requirements for bandwidth, power, etc. would make such an approach infeasible). Considering that crosslinks and on-board processing are primarily to address protracted nuclear war fighting requirements, and that such requirements seem out of place in the post-Cold War New World Order, these requirements should be re-evaluated.

Defense Support Program DSP-II / BE Synergistic System Overview (U)

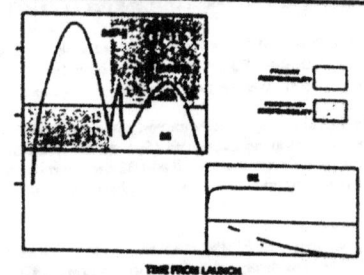

TIME FROM LAUNCH

DSP-II	BE SCANNER	BE STARER
• 4 Satellite Constellation	• Satellite Constellation	• Second AOI Revisit
• Geo-Synchronous Orbit	• km Orbit	• SWIR NET
• 10 Second Revisit Rate	• Second Revisit	• MWIR NET
ATH SWIR NET	• SWIR NET	• M-LWIR NET
8TH SWIR NET	• MWIR NET	• LWIR NET
• r BTH MWIR NET	• Target Capability	• VIS NET
• Target Capability	(Radius) Hot Spot	• Target Capability
• 1.5 Mbit S-Band Down Link	• DSP-II Cues To Other Areas	• BE Scanner Provides Cue
• 64 Kbit SDLS Down Link	• Direct Data To Users	• Direct Data To Users

• Centralized DSP-II And BE Data Fusion	• DSP-II Data Via Ground-Based Relays
• Discrete Reports For　　　argets	• BE Data Direct From BE Constellation
• Summary Reports For　　　argets	• Mobile Theater Segment Provides Survivability

Appendix E - DSP-II / Brilliant Eyes Synergy - April, 1993

Conclusions (U)

The DSP-II / BE synergistic system is capable of meeting both the GPALS and the FEWS ORD-specified performance requirements. Minor regrets in meeting some aspects of performance as specified by the draft FEWS ORD are more than offset by the utility afforded by the multi-spectral, high-sensitivity BE staring sensor which has capabilities well in excess of the proposed FEWS designs.

(U) The DSP-II / BE system does not meet all of the design and implementation detail specified in the draft FEWS ORD. Specifically, the DSP-II satellites do not employ crosslinks or on-board mission processing — Brilliant Eyes does, however. The requirements for crosslinks and on-board mission processing are driven by survivability concerns and reflect the Cold War mentality of engaging in a protracted massive global nuclear war with the Soviet Union. The Cold War is over and the Soviet Union no longer exists. These requirements must be re-evaluated in the light of the New World Order and defense budget realities.

(U) In addition to these issues, it is not possible to achieve a synergistic system by using crosslinks and on-board processing. This is because of the difficulty, if not impossibility of crosslinking the geosynchronous orbit DSP-II satellites to the Low Earth Orbit (LEO) BE satellites (requirements for bandwidth, power, etc. make this infeasible). Therefore, ground processing is the only way synergy can be achieved. Ground processing also maximizes the exploitation of other surveillance systems, including national assets and in-theater organic systems. The Global System provides for fusion of DSP-II / BE data with All-Source and Earth and weather imagery data to provide improved performance and capabilities. This cannot be achieved on-board since connectivity from these assets cannot be established to an on-board mission processor. The Theater System provides for fusion of DSP-II data with in-theater organic assets such as radars and passive sensor systems. This provides the theater commanders with enhanced organic capabilities. Again, this cannot be accomplished on-board.

FEWS, Brilliant Eyes, And Four-Satellite DSP-II Constellation 95-99 FYDP (U)

	FY 95	FY 96	FY 97	FY 98	FY 99	Total
FEWS ($ Million)	$385	$890	$1,042	$1,202	$1,370	$4,859
BE ($ Million)	$318	$295	$260	$445	$700	$2,018
DSP-II ($ Million)	$80	$120	$180	$340	$280	$1,000
FEWS + BE	$683	$1185	$1,302	$1,647	$2,070	$6,887
DSP-II + BE	$398	$415	$440	$785	$980	$3,018
Savings ($ Million)	$285	$770	$862	$862	$1,090	$3,869

Table UNCLASSIFIED -- FOR OFFICIAL USE ONLY

UNCLASSIFIED

Defense Support Program

Conclusions (U)

- **DSP-II / Brilliant Eyes Synergistic System Meets ITW&AA And GPALS Performance Requirements**
    - Meets Or Exceeds Draft FEWS ORD And GPALS Performance Requirements
        - Strategic And Tactical Missions

- **System Does Not Meet All Draft FEWS ORD-Specified Design/Implementation Details**
    - Cold War "Heroic" Survivability
        - No Crosslinks Between DSP-II Satellites
        - No On-Board Mission Processing On DSP-II Satellites
    - Requirements Should Be Re-Evaluated
        - Synergistic System Cannot Be Accomplished On-Board
            - Difficult To Crosslink Low-Earth Orbit And Geosynchronous Satellites
        - Do These Requirements Make Sense In The Post-Cold War New World Order?

- **Synergistic System Offers Potential For $10 Billion LCC Savings Compared With Separate FEWS And BE Acquisitions**
    - ≈ $4 Billion Savings In 95-99 FYDP
    - > $6 Billion Savings In 2000-2015

UNCLASSIFIED

Agenda (U)

- Executive Summary
- Potential BE Enhancements To Maximize Synergy
- DSP-II / BE Synergistic System Operational Concept
- Performance Assessment
- Cost Assessment
- Potential BE Cost And Risk Reductions
- Summary

Comparative Summary FEWS, DSP-II And BE (U)

(U) A comparative summary of FEWS, DSP-II and BE is shown in the table on the opposite page. FEWS, DSP-II, and BE costs and schedules are compared individually and in synergistic combinations. The life-cycle cost data for DSP-II was derived from quasi-independent assessments by The Aerospace Corporation and Tecolote (some specific sensor retrofit and RDT&E costs were also independently estimated by Aerojet Electronic Systems Division). The Brilliant Eyes cost data is from the BE SPC (it should be noted that the independent cost estimate prepared by Tecolote suggested that the SPO cost estimate was very optimistic). The FEWS costs are obtained from the FEWS COEA (adjusted to FY93 dollars). It should be noted that DSP-II and Brilliant Eyes life-cycle costs are for operations through 2015; the FEWS costs are for operations through only 2010 as specified in the FEWS COEA. No effort was made herein to project these costs through 2015. However, it is obvious that substantial additional satellite procurement, launch, and O&M costs can be expected for FEWS to operate through 2015.

(U) The 95-99 Five Year Defense Plan (FYDP) costs for DSP-II are shown in Appendix C - DSP-II Cost And Schedule on page C-13. The FEWS 95-99 FYDP costs are from the FEWS program plan dated February 1993. Brilliant Eyes FYDP costs are from the BE SPO. The by-year 95-99 FYDP costs are shown in the table below along with the savings from a synergistic DSP-II / BE versus a synergistic FEWS / BE. This table assumes a four-satellite DSP-II constellation. For a five-satellite DSP-II constellation, $0.1 Billion must be added to the FYDP. For FEWS, there would be little or no difference in the 95-99 FYDP costs for a four- or five-satellite constellation since FEWS is in the EMD phase during this time; FEWS life-cycle costs would change, but no effort was made herein to compute the delta. It should also be noted that the synergistic DSP-II / BE system has lower FYDP and life-cycle costs than the FEWS program alone without BE.

FEWS, Brilliant Eyes, And Four-Satellite DSP-II Constellation 95-99 FYDP (U)

	FY 95	FY 96	FY 97	FY 98	FY 99	Total
FEWS ($ Million)	$ 365	$ 890	$ 1,042	$ 1,202	$ 1,370	$ 4,869
BE ($ Million)	$ 318	$ 295	$ 260	$ 445	$ 700	$ 2,018
DSP-II ($ Million)	$ 80	$ 120	$ 180	$ 340	$ 280	$ 1,000
FEWS + BE	$ 683	$ 1185	$ 1,302	$ 1,647	$ 2,070	$ 6,887
DSP-II + BE	$ 398	$ 415	$ 440	$ 785	$ 980	$ 3,018
Savings ($ Million)	$ 285	$ 770	$ 862	$ 862	$ 1,090	$ 3,869

Table UNCLASSIFIED — FOR OFFICIAL USE ONLY

Defense Support Program
Comparative Cost And Schedule Summary
FEWS, DSP-II And BE (U)

Characteristic	FEWS	DSP-II	Brilliant Eyes	FEWS + Brilliant Eyes	DSP-II + Brilliant Eyes
Life Cycle Cost (FY 93 Dollars)	$ 18.4 (Bil)[1] (To 2010)	$ 9.6 (Bil) (To 2015)	$ 7.4 (Bil)[3] (To 2015)	$ 25.8 (Bil) (To 2010)	$ 17.0 (Bil) (To 2015)
95 - 99 FYDP[2] (FY 93 Dollars)	$ 4.9 (Bil)	$ 1.0 (Bil)	$ 2.0 (Bil)	$ 6.9 (Bil)	$ 3.0 (Bil)
Schedule For FOC		2003	2003		2003

[1] FEWS Cost (LCC To 2010) FEWS COEA Dated 17 September 1991 (Adjusted For FY 93 Dollars)
[2] The 1995 to 1999 Five Year Defense Plan (FYDP) costs are the required deltas to the existing DSP budget-line
[3] The Brilliant Eyes costs are from the BE SPO.

Appendix E - DSP-II / Brilliant Eyes Synergy - April, 1993

March 25, 1993

▉▉▉▉▉▉▉▉▉▉▉▉▉
Govt. Operations Committee, US House of Representat
Washington, DC.
Fax - 202-225-2373

Dear ▉▉▉▉▉▉▉▉
As per our conversation of 25 MAR 93, the following is my account of the happenings surrounding an incident involving Col Sanford Mangold, AF Space Command, Ansen, myself, and my husband, from the period beginning in Nov 1992 until present. This account is to clarify and expand upon our conversation of Dec. 1992.

On or about 17 April 1993, I attended a dinner party at the home of Lt Col ~~Larry Hung~~ of ORW in Colorado Springs, CO. ~~The guests at the party were the Directors of the~~ XP Organization of AF Space Command, and the head of that Organization, BGen Robert Dickman. On that evening I had two conversations concerning Col. Sanford Mangold.

The first conversation was with Col. Dick Cervie, the director of Manpower of the XP Organization. I had never met Col Corvic before that evening. He told me that it was a good thing that I had not gone to work in Col Mangold's organization at the Pentagon, because "he (Col Mangold) was not going to be around long". When I asked, why? He told me that Col Mangold was not taking care of the Command the way that he should, that he was difficult. I was told that the Command had sent him there and that the Command was unhappy with him, and were going to get rid of him. He used the term "the Command" and he used the term "we" in reference to who was going to get Col Mangold removed. I pointed out to Col Corvic, that when you arbitrarily remove the head of an organization, the people in that organization suffer. I told him that it was my understanding that Col Mangold hires "only the best people available". In mentally groping for a name to use as an example, the name that came to me was that of LtCol Jim Rooney — an officer that I had met, that would have been my supervisor had I worked in Col Mangold's organization and who I ~~scratched out~~ had been at Space Command prior to his assignment at the Pentagon. When I used Rooney's name as an example of someone that could potentially be damaged by removing his supervisor Cervic said, "don't worry about Rooney "we" are going to take care of him". He (Col Cervic) said," What we are trying to do is 'cut off the snake's head without killing the body'". Because of the graphic nature of the comment, it stuck in my mind. Other things were said, but this was what I remembered most vividly from the conversation.

My husband and I had ridden to the party with the Dickmans. On the way home from the party in Dickman's car I had the second conversation concerning Col Mangold. Ben Dickman was driving, with his wife Barbara sitting in the front seat my husband and I in the back. The conversation was between my husband and myself. I was telling my husband that "these guys really hate Sandy Mansell", that "they are going to get rid of him", that "he must really be a 'bad actor' for everyone to dislike him so much", "that there must be another side that he didn't show socially, that it was a good thing I hadn't gone to work for him because I would have been just as hated as he was by association." I believe I said something along the lines of these guys want him out nothing will happen because he is protected by Glosson. My husband was crushing my shoulder with his hand to shut me up, and was very uncomfortable with what I was saying to him. It was at this point that Ben Dickman turned in the seat and said, "don't worry about Sandy, Betsy. I have someone in his office gathering information to take him out." I believe that was exactly what was said, the verbage could be slightly diffrent but the meaning was very clear. I wrestled with my conscience for about 3 days, then I called Sandy's wife Karen. I told her that I believed that Sandy needed to be warned to be very careful, that people at the Command were very angry and I believed they were "out to get him". I told her that I thought he needed to be aware, so that he could put the professional relationships on track before something ugly happened. Sandy called back later and asked me for specific details to try to understand what was happening. These conversations took place in April. I learned that in June Col Mangold was removed from his job. The complaint was that he tried to "force" Anser Corp to hire a personal friend.

I would like to address this

issue, because I am the person that the change was centered around. It is my belief that I was used, that my name was used to damage Col Mangold and my husband, Col Worrell.

In November 1992 I submitted an SF 171 to the Pentagon. I was called by Capt Russo of Col Mangold's organization and told that he had a GS5 slot that he wanted to hire me for. We talked, he transferred me to Lt Col Rooney who basically did a interview over the phone, and told me that he thought we would work well together and wanted me to accept the job. My contact person was Capt Russo who was going to be doing the paper work associated with the hiring process. A week or so later, Capt Russo called to tell me that he was very sorry, but due to the freeze and cuts occurring in Civil Service, the slot that he wanted to hire me against had been out. He said that he felt very sorry that this had happened and asked for a civilian resume. He said he wanted to give my resume to some civilian companys. I thanked him for his concern, did not want to insult him by telling him that I was not interested in working for a contractor, and sent him a resume. I then submitted my 171 against other jobs from other services. A week later, I received an employment package from Ansen that included an application and a letter expressing interest in employing me. I didn't know for sure, but I suspected they had gotten my name from Capt Russo. I filled out the application & sent it in. Within a few days I received a call from Ansen personnel asking if I would come in for an interview the following week. I also received a call from Dept of Navy to schedule an interview the same week. (I interview and was hired) I arrived at Ansen on Tuesday, 17 Nov 1992,

I was taken to a personnel counselor who REVIEWED my paperwork and set up an escort for my interviews. I remember that she commented that I was being interviewed at a "very high level". I was interviewed by a Program Manager, Mr Pappanozi, a Vice President, Mr Adler, and a Senior Vice President, a Mr Mignorini (sp?) (or something like that). I was not told what job I was being interviewed for. I felt that collectively the attitudes were hostile, aggressive, arrogant, and in general unprofessional. My application clearly stated that I had not finished my degree - all of these men had that application. And every one of them told me that Anson "didn't hire people that didn't have a degree". No specific job was discussed - I was asked if I knew the ABDES System by Mr Pappanozi. I said no, but I was sure I could learn it.

I still didn't know what I was being interviewed for and no one told me. My interview with Adler was demeaning and I felt that he was overly aggressive in his demeanor. In particular I felt his question concerning "how did I expect to communicate with technical people when I was uneducated" was particularly offensive. The third interview was basically benign. I became truly incensed when I returned to the personnel counselor who went over the employment benefits with me that includes undergraduate tuition reimbursement for employees that do not have a degree. I felt as though I had been harassed and demeaned to make a point, but I really couldn't understand what it was—other than that Ansec had no intention of considering me for employment when they contacted me and they wanted to be sure I understood that I was not wanted by them - The feeling was mutual - at that point nothing on earth could have made me work for Anser - I called Capt Russo - told him how the interview had gone and told him to not do me any more favors by sending my resume to any more companys - At some point in this time frame I was told that the GS 5 slot of Capt Russo's that had been cut was put out as a contractor job and that Anser won the contract and had asked for the name of the person that had been hired for the slot before it was cut, to look at that person as a potential hire by them for that job. A few days after the interview with Anser Mr Adler called my home and told me that he had heard that I thought the interview was abrasive - he wanted to know who had gotten too aggresive with me and I told him "it was primarily you, Mr Adler"

I told him that my husband had come home from a lengthy TDY, that we had talked and that I understood what the problem was. I had asked my husband if Anser worked for him on any of his contracts in SDIO prior to accepting an interview with them. He told me that although Anser had worked for him in the past they no longer worked for him and that there was no conflict of interest. After the interview and my dismay at my treatment, I found out that my husband's dealings with Anser had been arbitrary. I am not sure of the details, but apparently Anser had been a support contractor on my husband's program in SDIO (Brilliant Pebbles). It was brought to his attention by one of his Directors (Doug APG) that a report had been changed at the direction of Anser Mgt to reflect favorably when the original results were unfavorable. The two Anser employees that prepared the report and were then told to change it went to the Director who went to my husband.

the Task Force Commander. who sent a letter citing Ansen for improper business practices and did not renew his contract with them. The two employees are no longer employed by Anser. I believe the reason was associated with this incident. I believe that the demeaning attitudes I experienced at the Ansen building and subsequent statements made by Ansen employees are in part a pay back to my husband and an attempt to involve and discredit him by alluding to a conspiracy between he and Col Mangold — the motive for this is, I believe, — revenge —

I asked my husband why he didn't tell me that he had had bad business dealings with Ansen before I went on this interview. he said "I thought they would be more professional than that".

Approximately 2 weeks later I learned that at a meeting between Ansen Executives and Col Mangold, my name was used.

freely and consciously by John Fabian who asked Col Mangold if he (Col Mangold) was trying to force Ansur to hire me. Hiring me was not an option for Ansur. I was unavailable for employment by them - Col Mangold, Capt Russo, and Mr Adler, who was present, knew that to be an absolute fact. I was incensed that my name was used and called the personnel counselor that I had initial contact with to make sure that they knew I was not available for employment by them. By this time my husband had gotten word that he would be going to Colorado Springs to the NTF. I told the young lady that I was moving out of the area, that I was moving to Colorado Springs whereupon she informed me that Ansur had an office there and perhaps I wanted to look at job in that office. I told her that I was not a good employment fit because it was my understanding Ansur didn't hire people that were non degreed. She said that was not true, and asked me who had

14

said that I told her "all three of the gentleman that interviewed me."

My husband began his job as the Director of the NTF on 22 Dec 92. After a lot of maneuvering on his part, Gen Dickman succeeded in having the facility put under him when it was transferred to the command. When I learned that my husband had been put under Gen Dickman, I did not want to move to Colorado. I had the feeling that my husband was going to be used and abused and I did not want to go through the emotional trauma of watching it, and having to deal with all of the social requirements that were going to be put on me. I did relent and move to Colorado the end of March. Within 2 wks of my arrival I went to the "dinner party". By the end of June I received word that Sandy had been removed from his job for trying to force Ansen to hire me. I expressed my displeasure to Capt Munk Abshire at being used and he told me that I shouldn't be upset - that I was not the reason Col Mangold was REMOVED. I was the tool that was used - that this was all "just political and that I shouldn't take it personally!" (Abshire was Dickmans & later I learned that in statements given by Jim Rooney, Harry Kingsbury, and John Fabian, all three used my husband's name - and, in my opinion, were very close to accusing him of conspiracy with Col Mangold to get his wife a high paying (GS5 equivalent job) job in Washington. When in fact all my husband wanted was for me to move with him because he was in the primary board for General Officer - In my opinion these allegations were made against him for exactly that reason. It is my belief that he was intentionally involved by Col Kingsbury, Lt Col Rooney, and John Fabian to discredit him before the General Officer board convened. It is my belief that the

16

person that gathering information on Col Mangold was directed to involve my husband. I have read Col Rooney's statement in which he says that he never spoke with me during the hiring process for the GS 5 job. This is a lie, he says that Col Mangold was trying to get Col Wornells wife a high paying job in Washington. I believe my husband has said in (Rooney's) presence that he wanted me to move with him to Colorado because he wanted to retire there. Col Kingsbury says that my husband introduced me to him as the person that was going to be working in his (Col Kingsbury's) office. Col Kingsbury introduced himself to me at a party and welcomed me to the organization. I told him that it had not worked out and that I was not going to be working there and he knew who my husband was because of the highly publicized program he directed. In my opinion both of these officers lied under oath to make a better case against

Col Mangold, and took the opportunity to secretly do a character assassination on my husband and myself as well.
I am sure that when this statement is used, I will be attacked and attempts will made to discredit me - I am also convinced that my husband will be harassed and his job will be in jeopardy, because he is the only person that anyone will be able to get to, and by destroying him, I too will be destroyed.

To the best of my knowledge my statements are true - my opinions are my own, and under penalty of perjury, I attest to the truth of his statement.

Lilia E. Darrell
3-25-93

Summary

- **Current requirements are not justified**
  - Developed when policy was nuclear warfighting
    - Requirements difficult to justify even under this policy
  - TMD requirements not rationalized in the context of overall TMD architecture
    - Role of radar (e.g. GBR) vs space-based IR
    - Counterforce requirements
    - Timeliness requirements
- **In particular, FEWS system drivers are highly questionable**
  - Sensitivity
  - Revisit
  - Processing

Summary (cont'd)

- DSP with stereo processing (DSP/TS) is adequate for both theater and strategic needs
  - Theater performance is somewhat fragile to hypothetical, but possible, threats
  - Major shortfall in theater is in impact point prediction
- DSP/TS revisit time, not sensitivity, is the weak link in performance
- (CLASSIFIED) is nice to have, but not required for TW/AA
  - DSP/TS can provide adequate timely detection of polar SLBM launches with the ATH array
  - DSP/TS is self-templating
- DSP/TS does not need Brilliant Eyes for TW/AA
  - BE relieves system fragility in theater
  - BE provides TI, polar capability

Summary (cont'd)

- **DSP-II is a technically sound, low risk concept**
  - It represents what a good program manager would come up with for fixing known problems and reducing life cycle costs if follow-on programs were not in the pipeline
  - It represents a fiduciary point for cost comparisons, if the requirements set that it meets is considered sufficient

Overall DSP-II Assessment

- **DSP with Talon Shield/TSD is a very capable theater sensor**
  - FEWS vs DSP cueing of GBR/THAAD shows little difference
  - DSP performance from actual experience
    - Performance under different circumstances needs verification
    - Gulf War environment not a "vanilla" set of circumstances for TW/AA
- **DSP-II is a sensible technical proposal**
  - It represents what a good program manager would come up with for fixing known problems and reducing life cycle costs if follow-on programs were not in the pipeline
  - It represents a fiduciary point for cost comparisons, if the requirements set that it meets is considered sufficient
- **DSP-II technical risks are low (subjectively)**
  - Keep as much of the DSP-I subsystems as possible
  - P3I approach

EGT vs DSP-II

- Aerospace internal evaluation faulted DSP-II for failing to meet FEWS ORD
- Technical approach assessed as "viable"
- Risk assessment subjective, and mostly consistent with DSP-II's own assessment of risk
  - DSP-II used NASA risk scale
  - EGT assessed risks on basis of subjective criteria (i.e. risk "medium" if hardware not in hand)
- Misunderstandings about DSP-II concept seem to be resolved (e.g. FPA layout vs thermal control)

FOR OFFICIAL USE ONLY

EXECUTIVE SUMMARY   1 NOV 1993
                                  (29 Dec 93 revision)

SUBJECT: Review of Accusations Pertaining to the Space Based Infrared
Budget Issue

TO: The Air Force Inspector General
    Washington, DC 20330-1000

1. Authority: An inquiry was conducted from 10-29 Oct 93 by Major General Marcus A. Anderson for the Inspector General of the Air Force, Washington DC 20330-1140 under the authority of letter of appointment, SAF/IG, dated 10 Oct 93.

2. The inquiry considered allegations from three sources. The following summarizes these allegations.

   a. The Secretary of the Air Force identified a set of five allegations in which AF officials were accused of releasing proprietary data to competing contractors, telling a contractor to "get on the FEWS team", inhibiting the flow of contractor data to OSD, suppressing information about program alternatives, and providing erroneous data to OSD.

   b. Aerojet Corporation cited several allegations surrounding an alternative to the Follow-on Early Warning System. They believed this information, in the form of an Aerospace Technical Operating Report, was suppressed and, further, given to their competitors even though it contained Aerojet proprietary data. In addition, they believed that the Air Force was not fairly evaluating cost in comparing the FEWS and DSP systems.

   c. Congressman Conyers requested that the DoD IG conduct an investigation into similar allegations. In documentation received from an unnamed source, it was claimed that senior Air Force officers suppressed information concerning a lower-cost alternative to FEWS, and that Mr Aldridge, CEO of The Aerospace Corporation, assisted in this suppression. Furthermore, it was alleged that senior AF officers passed false and misleading information to OSD decisionmakers on the FEWS and DSP systems. Based on agreement between SAF/IG and DoD IG, Congressman Conyers' concerns were addressed as a part of this report.

3. Certain allegations were referred to this inquiry which suggested the possibility of misconduct by senior Air Force officials. During the course of the inquiry into these allegations, we were guided by the policy and procedures contained in AFR 120-4. Despite a vigorous inquiry involving approximately 60 hours of recorded testimony from 36 witnesses, contractor and government alike, and several hundred pages of documents, we uncovered no substantiated

evidence of conduct which would constitute a violation of criminal law, standards of conduct, or would amount to an abuse of discretion, fraud, waste, or abuse, reprisal, or reflect adversely on a senior official's judgment. Given the above information, the following are significant findings with respect to senior Air Force officers identified from the allegations:

   a. CINCSPACE (Gen Horner) did **not** inhibit TRW from passing Multi-Spectral (MS) data to OSD. Although Gen Horner told TRW that he was concerned that they were sending mixed signals by proposing an MS alternative to FEWS, he did not direct TRW to withhold this data. During an interview, TRW said they made an "independent business decision" to not provide MS data to OSD/PA&E.

   b. The PEO for Space (MGen Schnelzer) did **not** suppress information about a lower cost alternative to the proposed $13B FEWS satellite program. While conducting a study on sensor alternatives (called Sensor Study I), MGen Schnelzer eliminated a concept called DSP-MLV since it did not meet user requirements which was a key groundrule for the OSD/Congressionally directed study. As groundrules on user requirements changed during the summer, this concept became one of several alternatives being reviewed within the Bottom-Up Review (BUR) process.

   c. Results of this inquiry reflect **no** wrongdoing by the SBEWS Program Director (██████). However, the allegation that ██████ provided a copy of the Aerospace TOR to Aerojet competitors was investigated by a separate inquiry which concluded that proprietary data was, in fact, inappropriately released.

4. Fifteen of the seventeen allegations noted from the three sources identified in paragraph 2 above were investigated. The two allegations not investigated deal with the release of Aerojet proprietary data to FEWS competitors which were investigated by Space and Missile Center. Of the 15 allegations reviewed, 10 are not substantiated. A summary of those substantiated in whole or in part follows:

   a. SAF-identified allegations:

      (1) "That USSPACECOM staff members told a defense contractor to 'get on the FEWS team or get out of the way', is substantiated in part. While no direct statement, as alleged, could be verified, TRW got a "message" from USSPACECOM that they should pay attention to their role in the FEWS program (one of two prime competitors).

      (2) "That the briefing charts and background information for the 5 Oct 93 Space-Based IR Sensor System capabilities budget issue briefing to Mr

FOR OFFICIAL USE ONLY

Deutch were released by USSPACECOM to space-based sensor competitors", is substantiated. The material was, in fact, provided to Lockheed, TRW, Grumman and Hughes; however, in the opinion of an expert witness, no proprietary data was released. On the other hand, POM data was included in the package and should not have been released. The actions were determined to be inadvertent.

b. Aerojet allegation, "That the Government attempted to discredit the Aerospace TOR" is substantiated. This is an unusual situation because the Government and the leadership of Aerospace Corporation (Mr Pete Aldridge) had good reason to discredit the report. It had not been coordinated with the user or the PEO, had been approved at an intermediate level at Aerospace, discounted JROC-validated requirements, and was written in an advocacy tone. Mr Aldridge was embarrassed with the report, as was the Air Force about the content and the way the report was coordinated and distributed.

c. Congressman Conyers-identified allegations:

(1) "That MGen Schneiter deleted from a Congressionally-mandated study an option (DSP-MLV) identifying improvements to the existing DSP as an alternative to the FEWS that could save up to $10B" is substantiated. Like the previous allegation, MGen Schneiter had a good reason to delete the DSP-MLV option since it didn't meet one of the key OSD/Congressional groundrules—options in the study must meet operational requirements as stated in the FEWS Operational Requirements Document.

(2) "That Mr Aldridge ordered the recall of the Aerospace TOR and assisted in the suppression of options from review by Congress. That Mr Aldridge interfered in a DoD IG investigation by requesting that the IG back-off on these issues", is substantiated in part. The part substantiated was that Mr Aldridge ordered the recall of the Aerospace TOR. He did so initially to read the report, then he affirmed the decision after review by an independent Aerospace team.

5. To summarize:

a. What brought us to this inquiry? In the space arena and perhaps across the acquisition spectrum, the intense competition for dollars in DoD and among its defense contractors ("survival" mentality) is producing distrust, suspicion, breakdowns in communications and ultimately allegations of impropriety, both from within the Air Force and from defense contractors.

(1) An event occurred in the February 1993 timeframe that was a catalyst for several of the allegations. That event was rejection of an option for Sensor Study I that had been prepared by a team from the DSP program office,

-3-

FOR OFFICIAL USE ONLY

FOR OFFICIAL USE ONLY

assisted by Aerospace and Aerojet. The rejection was made by MGen Schneiter (PEO for Space) who was in charge of the study. He made the decision for logical reasons, but the decision was not understood or accepted by those who had proposed the option. Thus, perceptions of favoritism toward FEWS, misleading/erroneous data being used, suppressing data in DSP, etc., ultimately became allegations in this inquiry.

    (2) Another key event was publication of the Aerospace Technical Operating Report (TOR) in April 1993. This report was purportedly done to document the results of the work done for Sensor Study I and to have an option available in case FEWS fell on hard times. In reality, the TOR became an advocacy document for those who felt "slighted" by the decision to reject a lower cost DSP option from Sensor Study I. The way in which this report was published and distributed caused a great deal of concern within the Air Force and Aerospace Corporation, and the actions taken resulted in several allegations addressed by this inquiry.

  b. Where do we go from here?. There's no simple fix. Given the environment as described above, the possibility of similar allegations from defense contractors is ever-present. Good communications will help, but will not guarantee success. Within the Air Force, we must listen to those with concerns, address them and attempt to achieve consensus. If consensus is not achieved, those with dissenting opinions need to understand why their position wasn't accepted. If they continue to push their position and perceive "no one is listening", future allegations will inevitably result.

HQ USAF/XOXJ 17 February 1994
Pentagon
Washington, D.C. 20330

Mr. Eric Thorson
Legislation and national Security Subcommittee
B373 Rayburn House Office Building
Washington, D.C. 20515

Dear Mr. Thorson

Attached are the answers to the questions given me on 2 Feb 94. As during my testimony, I am not speaking for the United States Air Force. The answers represent observations and professional judgments of events that occurred during the period from August 1991 until the present, during which time I served as the deputy, then the Chief of the Space/C3I/Nuc Deterrence Resource Allocation Team, as well as my experiences currently as an USAF Planner for Joint and NSC Issues.

SANFORD D. MANGOLD
Colonel, USAF

ATCH
Testimony (Q & A)

TESTIMONY (QUESTIONS & ANSWERS)

CONGRESSIONAL HEARING

2 FEBRUARY 1994

QUESTION:

Col Mangold, concerning your 26 Apr 93 letter to the Associate Deputy Assistant Secretary of the Air Force (Management Policy and Program Integration), what reaction did you get from the space acquisition community after this letter was published?

ANSWER:

The reaction from both the Associate Deputy Assistant Secretary (Mr. Blaise Durante) and from HQ USAF/AQS (Maj Gen Donald Hard) was immediate and harsh. What happened at this point was that the roof fell in on me. I was told that Mr. Durante and MGen Hard called my leadership and demanded an immediate retraction of the letter. Further, I was told that both individuals had openly labeled me as "insane." The letter was withdrawn, but my leadership told me I could pursue the matter again during the coming summer months when the FY 95 budget would begin development.

QUESTION:

Col Mangold, in your opinion why was MGen Hard's reaction so severe?

ANSWER:

MGen Hard and I had multiple disagreements over the course of the year in which I was the Team Chief. While such disagreements seemed natural between a cost-cutter (myself) and an acquisition specialist (MGen Hard), what I experienced at this point was an order-of-magnitude more animosity. In my opinion, the question of cutting FFRDC support meant far more to MGen Hard than merely reducing unnecessary technical support from an expensive, sole-source contractor - it meant affecting potential post-military employment. Only later did I realize the significance of my actions from MGen Hard's perspective, as upon his retirement from the Air Force, he went to work for the Aerospace Corporation. It was as if, when I started to get to post-government employment opportunities for senior individuals in the space acquisition community, I started to hit them where they lived. From 26 Apr 93 onward, my relationship with the space acquisition community, in general, and MGen Hard, in specific, deteriorated markedly.

QUESTION:

Col Mangold, did you ever mention cutting the FFRDCs' budget again?

ANSWER:

Yes, in the May-Jun 93 time frame, during a large meeting involving Team Chiefs, members of the acquisition community (SAF/AQ) and the USAF financial community (HQ USAF/FM & PE), I announced that I was going to reopen my attempts to cut the FFRDCs and believed I could potentially produce up to a $1 Billion dollar cost savings over the next five years.

QUESTION:

Col Mangold, what was the general reaction of the assembled individuals to your announcement?

ANSWER:

I would characterize the reaction from the acquisition community as "controlled enthusiasm." Actually, several individuals became irate and pointedly asked me how I expected Space and Missile Center (in Los Angeles, CA) to function without Aerospace support. I responded that for starters they might consider working more than 40 hours per week! I was accused of making a "cheap shot." (This exchange was documented in notes that Lt Col John O'Connor, HQ USAF/AQS, provided to his boss, MGen Donald Hard subsequent to this meeting.)

QUESTION:

Col Mangold, do you believe you stand on cutting the FFRDCs' budgets contributed to the loss of your job?

ANSWER:

Absolutely. In my opinion, it was the "straw that broke the camel's back." My adversaries realized that if I remained in my Team Chief position, I was going to initiate significant, permanent alterations to the way we acquire space systems. Although, the overall effect might result in major cost reductions, it would also most certainly result in post-military service employment opportunities for senior acquisition officials. This is because most of the regulations concerning conflict-of-interest prohibitions do not apply equally to FFRDCs as they do to "for-profit" companies. Regulations governing hiring practices for FFRDCs are much more liberal and open to a broad interpretation than in private industry. If my past track record for successful cost cutting was any indicator of how well I would do when I took on the FFRDCs, my adversaries knew that "once I had the FFRDCs in my sights, I would score a victory."

DEPARTMENT OF THE AIR FORCE
HEADQUARTERS SPACE AND MISSILE SYSTEMS CENTER (AFMC)
LOS ANGELES, CA

7 February 1994

SMC/SDS
160 Skynet Street, Suite 2315
Los Angeles AFB, CA 90245-4683

Mr Eric Thorson
Legislation and National Security Subcommittee
B373 Rayburn House Office Building
Washington, DC 20515

Dear Mr Thorson

    Attached are the answers to the questions given me, on 2 Feb 94. As during my testimony, I am not speaking for the United States Air Force. The answers represent observations and professional judgement of events during the period I served as DSP Program Manager.

Sincerely

EDWARD R. DIETZ, Col, USAF
Chief, Acquisition Development Division

Attachment:
Testimony (Questions & Answers)

Testimony (Question & Answers)
Congressional Hearing
3 February 1994

QUESTION:

Col Dietz, as DSP Program Manager during the time period covered by Mr Aru's opening statement, are your observations the same as his?

> **ANSWER:** Yes, I saw the same things, but I would like to emphasize different areas:
>
> First - Mr Aru stated that retribution was taken against the Aerospace Corp design team. I think it is worse than that. Although I don't know the motive, it is striking that the 3 senior managers who suggested a less expensive option were removed from their jobs. A Colonel in the Pentagon, a Colonel in California, and the DSP Program Manager at TRW Corp. Unfortunately, it may be worse than retribution. The central objective appears to have been to send a message to all employees ... keep your mouths shut if you want to keep your job. This is **unconscionable!**
>
> Second - Mr Aru is rightfully disturbed about the technical issues and the decisions that were made. I am more concerned about the ethics and integrity messages the USAF is sending to the public, and hundreds of young officers who watched this debate and saw that the only action take, was the replacement of 3 senior managers who suggested a lower cost solution. These young officers are learning that anything is OK if you sell a program, and 10 years from now they will be advocating programs based upon fraudulent arguments.

QUESTION:

Col Dietz, you are quoted as saying that General Horner was misinformed. What makes you believe this?

> **ANSWER:** In briefings to USAF leadership, and in the press, he incorrectly characterized FEWS and DSP. A few examples follow:
>
> 1. "FEWS makes launch location targetable" - **Not true!** Unless we use nuclear weapons. OSD's Everett Committee concluded "FEWS provides marginal advantage ... for counterforce (TBM)"
>
> 2. "FEWS is 10X more accurate" - **Wrong!** Current Army and USAF experience with DSP/Talon Shield has shown performance almost equal to FEWS specification, in addition:
>
> Launch point accuracy - "FEWS provides marginal advantage over DSP", OSD's Everett Committee.
> Impact point - **Irrelevant!** (Space Command doesn't care about impact point prediction), ref: Gen Horner testimony to OSD, Fall '93.
>
> 3. "FEWS is cheaper than DSP" - **Not true!** and the GAO agrees with me! Perhaps if you ignored the possibility of improving the current system or if you allowed all the specious cost additions to the DSP side of the cost account it would, but you'd also have to ignore OSD's findings, and numerous studies referenced by the GAO.
>
> 4. "FEWS detects even with high cloud cover" - **Sorely misleading!** This implies an all weather system that can track in clouds. Physics does not allow IR detection through the clouds. Neither DSP nor FEWS can do this.
>
> 5. FEWS detection of cruise missiles - **Unlikely.** Except for 1970 style weapons, under all but the most fortunate circumstances, and thus the military utility is questionable.
>
> 6. DSP current life expectancy - **Sorely Overstated!**

QUESTION:

Col Dietz, you have been quoted as being concerned that the cost comparisons were distorted. Do you have an example?

>**ANSWER:** Yes Sir. It is a continuing problem, and a number of obvious examples, worth billions, come to mid. Apparently the goal is to make the cost of improving DSP equal the cost of a new system.
>
>1. In testimony to Congress, the cost of improving DSP was said to "approach that of ... FEWS". Improving the old system is 1/2 the price of a new system. To me, approach means; close, or small difference. This is a 6 to 10 billion dollar savings we've ignored.
>
>2. Twelve unchanged DSPs were costed. Unreasonable! A small investment in life extension and producibility would yield billions is savings.
>
>3. DSP was costed with laser cross links - Ridiculous! We were actively pursuing elimination of the cross link, and Space Command had approved its deletion.
>
>4. $4 billion was added to the DSP cost estimate for data from a supporting system - Inexcusable! A classified program provided $.7 to $1.25 billion estimates to the Pentagon for this capability, the Navy plan discussed in the press was cheaper, and OSD confirmed my conclusion that it was not needed for missile warning.
>
>A simpler answer is: The OSD Everette Committee confirmed my assessment, found FEWS options significantly more expensive, and recommended canceling FEWS.

QUESTION:

General Hard stated in testimony to Congress that the cost of upgrading the DSP approached that of a new system (FEWS). Are there less expensive options for upgrade?

> **ANSWER:** Yes Sir! **Billions could be saved.** The upgrade presented was an unreasonable choice. It had little engineering behind it, was previously rejected by HQ Space Command, had poorer performance than the other upgrades, but it was almost as expensive as FEWS.
>
> A variety of significantly less expensive options have been presented to management (SPCMD, HQAF, OSD, PA&E) over the last few years. Major General Schnelzer and Major General Hard were frequent participants in these discussions until we were directed to stop talking about inexpensive upgrades.

QUESTION:

Col Dietz, you have been quoted as being concerned that performance comparisons have been intentionally distorted. Do you have any examples?

> **ANSWER:** Yes sir, this has been a continuing concern with many of us. It is however difficult to discuss specifics in an unclassified hearing.
>
> To give a feeling for the environment, I quote Aerospace Corp's Principle Deputy (Program Manager) for DSP, reviewing Gen Schnelzer's report to Congress:
>
>> "only the patently naive will accept..."
>> "utterly dependent upon a completely unknown..."
>> "...unbalanced in favor of FEWS"
>> "decision was being defended vs supplying accurate information"
>
> The performance of the new system appears to be systematically inflated, while the performance of the current system is deflated. For example:
>
>> 1. FEWS' unproven performance is quoted as better than the contract requires specification.
>> 2. DSP/Talon Shield, though operating superbly, is quoted as poorer than the contract specification.
>
> To summarize the situation, FEWS' performance is advertised as 10 to 20 times better than DSP. Not true! The OSD's Everett Committee concluded there is "marginal improvement".

QUESTION:

Col Dietz, you have been quoted as being concerned about witch hunts and retribution. Could you expand upon this?

> **ANSWER:** Yes sir. Who did what to who, and who allowed the study to be given to the Navy was more of a concern to senior management than ensuring an open technical debate about the options.
>
> I don't know if it was retribution, but it is striking to note the number of people who suggested a less expensive solution that have had their career terminated or major actions taken against their livelihood.
>
> A more disturbing possibility is that they were examples. The true intent was to send a message to 350 staff members, stifling any further discussion ... keep quiet or lose your job!

QUESTION:

Col Dietz, what are your central concerns in these hearings?

ANSWER: Three come to mind:

My primary concern is that USAF's silence on these ethics issues leads our young officers to believe we condone anything necessary to sell anew program.

The management team responsible for the problems we've talked about today is still in place, managing billions of dollars, and continuing to advise on the expenditure of billions more.

The only action taken by USAF is to remove senior managers for their involvement with a less expensive solution, that OSD ultimately endorsed.

QUESTION:

Col Dietz, the panel has discussed a number of different events, which appear to have a very disturbing central theme. Could you summarize these events and put them in context?

ANSWER:

A brief chronology will serve the purpose:

A small group of people under direction of Col Dietz found FEWS claims overstated, and they developed a less expensive alternative.

USAF management embarked upon a variety of inappropriate and illegal activities to protect the program (FEWS).

FEWS was canceled by OSD, after independent analysis confirmed Col Dietz's findings.

Typical inappropriate USAF acts:

- Proprietary data given to competitors, by USAF officers
- Cost of current system inflated to make new system seem cheaper
- Performance estimates distorted to make it seem a good idea to buy new system
- Congress mislead by being told cost of upgrading old system approaches cost of new system
- Cheaper solutions concealed from Congress
- Cheaper solutions concealed from HQ USAF budget analysts
- Attempts to destroy documents describing less expensive option
- Retribution taken against staff involved with cheaper option
  -- 2 Colonels, 1 Civilian, 7 Aerospace employees
- Document with cheaper solution withdrawn form circulation by Aerospace Corp.
- Incriminating documents given to USAF IG, in confidence, were leaked to the accused
- TRW Corp threatened by senior USAF officials.
- Analysis advising against buying new system (DSB, POET, GE, RAND, GAO) was suppressed and ignored
- Congress mislead concerning "public access" to cheaper DSP-2 solution
- Col Bailey not punished for illegal acts
- OSD access to TRW's competitive multi-spectral concept

obstructed by USAF
- OSD prohibited from seeing lower cost DSP-2 option
- Congress' request to investigate cheaper alternatives subverted by HQSPCMD. Direction to only evaluate top of the line choices they liked

Hearing on Strategic Satellite Systems
in a Post-Cold War World

February 2, 1994

Questions for the Record

Mr. Guido Aru

Question: Colonel Steve Stadler testified that DSP "got lucky" in Operation Desert Storm and was only able to detect the Scud launches due to favorable weather and viewing conditions. How do you respond?

Answer: Air Force Space Command and US Space Command have promulgated this story in order to justify a new early warning program. The facts, however, dispute their claim. DSP detected all of the Scud attacks in Desert Storm under varying weather, background, and night/day conditions. DSP had previously detected the Scud launches in the Iran/Iraq war, and routinely detects Scud and other tactical ballistic missile test launches in Russia, North Korea, and other countries. The Army's Joint Tactical Ground Station (JTaGS) and the Air Force's Talon Shield program will further enhance the DSP system's ability to detect and accurately report tactical ballistic missile launches. The attached Memo-Gram prepared by Mr. Jim Creswell, Talon Shield Principal Director, The Aerospace Corporation, dated 27 July 1993, provides a good summary of the issues of DSP's performance in Desert Storm.

(Insert Memo-Gram From Jim Creswell, dated July 27, 1993)

MEMO-GRAM

PLEASE RESPOND TO SENDER ON THIS ORIGINAL

Page 1 of 3

To: Col. (Sel) T. Crossey/MTT   Site: LAAFB   Bldg: 115   Date: 7/27/93

Attn:

Subject: Observation Conditions For Desert Storm

1. There have been statements by responsible AF representatives to acquisition review agencies that the SRBM boost phase detection results obtained by DSP during Desert Storm were the result of a "confluence of ideal conditions" and are likely not repeatable, even with Talon Shield and CTPE processing, i.e. the performance required by the Talon Shield CTPE is not likely to be attained because the ideal conditions are not likely to repeat.

2. Had the conditions been ideal and the results atypical, then they would indeed not provide a valid basis for the type of performance that can be expected from the Talon Shield program. (The Talon Shield minimum requirements for monocular sightings are to duplicate, or better, the Desert Storm results.) Conditions were, however, far from ideal.

3. The attached notes provide a brief summary of the observation conditions that _did_ prevail during Desert Storm. They support confidence in Talon Shield's performance requirements as reasonable, well-founded projections based on objectively interpreted experience.

Signature: N. Cresswell

Organization: TAP

Distribution:
Col. J. Bailey/MT
Col. E. Dietz/MTD
Col. J. Quirk/MTE
Maj. M. Remedes/DOXW
Cpt. J. Christoff/MTT

cc:
R. Allman/M5/647
E. Bersinger/M5/661
R. Broussard/Petefld
B. Ching/M5/657
T. Crites/Wash,DC
P. Enns/M5/660
K. Hines/M5/721
M. Jacobs/M5/653
D. Lavrie M4/041

T. Jerardi/POET
J. Kinsey/Herndon
J. Parsons/M5/664
A. Perella/POET
T. Polk/M5/624
T. Stocker/M5/624
F. Tomlinson/CoSpgs
R. Woodworth/CoSpgs
L. Zamos/M5/624

REPLY

To: Site: Bldg: Date:

Signature   Organization

1. Two and a half years after Desert Storm, folklore seems to be gaining credence over the facts. The latest "hearsay" is that the impressive space based IR sensing that provided warning of SRBM launches during Desert Storm was attributable to the ideal conditions afforded by the situation and environment. The implication: that the Desert Storm performance base used by Talon Shield has resulted in requirements that are too optimistic to be met, since the allegedly "ideal conditions" of Desert Storm are not likely to recur.

2. The reality of the situation was quite adequately summarized in Air Power In The Gulf: "As it worked out, the cloud cover was thirty-nine percent, the worst in the fourteen years that flight weather records have been kept on the Saudi peninsula". Quoting Air Force Secretary Rice on the same subject, "The fact is General Horner and his people had to plan attacks around unexpected cloud cover, winds aloft, thunderstorms, ice, you name it. It turned out during Desert Storm to be the worst weather in the fourteen or fifteen years of recorded weather history in that part of the world."

3. Apart from the weather, viewing conditions that contribute to the complexity of a detection include background, geometry (in terms of the satellite-earth center-missile angle commonly called Earth Central Angle, or ECA), aspect angle (the direction of the missile's flight relative to a satellite's line of sight), and the complexity of the situation presented to the operator in the loop to support him in his real/false discrimination task.

4. When absence of cloud cover and precipitable water vapor in the atmosphere allowed early missile detection, it also allowed transmission of the radiance from ordnance and target explosions. These were particularly heavy during the dark hours -- making the night backgrounds far from benign. (USAF daily fighter sorties averaged over 2500 per day during the forty-three day period.)

5. Fifteen of 88 SRBM launches were in daylight. These were as readily detected as the night launches.

6. The comment has been made that the target satellite proximities were ideal. The range of ECA's from the satellite stations do not support such a contention. In a possible range of 0 to 81.3 degrees ECA for below-the-horizon targets, the Desert Storm targets were at approximately 47 degree, 42 degree, and 62 degree ECA's for the three satellites used during hostilities. These ECA's are comparable to those that might be encountered at sixteen (16) other potential theater conflict areas. They are less advantageous than most, and only slightly better than might be encountered for the Baltic Republics area and parts of China or North Korea (e.g., approximately 47 to 67 for North Korea).

7. The aspect angles for the Desert Storm observations provided a range from adverse to reasonable. The station providing the best ECA also had nose on viewing (minimum apparent motion for a whole segment of the events).

8. Finally, the Desert Storm results were achieved with Operator-In-The-Loop as standard operating procedure. The advantages and detriments of that approach were absorbed with the resulting impressive record of detections and with only four false reports for the period.

9. Supporting details and statistics are a matter of record and are available in briefing materials at the SECRET level.

Questions for the Record - Mr. Guido Aru

Question: Air Force Space Command and US Space Command have stated that a new early warning program is required to provide improved launch location as well as detection of shorter-range tactical ballistic missiles than the Scud (e.g., SS-21 class missiles). How do you respond?

Answer: General Horner claims that the inability of the Collation Air Forces under his command during Desert Storm to register any confirmed kills of Scud TELs was a failure of DSP to provide adequate launch location information. However, the post-war assessments of the Scud TEL targeting problem find that the principal reason for this failure was with the organic sensor on-board the attack aircraft and their inability to distinguish TELs from decoys. A particularly thorough analysis can be found in "Defense Intelligence Assessment - Mobile Short-Range Ballistic Missile Targeting in Operation DESERT STORM", report number OGA-1040-23-91, dated November 1, 1991, prepared by the Joint Relocatable Target Program Office, Target Intelligence Division, Office for Global Analysis, classified Secret-NoForn-WNINTEL.

Irrespective of these conclusions, the fact is that FEWS will not provide any substantial improvement in missile launch location over DSP using the Army's Joint Tactical Ground Station or the Air Force's Talon Shield ground processing system. Analysis performed by the Space-Based Early Warning System Program Office using Desert Storm and simulated data proves this. Mr. Everett also validated this when his panel concluded that FEWS provides only "marginal advantage" for missile launch location and counter-force operations such as the Scud-hunting missions in Desert Storm.

As far as the detection of shorter-range tactical ballistic missiles than the Scud, every national panel that has reviewed this issues has concluded that the detection of these types of missiles (e.g., SS-21) is an inappropriate mission for a space-based infrared system such as DSP or FEWS. These panels include the SDIO Phase One Engineering Team (POET), The Institute for Defense Analysis, and Mr. Everett's technical support group. They have concluded this because such missiles burn-out below cloud cover and have extremely short flight times. The detection of these missiles should be handled by in-theater radar or passive location systems which, as Colonel Stadler himself testified, will be deployed anyway with US and allied forces to provide air surveillance.

Questions for the Record - Mr. Guido Aru   Page 3

Question: The Air Force IG concluded that the <u>exclusion</u> of the DSP-II (aka., DSP/MLV) alternative from the Congressionally-mandated Air Force Sensor Integration study as well as the <u>inclusion</u> of the DSP++ alternative was proper in that DSP-II failed to meet Draft requirements while DSP++ "approximated" the draft requirements close enough to merit inclusion. How do you respond?

Answer: I disagree. The Congressionally-mandated study specified that a combinations of systems should be evaluated for meeting <u>validated</u> ITW&AA requirements. In the case of DSP, a combination of DSP with Brilliant Eyes was to be evaluated. Specifically, an upgraded DSP combined with the "Government Baseline" Brilliant Eyes concept was to be developed which would meet the <u>approved</u> ITW&AA requirements which are documented in the Joint Requirements Oversight Council Memorandum 2-91 (JROCM 2-91). The DSP-II / Brilliant Eyes combined system concept would meet these requirements.

In a February 10, 1993 letter to Major General Garry Schnelzer, Brigadier General Dickman from Air Force Space Command identified six "validated" FEWS mission needs which he said the DSP and BE alternative must address. They are:

1. On-board data processing;
2. Satellite-to-satellite cross-links;
3. Worldwide collection and distribution of wide-band data back to the CONUS ground station;
4. Full satisfaction of all threat detection requirements as defined in the <u>unapproved</u> draft FEWS Operational Requirements Document;
5. Hardening/Jamming requirements equivalent to FEWS adjusted for the lower altitude Brilliant Eyes constellation; and
6. Collection, timing, and distribution of multiple Areas-of-Interest (AOIs) worldwide at varying revisit rates as well as sensitivities as defined in the <u>unapproved</u> draft FEWS Operational Requirements Document.

None of these six "validated" FEWS mission needs was ever approved by the Joint Requirements Oversight Council. Furthermore, DSP++ combined with Brilliant Eyes did not offer any more capability to address these six needs than DSP-II combined with Brilliant Eyes. Additionally, some of these needs could not be achieved by any space-based infrared system because they violate the laws of physics.

The DSP++ option was previously rejected by Air Force Space Command and the Air Force PEO/SP in 1991 because it was not cost effective. DSP-II showed that as much as $4 billion could be saved in the '95-'99 FYDP, with a total life-cycle savings through the year 2015 of approximately $10 billion when compared with the baseline FEWS program. In my opinion, information on DSP-II was withheld from OSD and Congressional decision makers because it was seen as a direct threat to FEWS. I believe the integrity of the acquisition process was compromised by Major General Schnelzer and by Brigadier General Dickman in order to preserve the FEWS program.

Once information on DSP-II was provide to OSD by the DoD IG, who seized a copy of the DSP-II report after a "Hot-Line" call, OSD commissioned several independent review teams to assess the situation. All of these teams agreed that FEWS was unnecessary, and that significantly lower cost alternatives were available. Furthermore, these panels concluded that an evolutionary upgrade of DSP (e.g., the DSP-II concept) represented the lowest cost and lowest risk alternative.

It should also be noted that when OSD requested that another DSP alternative (in addition to DSP++) be included in the Air Force Sensor Integration Study in late May 1993, Major General Schnelzer again ignored the DSP-II concept. He instead included a concept known as DSP-26 or DSP-Forever which offered no performance improvements or life-cycle costs reductions to the current DSP system. DSP-26, therefore, offered significantly less performance than DSP-II at a cost which approximated the FEWS program. Again, I believe this was a deliberate subversion of the acquisition process in order to justify the FEWS program. The Air Force IG failed to address this issue.

○

www.ingramcontent.com/pod-product-compliance
Lightning Source LLC
Chambersburg PA
CBHW060243240426
43673CB00047B/1867